CATHOLICI

CATHOLICISM

The Story of Catholic Christianity

by

Gerald O'Collins SJ

and

Mario Farrugia SJ

OXFORD
UNIVERSITY PRESS

OXFORD
UNIVERSITY PRESS

Great Clarendon Street, Oxford OX2 6DP

Oxford University Press is a department of the University of Oxford.
It furthers the University's objective of excellence in research, scholarship,
and education by publishing worldwide in

Oxford New York

Auckland Cape Town Dar es Salaam Hong Kong Karachi
Kuala Lumpur Madrid Melbourne Mexico City Nairobi
New Delhi Shanghai Taipei Toronto

With offices in

Argentina Austria Brazil Chile Czech Republic France Greece
Guatemala Hungary Italy Japan South Korea Poland Portugal
Singapore Switzerland Thailand Turkey Ukraine Vietnam

Oxford is a registered trade mark of Oxford University Press
in the UK and in certain other countries

Published in the United States
by Oxford University Press Inc., New York

British Library Cataloguing in Publication Data

Data available

Library of Congress Cataloging in Publication Data

Data available

ISBN 0–19–925994–1 (hbk.)
ISBN 0–19–925995–X (pbk.)

5 7 9 10 8 6 4

Typeset by Kolam Information Services Pvt. Ltd., Pondicherry, India
Printed in Great Britain
on acid-free paper by
Biddles Ltd., King's Lynn, Norfolk

PREFACE

The world's oldest and largest institution, the Catholic Church, is not limited to any particular class, race, or nation. With its geographical and cultural spread, it reaches out to all humanity. It lives up to its attribute, 'catholic': that is to say, it is worldwide and universal. It embraces all nations. A Catholic can join St Augustine of Hippo (354–430) in saying: 'I exist in all languages: my language is Greek, my language is Syrian, my language is Hebrew. My language is that of all peoples, for I exist in the unity of all peoples' (*Enarrationes in Psalmos*, 147. 19).

'Catholicity' belongs, of course, among the characteristics of the Church confessed by all Christians in the Nicene-Constantinopolitan Creed which is derived in its full form from the First Council of Constantinople (AD 381). Used at least sometimes every year by all Christians when they celebrate the Eucharist, this Creed declares a common faith in the 'one, holy, *catholic*, and apostolic Church'. That is the confession of many Protestants when they profess the Creed each Sunday, whether or not they meet for the Eucharist. Some people would prefer us to give this book the title of *Roman Catholicism*. After all 'Catholics' are those Christians who are in communion with the Bishop of Rome; they accept the authority of the Pope who lives in Rome and presides over the diocese of Rome. Nevertheless, when one speaks or writes of 'Catholics' or 'Catholicism', people almost invariably understand a reference to Roman Catholics. That surely was the presumption behind the request that we should write a book on 'Catholicism', and not one on 'Roman Catholicism'. At the same time, we appreciate the motives of some readers (e.g. some Anglican readers) who will add 'Roman' whenever we write of the Catholic Church and Catholicism, and who object to the Roman Catholic Church calling itself or being called 'Catholic' *tout court*. In any case, many elements of Catholic Christianity are found beyond the Catholic Church—a point to which we will return below. What is characteristic of Catholicism need not be always uniquely Catholic. Greek, Russian, and other Orthodox Christians share, for instance, the same range of seven sacraments.

Any claims by the Catholic Church to be the one, holy, catholic, and apostolic Church are contested by Orthodox Christians; their rival claims need to be heard by Western Catholics such as ourselves. In what follows, and especially in the chapter on the nature of the Church, we aim to reckon seriously with the force of the Orthodox position. Likewise, five hundred years of Protestantism have raised radical difficulties and alternatives for anyone who endorses the Roman Catholic claim to embody Christian and Catholic identity. We want to express a nuanced confessionalism, address historical issues as fairly as we can, and acknowledge critical, post-Reformation challenges that face Catholicism.

We write this book 'from the inside', as those who have been born into Catholic families and have tried to serve the Catholic (and wider) community as ordained priests and teachers of theology. Knowing the institution intimately, sharing a common faith, and identifying with the deep values of other Catholics, we hope to be able to understand and explain Catholicism competently, but without becoming biased and defensive. Some 'insiders' behave like that, but certainly not all. When it comes to music and drama, insiders who have years of study, experience, and personal commitment behind them help us to be more accurately informed about and skilfully guided through musical and dramatic compositions. In such areas detached outsiders may be able to communicate a wealth of facts, but at times the value of their judgements can be doubtful.

We draw encouragement here from *The Meaning of Revelation* (New York: Macmillan, 1960), in which Helmut Richard Niebuhr dedicates a chapter to the distinction between 'internal' and 'external' history, or history as lived from the inside and history as merely viewed from the outside (pp. 43–90). He illustrates clearly the advantages enjoyed by those who write history as they have lived it from the inside. Yet we must remain alert to reflections on Catholicism coming from 'outsiders'. To be sure, they may examine or want to examine Catholics as a purely historical rather than a spiritual phenomenon. Nevertheless, they sometimes pick up what insiders may not see very clearly if at all. An observer of genius such as Alexis de Tocqueville (1805–59) discerned forces that would remain central to life in the United States. We all need to join Robert Burns (1759–96) in the prayer, 'O wad some Pow'r the giftie gie us to see oursels as others see us!'

At points in this book we will relate the Catholic Church not only to other Christian communities but also to Judaism, Islam, and other world religions. But we cannot stop constantly to identify what is common (and what is different). Otherwise this book would become hopelessly long and far exceed the limits assigned to us. Nevertheless, we gladly acknowledge that such a detailed comparison and contrast would be eminently worthwhile, a valuable project for a team of experts.

In writing this book we want to be useful not only to our fellow Catholics but also to other Christians and to interested adherents of other faiths. Any evaluation of Catholicism presupposes some knowledge, but one must admit that it is not always there. Early last century an eminent Protestant scholar, Adolf von Harnack (1851–1930) deplored the ignorance of the majority of non-Catholic graduates about Catholicism:

I am convinced from constant experience of the fact that the students who leave our schools have the most disconnected and absurd ideas about ecclesiastical history. Some of them know something about Gnosticism, or about other curious and for them worthless details. But of the Catholic Church, the greatest religious and political creation known to history, they know absolutely nothing, and they indulge in its regard in wholly trivial, vague, and often directly nonsensical notions. How her greatest institutions originated, what they mean in the life of the Church, how easily they may be misconceived, and why they function so surely and impressively: all this, according to my experience, is for them, apart from a few exceptions, a *terra incognita* [an unknown land].

(*Aus Wissenschaft und Leben*, i (Giessen: Töpelmann, 1911), 97)

Von Harnack's judgement may have been excessively pessimistic. But what of today? A century later would he reproach non-Catholic (and, for that matter, Catholic) graduates from contemporary high schools, colleges, and universities with knowing little more about the 'unknown land' of Catholicism? Our own hope is to guide some of them through what may still be largely a *terra incognita*.

History has always been central to the life of the Catholic Church. The sense of being a Catholic has constantly involved retrieving a two thousand-year-old story. How should one construe the ups and downs, the fulfilments and disappointments of Catholics through the centuries? The first two chapters of this work offer an extended tour of that history. Then follow chapters that describe the central beliefs of the Catholic Church (Chs. 3–6), its sacramental life (Ch. 7), its constitution and mission (Ch. 8), and its moral doctrine (Ch. 9). The book will close by summarizing certain basic characteristics of Catholic Christianity (Ch. 10) and expounding some lively issues confronting the Catholic Church and its future (Ch. 11).

In telling the story of Catholicism, as so often elsewhere, every attempt to generalize is beset with enough exceptions to break the rule. But some generalizations will find much support: the coexistence from the very beginning of holiness and sinfulness; the recurrent tensions between the local community and a worldwide institution; and the Catholic Church's challenges to prevailing cultures along with widespread assimilation of them.

We begin this book both fascinated by its challenge and daunted by the enormous task it involves. Inevitably we will need to be constantly selective. Also we plan to give a certain preference to signs of grace rather than evidence of scandalous failures. In doing that, we are not aiming to produce a sanitized version of Catholicism and thus further some propagandistic agenda. Rather it is because we have long been convinced by a principle to which Aristotle repeatedly appealed: one should judge the nature of something from its best examples. Moreover, piling up stories of sinful failure always leaves the reader with the nagging question: if the Catholic Church is that bad, how on earth has it managed not only to survive but also to grow and flourish? Is the only explanation that the Holy Spirit has kept it going and spreading, despite its awful sins and deficiencies?

With deep gratitude we record our warm thanks to those whose expertise, suggestions, corrections, and questions have enlightened us when writing this book: Don Bolen, Ian Breward, Marcel Chappin, James Conn, Francisco Egaña, James Gobbo, William Henn, Jerome Hall, Brian Johnstone, Dorothy Lee, Giovanni Magnani, Margaret Manion, Hilary O'Shea, Maev O'Collins, John Radano, Francesco Paolo Rizzo, Philip Rosato, Jared Wicks, John Wilkins, and several anonymous advisers for the Gregorian University and for the Oxford University Press. We dedicate this work to the students and professors of the Gregorian University's faculty of theology. The translations from the Bible are our own.

G. O'C. and M. F.

Gregorian University, Rome
2 June 2002

CONTENTS

LIST OF ILLUSTRATIONS

ABBREVIATIONS

DH   H. Denzinger and P. Hünermann, *Enchiridion symbolorum, definitionum et declarationum* (Freiburg im Breisgau: Herder, 37th edn., 1991)

ND   J. Neuner and J. Dupuis (eds.), *The Christian Faith* (Bangalore/New York: Theological Publications in India/Alba House, 7th edn., 2001)

NT   The New Testament

OT   The Old Testament

PICTURE CREDITS

The authors and publishers wish to thank the following for their kind permission to reproduce the illustrations:

Abbas/Magnum Photos; Abegg-Stiftung; Riggisberg/Bridgeman Art Library; The Art Archive/Missions Etrangères Paris/Dagli Orti; Bibliothèque des Arts Decoratifs, Paris/Bridgeman-Charmet Collection; Catholic News Service; Sonia Halliday Photographs; Harris Museum and Art Gallery, Preston/Bridgeman Art Library; The National Gallery, London; Popperphoto; Carlos Reyes-Manzo/Andes Press Agency; Topham Picturepoint.

Picture research by Sandra Assershon.

I

The First Thousand Years

> We Catholics acknowledge readily...that Catholicism cannot be
> identified simply and wholly with primitive Christianity, nor even
> with the Gospel of Christ, in the same way that the great oak cannot
> be identified with the tiny acorn.
>
> (Karl Adam, *The Spirit of Catholicism*)

A classic passage from an English historian, Thomas Babington Macaulay
(1800–59), recalls the coming together in Catholicism of Greek and
Roman culture, the anointing in 754 of Pepin III (714–68) by Stephen
II (pope 752–757), St Gregory the Great (pope 590–604) sending
St Augustine in 596 to become the first archbishop of Canterbury, and St
Leo the Great (pope 440–61) confronting Attila the Hun and his forces in
452. Macaulay's evocation of Catholicism, written in 1840, runs as follows:

There is not, and there never was on this earth, a work of human policy so well
deserving of examination as the Roman Catholic Church. The history of that
Church joins together the two great ages of human civilisation. No other institution is left standing which carries the mind back to the times when the smoke of
sacrifice rose from the Pantheon, and when camelopards and tigers bounded in the
Flavian amphitheatre [i.e. the Roman Colosseum]. The proudest royal houses
are but of yesterday, when compared with the line of the Supreme Pontiffs. That
line we trace back in an unbroken series, from the Pope who crowned Napoleon in
the nineteenth century to the Pope who crowned Pepin in the eighth; and far
beyond the time of Pepin the august dynasty extends, till it is lost in the twilight of
fable. The republic of Venice came next in antiquity. But the republic of Venice
was modern when compared with the Papacy; and the republic of Venice is gone,
and the Papacy remains. The Papacy remains, not in decay, not a mere antique, but
full of life and youthful vigour. The Catholic Church is still sending forth to the
farthest ends of the world missionaries as zealous as those who landed in Kent with

Augustin[e], and still confronting hostile kings with the same spirit with which she confronted Attila. The number of her children is greater than in any former age. Her acquisitions in the New World have more than compensated for what she has lost in the Old. Her spiritual ascendency extends over the vast countries which lie between the plains of the Missouri and Cape Horn, countries which, a century hence, may not improbably contain a population as large as that which now inhabits Europe. The members of her communion are certainly not fewer than a hundred and fifty millions; and it will be difficult to show that all other Christian sects united amount to a hundred and twenty millions. Nor do we see any sign which indicates that the term of her long dominion is approaching. She saw the commencement of all governments and of all the ecclesiastical establishments that now exist in the world; and we feel no assurance that she is not destined to see the end of them all. She was great and respected before the Saxon had set foot on Britain, before the Frank had passed the Rhine, when Grecian eloquence still flourished in Antioch, when idols were still worshipped in the temple of Mecca. And she may still exist in undiminished vigour when some traveller from New Zealand shall, in the midst of a vast solitude, take his stand on a broken arch of London Bridge to sketch the ruins of St Paul's.[1]

Macaulay's rhetoric suggests that history could be the best way into the subject of this book. Hence our two opening chapters will review significant events and persons who show us Catholicism in its strength and in its weakness. Our principal aim is to illustrate the origin and development of important Catholic beliefs and practices that are still with us. The first chapter will be structured in three major sections. It will outline events culminating in the Christian freedom granted by Emperor Constantine in 313, then move on to the Council of Chalcedon in 451, and finally to the split between Eastern and Western Christianity expressed by the mutual excommunications of 1054 pronounced by Cardinal Humbert of Silva Candida (d. 1061) and Michael Cerularius, the patriarch of Constantinople (d. 1058).

BEFORE CONSTANTINE

Catholic Christianity, which began in Jerusalem with the resurrection of the crucified Jesus (most likely in April AD 30) and the coming of the Holy

---

[1] Essay on Ludwig von Ranke's *History of the Popes*, in *Critical and Historical Essays*, iii (London: Longman, 7th edn. 1952), 100–1. The Venetian Republic originated in the fifth century (when people fled from the forces of Attila the Hun to the safety of some islands) and was finally overthrown by Napoleon in 1797. At the end of the first century AD, Antioch, now occupied by the Turkish town of Antakiyah, was (after Rome, Alexandria, and Ephesus) the fourth largest city of the Roman Empire. In June AD 630 Muhammad (c.570–632) took over Mecca and put an end to the idolatry against Allah that he found there.

Spirit, emerged from Judaism. During his public ministry, or what one might call the period of proto-Christianity, Jesus led a revival movement that had some surprising features (e.g. the presence of women who travelled in his company) but that remained largely within Judaism itself. He gathered a core group of twelve men (all Jews) and a wider group of disciples who seem to have included some non-Jews (e.g. Matt. 8: 5–13; Mark 7: 26; Luke 17: 11–19).[2]

After Pentecost

In the post-Pentecost situation, the first Christians expected the risen Christ's glorious second coming, and formed a messianic, millennial group within Judaism. They fashioned their proclamation and interpretation of Jesus by putting together two elements: on the one hand, their experience of the events in which Jesus was the central protagonist and, on the other, the images, concepts, expectations, and practices that they found to be relevant and illuminating within the Jewish scriptures. To articulate their convictions about Jesus and his role in fulfilling the divine purposes, they depended in part upon their Jewish background. Thus the initiation rite of baptism took over some values from the purificatory rites of Judaism, not least from the baptism for the forgiveness of sins practised by John the Baptist. All Jesus' followers continued to find in the Jewish psalms their main prayer-book—something that was to be anathema in the second century to Marcion, who, as we shall see, wanted to eliminate the OT altogether. Some or even many of them continued to worship as Jews or in the Jerusalem Temple until excommunicated from Palestinian (and other?) synagogues towards the end of the first century. At least to begin with, Jesus' followers were unsure about the need to observe the Torah or Jewish law (especially on

---

[2] Since here and in some later chapters we draw on the Gospels, we want to make some points clear from the outset. (1) We agree with the widely accepted scheme that there were three stages in the transmission of Jesus' words and deeds: the initial stage of his sayings and doings in his public ministry; the handing on, by word of mouth or in writing, of traditions about him; the authorial work of the four evangelists. (2) We also agree that one can use such criteria as multiple attestation or multiple witness in arguing that the accounts of certain words and deeds go back substantially to the first stage: i.e. to Jesus himself. (3) When we draw on the Gospels, we will indicate whether we understand some passage to report what Jesus said or did at stage one (e.g. in his choice of the Twelve), or whether we use the passage to illustrate how a particular evangelist at stage three (and/or the tradition behind him at stage two) understood Jesus' identity or work. (4) We cannot stop every time to justify why we and others hold some saying or deed to have its historical origin in what Jesus said or did.

circumcision and dietary requirements) and to proclaim the good news of the risen Christ to the Gentiles. Paul's letters (e.g. Romans and Galatians) and the Acts of the Apostles (e.g. Acts 10: 1–11: 18; 15: 1–39) reflect these initial hesitations. But Jesus' followers differed from (other) devout Jews by administering baptism 'in the name of Jesus' (e.g. Acts 2: 38) and celebrating together 'the breaking of the bread' or the Eucharist (e.g. Acts 2: 42, 45).

In the Acts of the Apostles Luke tells the story of the origins and early spread of Christian faith. Among Jesus' disciples the first prominent figure is St Peter, who functions as the head of the twelve apostles, the core group of public witnesses to Jesus' life, death, and resurrection. With his dramatic calling or conversion on the road to Damascus around AD 36, St Paul enters the Acts of the Apostles in ch. 9 and takes over the narrative from ch. 15. According to that book, when Paul returns to Jerusalem in ch. 21, he meets St James and 'all the elders'. But there is no mention of Peter still being in Jerusalem. Acts ends with Paul arriving in Rome several years before he and Peter died there as martyrs, some time between AD 64 and 67. In 62 James, the leader of the Mother Church, had already been martyred in Jerusalem.

These first decades of Christian history featured the tension between two 'constituencies', the foundational Jerusalem Church with its vision of a Torah-observant community and the non-Torah-focused vision of Paul and others. The latter vision shaped the Catholic or universal identity of the early Church and lifted it beyond being merely a millennial group within Judaism. Paul loved the Jerusalem community, and showed that love by collecting money for the Mother Church from other (local) churches (e.g. 2 Cor. 8: 1–9: 15). Nevertheless, as Raymond Brown and John Meier showed, Catholic identity in Antioch, Rome, and other centres was formed in tensional relationship with the Jerusalem community.[3]

Paul spearheaded missionary activity around the Mediterranean world, and spread faith in Jesus as Lord and Saviour. Luke understands this original Christian expansion as opening up an indefinitely long period which will close when Jesus appears again in his glory. In the meantime, as Acts repeatedly indicates, the risen Jesus and his Holy Spirit constantly guide and empower Christian life and mission. But by the 60s, despite

---

[3] See R. E. Brown and J. P. Meier, *Antioch and Rome* (New York: Paulist Press, 1983).

some optimistic statistics from Luke (Acts 2: 41; 4: 4), there were probably not more than three thousand Christians.[4]

By then Jesus' followers had come to be called 'Christians' (Acts 11: 26). Through baptism 'in the name of Jesus Christ' (Acts 2: 38) they knew their sins to be forgiven, received the Holy Spirit, entered the community of the Church, and celebrated the Eucharist (1 Cor. 11: 23–6). When praying, they used not only the psalms but also the Lord's Prayer and other such prayers as the *Benedictus* and the *Magnificat* (Luke 1: 46–55, 68–79), which were originally in Greek like the rest of Luke's Gospel but were subsequently known by Latin titles. They learned the teaching of Jesus that reached them through their apostolic leaders. The risen and exalted Jesus, now confessed as Messiah, Lord, and Son of God, was together with God the Father, experienced as having sent the Holy Spirit into the world. Luke names devout people from different parts of the known world—from 'Parthians, Medes, and Elamites' to 'Cretans and Arabs' (Acts 2: 9–11) as key spectators of Pentecost. Luke knows that the Spirit is offered to all peoples; salvation no longer requires circumcision and the practice of the Mosaic law in all its details.

Paul's letters likewise defend God's gift of salvation to all alike; justification is not gained through human efforts at fulfilling the law. Faith and baptism incorporate people into the Church, the body of Christ, and put an end to distinctions between Jew and Gentile, slave and free, male and female (Gal. 3: 26–9). Faith in God the Father, in Jesus as Son of God and divine Lord, and in the Holy Spirit brings all believers together in the unity of baptism, the Eucharist, and a common life. The apostle insists that sharing in the one eucharistic bread and in the one cup entails belonging to the one body of Christ (1 Cor. 10: 16–17). A fifth-century prayer (from the *Liturgy of St Basil*) expresses beautifully Paul's desire for Catholic unity: 'May all of us who partake of this one bread and chalice be united to one another in the communion of the same Holy Spirit.'

[4] R. Stark, *The Rise of Christianity* (San Francisco: HarperCollins, 1997), 185. On the rise of Christianity see also D. Boyarin, *Dying for God: Martyrdom and the Making of Christianity and Judaism* (Stanford: Stanford University Press, 1999); P. Brown, *The Rise of Western Christendom. Triumph and Diversity A.D. 200–1000* (Oxford: Blackwell, 1996); C. M. Cusack, *The Rise of Christianity in Northern Europe, 300–1000* (London: Cassell, 1998); P. F. Esler (ed.), *The Early Christian World*, 2 vols. (London: Routledge, 2000); H.-J. Klauck, *The Religious Context of Early Christianity* (Edinburgh: T. & T. Clark, 2000); J. T. Sanders, *Charisma, Converts, Competitors* (London: SCM Press, 2000). On Stark's book see the symposium in *Religious Studies Review*, 25 (1999), 127–39. Not all reviewers have been persuaded by Stark's numerical estimates and interpretation of Christianity's development.

In emphasizing the holy unity of the baptized, the apostle's letters, even more than the Acts of the Apostles, let us glimpse the moral failures of early Christians. The First Letter to the Corinthians reveals how some suffered from factionalism, indulged doubts over the central truth of the resurrection, committed fornication, incest, and drunkenness, and showed a selfish unconcern towards poorer Christians. The reproaches coming from Paul challenge illusions about a hypothetical golden age of Catholic Christianity which practised heroic ideals on all sides. From its outset the Church suffered from scandals and divisions. The Book of Revelation, with its opening letters to the seven churches, joins the apostle in testifying to the mixture of holiness and sinfulness that characterized Christianity from the beginning (Rev. 2: 1–3: 22). The Gospels also repeatedly imply and even frankly point to sinful conduct to be found in the early communities; even prophets, exorcists, and miracle-workers could do evil and fail to follow the will of God (Matt. 7: 15–23).

Along with holiness and sinfulness, after the initial hesitations (see above) a missionary outreach characterized early Christianity. The Acts of the Apostles and Paul's letters name with respect missionaries who spread the good news about Jesus as Saviour of the world: Barnabas, Epaphroditus, Timothy, Titus, and, not least, Prisca (or Priscilla) and Aquila. This married couple, when they lived in Ephesus and Rome, gathered believers in their home, and were also known to the Christians of Corinth (1 Cor. 16: 19; Acts 18: 2–3, 26). Paul calls this couple his 'fellow workers' (Rom. 16: 3). When listing other collaborators on the mission for Christ, he names Andronicus and Junia (another married couple?) as 'distinguished among the apostles' (Rom. 16: 7). Unlike Luke, who generally identifies 'apostles' with the twelve, Paul also gives the former title to itinerant evangelists who are commissioned, sent by a church, and found another (local) church, as apparently Prisca did in Corinth with her husband Aquila.

Early Leadership and Life

In concluding his Letter to the Romans, Paul begins with 'our sister Phoebe, a deacon of the church', speaks of those who 'work' to spread the good news, and greets twenty-six people, twenty-four of them by name. As much as any passage in the NT, the final chapter of Romans raises the question: was the Church meant to be a completely egalitarian community, free of any kind of subordination to office-holders and hierarchical authorities? Did the vision of Jesus and the spontaneous direction of the Holy Spirit exclude the

FIG. I. A fifteenth-century mural of the 'mystical supper' from Paleochorio (Cyprus) shows Jesus majestically celebrating the Passover on the night before he died. (Sonia Halliday Photographs.)

institutionalized leadership, which occurred in the subsequent transmission of a threefold ministry of bishops, priests, and deacons? Did that historical development betray Jesus' original dream of a community of male and female disciples as co-partners variously empowered by the Holy Spirit to minister to the whole community? In its normative, first-century period was the Church directly governed by the Holy Spirit and did it flourish without supervisory authorities or any official establishment? Or was there always some kind of leadership which rightly developed and was handed on to successive generations for the good of all? We can put the issue in terms of the thesis proposed by Willi Marxsen, Siegfried Schulz, and some other twentieth-century scholars: 'early Catholicism', a deterioration they already detect in Acts, the Pastoral Letters, and other NT writings. This thesis claims that the good news proclaimed by Jesus and Paul suffered inasmuch as a structured institution emerged to dispense salvation through ministerial ordination, a hierarchical succession of leaders, set forms of doctrine, and a re-established law.[5] Without thinking their way through any such sophisticated thesis as 'early Catholicism', some instinctively presuppose that the earlier situation must, *for that very reason alone*, be the more authentic. Some (or even many?) continue to subscribe, unthinkingly, to the old myth of an original purity, corrupted by a subsequent history of decline. The 'real' or the 'true' is found only at the start. On our guard against such a myth, what can we discern about the situation of Jesus and the post-resurrection developments?

If we begin with the Gospels, we find multiple witness for the fact that during his ministry Jesus chose twelve disciples from among the wider ranks of his followers and gave them some kind of authoritative office and leadership role. In so doing, Jesus revealed his intention to reform and transform the people of Israel, understood to constitute twelve tribes or groups descended from Jacob (Gen. 35: 22–6). Mark attests the original call and subsequent mission of the twelve (Mark 3: 13–19; 6: 7–13). Q, a collection of sayings of Jesus that both Matthew and Luke draw from,[6]

---

[5] See J. D. G. Dunn, *Unity and Diversity in the New Testament* (London: SCM Press, 2nd edn. 1990), 341–66; G. O'Collins and D. Kendall, *The Bible for Theology* (Mahwah, NJ: Paulist Press, 1997), 101–16.

[6] Although some NT scholars dispute the existence of such a collection of sayings behind the Gospels of Matthew and Luke, Q still seems to most scholars the best working hypothesis about the immediate origin of sayings that are common to these two Gospels. See F. Neirynck, 'Synoptic Problem', in R. E. Brown *et al.*, *New Jerome Biblical Commentary* (Englewood Cliffs, NJ: Prentice-Hall, 1990), 587–95.

reflects the existence of this core group (Matt. 19: 28 = Luke 22: 30). They are 'in place' to receive a foundational appearance of the risen Christ, a fact first attested by a traditional formula cited by Paul (1 Cor. 15: 5) and subsequently narrated in varying ways by the Easter chapters of the Gospels. The Twelve are given by Christ authority to lead and teach in his name, an authoritative role for which, as Luke and (in his own way) John indicate, they are empowered by the Holy Spirit. Their apostolic mission shares in and comes from the mission of the Son and the Holy Spirit.

What do the Pauline letters indicate about leadership in the Church? A dramatic encounter with the risen Christ (and not as such with the Holy Spirit) made Paul himself an apostle who proclaims the resurrection of the crucified Jesus (1 Cor. 9: 1–2; 15: 8–11; Gal. 1: 11–12, 15–17). Paul's forceful sense of his own apostolic authority comes across clearly, not least in his Letter to the Galatians. After founding communities, he exercises remote-control authority over them through his letters and occasional visits. But how does he understand the authority of others in the growing Church? In his first letter Paul distinguishes between those who 'preside' and those who 'defer' (1 Thess. 5: 12). A little later he notes how, within the whole 'body of Christ', God has appointed various persons to be apostles, prophets, teachers, workers of miracles, healers, helpers, administrators, and speakers in different kinds of tongues (1 Cor. 12: 8–12, 28–30). The apostle's language in 1 Corinthians 12 has encouraged some to envisage a Spirit-filled community with no permanent institutions and ordained officers, a charismatic 'pneumatocracy' as opposed to an institutional 'christocracy'. But does Paul in 1 Corinthians 12–14 intend to make permanent prescriptions for the Church's ordering, by opposing charisms to institutions and offices or what is pneumatological and charismatic to what is christological and institutional? It seems rather that he intends to give some practical advice to the Corinthian community and help solve some particular challenges facing them.[7] The eight ministries of 1 Corinthians 12: 28 become five in another list, from a 'deutero-Pauline' letter or one perhaps written by an associate of the apostle after his death: 'his [Christ's] gifts were that some should be apostles, some prophets, some evangelists, some pastors and teachers' (Eph. 4: 11). The list now includes

---

[7] See E. Nardoni, 'Charism in the Early Church since Rudolph Sohm: An Ecumenical Challenge', *Theological Studies*, 53 (1992), 646–62.

the 'evangelists' or official messengers/preachers of the good news (see Rom. 10: 8–17).

The foundation of many local churches by apostles and others brought a shift in leadership, when settled pastors (called 'overseers', 'elders', and 'deacons') took over from the missionary apostles, the other evangelists, and the founders among whom had been the 'pillars' of Galatians 2: 9. A range of NT sources reflect this movement from missionary preachers to settled, pastoral leaders (Acts 20: 17, 28; Phil. 1: 1; 1 Pet. 5: 1–4; the Pastoral Letters to Timothy and Titus), even if many details about the appointment of the latter, their leadership functions, and their relationship to the travelling missionaries remain obscure.

The Pastoral Letters, when recording a more developed organization of ministries, speak of 'overseers' or 'bishops' and their qualifications (1 Tim. 3: 1–7; see Titus 1: 7–9), of the 'elders' or 'presbyters' to be appointed by Titus 'in every town' (Titus 1: 5–6; see 1 Tim. 5: 17–20), and of the qualities appropriate for 'deacons' (1 Tim. 3: 8–10, 12–13), and apparently also for deaconesses (1 Tim. 3: 11).[8] There is some indication about succession in teaching authority (2 Tim. 2: 2). Much is stated about the teaching, preaching, defence of sound doctrine, administration, and domestic behaviour expected from leaders. But apart from some passing regulations concerning worship (1 Tim. 2: 1–2, 8) and several references to the 'laying on of hands' (1 Tim. 5: 22; see 1 Tim. 4: 14; 2 Tim. 1: 6), nothing further is said about the liturgical life of the community and, for instance, about the roles taken by these leaders (or others) in baptizing and celebrating the Eucharist.

An examination of the NT supports then the conclusion: the Christian communities, both in the apostolic situation (AD 30–70) and in the sub-apostolic situation (AD 70–100), were characterized by a measure of organization which, along with the basic equality of all the baptized, comprised the leaders (with their gifts and institutionalized offices) and the led (with their personal charisms). These communities were not simply egalitarian. Today some Christians read the scriptures with deep

---

[8] Acts reports 'elders' alongside 'the apostles' in Jerusalem (Acts 11: 30; 15: 2, 4, 6, 22–3; 16: 4). When Paul visits Jerusalem for the last time, no 'apostles' are mentioned but only 'all the elders' alongside James (Acts 21: 18). Acts 6: 1–6 reports the appointment of seven men to 'serve' (*diakonein*) in the administration of the Jerusalem community. One of them (Stephen), however, works wonders and proves an outstanding speaker (Acts 6: 8–10) before being put on trial and martyred. Another (Philip) becomes a wandering preacher and miracle-worker (Acts 8: 4–40).

suspicion, play down the role of the Holy Spirit in guiding the foundational period of the Church, and deny the authority of some, especially the later, books of the NT. A sharp, anti-Gnostic observation of St Irenaeus (*c.*130–*c.*200) may apply here: 'When the heretics are refuted from the scriptures, they turn to accusing the scriptures themselves, as if there was something amiss with them' (*Adversus Haereses*, 3. 2). Irenaeus encouraged allegiance to the normative voice of the scriptures when facing the question of the Church's structure and other such critical issues. We return to him shortly.

The last paragraph may have put matters too sharply. But we meet here what we might call a 'Protestant' and 'Catholic' parting of the ways. A 'Protestant' reading can dismiss the later NT books as representing a regrettable decline into 'Early Catholicism' and appeal to the earliest forms of Christian community, to the extent that they can be identified and recovered. A 'Catholic' reading is comfortable with the patterns of organization emerging in the later NT writings and flowing into the post-NT developments.

We find in St Ignatius of Antioch (d. *c.*107) a key witness to the emerging organization of Catholic Christianity. The first to have used the expression 'the Catholic Church' (*Epistle to the Smyrnaeans*, 8. 2), this martyr stressed unity of Christians and obedience to their monarchical or single presiding bishop. Evidently by the early second century bishops headed the various Christian communities in Asia Minor. Ignatius understood the bishops not only to lead the celebration of the Eucharist and maintain (against early Gnostics) the centrality of Christ's bodily incarnation but also to approve the marriages of Christians. He wrote in his *Epistle to Polycarp*: men and women who marry should 'enter the union with the consent of the bishop; thus their marriage will be acceptable to the Lord and not just gratify lust' (5. 2). Ignatius was put to death in Rome, where he recognized 'a Church worthy of God, worthy of honour', and 'presiding in love' (*Epistle to the Romans*, opening greeting). But he mentioned no bishop of Rome, which—along with other evidence—may suggest that the system of a monarchical bishop at the head of the local community had not yet clearly developed there as the normative form of Church government.[9]

[9] See E. Duffy, 'Was there a Bishop of Rome in the First Century?', *New Blackfriars*, 80 (1999), 301–8. Whatever we conclude about Rome, Ignatius of Antioch states firmly that one cannot speak of a 'church' unless it has a *bishop*, presbyters, and deacons (*Epistle to the Trallians*,

By the late second century Irenaeus was to defend episcopal succession, with bishops enjoying the sanction of apostolic authority, on the basis of the 'rule of faith'. His championing of a public rule entailed (*a*) rejecting the new, Gnostic 'scriptures', (*b*) recognizing the mainstream Christian scriptures (in particular, the four Gospels), and (*c*) defending the episcopal office held in succession when the ministry of the apostles gave rise to a continuous line of ordained bishops. Irenaeus acknowledged an authoritative continuity in the orthodox teaching of bishops succeeding one another and proclaiming the one faith and one tradition of the apostles. This rule of faith belonged to the worldwide Church, in which episcopal succession could be traced back to the apostles—something Irenaeus did for the sees of Ephesus, Smyrna, and Rome, 'the greatest and oldest church' (*Adversus Haereses*, 3. 1–4). He criticized fiercely the secret, anti-hierarchical, and anti-apostolic position of the Gnostics:

They oppose tradition, claiming to be wiser not only than the presbyters [i.e. the bishops] but even than the apostles, and to have discovered the truth undefiled. The apostles, they say, mingled with the Saviour's words matter belonging to the Law; and besides this, the Lord himself uttered discourses some of which derived from the Demiurge, some from the intermediate Power, some from the Highest, whereas they themselves know the hidden mystery without doubt, contamination, or admixture. (Ibid. 3. 2. 2)

In Ch. 3 we will return to the issue of scripture and tradition, which was central in Irenaeus' polemic against the Gnostics. His understanding of the Holy Spirit was not yet sufficiently elaborated to appreciate clearly the Holy Spirit as the primary bearer of the Church's tradition and life. His principle, 'where the Church is, there is the Spirit of God' (ibid. 3. 24. 1), formed a sound starting-point but needed considerable filling out.

Respect for authority and concern for unity identify Catholic Christianity from the time of Paul, Ignatius, and Irenaeus. The NT Letter to the Ephesians celebrated the unity of first-century believers: 'There is one Body and one Spirit, even as you were called to the one hope which belongs to your call, one Lord, one faith, one baptism, one God and Father of us all, who is above all and through all and in all' (Eph. 4: 4–6). But how were the scattered communities to remain together in the 'one faith' and 'one hope' to which they knew themselves to be called? By the end of the first century

3. 1). On the development of the episcopacy in the early Church, see F. A. Sullivan, *From Apostles to Bishops* (Mahwah, NJ: Paulist Press, 2001); on Rome, see P. Lampe, *Die stadtrömische Christen in den ersten beiden Jahrhunderten* (Tübingen: Mohr-Siebeck, 1987).

AD there were probably less than 10,000 Christians, who made up around fifty communities—from Spain (perhaps), southern France (perhaps), Italy, Greece, Asia Minor, North Africa, Egypt, the Middle East, and beyond in Iran and India. Besides the work of such itinerants as Prisca and Aquila, Christian leaders met the challenge of maintaining contact and unity in basic beliefs and practice by a steady exchange of letters. Paul had left an extraordinary example, with letters that strikingly exceeded in length what was customary in the ancient world. Even his shortest letter, that to Philemon (only 25 verses), went beyond the average letter composed by Greek- and Latin-speaking writers of his time. As well as the Pauline correspondence, the NT contains seven letters attributed to others, one of which, First Peter, was sent from Rome to the Christians dispersed here and there in Asia Minor or what is now Turkey. The author of the Book of Revelation sent his work from the island of Patmos to seven Christian communities, also found in what is now Turkey (Rev. 1: 9). A few years later, on his way to be martyred in Rome, Ignatius, the bishop of Antioch in what was then the Roman province of Syria, wrote seven letters: six to particular Christian communities and one to Polycarp, bishop of Smyrna, who was himself to be burned alive about AD 156. Recalling Peter and Paul, the two great leaders martyred in Rome some forty years earlier, Ignatius pleaded with the Roman Christians not to hinder his martyrdom: 'Suffer me to become the food of wild beasts; through them I can reach God. I am God's wheat, and I am to be ground by the teeth of wild beasts that I may become the pure bread of Christ' (*Epistle to the Romans*, 4. 1).

Persecution and martyrdom, particularly that of leaders, began very early in the history of Christianity. In AD 44 James the son of Zebedee suffered martyrdom by being beheaded by Herod Agrippa I. Paul lists the imprisonments, floggings, and other sufferings he had already undergone by the late 50s (2 Cor. 11: 23–7). Before his Damascus Road encounter with the risen Christ, he himself had acquiesced in the stoning of Stephen (Acts 7: 55–8: 1). In AD 62 the Jerusalem community lost its leader when St James was stoned to death. In his *Annals* (15. 44) the Roman historian Tacitus tells the gruesome story of Christians killed as scapegoats by the Emperor Nero in AD 64. Right from the first centuries various authentic records of martyrdoms have survived. The *Passion of St Perpetua* describes how she and other Christians in Carthage were mauled by wild beasts and then had their throats cut in AD 203, during a persecution under the Emperor Septimius Severus.

When Church leaders met for the First Council of Nicaea in AD 325, not a few of them showed the marks of recent persecution on their bodies. The hands of Paul of Neocaesarea had been paralysed by hot irons. Hosius, the bishop of Cordoba (d. 360) who acted as Emperor Constantine's adviser at the Council, and St Eustathius (bishop of Antioch 324–30) had both suffered during the cruel persecution of Maximin Daza (d. 313). Two Egyptian bishops had each lost an eye. One of them, St Paphnutius (d. 360), had also been hamstrung. His scarred body evoked the veneration of the bishops and others present; Emperor Constantine showed respect by kissing his mutilated face.

Catholic Christianity has regularly been marked by suffering and martyrdom. In fact, while the brutal persecution of Christians in the Roman Empire was haphazard and often limited to their leaders, it repeatedly proved to be much worse elsewhere and in later centuries. In 1597 twenty-seven Japanese Catholics were crucified at Nagasaki; in the following decades thousands of other Japanese and some foreigners suffered death for their faith. The eighteenth- and nineteenth-century persecution in Vietnam resulted in thousands of martyrs. On a visit to South Korea in 1984, Pope John Paul II canonized 103 Catholic Christians who died during persecutions in 1839–46 and 1866–7. From the end of the eighteenth century through to the middle of the nineteenth century, the Korean Catholic Church counted up to 10,000 martyrs, headed by St Andrew Kim Taegon. During the Ugandan persecution (1885–7) St Charles Lwanga and twenty-one companions were burned to death or killed by the sword. The king of Uganda executed numerous Anglican Christians as well as these Catholics. During the fourteenth century under Mongol rulers, especially Tamerlane (1336–1405), the Church of the East (often called the Nestorian Church) suffered a savage persecution. The tyranny of Joseph Stalin (1879–1953) brought death to numerous Orthodox Christians, both in the USSR and (immediately after the Second World War) in satellite Communist countries. Catholic Christians have certainly not been alone in dying for their faith, but they have done so in large numbers—not least in the twentieth century.

It has often been said, and may well be true, that more Catholics and other Christians suffered imprisonment and martyrdom in the twentieth century than in all previous ages put together. We are still waiting for complete martyrologies or lists of those men and women who have given their lives for their faith in Jesus and, one must add, in the exercise of their discipleship. Many laypeople, religious women, priests, and bishops have died as 'martyrs of charity', followers of Christ who, often in situations of extreme danger, set themselves to serve others unselfishly. A letter written by an Italian nun, Sister Erminia Cazzaniga, shortly before she was killed in September 1999 by the militia in East Timor, spoke for these martyrs of charity. She wrote of her determination to stay with the East Timorese people, despite the threat of violence: 'Today our mission consists not only in helping but also, as St Paul says, in weeping with those who weep, sharing with those in need, and giving much hope and confidence in God the Father who does not abandon his children.'

Following this excursus on later martyrs, let us go back to the early Church and sketch something of the lives of Christians in the pre-Constantine period, and then outline the enduring contributions to Catholic Christianity that came from five outstanding figures: Justin, Irenaeus, Tertullian, Origen, and Cyprian.

Baptism 'in the name of the Father and of the Son and of the Holy Spirit', reported at the end of Matthew's Gospel, rapidly became and remained the standard formula for the basic sacrament of Christian initiation (Matt. 28: 19). The *Didache*, written probably around AD 90, and so one of the earliest Christian works outside the NT, instructs those who baptize to do so using the trinitarian formula (7. 1–3). This invocation of the Trinity provided the creative ground-plan for constructing the questions concerning the tripersonal God ('Do you believe in the Father?' and so forth) and answers that encouraged the formation of creeds. Such questions evoked the threefold baptismal profession of faith in the Trinity recorded by the *Apostolic Tradition* of St Hippolytus of Rome (*c.*170–*c.*236) that dates from *c.*216 (DH 10; ND 2). Baptismal creeds, (with the Old Roman Creed crystallizing around the middle of the third century and giving rise to other creeds), emerged in the West and in the East and were then followed by conciliar creeds, the earliest being those from the Council of Antioch (325) and from the First Council of Nicaea (325). The evidence from the second and third centuries records the faith of the catechumens and the communities that welcomed them, when in a dramatic experience of deep personal relevance they confessed their faith and were united to the tripersonal God.[10]

---

[10] See J. N. D. Kelly, *Early Christian Creeds* (London: Longman, 3rd edn. 1972); W. Kinzig and M. Vinzent, 'The Origin of the Creed', *Journal of Theological Studies*, 50 (1999), 535–59.

The celebration of the Eucharist on Sunday or the Lord's Day reaches back to the start of Christianity. Paul (1 Cor. 11: 23–6) and Luke (Acts 2: 42; 20: 7) witness to that. The *Didache* seems to refer to the eucharistic liturgy in a prayer: 'As this broken bread was scattered over the hills and then, when gathered, became one mass, so may your Church be gathered from the ends of the earth into your kingdom' (9. 4). A few years later St Justin Martyr (*c*.100–*c*.165) wrote a fairly detailed account of eucharistic worship on Sundays (*First Apology*, 65–7). (Here he also indicated the practice of collecting money for the relief of widows, orphans, prisoners, the sick, and others in need. Of this more anon.) The *Apostolic Tradition* of Hippolytus, from the beginning of the third century, includes a eucharistic prayer, which (with slight adaptations and the addition of the 'Holy, Holy, Holy' or 'Sanctus') became after the Second Vatican Council (1962–5) the second eucharistic prayer for Catholics of the Latin or Western rite. Then, as now, the Eucharist comprises two parts: the Liturgy of the Word, which followed the pattern of Jewish synagogue services, and the Liturgy of the Eucharist, which centred on Jesus' words of institution at the Last Supper and included an invocation of the Holy Spirit (the 'Epiclesis').

The first Christians held services in private homes or house churches. The oldest Christian building known to be used exclusively for religious functions seems to be a house remodelled extensively for such purposes around AD 235 in Dura Europos, an ancient city on the right bank of the Euphrates, north-west of Baghdad. When public freedom arrived with the Emperor Constantine, Christians built their own churches or restructured former pagan temples for their worship. Christian art then developed more freely. It had begun in the catacombs of Rome, with representations of Christ as the Good Shepherd, of the Last Supper, of the Virgin Mary, and of the Magi on their way to find Jesus. That earliest Christian iconography included no scenes of the birth of Jesus or his crucifixion. It took hundreds of years before artists directly expressed his crucifixion with all its pain, and his resurrection into glory.

Christians defended high ideals for the family and provided a happier, more secure way of life, especially for women. They held the marriage bond to be sacred, excluded polygamy, divorce, and incest, and rejected a double standard that accepted various forms of sexual licence for pagan men. Right from the time of the *Didache* they condemned abortion and infanticide (2. 2). Non-Christians limited population by practising abortion (which often brought death to the mother and caused infertility to those women who survived). Domitian (Emperor of Rome 81–96), for example, made his niece Julia pregnant and then ordered her to have an abortion, from which she died. Pagans were also ready to kill newborn children, especially baby girls. As Christians did not follow suit, many Christian women survived to intermarry with pagan men and create new households of believers.[11]

Right from the first century (Acts 6: 1; 1 Tim. 5: 3–16), Christian communities respected and financially supported widows. Their expanded sense of family and family obligations was strikingly reflected in Paul's letters and his concern for the poor Christians in Jerusalem. To relieve their misery he repeatedly encouraged believers elsewhere to contribute generously (Rom. 15: 25–7; 1 Cor. 16: 1–4; 2 Cor. 8: 1–9: 15; Gal. 2: 1–10). The Christians of Rome exercised a notable ministry by supporting with their money needy communities elsewhere in the Mediterranean world. This social concern extended beyond the ranks of the believers to all those in great need (see Matt. 25: 31–46). A story about St Laurence (d. 258), one of the seven deacons responsible for the goods of the Roman community and the distribution of alms to the poor, enjoys legendary accretions but expresses nicely the tradition of social service:

When the Prefect of Rome was informed of these charities, imagining that the Christians had hid considerable treasures, he wanted to secure them: for he was no less a worshipper of gold and silver than of Jupiter and Mars. With this in view he sent for St Laurence and said to him, 'Bring out your treasures; the Emperor has need of them to maintain his forces. I am told that according to your doctrines you must render to Caesar the things that belong to him.' Laurence went all over the city, seeking out the poor who were supported by the Church. On the third day he gathered together a great number of them, and placed them in rows, the decrepit, the blind, the lame, the maimed, the lepers, orphans, widows and maidens; then he went to the Prefect and invited him to come and see the treasure of the Church. The Prefect, astonished to see such an assembly of misery and misfortune, turned to the deacon with threatening looks, and asked him what all this meant, and where the treasures were that he had promised to show him. St Laurence answered, 'What are you displeased at? These are the treasure of the Church.'[12]

---

[11] On the role of women in the growth of Christianity, see M. T. Malone, *Women and Christianity* (Dublin: Columba Press, 2000); Stark, *Rise of Christianity*, 95–128.

[12] H. Thurston and D. Attwater (eds.), *Butler's Lives of the Saints*, iii (London: Burns & Oates, 1956), 2978; slightly edited.

Many pagans who survived severe epidemics owed their lives to their Christian neighbours. Two such epidemics, in particular, should be recalled. By courageously caring for the sick, Christians helped to mitigate the epidemics of 165–80 and 251–66, which destroyed up to one-third of the population of the Roman world. These calamitous crises became the occasion of conversions to and growth of the Church. From probably being less than 10,000 in AD 100, Christians passed the 100,000 mark around AD 180, were well over six million by AD 300, and, with around thirty-four million adherents had become more than half the population of the Roman Empire by AD 350.[13]

From Justin to Cyprian

To complete this account of elements from pre-Constantinian times that retain their importance for those who appreciate Catholic Christianity, we wish to retrieve some items from the witness of five writers. We begin with Justin. Among the distinctive features of his writings, two have shown their face in twentieth-century Catholicism. First of all, his *Dialogue with Trypho* illustrated how Catholic thinking should flow naturally towards Judaism. Justin shared the Hebrew scriptures with the Jew Trypho, and never belittled the faith of his debating partner. For several centuries dialogue with Jews and a mission to the Jews were to enjoy a high priority among Christians, not least because Jews remained a significant source of Christian converts.[14] In the third century Origen, one of the greatest Christian scholars of all time, engaged in theological debate with Jews. A section of the *De Incarnatione Verbi* (7. 33–40) by St Athanasius (*c.*296–373) shows how such debate with Jews still mattered to a bishop of Alexandria, a city that had enjoyed one of the largest Jewish communities in any of the ancient world. As a hermit in the Syrian desert, St Jerome (*c.*342–420) learned Hebrew from a Jewish scholar. Hence in producing what came to be called the Vulgate, the most widely used Latin translation of the Bible, he could translate the Hebrew scriptures directly from the original texts. But, sadly, by the fourth century the misinterpretation of the blood curse from Matthew 27: 25, the polemic against 'the Jews' in John's Gospel, some severe language from Paul (e.g. 1 Thess. 2: 14–16), and other texts and factors had encouraged anti-Jewish attitudes among

---

[13] On the growth of Christianity in the aftermath of the epidemics, see Stark, *Rise of Christianity*, 73–94.

[14] Ibid. 49–71.

Christians. With St John Chrysostom (*c.*347–407) anti-Jewish polemics firmly set in; and through the centuries Catholics committed terrible crimes against Jews or remained guilty bystanders of such crimes. The Second Vatican Council called for repentance and denounced 'the hatred, persecutions, and displays of anti-Semitism directed against the Jews at any time and from any source' (*Nostra Aetate*, 4). The thought of Justin and some of his successors deserves to be recovered in the cause of healing religious and human relations between Catholics and the Jewish people—as Pope John Paul II (b. 1920) has led the way in doing.

Justin also merits retrieval for a second thrust of his teaching: a sense of the presence of the 'generative' Word's 'seeds' that have been 'dropped' everywhere. In one way or another, all human beings share in the Word (or Logos) of God. Christians have received the full knowledge of Christ, but others enjoy the presence of the Logos at least in fragmentary ways. Thus Justin interprets Greek history as a prelude and preliminary to Christ and Christianity:

> Plato's teachings are not contrary to Christ's but they are not in all respects identical with them. This is the case with the doctrines of others: the Stoics, the poets, and the prose authors. For each, through his share in the divine generative Logos, spoke well, seeing what was suited to his capacity... Whatever has been spoken aright by anyone belongs to us Christians; for we worship and love, next to God, the Logos, who is from the unbegotten and ineffable God... All those writers were able, through the seed of the Logos implanted in them, to see reality [at least] darkly. For it is one thing to have the seed of a thing and to imitate it up to one's capacity; far different is the thing itself, shared and imitated in virtue of its own grace. (*Second Apology*, 13)

Several decades later Origen was to say something similar, as was Athanasius in the fourth century.[15] Justin's theme of the seeds of the Word returned in the teaching of the Second Vatican Council (the decree *Ad Gentes*, 11), in a 1975 apostolic exhortation from Pope Paul VI (*Evangelii Nuntiandi*, 53), and in further texts and documents from Catholic leaders and theologians as they struggled with the issue of the Church's mission to and dialogue with the members of other religions. It is this context which has configured Jacques Dupuis's reflections on the universal and powerful presence of the Word of God.[16]

[15] See G. O'Collins, *The Tripersonal God* (Mahwah,NJ: Paulist Press, 1999), 93.
[16] See J. Dupuis, *Toward a Christian Theology of Religious Pluralism* (Maryknoll, NY: Orbis, 1997), 57–60, 70–7; id., *Christianity and the Religions* (Maryknoll, NY: Orbis, 2002), 147–56.

Early intimations of themes that have remained dear to Catholics thread through the work of Irenaeus, who preached and expounded his faith in a largely hostile environment. He lived through cauldron years as the second century went to its close. He took over the diocese of Lyons which had suffered from its bishop and others being killed in a Roman persecution of 177. As well as being threatened by external forces, the Church was menaced from within by such Christian heretics as Marcion and the Gnostics. Let us pick out six themes from Irenaeus that Catholics have cherished and developed through the centuries. First of all, he proudly proclaimed the worldwide unity of the one Catholic faith. 'Although scattered throughout the whole world even to the ends of the earth', the Church maintained the essential teaching received from the apostles. 'Although there are many different languages in the world', Irenaeus announced, there were 'no different beliefs or traditions in the churches established in Germany, or in Spain, or among the Celts, or in the East, or in Egypt or Libya, or among those established in the centre of the earth' (i.e. either Italy or Palestine) (*Adversus Haereses*, I. 10. 1–2).

Second, he set his face against the aberrations of Marcion, who rejected the Creator God of the OT as a cruel deity, not to be identified with the Father of our Lord Jesus Christ. Marcion excluded the Jewish scriptures and accepted only an emended version of Luke's Gospel and ten Pauline letters. In effect, Marcion stripped the Christian scriptures of those books (for instance, Matthew's Gospel) that were particularly concerned to justify Christian faith in the light of the OT history and scriptures. Against such errors Irenaeus championed not merely the four Gospels but also the enduring authority of the Jewish scriptures and, in particular, their doctrine of God. There is only one God, who created the material world and human beings made in the divine image and likeness (Gen. I: 27). In excluding the Jewish God and the value of Jewish history, Marcion opened the door to anti-Semitism; Irenaeus strenuously resisted any such belittling of the history of salvation and creation that reached back through Abraham to the beginning of the human story.

Third, through their sin human beings lost the divine likeness but remained in the image of God, even if this was not yet properly manifested until the divine Word came among us. St Augustine of Hippo (354–430) and the Council of Trent (1545–63) were to take further the doctrine of 'original sin' or the loss of grace and wounding of nature suffered by our 'first parents', which affected all later generations of men and women. At times original sin turned into a compromised concept, especially among those who overstressed its evil effects and even maintained the thesis of total depravity, according to which human beings were radically corrupted by the fall into sin. Irenaeus has always remained a secure guide: the loss of the divine *likeness* by Adam and Eve was passed on to their descendants but their sin did not destroy the divine *image*. God's loving pedagogy was to bring our restoration through Christ.

Fourth, Irenaeus developed Ephesians 1: 9 and called this restoration 'recapitulation'. In the guise of the New Adam, the Son of God more than restored what human beings had lost. He reunited all men and women when he crowned and consummated the loving divine plan for all creatures. In this unified version of creation and redemption Irenaeus saw everything as one great drama of God's self-communicating goodness, a vision that in part anticipated the theology of St Maximus the Confessor (*c*.580–662), Blessed John Duns Scotus (*c*.1266–1308) and the optimistic, evolutionary perspective of Pierre Teilhard de Chardin (1881–1955). Even more than Irenaeus' unitary view of creation and redemption, his image of Christ as Last/New/Second Adam has prospered in Catholic Christianity. It was adopted by John Henry Newman (1801–90) in *The Dream of Gerontius*, entered into the last and longest document from the Second Vatican Council (*Gaudium et Spes*, 22), and surfaced in the teaching of Pope John Paul II (e.g. in his 1979 encyclical *Redemptor Hominis*, 8). Catholic liturgy and art has repeatedly developed the same theme. By referring twice to Adam, the *Exultet* or Easter Proclamation, which has been sung for well over a thousand years at the Easter Vigil, implies Christ's role as Last Adam. Icons used by the official liturgy of the Eastern Christian tradition, both Catholic and Orthodox, picture Adam, Eve, and their descendants being released from a long bondage to sin and death when the New Adam comes to rescue them.

Fifth, Irenaeus went beyond Paul's teaching about the 'Last Adam' (Rom. 5: 12–21; 1 Cor. 15: 21–2, 45–9) and acknowledged the role of the obedience of Mary, the Second Eve, in the story of human salvation. Irenaeus' interest in Mary made him one of the first Christians to elaborate the idea of the Word's double generation: the eternal generation from the Father and the generation in time from the Virgin Mary. Already present in the Nicene-Constantinopolitan Creed (AD 381), this theme of the divine and human generation of God's Son was to be taken up very clearly by the teaching of the Council of Chalcedon (AD 451). That council echoed Irenaeus' language about the Word of God being 'one and the same' as the earthly Jesus. The Chalcedonian language of one 'person' or 'subsistence' was not yet available to Irenaeus, but in his simpler way he upheld the personal unity of the incarnate Son of God, a unity that supports the Marian title of 'Mother of God (*Theotokos*)'. We return to this point later in this chapter.

Sixth, where Marcion drastically reduced the authoritative scriptures, the Gnostics added new texts, allegedly the fruit of further divine revelation, in support of their 'spiritualized' version of Christianity. Gnosticism took human redemption to mean the spirit escaping from the body and from the evil, material world. Against such aberrations Irenaeus refused to downplay matter. He insisted on the goodness of the created world in general, and of the human body in particular. Not only its origin (in God's creation) and its destiny (in the resurrection to come) but also (and even more) the incarnation of the Son of God conferred an essential dignity on human bodiliness. Predictably the affirmation of John 1: 14 ('the Word became flesh') assumed a central position for Irenaeus. By assuming 'flesh' (the complete human condition of body and spirit), the Son of God ratified the value of men and women created in God's image and likeness. When they are baptized into Christ and receive him in the Eucharist, their intimate contact with the incarnate and risen Lord will bring them to their own resurrection. One can trace a clear trajectory from Irenaeus' championing of the 'enfleshment' of God's Son and the dignity of our bodily humanity down through the centuries, not least down to Christmas cribs in Italy and elsewhere and Italian art's portrayal of the child Jesus at Mary's breast—both forceful ways of bringing out the true (bodily and spiritual) humanity of the incarnate Word of God.

The brilliant, lapidary expressions of Irenaeus' younger contemporary, Tertullian (*c*.160–*c*.225), have become commonplaces in the talk of Catholics and other Christians.[17] 'The blood of martyrs', he wrote, 'is the seed of Christians' (*Apologeticus*, 50). He spoke of 'the flesh' as 'the hinge of salvation' (*De Resurrectione Carnis*, 8. 2): 'caro cardo salutis'. The memorable statement with which he began this last work characterized the deepest concerns of believers then and later: 'Fiducia Christianorum resurrectio mortuorum, illam credentes hoc sumus (The resurrection of

---

[17] Sadly, later in his life Tertullian joined the Montanists, a Spirit-inspired, anti-institutional movement that encouraged a very ascetic life in expectation of the imminent end of history.

the dead constitutes the confidence of Christians. By believing it, we are what we claim to be).' For decades after Tertullian, Christian tombs used such figures as the three young men surviving their stint in the fiery furnace (Dan. 3: 1–30), Daniel rescued from the lions' den (Dan. 6: 1–28), Susanna saved from a death plotted by two lustful elders, Jonah emerging from the great fish, and Lazarus resurrected by Jesus, to express a hope for a glorious salvation in the risen life to come. Tertullian's statement and ancient Christian sepulchral art anticipated the resurrection hope that Catholics and other Christians would continue to express in later centuries—in particular, through signs and symbols in cemeteries around the world.

To Tertullian we owe the language of God as 'Trinity' and that of 'three persons and one divine substance' or nature. Along with the theological clarity of his language went a certain disparaging of philosophy as productive of heresies. In what was to become a classic formulation, he denounced Greek philosophers and the heirs of Plato's Academy: 'What has Athens to do with Jerusalem? What has the Academy to do with the Church? What have heretics to do with Christians?' (*De Praescriptione Hereticorum*, 7). Fortunately, down through the ages Catholic thinkers have followed the lead of St Basil of Caesarea (*c.*330–79) in his *Address to Young Men on Reading Greek Literature*, and respected the contributions of high culture. They have supported St Thomas Aquinas (*c.*1225–74) in letting philosophy live together with theology. The relationship between living faith and cultivated reason need not turn sour, as the 1998 encyclical letter of John Paul II, *Fides et Ratio*, argued vigorously. Some people regrettably continue to assume that faith is *against* reason, or at least that faith should, schizophrenically, be separated from reason. They should read Dante Alighieri and other outstanding witnesses from the Catholic tradition, whether ancient, medieval, or modern, who espouse faith *and* reason. Divine revelation should be embraced in faith, together with the best that human learning offers.

Our next pre-Constantinian writer, Origen (*c.*185–*c.*254), by his constant attention to the scriptures underwrote their indispensable role for Catholic and all Christian life and thought. The Second Vatican Council drew on Jerome for the concise statement: 'Ignorance of the scriptures is ignorance of Christ' (*Dei Verbum*, 25). Origen had already endorsed this sentiment, and would reproach any Catholics who drift away from letting the scriptures constantly illumine their existence. His interest in prayer and the spiritual life went hand in hand with his biblical scholarship. His commentary on the Song of Solomon initiated a lasting Catholic interest in that anthology of love poems as an allegory of God's relationship with the Church and individual believers. St Bernard of Clairvaux (1090–1153) dedicated eighty-six homilies to the Song of Solomon, and later Catholic mystics also drew from this book when articulating their profound experiences of God.

In our résumé of pre-Constantinian figures, the final one to be retrieved for his continuing Catholic relevance is St Cyprian, who received baptism in 246, was elected bishop of Carthage two years later, and suffered martyrdom in 258. He wrote his famous treatise on Church unity (*De Catholicae Ecclesiae Unitate*), when faced with the issue of Christians who denied their faith under the pressure of persecution and then wished to be reconciled. Some rigorists such as Novatian, a rival bishop of Rome at the time of St Cornelius (pope 251–3), imposed lifelong excommunication or even rebaptism on such apostates. Against such rigorous schismatics Cyprian insisted on divine grace being mediated through the Church: 'You cannot have God for your Father, if you do not have the Church for your mother' (*De Catholicae Ecclesiae Unitate*, 6). The one Church communicated salvation, and the unity of the worldwide Church, founded on and symbolized by Peter, was incompatible with competitive bishops. Apparently Cyprian himself left two versions of a key passage in ch. 4 of his treatise on unity. The shorter, first version ran as follows: 'If someone deserts the Chair of Peter upon whom the Church was built, has he still confidence that he is in the Church?' The longer, second version was apparently written not so much to challenge the rigorists as to sound less 'papalist' when Cyprian was in dispute with St Stephen I (pope 254–7): 'If someone does not hold fast to this oneness of the Church, does he imagine that he still holds the faith? If he resists and withstands the Church, has he still confidence that he is in the Church?'

These questions could be applied to inflexible movements that have recurrently emerged down to the late twentieth century. In Cyprian's own case, an ironical aspect of his work on Church unity emerged in his controversy with Pope Stephen I over baptism administered 'outside the Church'. Like other African and some oriental bishops, Cyprian argued that such baptism had no value. The Church of Rome held, however, that both schismatics and heretics could validly administer baptism. Persecution cut short the controversy and Cyprian died a martyr in 258. In a later chapter on the sacraments we return to this issue.

These last few pages have been dedicated to Justin, Irenaeus, Tertullian, Origen, and Cyprian. Many Christians, and not just Catholics, retrieve with gratitude numerous ways in which they articulated their inherited faith. But certainly Catholics find much to claim and reclaim in their writings and lives. It is no accident that the 1992 *Catechism of the Catholic Church* quotes from or refers to them frequently.

So far in this chapter we have dealt with the emergence of the world-wide Church, its early life and leadership, and five pre-Constantinian figures who shaped the faith and practice of Catholic Christianity in times of persecution. We turn now to Emperor Constantine (d. 337) and the radical change he brought.

THE ROAD TO CHALCEDON

Constantine's decisive victory of 28 October 312 on the outskirts of Rome, either at the Milvian Bridge or further up the River Tiber at Saxa Rubra (now a centre for RAI or the Italian national television and radio authority), made Constantine the emperor of the Western Empire. Before engaging the forces of Maxentius, his rival for power, Constantine reputedly saw in a dream or a vision Christ's cross and the words: 'In this sign you will conquer (*in hoc signo vinces*).' With the sign of the cross on his own helmet and his soldiers' shields, he believed that the one, all-powerful God guaranteed the military triumph. The 313 Edict of Milan, a verbal agreement reached between Constantine and Licinius, the emperor of the Eastern Empire, pledged religious freedom for Christian believers and the restitution of goods confiscated from them during the severe persecution that had been decreed by Emperor Diocletian in February 303 and continued until 310.[18]

Christians experienced a startling reversal of fortune when Constantine initiated a long series of legislative acts that they supported. On 13 May 315, for example, he decreed financial help for poor people so as to check the practice of abandoning newborn children to death. That same day he proclaimed that Catholic churches would be supported by imperial funds. On 23 June 319 he ordered that decisions taken by the courts of bishops were to enjoy a civil effect. On 3 March 321 he decreed Sunday to be a day

---

[18] For ways in which art reflected the Constantinian change, see J. R. Elsner, *Imperial Rome and Christian Triumph. The Art of the Roman Empire AD 100–450* (Oxford: Oxford University Press, 1999).

of rest, and a few months later ordered courts to remain closed on Sundays. A decree of 18 April 321 made the emancipation of slaves easier—by means of a Church procedure. In 324 public money became available for the construction of churches, and in 326 Constantine, encouraged by his elderly mother, St Helena (*c.*255–*c.*330), began building the central shrine of Christendom, the Church of the Resurrection in Jerusalem. The Emperor had already started building St Peter's Basilica in Rome, sited on the place of the apostle's martyrdom and burial, and completed in 328. A decree of 14 June 326 forbade married men to keep a concubine at home. In late 330 bishops and priests, along with Jewish clergy, were exempted from a range of public duties.

How deeply Christian was Constantine's faith? To what extent did he prove himself a political opportunist, who—in the spirit of 'if you can't beat them, join them'—made an ally out of the Church, which by his time had become a large state within the state? The very titles of books, such as Paul Keresztes's *Constantine: A Great Monarch and Apostle* (Amsterdam: J. C. Gieben 1981) and Alastair Kee's *Constantine versus Christ: The Triumph of Ideology* (London: SCM, 1982), reflect the sharply divergent answers scholars have given to the question of Constantine and Christianity. What cannot be reasonably doubted is the depth of the basic religiosity, which, together with much immoral behaviour, characterized his life. Eventually he received baptism shortly before he died in 337.[19] In the meantime that 'Father of Church History', Bishop Eusebius of Caesarea (*c.*260–*c.*340), who attended the dedication of the Church of the Resurrection in Jerusalem, had been busy encouraging the notion of the Emperor as the providential instrument of divine salvation and even as vicar of God the Father on earth. Whatever else it did, Constantine's toleration of Christianity brought no separation of Church and state. This first Christian emperor of the Roman Empire convened, funded, and (at least initially) presided at the first General Council, that of Nicaea I in 325; he legislated for orthodox faith, outlawed heresy, and preached weekly sermons to his courtiers. Church leaders frequently agreed with him and with other civil authorities that heretics could be punished by fines, confiscation of property, torture, and even death.

---

[19]   See H. A. Drake, *Constantine and the Bishops: The Politics of Intolerance* (Baltimore: Johns Hopkins University Press, 2000); S. N. C. Lieu and D. Montserrat (eds.), *Constantine: History, Historiography and Legend* (London: Routledge, 1998).

Henceforth Christianity and, in particular, Catholic Christianity would continue to struggle with Church–state relations—under monarchies, dictatorships, oligarchies, democracies, and all manner of variants in these systems of government. Eusebians of all centuries have expected the state and the Church to work closely together for the glory of God. Despite the changes, 'the state' could also work against 'the Church': e.g. St Athanasius of Alexandria had to go into exile five times and St John Chrysostom (d. 407) was twice deposed from his see (Constantinople) by the imperial court. Others have stressed the relative independence of civil and religious spheres. Until 313 numerous writers such as Tertullian had expressed the sense of Christians being citizens of heaven and hence strangers on earth. They obeyed the state where essential civil duties were involved, but preferred to distance themselves from Caesar and his concerns. Now the situation was changed forever. The relations between St Ambrose of Milan (*c.*339–97) and Emperor Theodosius I (*c.*346–95) exemplify the new complexity.[20]

In 388, after a mob encouraged by their bishop had burned down a synagogue at Callinicum on the Euphrates river, Theodosius ordered the bishop to pay for the rebuilding of the synagogue. Ambrose protested to the Emperor: a Christian could not do such a 'favour' to some Jews (*Epistola*, 9). Theodosius insisted that the synagogue should be rebuilt but did not insist on the guilty bishop receiving the bill: the state would pay for the reconstruction. At a Mass celebrated in the Emperor's presence Ambrose challenged Theodosius to cancel the order for the rebuilding of the synagogue and used his popularity to extract this volte-face from the reluctant Emperor. In 390, after Theodosius had permitted (or even ordered) a massacre in Thessalonica to avenge the killing of one of his generals, Ambrose refused him communion until he had done public penance. The Emperor did so, and was publicly reconciled at Christmas 390.

While Ambrose could bring such effective influence to bear on Theodosius, he could not always do so with Magnus Maximus, the emperor who from 383 until 388 controlled Britain, Gaul, and Spain. Maximus persecuted Priscillian (a one-time bishop of Avila) and his followers. Their dualistic heresy was borrowed from Gnosticism and followed Sabellian

---

[20] On Ambrose and his times see J. Moorhead, *Ambrose: Church and Society in the Late Roman World* (Reading, Mass.: Addison-Wesley, 1999).

tendencies by interpreting 'Father', 'Son', and 'Holy Spirit' as merely three modes or facets of the one, mono-personal God. (A shadowy third-century figure, Sabellius had apparently explained trinitarian language in terms of three kinds of divine actions and denied any personal distinctions within the divinity.) Priscillian's false ideas included a moral rigorism which went as far as to condemn marriage. Despite the protests of Ambrose and St Martin of Tours (d. 397), the imperial authorities, encouraged by some Gallic bishops, executed Priscillian at Trier in 388. Ambrose reacted by excommunicating Maximus and the bishops who had supported the prosecution and execution of Priscillian and his friends.

As the fourth century went on, Christians—but not necessarily all their leaders—had become more privileged and less tolerant. Towards 400 their faith had become a qualification for public office, and Christianity the state religion. Increasingly restrictions were placed on pagan worship. In 415 a Christian mob in Alexandria lynched the outstanding Neoplatonist philosopher, Hypatia. Their archbishop, known to history as St Cyril, was suspected of being party to her killing, but this was never proved. Certainly he encouraged the destruction of synagogues. As we shall see, his intolerance could also be aimed at Christian bishops like Nestorius of Constantinople.

When Constantine's victory sealed public freedom for Christians, the Roman Empire, despite recurrent crises, still looked uniquely stable. Yet from 400 its frontiers began collapsing in an alarming fashion. In 410 a shock ran through the Empire when the Visigoth leader Alaric, an Arian Christian, captured Rome. St Jerome wrote from Bethlehem: 'Rome, capturer of the world, fell captive' (*Epistola*, 127. 12). The Vandals, led by Gaiseric, also an Arian Christian, had overrun North Africa by 429. In 442 the Roman legions abandoned Britain. Between 410 and 463, invading forces had put Rome itself under siege eight times, occupied the city six times, and sacked it twice (in 410 and 455). It was Pope Leo I, and not a Roman emperor, who persuaded Attila, king of the Huns (known as 'the Scourge of God'), not to sack Rome in 452, the year after Leo's teaching on Christ had been solemnly endorsed at the Council of Chalcedon. Let us now pull together some of the major achievements for Catholic Christianity from Constantine in 313 to Leo in 451. We do so under the headings of 'Councils and Controversies' and 'Lights and Shadows'.

Councils and Controversies

Toleration had hardly arrived before Christians found themselves embroiled in a long and decisive struggle for their faith in Christ. Born shortly after Origen died, Arius (*c.260–c.336*) inherited Origen's trinitarian teaching about the Father, the Son, and the Holy Spirit as three *hypostaseis* or distinct individuals who share in the one divine nature but manifest a certain subordination (of the Son and the Spirit to the Father).[21] Arius apparently wanted to push this subordination much further. He spread his views not only by preaching powerfully but also by composing popular verses and songs. He held that the Father is absolutely beyond the Son and, being unbegotten, is the only true God. Any generation 'from the substance (*ousia*)' of the Father would misinterpret the divinity in physical categories and wrongly suggest the divine substance being divided into two or three parts. Like the followers of Sabellius, Arius and his group wanted to preserve the absolute 'mon-archy (one principle)' of God. But unlike the Sabellians, they held on to the real difference of identity between the Father and the Son. (Arius had almost nothing to say about the Holy Spirit.) Where Sabellians asserted a strict unity of the divine essence without any real distinction of subjects (so that 'Father', 'Son', and 'Holy Spirit' were simply three different modes in which the strictly mono-personal God acts and is revealed), the Arians distinguished the subjects while denying their unity of essence. They considered the Son inferior to and, in fact, infinitely different from the Father.

In an incoherent statement ridiculed by Athanasius, who attended the Council of Nicaea in 325 and became bishop of Alexandria in 328, Arius described the Son as being created out of nothing and by the will of the Father, but not created 'like one of the creatures'. Using a phrase repudiated by Origen in the previous century, Arius denied that the Son was co-eternal with the Father: 'there was [a time] when he was not'. Arius insisted that the Son's being 'generated' was in effect a creation. The only creature directly created by the Father, the Son carried out the will of the Father by creating everything else and so acting as a kind of demiurge, a Logos

---

[21] On Arius and Arianism see D. E. Groh, 'Arius, Arianism', *Anchor Bible Dictionary*, i. 384–6; R. Williams, *Arius: Heresy and Tradition* (London: Darton, Longman & Todd, 1987). For clear guides to the early councils, see W. Portier, *Tradition and Incarnation* (Mahwah, NJ: Paulist Press, 1994), 160–206, and N. Tanner, *The Councils of the Church: A Short History* (New York: Crossroad, 2001), 13–33.

exercising power between God and the universe. Hence the One who became incarnate was less than God and not truly divine. It was this challenge to Christ's divinity that the Council concerned itself to rebut.

Nicaea I confessed in its creed that the Son is 'of the substance/being (*ousia*) of the Father, God from God, Light from Light, true God from true God, begotten, not made, of one substance/being (*homoousios*) with the Father'. The Council anathematized those who said of the Son 'there was [a time] when he was not', and that 'he was created out of nothing and is of a different *hypostasis* or *ousia* from the Father' (DH 125–6; ND 7–8). This amounted to holding that the Son is truly Son of God and not less than God: in the generation (not creation) of the Son, the substance of the Father has been fully communicated, and the Son is co-eternal with the Father.

The Council of Nicaea spoke out clearly for the divinity of Christ, but used three terms that continued to run into difficulties: *homoousios, ousia*, and *hypostasis*. Many bishops and others remained uneasy about or even antagonistic to the term *homoousios*. It was not biblical. It had a chequered background, and, in particular, could be misunderstood in a Sabellian sense, as if the Father and the Son were identical not only in substance/ nature but also as personal subjects. *Homoousios* might also be applied to material substances such as a whole mass of bronze that can be cut up into parts and made into such particular, separate objects as coins. Some of the early 'material' analogies for the relationship between Father and Son were open to this misunderstanding. Furthermore, at least some bishops understood *homoousios* in a generic sense, as if the Father and the Son shared the *same kind* of being but not an *identical* being. In ancient Greek, as in modern English, 'same' does not necessarily mean 'numerically identical' or 'one and the same'. In any case a number of bishops, while opposed to Arius, continued to prefer a term that had been discussed and rejected at the Council, *homoiousios*, in the sense of the Son 'being of like substance' with the Father.

As used both in the NT and in (Platonic and Stoic) philosophy, the relevant range of meanings for *hypostasis* tended to cluster under two headings: *hypostasis* as (1) the primordial essence, or as (2) the individuating principle, subject, or subsistence. In the third century Origen confronted Sabellian modalism by speaking (in the latter sense) of the triune God as three individual *hypostaseis*. The terminological problem was bedevilled by the fact that Western (Latin) Christians, ever since the time of Tertullian, understood the Greek *hypostasis* to correspond to their Latin term *substantia*: that is to say, they took *hypostasis* in sense (1) above. Hence when Eastern (Greek) Christians acknowledged the three *hypostaseis* of God, Westerners were easily shocked as they interpreted such a statement to mean three separate divine substances. However, from their point of view, the Greeks could misunderstand Latin talk about the one divine *substantia* as lapsing into the modalist position of one *hypostasis* in sense (2) of the word and hence as a denial of any personal distinctions within God.

The upshot for Nicaea of this inherited ambiguity about *hypostasis* was that taking *ousia* and *hypostasis* to be equivalents, as the Council did, ran the risk of *homoousios* being misunderstood in a Sabellian way. Father and Son are not only of the same *ousia* but also of the same *hypostasis*—in sense (2). Then there would be no real distinction between Father and Son; they would not be distinct individuals.

Uncompromising in championing the teaching of Nicaea I and in opposing Arius and the Arians, Athanasius suffered much during his forty-five years as bishop of Alexandria (328–73) and was driven five times into exile or hiding. An eloquent and learned hermit turned bishop, St Basil of Caesarea (*c.*330–79) and others joined Athanasius in support of *homoousios* and its right interpretation. The term pointed to the numerical identity of essence between the three divine persons. In particular as regards the 'substance' of God, the Father and the Son are the 'same one'. Those decades of controversy left indelibly imprinted on the conscience of Catholics (and many other Christians) a deep faith in Christ's divinity. This faith remained for them an utterly non-negotiable truth.

Basil, St Gregory of Nazianzus (329–89), and their associates in Cappadocia not only helped secure the triumph of Nicaea's teaching on the common essence, substance, or *ousia* shared by Father and Son (and Holy Spirit) but also a switch away from the Council's terminology. They no longer used *ousia* and *hypostasis* as synonyms. The Cappadocians wrote of one *ousia* (numerically identical essence or substance), divinity, or power shared by three *hypostaseis* (individual subsistences) or *prosopa* ('persons'). This group of saintly theologians helped put their trinitarian language firmly in place at the First Council of Constantinople (381), which reaffirmed and expanded the teaching of Nicaea to give the Church, the enduringly successful Nicene-Constantinopolitan Creed. It became the sole baptismal confession of the East and the eucharistic creed of all Christians.

Constantinople I, in particular, defended the existence of the Holy Spirit as a distinct and equal divine person, and did so by enlarging massively the third article of the Creed which Nicaea I had left brief and cryptic ('we believe in the Holy Spirit'). Probably because the majority of the bishops and Emperor Theodosius I (who had convened the Council in the hope of putting an end to the disputes about the divinity of the Son and the Holy Spirit) recognized the anger roused in some circles by Nicaea's term *homoousios*, they declined to apply this term to the Holy Spirit in the Creed. They preferred instead to acknowledge the Spirit's divinity in more biblical terms as 'the Lord and Life-giver', who 'proceeds from [but is not created by] the Father', who is 'worshipped and glorified' together with the Father and the Son, and who 'spoke through the prophets'.

As regards Christ, Constantinople not only confirmed Nicaea's teaching on his divinity but also maintained his full and perfect humanity. This was done by condemning the teaching of Apollinarius of Laodicea (*c*.310– *c*.390) (DH 151; ND 13). He had been so intent on defending the Nicene faith in Christ's divinity that he held that in the incarnation, the Logos or Word of God assumed a body but took the place in Christ of the higher (spiritual and rational) soul. Hence Apollinarius did not acknowledge a complete humanity in Christ; he was truly divine but not fully human. In his rejection of Apollinarianism, Gregory of Nazianzus gave classical expression to a theme that goes back at least to Origen, when he argued that to have saved us, Jesus must be also fully human: 'the unassumed is the unhealed' (*Epistola*, 101. 32). To have healed human nature in its entirety (including our rational soul), the Logos must have assumed a complete nature when taking on the human condition.

Granted then that Christ is truly divine (Nicaea I, also reaffirmed by Constantinople I) and fully human (Constantinople I), how is the union between his divinity and humanity to be understood and interpreted? One could state this union weakly to the point of seeing two subjects, the human Jesus and the divine Logos, who coexist and collaborate in a union of love. One could also maximalize the union to the point of eliminating the real distinction between the two natures. Decades were to pass before the Council of Chalcedon made it clear that the union should be seen as taking place in the person and not in the natures. The unity is due to the one person, the duality to the natures.

Twenty years before Chalcedon, matters came painfully to a head in the controversy between Nestorius (d. *c.*451) of Constantinople, and St Cyril of Alexandria (d. 444, and bishop of Alexandria from 412), which climaxed at the Council of Ephesus in June 431. Unguarded in his theological language, Nestorius laid himself open to the accusation of turning the distinction between Christ's two natures into a separation and proposing a merely moral unity between the eternal Son of God and Jesus as adopted son. Implacable in his opposition to Nestorius, Cyril himself was accused of confusing or 'mixing up' Christ's divinity and humanity. A certain absence of clarity in the use of terms bedevilled the whole situation. Moreover, Nestorius found it hard to attribute to the Word of God the events of Jesus' human life: in particular, his human birth from Mary. Hence Nestorius declined to call Jesus' mother 'the Mother of God' (*Theotokos*). This popular Marian title had probably been used by Origen and had been commonly employed by Athanasius, Gregory of Nazianzus, and other fourth-century figures. Nestorius at first proposed 'Mother of Christ' (*Christotokos*) and eventually was ready to accept *Theotokos*. But by then it was too late. His leadership of the see of Constantinople had been fatally jeopardized by his excessive insistence on the integrity and distinction of Christ's two natures and his failure to appreciate the unity of the one acting subject that justified calling Mary the Mother of (the Son of) God. A sense of this unity in Christ led the Council of Ephesus to champion the Marian title of *Theotokos* and depose Nestorius. Cyril and the Council had the Nicene-Constantinopolitan Creed on their side: it attributes to one and the same subject divine and human attributes. This implies the appropriateness of confessing that the eternal Word of God was born, suffered, died, and rose from the dead. The law of prayer was the law of belief (*lex orandi lex credendi*). Hence the Council of Ephesus confessed that '(the Son of) God was born', just as in 553 the Second Council of Constantinople would confess that '(the Son of) God suffered/ died in the flesh' (DH 432; ND 620/10; see DH 401; ND 617).

The Council of Ephesus indicated clearly that the divinity and humanity of Christ are not separated. If so, are they really to be distinguished? And, if not, how are they united? These questions remained to set the agenda for the Council of Chalcedon in 451.

In an important (but fateful) letter of April 433 to John the patriarch of Antioch, Cyril had written of 'the difference' between Christ's two natures, 'from which came the union'. Shortly after Cyril's death in 444, this language was pushed to an extreme by the head of a large monastery in Constantinople, Eutyches (*c.*378–454). When interpreting the union effected by the incarnation, he apparently argued that after the union the human nature is absorbed by the divine nature. Hence Christ is 'from' two natures but not 'in' two natures. Only one 'nature (*physis*)' remains after the union, and Christ cannot be said to be and remain 'consubstantial' or of the same nature with human beings. The crisis occasioned a famous letter from Pope Leo the Great to the patriarch of Constantinople, his *Tomus* to Flavian. Leo maintained a wonderful balance when describing the undiminished duality (and distinctive properties) of Christ's two perfect natures and the unity of his one person.

Leo believed that his *Tomus* sufficed. But, after Theodosius II, who had supported Eutyches, fell from his horse and died, the new emperor, Marcian, insisted on convoking the Council of Chalcedon. After confirming the Nicene-Constantinopolitan Creed and other earlier doctrinal statements, the Council affirmed the one person (*prosopon* or *hypostasis*) of Christ *in* (not 'out of' or 'from') two natures (*physeis*), divine and human. It specified that 'the one and the same Christ, Son, Lord, and Only begotten' was made known in these two natures that both maintain their full characteristics, and so exist after the incarnation 'without confusion or change, and without division or separation' (DH 300–2; ND 613–15). 'Without confusion or change' aimed to exclude the current error of Eutyches in merging Christ's two natures, 'without division or separation' to exclude the error attributed to Nestorius of separating the two natures. The Council of Chalcedon was attended by 520 bishops; Emperor Marcian himself read out the final draft of Chalcedon's definition.

In teaching that Christ is one person and has two natures, Chalcedon proved a lasting success in regulating language about Christ. But it left some, even much, unfinished business: for instance, the analysis and definition of 'person'—a task that belongs in any case to theologians and philosophers rather than to the work of an ecumenical council. Moreover, unlike Arius and Apollinarius (condemned with their followers in 325 and 381 respectively), the groups who remained unreconciled to the teaching at Ephesus in 431 and at Chalcedon in 451 still have their followers—known, respectively, as Nestorians (who call themselves, however, 'Assyrians' or 'the Church of the East') and Monophysites (now generally named 'Oriental Orthodox'). In November 1994 a common declaration signed by Mar Dinkha IV, the patriarch of the Assyrian Church of the East, and

Pope John Paul II laid to rest, at least officially, differences between the Catholic Church and the followers of Nestorius over their belief in Christ (ND 683). In May 1973 a joint declaration between Pope Paul VI and the Coptic pope, Shenouda III of Egypt, had already effected an official reconciliation over the language and teaching of Chalcedon between Catholics and some of those who rejected that Council's 'Dyophysite' (two natures) teaching about Christ (ND 671a).

Between Emperor Constantine's official toleration of Christianity in 313 and the Council of Chalcedon in 451, the controversies we have summarized laid down Catholic faith in Christ and the tripersonal God. Some other controversies clarified other characteristically Catholic beliefs about Christ and the tripersonal God. The rigorism that Novatian exemplified in the third century flared up again around 311: a new bishop of Carthage was to be consecrated by a bishop who was accused of being a traitor during Emperor Diocletian's severe persecution. The dissenting bishops chose a different candidate, later succeeded by another bishop, Donatus (hence the name of the schism, Donatism), who resisted any compromise and was killed in 347 during an assault on his basilica in Carthage. The Donatists seem to have denied the validity of sacraments conferred by unworthy ministers, to have required rebaptism of Christians who lapsed back into sin, and held that only holy persons belonged to the Church. St Augustine of Hippo (354–430) opposed the Donatists with love, but with a firmness that went as far as approving violent measures (*Epistolae*, 93; 105; 185). A conference at Carthage in 411 attended by 284 Donatist bishops and 286 Catholic bishops weakened the Donatists; and they finally disappeared when the Muslims overran Christianity in North Africa. In their conflict with Donatism, Catholic leaders stood not only for a worldwide Church over a merely African Church, but also against any attempt to turn the Church into a community that admits and maintains only saintly men and women.

Augustine also had to contend with the heresy of Pelagianism, a 'do-it-yourself' version of Christianity which held that we can move towards salvation through our sustained efforts, and that we do not rely from the start on divine grace or transforming help freely and lovingly given by God. A theologian and biblical scholar from the British Isles, Pelagius taught in Rome in the late fourth and early fifth century before heading down to North Africa when Rome became menaced by the Goths. Because of their nature created by God, human beings, he argued, always have the power to choose what is good. His followers explained original sin as no more than the bad example of Adam and Eve, which did not interiorly harm their descendants and left intact the natural exercise of free will. Pelagius himself encouraged a strongly ascetical life and the development of a moral elite. Vigorously opposed by Augustine who recognized how much human freedom has been weakened by inherited sin, Pelagianism was condemned by two local councils in North Africa (DH 222–30; ND 501–2, 1901–6) and by the Council of Ephesus (DH 267–8). Some later Catholic spiritual teachers were to say, 'Act as if everything depended on you, but pray as if everything depended on God.' But the latter sentiment, the primacy of grace, outweighed the first. Mainstream Catholicism never wavered in the conviction it drew from Augustine: 'When God crowns our merits, he does nothing else than crown his gifts.'

In the great scheme of Catholic things, Augustine's contribution went far beyond what he did in the Donatist and Pelagian controversies.[22] Generations have treasured, for instance, his touching account of the death of his mother. St Monica (*c*.331–87), who died in Ostia (the port of Rome) when she and her sons were waiting to return by ship to North Africa. Her words to Augustine catch the very heart of the communion of saints, the spiritual union between Christ and all Christians, whether already in heaven (or purgatory) or still living on earth: 'This only I ask of you that you should remember me at the altar of God' (*Confessions*, 11. 27). Monica's words affirmed her belief in purgatory, the state of those who die in God's friendship but who still need to be fully cleansed (through Christ's merits) from the effects of their sins and to grow spiritually before enjoying the final vision of God. Through their prayers for the dead (attested at least since the second century) and celebration of the Eucharist for the dead (attested at least since the third century), Christians expressed their loving concern for their dear ones who had died but who remained united with them in God. Praying for the dead was to remained a typical feature of Eastern and Western worship. The words of Augustine's dying mother became perhaps the loveliest witness from all times to this

[22] See A. D. Fitzgerald (ed.), *Augustine Through the Ages* (Grand Rapids, Mich.: Eerdmans, 1999); C. Harrison, *Augustine: Christian Truth and Fractured Humanity* (Oxford: Oxford University Press, 2000). For a summary of Augustine's achievements see 'Augustine, St, of Hippo', *Oxford Dictionary of the Christian Church*, 128–30; to the list of scholars whose publications on Augustine feature in the excellent bibliography, one should add such names as M. R. Barnes, R. Dodaro, G. P. Lawless, R. J. O'Connell, B. Studer, and, in particular, A. Trapé.

practice. On prayers for the dead and so much more, Augustine profoundly influenced later Christian thought and practice.

Lights and Shadows

This summary of the years between Constantine and Chalcedon would
remain patently incomplete without an account of some developments
that were to cast lights or shadows over the Catholic centuries to come.
The lights included the rise of monasticism and pilgrimages, while
shadows showed up in some areas of authoritative administration.

Monasticism may be described as a movement among baptized Christians who respond to Christ's call for perfection (Matt. 5: 48; 19: 16–26) by
giving themselves through poverty, celibacy, and obedience to a life of
prayer, common worship, and service of others. Towards the end of the
Roman persecutions, an ascetic existence (involving prayer, penance, and
manual work) in the deserts of Egypt, Palestine, and Syria began to
provide a heroic alternative to real martyrdom. In Egypt St Antony the
Hermit (c.252–356) and St Pachomius (c.290–346) organized their followers around a way of life led by spiritual guides, thus preparing the way for
the two standard forms of monasticism: the life of hermits and life in
common. Deeply influenced by Basil of Caesarea, Eastern monasticism
helped to promote Western monasticism through such writings as *The
Life of St Antony* by Athanasius of Alexandria and the *Conferences* of St
John Cassian (c.360–435). The monastic life of Augustine of Hippo and
his community also exercised a big influence over coming developments.

Journeys of devotion to holy places have been practised by Christians
and adherents of other religions. After freedom came with Constantine,
pilgrimages to the Holy Land and to the tombs of the Roman martyrs
increased. In her old age Helena, the saintly mother of Constantine,
visited the Holy Land and founded basilicas on the Mount of Olives
and at Bethlehem. A tradition that dates from about seventy years after her
pilgrimage in 326 told of her discovering the cross on which Christ died. A
work from the end of the fourth century, the *Pilgrimage of Etheria*, gives
the story of a Christian pilgrim (probably a Spaniard) who visited Jerusalem and its neighbourhood. She described in detail the liturgical ceremonies: not only the daily and Sunday offices but also the services for the
Epiphany, Holy Week (including the procession of palms to the Mount of
Olives and the veneration of the cross), Easter, and Pentecost. Other
traditional and modern places of Christian pilgrimage came to include

BERNADETTE

FIG. 2. An anonymous picture expresses the intensity of St Bernadette Soubirous at prayer. Her visions of the Virgin Mary in 1858 made Lourdes into one of the world's most popular places of pilgrimage. (Bibliothèque des Arts Decoratifs, Paris/Bridgement-Charmet collection.)

Santiago de Compostela (Spain) and the Marian shrines of Czestochowa (Poland), Fatima (Portugal), Guadalupe (Mexico), Loreto (Italy), Lourdes (France), and the island of Tinos, where the Orthodox celebrate in a special way the 'dormition' (or falling asleep in death) of Our Lady.

Under Diocletian (emperor 284–305) the Roman Empire was reorganized into fifteen 'dioceses', or administrative divisions. In the Western Church this became the standard term for the territory under the authority of a bishop or archbishop. Even earlier, Catholic Christianity had already taken over some symbols and terms of public administration. Thus from the third century the seat, or 'cathedra', of Roman magistrates was adopted to symbolize the authority of bishops in teaching, preaching, and presiding at worship in their 'cathedral', the chief church in a diocese where the bishop has his throne or cathedra. Terms used in the public adminstration of the Empire passed into common Christian usage. Thus ministers were spoken of as 'ordained' (or initiated into office), and gatherings of bishops came to be called 'synods'.

The political authority of Rome made it easier for Christians and their leaders to accept the distinctive ministry of leadership invested in St Peter's successor, the bishop of Rome. A sense of the primacy of authority enjoyed by the bishop of Rome developed notably in the fifth century. At the Council of Chalcedon the bishops greeted 'for the confirmation of the orthodox faith, the letter [*Tomus*] of the Ruler of the greatest and elder Rome, the most blessed and most holy Archbishop Leo . . . since it agrees with the confession of the great [St] Peter and is a pillar of support to all against the heterodox'.[23]

Inevitably there were already shadows over the history of the bishops of Rome. The worldly and politically canny Damasus (pope 366–84) is remembered as St Damasus. But the murderous strife that accompanied his election and left at least 137 people dead in what is now the Basilica of Santa Maria Maggiore hinted at the renaissance popes and scandalous times to come. Earlier in the fourth century Constantine had founded Constantinople (or the 'New Rome') on the site of old Byzantium. Little by little the division between the Western and the Eastern Empire would entail a separation between the pope in Rome and the bishop of Constantinople, who, despite Pope Leo's objections, formally received patriarchal powers at

---

[23] J. Stevenson and W. H. C. Frend, *Creeds, Councils and Controversies* (London: SPCK, 1989), 352.

the Council of Chalcedon in 451. Previously the Church of Alexandria had striven for pre-eminence with Constantinople. After 451 tension was to grow between Rome and the patriarch of Constantinople, acknowledged from the sixth century as the ecumenical patriarch of the East.

DEVELOPMENTS AND TENSIONS

Missionary outreach, political changes, doctrinal developments, and monastic growth can serve as headings to bring together some of the major changes in Catholic Christianity from the middle of the fifth century up to the close of the first millennium.

Missionary Outreach

A story of loss and gain, those centuries featured some outstanding missionaries, who followed in the footsteps of such earlier evangelists as St Gregory Thaumaturgus (*c.*213–*c.*270), St Gregory the Illuminator (*c.*240–332), and St Martin of Tours. Converted to Christian faith when he spent several years in Palestine with Origen, Gregory Thaumaturgus (wonder-worker) returned to Pontus and his native city of Neocaesarea. He soon became its bishop and made Christians of its population. Among those whom he instructed in the Christian faith was the grandmother of St Basil the Great and St Gregory of Nyssa (*c.*330–*c.*395). He was remembered not only for working many miracles but also for being the first recipient of a vision involving the Blessed Virgin Mary. Gregory the Illuminator, the 'Apostle of Armenia', returned from exile to Armenia and eventually converted the king to Christianity, who around 301 made Christianity the official religion of the country. For some generations the family of Gregory supplied the bishop or 'Catholicos' for Armenia. This tradition began when he consecrated his son to succeed him; this son was among the bishops who attended the Council of Nicaea in 325. Martin of Tours, as well as encouraging the spread of monasticism in Gaul, did something new by preaching in the countryside and introducing there an early form of parish structure. Although Jesus had largely avoided the towns and preached in villages or out in the countryside, Christianity quickly became an urban religion. It often took centuries before the rural population or the 'pagans' (those who lived in country villages) were evangelized. It was not until around 1400 that the majority of Europe's population was Christian.

In summarizing the missionary outreach of Catholic Christianity during the first thousand years, we will concentrate on Western, Eastern, and Northern Europe. But first a word about Africa and Asia. In the Book of Acts, Luke tells the story of an official in the service of the queen of the Ethiopians being baptized on his way home from Jerusalem (Acts 8: 26–39). In the fourth century St Frumentius (*c*.300–*c*.380), then a young Christian accompanying a merchant on his way back from India, was captured by some Ethiopians but came to assist the king of Abyssinia in matters of government. He took the opportunity to carry on mission work and around 350 was consecrated bishop by St Athanasius of Alexandria. Christianity soon became the state religion. The Ethiopian Church did not, however, accept the christological teaching of Chalcedon. Apart from brief periods in the fifteenth and seventeenth centuries, it has not since been in communion with the bishop of Rome.

Even before the Council of Ephesus in 431, communion with the Western Church and the bishop of Rome had already been problematic for those who became known as Assyrian Christians or the Church of the East (that is to say, East of the Roman Empire). Political divisions, geographical separation, and misunderstandings helped to harden the break for many centuries. In the meantime, however, from the early sixth century the Church of the East had sent missionaries as far as China and India. Inscriptions on the Sigan-Fu Stone, erected in northwest China in 781, bear witness to the success of those missions. (Replicas of this stone are to be found in the Vatican Museum, the Gregorian University (Rome), and the Metropolitan Museum of Art (New York).) In his travels to China, Marco Polo (d. 1324) found Assyrian Christian communities in almost all the cities he visited. Assyrian Christians made contact with the Malabar or St Thomas Christians of south-west India, apparently evangelized in the first century by St Thomas the Apostle before he died a martyr's death. From the eighth to the sixteenth century the patriarch of the Church of the East in Baghdad used to send the Malabar Christians their metropolitan or bishop who exercised authority not only in his own diocese but over the whole area or province.

Let us turn now to missionary work in the British Isles and other parts of Europe. The first Christians in Ireland were prisoners of war brought there from Roman Britain. Apparently born in Roman Britain, St Patrick (*c*.389–*c*.461) spent time as a slave in Ireland before escaping. He returned as a bishop, made Armagh his episcopal see, and set himself to evangelize the whole island. The daughter of one couple he baptized, St Brigid (d. *c*.523), founded at Kildare the first nunnery in Ireland and exercised much influence in the growth of Catholic Christianity. After Patrick she was to become the second patron saint of Ireland.

Originally the Church's organization followed the divisions of the tribal kingdoms of Connaught, Leinster, Meath, Munster, and Ulster; Dublin (founded only in the tenth century) did not yet exist. In the sixth century large monasteries started to grow and for many centuries ecclesiastical authority was exercised by the abbots of these monasteries. Church government developed around monastic districts rather than diocesan territories. Such abbots as St Columba (*c*.521–97) and St Columbanus (*c*.543–615) left Ireland and proved highly successful missionaries abroad: the former in Scotland, and the latter in Gaul, Switzerland, and Northern Italy. These Celtic monk-missionaries, along with their Anglo-Saxon counterparts, established new monasteries (such as Columba's foundation on the Island of Iona, off the Scottish coast) and spread the practice of 'private' penance or 'auricular' (in the ear) confession of sins. Eventually, especially after the Fourth Lateran Council of 1215, such private confession of sins became standard and definitively replaced the original system of public penance (of which more in Ch. 7).

Some of these missionaries, such as the Irish bishop St Kilian (d. *c*.689) who converted the ruler and much of the population around Würzburg, and the British bishop St Boniface (680–754), died as martyrs in Germany. Boniface, in particular, enjoyed a wide and enduring success in spreading Christianity and organizing the Church in Germany; he more than deserved to be called 'the Apostle of Germany'. One of his disciples founded the abbey of Fulda to assist missionary work among the Saxons. Boniface's tomb turned it into a notable centre of pilgrimage. It is not far from Geismar, where Boniface had made his courageous mark on history by cutting down an oak sacred to the god Thor. The area, still called 'Eichsfeld (the Field of the Oak)', remained very Catholic and, after the Second World War (1939–45), was a centre of opposition to the Communist regime during the years of the German Democratic Republic which collapsed in 1989 with the reunification of Germany.

Boniface's mission in Germany received strong papal support, especially from 722. More than a century earlier, St Gregory the Great (pope 590–604) did much to refound Catholic Christianity in Britain. After he supposedly saw some young Anglo-Saxon slaves in Rome and commented, 'not Angles but angels', he sent St Augustine (d. 604 or 605) to England where he landed in Kent during the summer of 587. There were difficulties between this somewhat timid monk and representatives of the ancient Celtic Church. But the success of Augustine's mission was sealed when he was consecrated the first archbishop of Canterbury. An English Christianity emerged that happily mingled Anglo-Saxon, Celtic, and Roman elements.[24]

Papal support backed other missionaries who fanned out across Europe, such as the English monk St Willibrord (658–739), 'the Apostle of Frisia' (part of the modern Netherlands). Consecrated by St Sergius (pope 687–701), he became the first bishop of Utrecht, collaborated in missionary work with Boniface, and preached as far north as Denmark. A century later another monk-missionary, St Anskar (801–65), went as far north as Sweden, where he built the first Christian church. To further his work Gregory IV (pope 827–44) appointed him bishop of Hamburg and then archbishop of Bremen. Civil wars destroyed the work of Anskar in Sweden, where it was only in the eleventh century that English missionaries were able to undertake the systematic conversion of the country.

Anskar's younger contemporaries, St Cyril (826–69) and St Methodius (c.815–85), brothers from Greece who came to be known as 'the Apostles to the Slavs', were sent by Emperor Michael III from Constantinople to evangelize Moravia (part of what was to become Czechoslovakia). Cyril invented the Glagolithic or Cyrillic alphabet, thus founding Slavonic literature, introduced Slavonic for church worship, and circulated a Slavonic version of the scriptures. After Cyril died on a visit to Rome, Methodius was consecrated a bishop and returned to Moravia with the full backing of the pope. Despite that, the German bishops imprisoned him and it took two years before John VIII (pope 872–82) could secure his release. It was probably from Moravia that Christianity spread to Poland in the second half of the tenth century. Missionary contacts with Constantinople brought Christianity to Russia. In 988 Prince Vladimir of Kiev was baptized and made Christianity the official religion of his realm. But by that time political upheavals had dramatically changed the face of Christianity.

---

[24] See B. Ward, *High King of Heaven: Aspects of Early English Spirituality* (Kalamazoo, Mich.: Cistercian Publications, 1999).

Political Changes

Under Justinian I (Roman emperor 527–65), the decline of imperial power was reversed for a time. He reconquered North Africa from the (Arian) Vandals and Italy from the Ostrogoths, who were also Arian Christians; he also re-established imperial authority in part of Spain, where the (Arian) Visigoths had dominated. He built many magnificent basilicas, including the majestic Santa Sophia in Constantinople. Dedicated to the person of Christ as 'Holy Wisdom', it was to be converted into a mosque when the city fell to the Turks in 1453. A champion of orthodox Christianity, Justinian persecuted the Montanists and in 529 closed pagan schools of philosophy. They included the celebrated Academy or Platonic school, which had met in the gardens and olive groves of Academe (on the North-West side of Athens) since the days of Plato and provided a name for countless other academies in modern times. Justinian answered Tertullian's questions ('What has Athens to do with Jerusalem? What has the Academy to do with the Church?') by closing the Academy and forcing many pagans to accept baptism. Through the Second Council of Constantinople (553) the Emperor unsuccessfully tried to end the break between mainline Catholicism (which accepted the Council of Chalcedon's teaching about Christ's two natures) and the Monophysites. (We return to this issue below.) His failure to heal the divisions between the Chalcedonian and the non-Chalcedonian Churches weakened Christianity and made the Muslim takeover much easier in such countries as Egypt. The Emperor's codification of Roman law, the Code of Justinian, was to exercise a great influence on legal systems (both civil and ecclesiastical) in Europe and on subsequent relations between the Church or the 'priesthood (*sacerdotium*)' and the state or imperial authority, the *imperium*. On his Eastern frontiers, Justinian spent years in unsuccessful or at least indecisive conflicts with the Persians. Within a century of his death the whole landscape was changed through the rise of Islam.

After the death of Muhammad in Medina (Arabia) in 632, the Arab conquests of Palestine, Syria, Persia, Egypt, and North Africa moved ahead fast. In the eighth century Muslim forces conquered Spain but were stopped from overrunning the kingdom of the Franks by the victory won near Poitiers in 732 by the forces of Charles Martel (*c.*690–741). Armed conflict, as well as a measure of religious and cultural dialogue, were to characterize Christian–Muslim relations in the centuries to come.

We return to this theme below (in the context of the Iconoclastic controversy) and in the next chapter.

The grandson of Charles Martel, Charlemagne (*c.*742–814, and sole ruler of the Franks from 771), proved highly successful in extending his kingdom, creating good state administration, reforming the clergy, and stimulating learning. He became the first emperor of the Holy Roman Empire when crowned by Pope Leo III on Christmas Day 800 in the old Basilica of St Peter's. The following year his campaign to win back Spain from the Muslims achieved its first notable success when Barcelona was captured. By that time, through defeating the Arian Lombards who had overrun the Italian peninsula at the time of Gregory the Great, Charlemagne had swept away the last dominion of Arian Christianity. But his coronation as the first 'Holy Roman emperor' permanently strained relations with the Eastern emperor (in Constantinople) and the Eastern Church. Under Charlemagne the Nicene-Constantinopolitan Creed began to be chanted regularly at Mass throughout his empire, with the fateful words added about the Holy Spirit proceeding from the Father 'and from the Son' (*Filioque*). Not part of the original Creed, the one word in Latin (which becomes four in English) had been added probably in 675 at the Fourth Synod of Braga (in modern Portugal). This issue comes up in the next section, on doctrinal developments.

Doctrinal Developments

The Council of Chalcedon provided a 'logical' conclusion to the first three ecumenical councils. Against Arianism, Nicaea I used the term *homoousios* to reaffirm 'Christ is (truly) divine'. Against Apollinarianism, Constantinople I insisted 'Christ is (fully) human'. Against what were understood to be the errors of Nestorius, Ephesus professed that Christ's humanity and divinity are not separated. Against Eutyches, Chalcedon taught that, while belonging to the one (divine) person, the two natures of Christ are not merged or confused. Thus the first four councils became acknowledged as representing the essential and orthodox norm for understanding and interpreting the NT's witness to Christ (and the Trinity). In speaking of NT witness, one must add that it provided a starting-point but remained much less specific than were later christological and trinitarian doctrines.

Five months after his election to the papacy, Gregory the Great in a circular letter of February 591 to five Eastern patriarchs (those of

Constantinople, Alexandria, Antioch, Jerusalem, and the former patriarch of Antioch) declared that he received and venerated the first four councils just as he received and venerated the four Gospels (DH 472).[25] Even so late in the day, his endorsement of the second council, Constantinople I, was important. (Having been a papal envoy to Constantinople before becoming a bishop, Gregory showed a proper sensitivity to East–West tensions.) Before recognizing Constantinople I, in which none of its bishops had taken part, the Western Church had shown some resistance. In his letter Gregory also indicated his unqualified acceptance of the fifth council. But this endorsement of Constantinople II was motivated by his fidelity to the first four councils. They remained the touchstone for essential orthodoxy in teaching about Christ and the Trinity.

But, despite proving a logical conclusion to the first three general councils, Chalcedon left some, or even much, unfinished business. For instance, in the innovative part of its teaching it did not define 'person (*prosopon* or *hypostasis*)'. Half a century later, Boethius (*c*.480–524) influenced all later Western teaching on Christ (and subsequent Western philosophy) by defining person as 'an individual substance of a rational nature'. In the meantime, however, a sad division emerged between the Catholic Church and the hardline followers of Cyril of Alexandria, who remained dissatisfied with the Chalcedonian formula of 'two natures'. In an unsuccessful attempt to win them back, Emperor Justinian promoted Constantinople II (553) and a regrettable, posthumous condemnation ('Three Chapters') of three authors who supposedly favoured errors that Cyril had opposed. By using Cyril's 'one nature' and Chalcedon's 'two natures' as equivalent expressions (DS 429; ND 620/8) and presenting the union between 'God the Word' and 'the flesh' as taking place 'hypostatic-ally' (DS 424–6, 429–30; ND 620/4, 5, 8), Constantinople II highlighted the unity of Christ's person over the distinction of the natures. This also came through notably when Chalcedon's 'in' two natures was replaced by Cyril's 'from' two natures (DS 429; ND 620/8). This championing of Cyril also led the Council to remove any possible lingering ambiguity about Christ's divine identity by calling 'our Lord Jesus Christ' 'one of the Holy Trinity' (DS 424, 426, 432; ND 620/4, 5, 10). In line with its stress on the union of divinity and humanity in Christ, the Council anathematized

---

[25] See R. A. Markus, *Gregory the Great and his World* (Cambridge: Cambridge University Press, 1997).

those who would not 'venerate in one act of worship God the Word made flesh together with his flesh' (DS 431; ND 620/9).

With still no peace in sight between the Monophysites (who championed Cyril's language) and the mainstream Dyophysites (who followed Chalcedon's teaching on 'two natures'), Sergius (patriarch of Constantinople from 610 to 638 and himself the son of Monophysite parents) proposed a compromise with his formula of Christ's two natures but 'one energy'. In a correspondence with Sergius, Pope Honorius I (d. 638) wrote of their being only 'one will' in Christ. Defenders of Honorius may explain how he did not lapse into heresy: he was not talking 'ontologically' (as if Christ's human nature literally lacked a human will) but merely 'morally' (in the sense that Christ's human and divine wills worked in such perfect harmony that it was as if they were one). Nevertheless, one can hardly acquit Honorius of being gravely imprudent in his two letters to Sergius (DH 487–8). His 'monothelite' ('one will') language threatened belief in Christ's full humanity, as if the human nature of Christ lacked an essential faculty, its will. The monothelite view transposed Monophysite reductionism from the level of human nature as such to that of human faculties, and represented Christ's human will as being 'absorbed' by his divine will. Patriarch Sergius' 'one energy' formula, in effect, did the same. It slipped over the fact that Christ's 'energy' or modes of activity comes from his natures and not as such from his person. Hence to assert 'one energy' was tantamount to asserting 'one nature'. This amounted to a Monophysite view of Christ's activity, as though his human action were absorbed by the divine principle of activity.

The Third Council of Constantinople (680/1) took a firmly Chalcedonian line by condemning Honorius' monothelite teaching (DH 550–2) and distinguishing the two natures of Christ in terms of their willing and acting. It taught that Christ enjoyed a human and a divine will (the two wills being in perfect harmony with each other) and two 'energies' or 'natural operations'. Applying Chalcedonian terminology to the problem it faced, Constantinople III insisted that the two wills and 'natural operations' were neither separated from each other nor blended together (DH 556–8; ND 635–7). Thus at the level of Christ's will and 'natural' activities, the Council upheld the Chalcedonian balance between a Nestorian separation and a Eutychian blending.

The vindication of Christ's complete humanity was motivated by soteriological considerations. Without a human will, not only would his true 'consubstantiality' with us have been defective but also the reality of the salvation he mediated would have become suspect. Lacking a human will, Christ could not have freely accepted also 'on our side' (and for our sake) the redemptive mission that he carried through.

The Second Council of Nicaea (787) formed an epilogue to the previous six councils by putting an end to the Iconoclastic heresy, a movement which, not long after Jerusalem had come under Muslim control in 638, opposed the use of images in Christian worship and disturbed the Eastern Empire from c.725 to 843. Various causes triggered off this movement: some Christians, for example, played down the importance of Christ's humanity and hence any visual images of him; others believed that the use of icons hampered the conversion to Christianity of Jews and Muslims. In a first phase, icons were destroyed as fostering superstitious practices and even being idols that were incompatible with Christian faith. From the monastery of St Sabas near Jerusalem St John Damascene (c.675–c.749) argued that using images to represent Christ and other sacred persons was a necessary consequence of the incarnation. They visibly expressed faith in the Word of God taking 'flesh' and assuming human existence in our material world. Nicaea II restored images and their veneration (DH 600–3; ND 1251–2). By endorsing iconic expression of belief in the incarnation, the Council summarized and drew to a close the christological teaching of seven ecumenical councils. Not long after Nicaea II, in 843 the Feast of Orthodoxy was established to mark the triumph over Iconoclasm, in particular, and over (christological) heresy, in general. Eastern Christians, both Orthodox and Catholic, still celebrate this feast on the first Sunday of Lent.

Tensions between Eastern and Western Christianity flared up in the ninth century with a brief schism involving Photius (c.810–c.895), who was appointed, deposed, reappointed, and once again deposed as patriarch of Constantinople. Many details of the controversy, which involved several popes and Eastern emperors, remain obscure. But Photius entered history by being the first Eastern theologian to accuse Western Christianity of unilaterally tampering with the Creed by adding the Filioque or teaching about the Holy Spirit 'proceeding' not only from the Father but also from the Son. As regards the government of the Church, the Photian schism encouraged Eastern Christians to be even less willing to accept papal authority. From the time of Charlemagne's coronation in 800 until around 1050, popes often depended far too much either on the Western emperor or on the local or regional nobility in Rome or Italy, respectively. Apart from Nicholas I (pope 858–67) and Sylvester II (pope 999–1003), outstanding popes were sadly lacking. Sergius III (pope 904–11) was said to have murdered his two predecessors, and John XII (pope 955–64) was given the papal office at the age of 20 through the power of his father, the real ruler of Rome. Between 882 and 984 nine popes were murdered: by poison, strangulation, and other methods. That deplorable period in the history of the papacy also played its part in preparing the ground for the break between Western Catholicism and Eastern (Orthodox) Christianity, which is conventionally dated as 6 July 1054.

A monk who became patriarch of Constantinople in 1043, Michael Cerularius (d. 1058), strongly attacked the addition of the Filioque to the Creed and the (Western) use of unleavened bread for the Eucharist. An attempted reconciliation was doomed to failure, since an equally violent personality led the legation from Rome, Cardinal Humbert of Silva Candida. On that fatal 6 July 1054 the Cardinal laid on the altar of Santa Sophia a bull excommunicating Cerularius, who responded by excommunicating the Cardinal. In the long run that clash came to be seen as the beginning of a lasting schism. (The mutual excommunications were to be officially lifted only in December 1965.) But in the short run Eastern and Western Christians continued to have much in common, not least in the area of monastic life.

We have already seen above something of the fruitful story of Eastern and Celtic monasticism. Let us complete this chapter by a postscript on monasticism, which may over time do much to heal the divisions between East and West.

Monastic Growth

In the West St Benedict of Nursia (*c*.480–*c*.550) emerged as the great leader of Western monasticism. After living as a hermit in a cave at Subiaco (outside Rome) for some years, he gradually gathered followers and founded twelve monastic communities, each with twelve monks and an abbot appointed by Benedict. Local problems led Benedict to move south with a small group of monks to Monte Cassino, where he died and is buried. His sister, St Scholastica (*c*.480–*c*.543), who founded a convent a few miles from Monte Cassino, is buried in the same grave as her brother. Benedict's enduring legacy was his monastic rule of life. Drawing on earlier rules for monks fashioned by Basil, John Cassian, Augustine of

Hippo, and others, Benedict composed a spiritually profound and very practical rule for a monastic way of life. The Benedictine motto of 'pray and work (*ora et labora*)' made room for education.

Centuries before the foundation of Western universities, sacred and secular learning remained alive, thanks to such leaders as St Hilda of Whitby (614–80), St Bede 'the Venerable' (*c.*673–735), and many other men and women who followed the monastic way of life. The thousands of finely ornamented manuscripts they lovingly created still glow like jewels in museums around the world. Dated from around 800, the glorious writing and illustrations of the Book of Kells (from a monastery in County Meath but preserved in Trinity College, Dublin) set forth the four Gospels. It bears lasting witness to the monastic love for the inspired scriptures in general, and the life of Christ in particular.

One must never tamper with a masterpiece. Yet Macaulay's vivid evocation of Catholicism with which this chapter began might have benefited from some references to the monastic way of life. Or else one should write a companion piece and celebrate the lasting achievements of Benedict and Basil, Scholastica and Hilda, and the army of men and women who have left the world in their debt through following a monastic rule of life.

So we close our account of the first thousand years of Catholic Christianity. Much remains that is very familiar: the celebration of baptism and the Eucharist; the main lines of faith in Christ and the Trinity (as expressed in the Nicene-Constantinopolitan Creed of 381); the central role of the Gospels, the psalms, the letters of Paul, and the other scriptures (both OT and NT) for our common worship and personal lives; the organization of the worldwide Church into dioceses (called 'eparchies' by Eastern Christians) headed by bishops; the use of images for Christ and his saints (endorsed in 787 by Nicaea II); monastic life for a small but significant number of Catholics (and other Christians); the example of heroic martyrs; and then some basic beliefs championed by St Augustine. Against the Donatists he insisted that the Church embraces saints *and* sinners, and against the Pelagians that, from the beginning to the end of the drama of our redemption, we rely utterly on God's saving grace. We move next to the story of the Catholic Church in the second millennium.

2

The Second Thousand Years

Thousands of years hence Catholicism will probably be even richer,
more luxuriant, more manifold in dogma, morals, law, and worship
than the Catholicism of the present day. A religious historian of the
fifth millennium A.D. will without difficulty discover in Catholicism conceptions and forms and practices which derive from India,
China, and Japan.   (Karl Adam, *The Spirit of Catholicism*)

Contemporary theology must consider the fact that the Reformation
was not only a religious gain but also a religious loss. Although my
system is very outspoken in its emphasis on the 'Protestant
principle', it has not ignored the demand that the 'Catholic substance' be united with it.   (Paul Tillich, *Systematic Theology*)

The point of arrival of this chapter imposes itself automatically: the year
2000. But what middle point should we decide upon? It is tempting to
find the half-way mark at 31 October 1517 and the ninety-five theses that
Martin Luther (1483–1546) published as a call for reform in the Church
but which triggered the Protestant Reformation. Any version of the
second thousand years of Catholicism must deal with the sad divisions
that followed and the latterday attempts to heal these wounds. Nevertheless, what we quoted from Thomas Macaulay at the beginning of Ch.
1 suggests a different breakpoint and another October date: the discovery
on 12 October 1492 of the Americas by Christopher Columbus (1451–
1506). As the British historian put it, the Catholic Church's 'acquisitions in
the New World . . . more than compensated for what she lost in the Old'.

Inevitably any accounting of the Church from the eleventh to the
end of the fifteenth century will concentrate on Europe and European
Catholicism. That was where the overwhelming majority of Catholics

then lived. But Columbus' achievement and other subsequent events had made the situation dramatically different at the end of the twentieth century. By the year 2000 over three-quarters of the world's one billion Catholics were living in the Americas (North, Central, and South), Africa, Asia, and Oceania. Let us begin with the period before Columbus and 1492.

BEFORE COLUMBUS

The elements that expressed and shaped European Catholicism during the five centuries on which the first half of this chapter focuses include building programmes, religious foundations, the sacramentalizing of daily life, crises in leadership, reform movements, and the rise of national states. Some of these developments within the Catholic Church showed style and staying power. They are with us today, and we do not need to plunge back through the centuries to glimpse them.

Building Programmes

A visit to the basilica of St Mary Major leaves the deepest impression on some travellers to Rome—not least through the sweep of Catholic history it incorporates. In a square outside, the fluted column that carries a seventeenth-century statue of the Virgin Mary came from a fourth-century public building constructed by Emperor Constantine. Completed by 440, the interior of the church retains its original magnificence with thirty-six marble columns and four granite ones dividing the nave from the aisles and following the style of a Roman basilica or hall for public adminstration. Exquisite fifth-century mosaics along the nave and over the triumphal arch depict scenes from the life of the Old Testament patriarchs, the life of Moses, and the early life of Christ. Down to the nineteenth century generations have added their statues, pavements, mosaics, chapels, altars, tombs, and the rest, as well as feeling free to adjust or add to the original basilica. One twelfth-century mosaic sets the Virgin Mary on the same throne as Christ and recalls how the Council of Ephesus declared her to be *Theotokos* or Mother of God. What one sees in St Mary Major evokes so many episodes in the history of the Church and the world. For instance, the basilica contains the first figures ever made for a Christmas crèche or crib, those created by Arnolfo di Cambio and his assistants (late thirteenth century). The elaborate ceiling of St Mary

Major, gilded with what is said to be the first gold brought back by Christopher Columbus and presented to Alexander VI (pope 1492–1503) by Ferdinand V of Aragon (1452–1516) and Isabella of Castile (1451–1504), evokes the grim and glorious story of the conquest of the Americas.[1]

Church buildings from the eleventh to the beginning of the sixteenth century bear eloquent witness to the Catholicism of those centuries, when all classes of society conspired to express their faith through mosaics, carvings, paintings, stained-glass windows, and the magnificent churches and monasteries that housed them. From around AD 1000 until the thirteenth century, Romanesque style (and its variant in Norman style) dominated—with massive walls, relatively small windows, and round arches and vaults. The Romanesque basilica of Vézelay (south-east of Paris) and the Norman (with Arab decoration) Abbey of Monreale (near Palermo) offer outstanding examples from those centuries. The twelfth-century mosaics of the Abbey of Monreale represent an entire cycle of OT and NT stories and figures, with a gigantic Christ conferring his blessing and enthroned in the central apse. Gothic style began with the rebuilding of the royal abbey church of Saint-Denis (near Paris), which was dedicated in 1144. Pointed arches, soaring towers, and the light that streamed through the walls of brilliant stained glass lifted believers' minds and hearts to God. The Gothic cathedrals of Chartres (begun 1145) and Amiens (begun 1220) became models for churches right across Europe. The rich sculpture, stained glass, and luminous structure of Chartres Cathedral (south-west of Paris) have always inspired superlatives. A descendant of two American presidents, Henry Adams (1838–1918), wrote in *Mont-Saint-Michel and Chartres*: 'If you want to know what churches were made for, come down here on some great festival of the Virgin, and give yourself up to it; but come alone! That kind of knowledge cannot be taught and can seldom be shared.'[2] Charles Peguy (1873–1914), who died at the front in the opening weeks of the First World War, helped to maintain Chartres Cathedral as a goal of modern pilgrims.[3] Its forty-four window groupings depict a vast array of OT and NT scenes; its hundreds of carved figures express Christian faith and life in a very lifelike way.

---

[1] Another church building in Rome that illuminates wonderfully the Christian faith is the Basilica of Sant'Agnese on the Via Nomentana; see Margaret Visser, *The Geometry of Love* (New York: Farrar, Straus & Giroux, 2000).

[2] H. Adams, *Mont-Saint-Michel and Chartres* (New York: Doubleday, 1959), 117.

[3] See G. O'Collins, 'In Praise of Cathedrals', *America*, 22 November 1997, 12–15.

Few writers evoke so skilfully and affectionately such astounding monuments of faith as does Simon Jenkins.[4] When presenting his thousand 'best' examples in England, he draws overwhelmingly from the (roughly) eight thousand Anglo-Saxon, Norman, and Gothic pre-Reformation churches that have survived. Those who want to know what European Catholicism was like from the eleventh to the sixteenth century could well be guided by Jenkins and others and look at the testimonies left in stone, wood, and glass. In those permanent ways medieval believers set down their stories for us.

The dramatic frescoes of Cimabue (1240–1302) in Assisi and those of Giotto (1266–1337) in Assisi and Padova bear witness to a faith grounded in the biblical stories and supremely actualized in the lives of saints. Duccio (*c.*1255–1344) testified to the eucharistic belief he shared by the marvellous altarpiece in Siena cathedral. The bronze doors that Lorenzo Ghiberti (1378–1455) created for the baptistry of Florence evoke stories from the OT, the life of Christ, and his passion, and prompted Michelangelo (1475–1564) to declare one of them worthy of being 'the Gate to Paradise'. The scriptures provided central themes for the sculptures of Donatello (1386–1455) and the glazed terracotta figures by Luca della Robbia (1400–82), his nephew, Andrea della Robbia (1435–1525), and Andrea's descendants. A fresco by Masaccio (1401–28) in Santa Maria Novella, Florence, remains a hauntingly effective image of the Trinity revealed through the death and resurrection of Christ. A few blocks away in the Monastery of St Mark the sunlit simplicity of the frescoes by Beato Angelico (*c.*1400–55) continue to touch the heart through their beauty and faith. Florence led the way in the fifteenth century. But artists of genius worked elsewhere: Mantegna (1431–1506) in Mantua, his brother-in-law, Giovanni Bellini (1430–1516), in Venice, and Piero della Francesca (*c.* 1416–92) in Arezzo, San Sepolcro, and Urbino. The twentieth century learned to appreciate again the harmony and serenity of Piero's images of Christ at his baptism and resurrection. The greater and lesser artists of the Italian Renaissance testify to the Catholic life and faith of their times.

The annunciation to Mary of Christ's coming birth (Luke 1: 26–38), his nativity, John's account of his death (John 19: 25–30), and Luke's account of the first Pentecost (Acts 1: 12–13; 2: 1–4) provided themes for Beato

---

[4] *England's Thousand Best Churches* (London: Penguin, 1999).

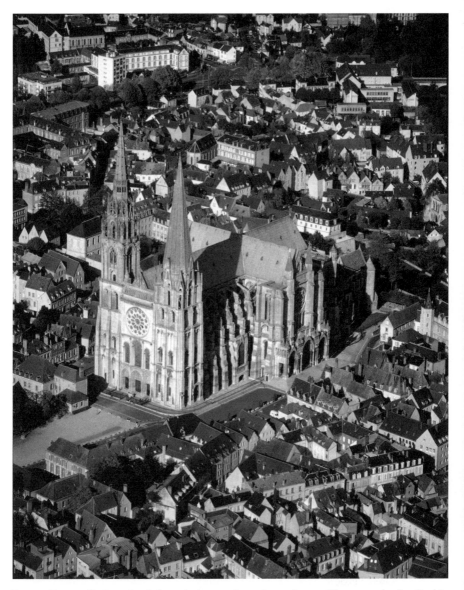

FIG. 3. Famous for its stained-glass windows and exterior sculpture, Chartres embodies Gothic cathedrals at their best, and humanity rising towards God. (Sonia Halliday Photographs.)

Angelico, Bellini, Piero, and other artists to represent the Virgin Mary with her Son and with those who believe in him. After the Council of Ephesus's official endorsement in 431 of the Marian title 'Mother of God' (*Theotokos*), devotion to her in the Christian East and then in the West took off. In Christian art, the small group around Mary at the foot of the cross and the larger group of disciples gathered with her at Pentecost conveyed the sense that the Church cannot exist without being in fellowship with her. The *Annunciation* by the late-Gothic artist Jan van Eyck (1390–1441), now found in the National Gallery of Art, Washington, sets the scene in an elaborate church interior and presents Mary as an archetype of the whole Church community.

Along with the visible heritage of Catholicism, one should not forget the rich musical life that flourished in Eastern and Western worship. Liturgical hymns, going back to the fifth and sixth centuries, continue to inspire devotion in those who attend the liturgies of Eastern Christianity, whether Orthodox or Catholic. The 'Akathistos', a long song of praise to the Mother of God that dates at least from the seventh century, remains among the most moving hymns in all Christian worship. One of the glories of Western civilization, the medieval repertoire of plainsong has not lost its evocative religious power. In the late twentieth century, the 'Canticles of Ecstasy' and other musical compositions from St Hildegard of Bingen (1098–1179) have enjoyed an extraordinary revival.

Religious Foundations and Movements

The closing pages of Ch. 1 sketched the growth of monasticism initiated by Benedict and his sister Scholastica. By the time of Emperor Charlemagne (d. 814) the Rule of Benedict had spread across Europe and provided a visible link between autonomous abbeys. Boniface (d. 754), a British missionary monk, not only preached Christianity in Germany but also established or helped to establish Benedictine houses there, most notably the Abbey of Fulda. Convents of Benedictine nuns continued to be established, and would boast of such notable figures as Roswitha of Gandersheim (Saxony), a tenth-century writer of poetry and plays. Great mystics such as St Hildegard of Bingen and St Gertrude of Helfta (1256–c.1302) followed the more austere Cistercian rule.

By their time, reform movements among Benedictine monks had led to the foundation of new communities where stricter observance prevailed. Thus the Cistercian Order emerged, its name coming from its mother house of Citeaux (founded in 1098, the year of Hildegard's birth), where St Bernard (1090–1153) became a novice in 1112. His immense influence played a major part in disseminating the new order right across Western Europe.[5] By the close of the twelfth century 530 Cistercian abbeys had been established and there would be another 150 foundations in the next century. Bernard sent a group of monks to found the Abbey of Rievaulx in Yorkshire. By the time of St Aelred (abbot 1147–67 and called the 'Bernard of the North') this community numbered around 600 monks. Like Rievaulx, Cistercian houses were normally erected in remote areas. They followed strict rules on silence, diet, and manual labour, fostered plain architecture, and practised good farming methods.

After the seventeenth century this order came to be divided into the Cistercians of the Common Observance or simply the Order of Cistercians (O.Cist.) and Cistercians of the Strict Observance (OCSO), popularly called 'Trappists' (from the rigorously ascetical Abbey of La Trappe in France). At the end of the twentieth century there were 169 houses of Trappist monks and nuns in various countries, and 160 houses of monks and nuns of the Common Observance. Cistercians, both men and women, continue their witness by a lifestyle of prayer, study, silence, and Christian simplicity, as do thousands of Benedictine monks and nuns around the world.

In the twenty-first century the mendicant ('living by begging') orders of Franciscans and Dominicans also continue to offer visible testimony to saints and their companions who revitalized medieval Catholicism. St Dominic (*c.*1174–1221), the founder of the Order of Preachers (commonly called the Dominicans), worked untiringly to spread correct Christian doctrine—which involved him in efforts to win the Albigensians (of whom more anon) back to mainstream Catholicism. A courageous and efficient leader, he parted ways with the careerism of many upwardly mobile priests by three times refusing to accept nomination as a bishop. His followers were to include such eminent figures as St Thomas Aquinas (*c.*1225–74) and St Catherine of Siena (1347–80), who will return later in this chapter. Even though it was probably not introduced by Dominic himself, Dominican preachers popularized the practice of the rosary, still a very common devotion among Catholics and some other Christians (e.g. some Anglicans). It commemorates events involving Christ or his mother

---

[5] See G. R. Evans, *Bernard of Clairvaux* (Oxford: Oxford University Press, 2000).

Mary and requires a string of beads to count the particular prayers it involves. The five 'joyful mysteries' centre on Christ's birth and child-hood. The five 'mysteries of light' begin with Christ's baptism and end with his institution of the Eucharist. The five 'sorrowful mysteries' begin with Christ's agony in the garden and end with his death on the cross. The five 'glorious mysteries' start with Christ's resurrection and end with Mary's sharing in her Son's victory over death. Each mystery includes the 'Our Father' (once), the 'Hail Mary' (ten times), and the 'Glory be to the Father' (once). Because of its repetitions, the rosary has sometimes been called the 'Jesus prayer' of Western Catholicism.

The Dominicans propagated the rosary; the Franciscans did the same for the Christmas crib and the Stations of the Cross (a devotion in which the participants prayerfully move around fourteen scenes from the suffer-ing and death of Christ). The background to these touching and enduring devotions was a kind of sea change that had occurred around AD 1000 and brought a heightened sensitivity to Jesus' humanity, along with a new openness to deeply felt interpersonal relationships—the sense that, as Aelred of Rievaulx put it, a friend 'is the best medicine in life'. St Anselm of Canterbury (c.1033–1109) prayed to Jesus as like a mother hen who gathers her chickens under her protective wings. Bernard and, even more, Julian of Norwich (c.1342–after 1413) helped to encourage this tender, motherly talk. Christ was understood to act like a mother in loving, feeding, and instructing his friends.[6] A widespread interest in the Song of Songs encouraged very affectionate language in talking to and about Jesus, our mother, lover, and friend. A prayer by St Richard of Chichester (c.1197–1253) captures the new tenderness:

Thanks be to thee, my Lord Jesus Christ, for all the benefits which thou hast given me—for all the pains and insults thou hast borne for me. O most merciful Redeemer, Friend, and Brother, may I know thee more clearly, love thee more dearly, and follow thee more nearly.

A parallel readiness by painters and sculptors to go beyond older, more stylized representations and present graphically the events of Jesus' life, passion, death, and resurrection vividly articulated and powerfully pro-moted a warm devotion to Jesus. The use of the crucifix or an image of Christ crucified grew, and with that a new devotion to the five wounds of Christ emerged in the twelfth century. Eventually the extraordinarily

---

[6] See C. W. Bynum, *Jesus as Mother* (Berkeley, Calif.: University of California Press, 1982).

popular *Imitation of Christ* by Thomas à Kempis (1380–1471) was to put across for all ages what a Jesus-centred life entails: 'Blessed are those who know how good it is to love Jesus... Love him and hold him for your friend; for, when all others forsake you, he will not forsake you or suffer you finally to perish' (2. 7). In short, 'to be without Jesus is the pain of hell, and to be with him is a delightful paradise' (2. 8).

Three centuries earlier St Francis of Assisi (1181/2–1226) epitomized forever the Christ-centred life. By celebrating Christmas in a barn with animals and straw, he conveyed the deep meaning of Jesus' birth and encouraged the widespread practice of using various figures to represent that birth with which the Gospels of Matthew and Luke begin. Love for the human story of Jesus led Francis and his followers not only to celebrate, with what we know as Christmas cribs, the birth of Jesus but also to recall the end of that story in his passion and death. During an ecstatic experience two years before his death Francis received the stigmata—wounds on his hands, feet, and side that corresponded to those of the crucified Jesus and completed the Christlike image he presented. His followers took over in 1342 the custody of shrines in Jerusalem associated with Christ's suffering and death. For those Christians unable to visit the Holy Land, Franciscans and others erected innumerable Stations of the Cross as a means for sharing through prayer in the passion, death, and burial of Jesus. A Franciscan, St Leonard of Port Maurice (1676–1751), set up more than five hundred sets of Stations, the most famous being the one in the Colosseum of Rome where Pope John Paul II regularly led the faithful in prayer on Good Friday evening. Like the Stations of the Cross, the medieval passion plays elaborately presented the story of Jesus' suffering and death and so fostered devotion to the crucified and risen Christ. Along with the Stations of the Cross, such religious dramas have enjoyed a striking revival since the nineteenth century—not least through the continuing success of the Oberammergau Passion Play (southern Bavaria), which has been staged more or less every ten years since 1634 and which over the last thirty years has shed some of its anti-Semitic elements.

The influence of Francis and his associate, St Clare (1194–1253), has endured through such remarkable figures as St Antony of Padua (1195–1231), Blessed Angela of Foligno (c.1248–1309), Saint Pio of Pietralcina (1887–1968), and many other Franciscan mystics and missionaries. The unaffected faith, deep humility, total poverty, gentleness with the vulnerable, and Christlike love practised by Francis have made him one of the most popular saints of all times. At Assisi in the Basilica of St Francis twenty-eight frescoes by Giotto, which line the walls of the nave in the Upper Church, tell the story of the saint: the sorrows, joys, and miracles of Francis's life are easily understood by the pilgrims who have always thronged to that holy place. Catholics and other Christians continue to feel his influence, not least the love of creatures expressed by his 'Canticle of Brother Sun', which celebrates 'brother sun, sister moon, brother wind, sister water, brother fire, and sister earth'. A world suffering from environmental degradation and threatened even with the death of the planet may still find a saving message in Francis's lyrical feeling for the beauty and goodness manifested in all creation.

Dominicans, Franciscans, and members of other religious orders, by providing professors and erecting their own study centres, contributed to the growth of European universities: in Bologna (eleventh century), in Paris (twelfth century), in Oxford (second half of the twelfth century), in Padua (1222), Cambridge (late thirteenth century), Prague (1348), and elsewhere around Europe. Wisdom had no frontiers in the medieval period. The Franciscans Alexander of Hales (*c*.1186–1245), Roger Bacon (*c*.1214–*c*.1292), and William of Ockham (*c*.1285–1347) were English. So too was that distinguished friend of Dominicans and Franciscans, Robert Grosseteste (*c*.1170–1253), a scholar and bishop famous for his learning in theology, biblical studies, physics, and astronomy. The Franciscan Blessed Duns Scotus (*c*.1265–1308) was a Scot; Siger of Brabant (*c*.1240–*c*.1284) came from what is now part of Belgium and Holland; the Dominican St Albert the Great (*c*.1200–80) was German; the more mystical Franciscan St Bonaventure (*c*.1217–74) and the toughly realistic Dominican St Thomas Aquinas (*c*.1225–74) were Italians. Aquinas typified the mobility and internationality of the new learning that had been pioneered by Anselm and Peter Abelard (1079–1142), sharpened by the rediscovered metaphysical writings of Aristotle, and inspired by the desire to relate faith and reason. As student and teacher, Aquinas spent time in Paris, Cologne, and intellectual centres in Italy (Anagni, Orvieto, Rome, and Viterbo). The last two years of his life were spent setting up a Dominican school in Naples and working on his *Summa Theologiae*, a masterwork of Christian humanism and compendium of systematic theology to be used by students.

Like the Gothic cathedrals of his age, Aquinas's theology aimed to synthesize what could be drawn from divine revelation (expounded by scriptures and councils, and interpreted through such classic authorities as Augustine of Hippo, John Damascene, and Anselm of Canterbury) and best insights of human philosophy. Let us comment briefly on Aquinas's achievements in Christology (or the doctrine of Christ) and in teaching on the sacraments.[7]

The primary motive for the incarnation of God the Son, he argued, was to remit and remedy sin. Hence if human beings had not sinned, the incarnation would not have taken place. Nevertheless, Aquinas endorsed as well the Neoplatonic principle that 'good diffuses itself' and presented the incarnation as God's supreme act of self-communication. Further, in a way that almost anticipated the lines along which Karl Rahner (1904–84) was to develop an 'evolutionary' christological view that owed something to Pierre Teilhard de Chardin (1881–1955), Aquinas also represented the personal union between the Word of God and an individual human nature as the 'fitting' consummation of human perfection. Any summary of Aquinas's christological teaching should include at least five items. (1) Far from picturing Christ as a merely passive victim, Aquinas followed the lead of Constantinople III and integrated into his doctrine of redemption the essential role of Christ's human will in his free consent to the passion and cross. Salvation came not only from the outside (from the initiative of God) but also from within the human race. (2) Even if one may question how far Aristotelian thought (e.g. about efficient and formal causality) shaped and structured Aquinas's Christology or simply remained a useful language and 'merely' surface terminology, nevertheless, here as elsewhere, he combined two 'bests': the best biblical exegesis of his time and the best philosophy of his time. (3) In unfolding the different facets of redemption's mediation, Aquinas endorsed a triple scheme founded in the Hebrew scriptures: Christ as the anointed priest, prophet, and king. (4) His attention to various episodes of Christ's life (e.g. the baptism with the subsequent preaching and miraculous activity) stood in judgement over many subsequent Christologies and their neglect of Jesus' human story. (5) Aquinas's Christology, which followed the Johannine path of 'the Word

---

[7] On Aquinas see J. Jenkins, *Knowledge and Faith in Thomas Aquinas* (New York: Cambridge University Press, 1997); N. Kretzmann and E. Stump (eds.), *Cambridge Companion to Aquinas* (New York: Cambridge University Press, 1993). On Aquinas's Christology see E. Stump, 'Aquinas' Metaphysics of the Incarnation', in S. Davis, D. Kendall, and G. O'Collins (eds.), *The Incarnation* (Oxford: Oxford University Press, 2001), 197–218; G. O'Collins, *Christology* (Oxford: Oxford University Press, 1995), 203–7; P. E. Persson, *Sacra Doctrina: Reason and Revelation in Aquinas* (Oxford: Blackwell, 1970).

FIG. 4. Through the face and right hand of St Thomas Aquinas (d. 1274), Sandro Botticelli (d. 1510) suggests the spiritual strength and verbal precision of the great theologian. (Abegg-Stiftung, Riggisberg/Bridgeman Art Library.)

descending to become flesh', obviously highlighted the incarnation. At the same time, however, he did not allow an all-absorbing theology of the incarnation to take over. He stood apart from many of his predecessors (e.g. Anselm) and successors (e.g. numerous authors of pre-Vatican II Christology) in treating Christ's resurrection at considerable length.

The saving 'work' of Christ is mediated (albeit not exclusively) through the sacramental life of the Church: through baptism, the Eucharist, and the other five sacraments. In his sacramental theology, among other things Aquinas strikingly exploited the Aristotelian notions of substance and accidents in expounding as 'transubstantiation' the eucharistic presence of the risen Christ under the appearances of bread and wine. Here Aquinas's theology coincided with a renewed devotion to the Eucharist and the establishment of the Feast of Corpus Christi in 1264. He himself was probably the author of a sequence, or chant then sung at Mass before the Alleluia verse for the feast ('Lauda Sion'), a hymn ('Pange lingua'), and other texts composed for the newly instituted feast. Besides celebrating Christ's eucharistic presence, the feast supported a sense of the Mass as an expiatory sacrifice for sins. That also meant fostering faith in the sacrificial and expiatory death on the cross. The infinite merits of that once-and-for-all death, made available pre-eminently through the Eucharist, could supply for the penance that living and dead sinners have failed to perform.[8]

Aquinas provided much 'food for verse', not least on the theme of divine love, for Dante Alighieri (1265–1321), the most famous medieval poet and with William Shakespeare (1564–1616) arguably the greatest poet of all time. Born in Florence, Dante was 25 when his beloved Beatrice died. Her death triggered a profound crisis, from which a vision of Beatrice in 1296 roused him to fulfil his promise that he would write a poetic work 'such as had been written for no lady before'. Just before he died, he finished the last canto of the *Divine Comedy*, which ends by celebrating 'the love that moves the sun and the other stars'. That canto opens with St Bernard praying to the Virgin Mary ('Maiden, yet a Mother, Daughter of thy Son') that Dante might be enabled to see God. The poet's earthly love for Beatrice has brought him to the vision of the all-loving God.

So far in this chapter we have recalled how building programmes and religious orders (which also contributed to the rise and growth of medieval

---

[8] See M. Rubin, *Corpus Christi: The Eucharist in Late Medieval Culture* (Cambridge: Cambridge University Press, 1991).

universities) helped to shape what we continue to see in Catholic Christianity (and beyond), and—for that matter—to hear in an astonishing musical heritage. We look now at the sacramentalizing of daily life, through pilgrimages and other activities.

Pilgrimages

At the age of 35 Dante joined other pilgrims by coming to Rome for the Jubilee Year of 1300, the first of twenty-five Jubilee Years that have brought believers to Rome down to 2000, a unique Jubilee in that it coincided with the end of the second millennium. Pilgrimages stretch back to the origins of the whole Jewish-Christian story. Abraham and Sarah left Ur of the Chaldees and became nomads for God. New Testament books such as the Letter to the Hebrews and the First Letter of Peter saw life as a journey to a heavenly homeland. By AD 250 the popular cult of Peter and Paul began to flourish in Rome and draw pilgrims to their tombs. Dante used the pilgrimage theme to open the *Comedy* ('In the middle of our life's road I found myself in a dark wood—the straight way ahead lost'); the spiritual transformation of the pilgrim takes him through hell and purgatory to heaven. Along with Jerusalem and Santiago de Compostela (with its tomb of St James the Apostle), both before and after 1300 Rome attracted pilgrims at all times and especially during Jubilee years. For one of those early Holy Years (1350) the influential mystic St Bridget of Sweden had come on pilgrimage to Rome and stayed to be a reformer.

Not as exalted a poet as Dante, Geoffrey Chaucer (1340–1400) pictured in *The Canterbury Tales* a group of twenty-nine pilgrims on their way to the shrine of St Thomas Becket (*c.*1120–70) in Canterbury Cathedral. This assorted group of men and women allowed Chaucer to describe the saints and sinners who made up the Catholic Church of his day. Their virtues and vices exhibit the way in which the baptized of those days behaved or misbehaved themselves. At a time when the vast majority of men and women were still illiterate and when the mass entertainment of modern television, radio, and cinema was never imagined, the spiritual tourism of pilgrimages exercised a strong pull. Those shared journeys to the shrines of saints embodied a common faith and strengthened a common sensibility.[9] One could argue that, at least in part, European consciousness arose through the pilgrimages of the Anglo-Saxon, Celtic, Germanic, Latin,

---

[9] See Diana Webb, *Pilgrims and Pilgrimages in the Medieval West* (London: Tauris, 1999).

FIG. 5. Young people holding high the cross on their annual pilgrimage to the shrine of Maipu, Chile. (Alonso Rojas/Andes Press Agency.)

and Slavic peoples.[10] Stone crosses along the roads sacralized the journey, and at the journey's end the venerated sanctuary renewed the sense of communion with Christ and his saints. The ancient Celts named such shrines 'thin places'; time and again they experienced there close communication between God and themselves.

Such pilgrimages reinforced the consciousness of life as a spiritual journey, a preparation for death and eternal life. *Everyman*, an English morality play of the late fifteenth century, reflected that sense. The hero encounters the person of Death, who summons him to God and judgement. The changing seasons of Advent, Christmas, the Epiphany, Lent, Holy Week, Easter, and Pentecost also played their part in sustaining a feeling of human life moving through sacred time to a final meeting with God. Along with the impact of this liturgical cycle, feasts of saints recurred year by passing year and fostered the devotion of towns, guilds, and other groups who cherished their heavenly patron.[11] Movements that practise forms of neighbourly love continue in such organizations as the St Vincent de Paul Society, founded in Paris in the mid-nineteenth century for laypersons to serve the poor, and the San Egidio Community, founded in Rome in 1968 for common prayer and service of others.

We leave now the world of Dante and Chaucer and the lives of laymen and laywomen. We need to examine the roles of bishops and popes, and not least in their relationships with rulers.

Bishops, Princes, and Popes

During the early centuries of Christianity, the clergy and people of a local church picked their own bishop. A famous choice was that of Ambrose of Milan, the governor of the city and region, who had not yet been baptized when the people called for him after Bishop Auxentius died in 373 or 374: 'Ambrose for bishop!' In those centuries neighbouring bishops gave (or

---

[10] This view is sometimes mistakenly attributed to Johann Wolfgang von Goethe (1749–1832). What we find in Goethe's *Noten und Abhandlungen* is rather a little paragraph appended to the *West-östlichen Divan*, in which some heavily ironical sentences tell the reader to be grateful for the fanaticism of pilgrims and crusaders, since they preserved our 'cultivated European conditions' from contamination by the East. The whole point of the *Noten und Abhandlungen* is in fact to represent the non-Christian Orient as vastly more civilized than contemporary Europe. We thank Professor Nicholas Boyle for this information and reference.

[11] Dante's Florence, after Paris the second largest city in Europe, had (1) major merchant guilds for bankers, judges, and the like, and (2) medium and minor guilds for bakers, shoemakers, hotel-keepers, and the like—eventually seven of group (1) and fourteen of group (2).

withheld) their assent to the nomination of new bishops. Gradually, however, bishops began playing a bigger role in selecting new bishops, and largely reduced the role of the laity to a formality. This development met with criticism from Augustine of Hippo and a number of popes. Leo the Great, for instance, wrote to the bishops of Gaul, insisting that for the nomination of a bishop there should be 'the written opinion of the clerics, the testimony of the (civil) authority, and the agreement of the people and of the priestly order. He who is to preside over all should be elected by all' (*Lettera*, 10. 6). Before the ninth century the popes were concerned with the naming of bishops only for the dioceses of central Italy. From the eleventh century, and especially from 1300, the See of Rome became involved in cases of disputed elections of bishops. After 1500 the Holy See was to recognize the 'right' of many sovereign rulers to name bishops, but from the nineteenth century took on more and more the role of naming bishops in the Latin rite. Eventually, with the exception of some dioceses (in Switzerland and some German-speaking areas), the Pope was to have the sole control in the naming of bishops for Western Catholics.

Being considered married to their dioceses, bishops could not be transferred from one diocese to another. The First Council of Nicaea (325) required that bishops (like priests and deacons) should remain in the diocese where they had been ordained (canon 15). It was only in 882 that someone already a bishop was first elected bishop of Rome, Pope Marinus I. The non-transferable state of bishops in the ancient Church contrasts with what regularly happens today in the (Western) Catholic Church, in which a bishop may move from one diocese to another and sometimes even shift on to a third—often thereby 'moving up the episcopal ladder' from a smaller and poorer diocese to a larger and richer one. Or perhaps one should talk about promotion to a more significant diocese following a successful episcopal apprenticeship in a less significant one?

For many centuries, both in the East and in the West, kings and emperors involved themselves in church affairs and could exercise great pressure in the appointment of new bishops. This happened in the case of Anselm, abbot of Bec (in Normandy), and with happy results for the See of Canterbury. Ronald Knox tells the story:

[Anselm], with some misgiving, came over to visit a sick friend in England at a time when the archbishopric of Canterbury had long been left vacant, so that King William Rufus and his creatures might enjoy the sequestrated revenues of the See...At Christmas 1092, the clergy were allowed to pray for a remedy for the misfortunes of the Church . . . Early in 1093 King William fell sick and was evidently at the point of death . . . fortunately for himself, the Norman king was more prompt in seeing the point of the situation. He promised amendment and restitution of every possible kind, and sent for Anselm at once as the obvious person to be elected archbishop. And then began a scene which has been enacted with various results a thousand times in the history of sanctity, but seldom with so much publicity or so much dramatic interest as in Anselm's case. When you try to make a saint accept a bishopric, it is like trying to make a child take medicine; the result is a perfect fury of dissent . . . In this case not merely the ordinary considerations but the whole welfare of a long-widowed Church and, as seemed probable, the life of a notorious sinner were depending upon St Anselm's acceptance, and he simply refused . . . It was only by the use of physical force that they dragged the saint to the King's bedside; and there, pressing the crozier against the knuckles that would not open so as to hold it, they elected the Archbishop of Canterbury.[12]

King William II recovered and, even before Anselm was consecrated archbishop in December 1093, initiated violent disputes with him over property and over relations with the papacy. After William II eventually died in 1100, Anselm ran into conflicts with the new king, Henry I, who wanted him to consecrate bishops whom Henry had 'invested'—that is to say, given the symbols of their office, the ring and crozier. Controversies between lay rulers and popes over such 'investiture' by kings and emperors flared up during the papacy of St Gregory VII (pope 1073–85) and lasted for decades in England, France, and Germany.

Even after the investiture controversy ended, conflicts continued to break out between rulers and bishops: for instance, between King Henry II and a friend whose election as archbishop of Canterbury Henry had promoted, St Thomas Becket (c.1120–70). From 1164 Becket had to live in France. When he returned from exile, he refused to absolve some bishops who had assisted at the coronation of Henry's son unless they agreed to do penance for this illegal act which infringed the rights of Canterbury. Henry exploded with rage and uttered words that led four knights to ride at once to Canterbury and kill Becket in his cathedral. This murder symbolized for later ages, albeit in different political and ecclesiastical contexts, the struggles between lay rulers and bishops that have continued to result in such martyrdoms as that of Archbishop Oscar Romero of San Salvador (1917–80). During his three years as archbishop, he spoke out for the human rights of the poor and the powerless—a

---

[12] R. A. Knox, *Occasional Sermons of Ronald A. Knox* (London: Burns & Oates, 1960), 30–1.

'crime' for which he was gunned down at the altar while saying Mass. But, over the clash between Henry II and Thomas Becket, we are getting ahead of ourselves. We need to retrace our steps to the 'Gregorian reforms' and their background.

The second thousand years of Catholicism had begun, however, with a pope who was a loyal servant of the German emperor: Sylvester II (pope 999–1003), the first Frenchman to be elected to the papacy. A brilliant scholar, this pope was also deeply involved in promoting Christian life and growth in Poland, Hungary, and Russia. He chose to be called 'Sylvester' because he wished to imitate St Sylvester I (pope 314–35), the spiritual collaborator of Emperor Constantine. Just as Sylvester I and Constantine had done in the fourth century, Sylvester II aimed to promote the imperial rule and the healthy state of the Church.

But such friendly relations between popes and rulers hardly remained the norm. Gregory VII, known from childhood as 'Hildebrand', practised an austere, monastic lifestyle and gave himself to reviving the Church morally—in particular, by reforming money-hungry and sexually immoral clergy. He fought against outside influence in the election of bishops and internal corruption in the shape of clerical simony and unchastity. Simony—that is to say, the buying or selling of ecclesiastical privileges—Gregory described as akin to prostitution. It came in three forms: not merely the vulgar *a manu* where money changed hands, but also in the subtler *ab obsequio* where some other service or favour paved the way for a nomination, and the more insidious *a lingua* where support of one kind or another did the trick. The German emperor, Henry IV, opposed some of the papal reforms and went so far as to hold two synods that declared Gregory deposed. In the unprecedented act of a pope excommunicating an emperor, Hildebrand responded by deposing Henry and declaring the Emperor's subjects free of their oath of allegiance to him. A year later Henry submitted to the Pope at Canossa (in Northern Italy), did penance, and was absolved from the censures imposed on him. When Henry failed to keep the promises he made at Canossa, the Pope once more excommunicated him. The Emperor marched on Rome, briefly occupied the city, and set up an antipope, Clement III. Gregory fled south and died at Salerno. His last words are supposed to have been: 'I have loved righteousness and hated iniquity; therefore I died in exile.'[13]

[13] See H. E. J. Cowdrey, *Pope Gregory VII, 1073–1085* (Oxford: Clarendon Press, 1998); C. Morris, *The Papal Monarchy* (Oxford: Oxford University Press, 1991).

The Gregorian reforms, while being on balance very much a 'good thing', suffered from their ambiguities—within the Catholic Church and beyond. Relations with those 'beyond' featured a remarkable letter of 1076 (*Epistola*, 21) to Anzir, the Muslim king of Mauretania, whom Gregory VII thanked for freeing some prisoners and promising to free some more. Anzir had even sent a candidate to be consecrated a bishop and so take care of his Christian subjects. Nearly nine hundred years later, in its declaration on the Relation of the Church to Non-Christian Religions (*Nostra Aetate*, 3 n. 1), the Second Vatican Council recalled this letter, which recognized how Christians and Muslims honour Abraham and adore one and the same God. Yet two years earlier, in 1074, Gregory had unsuccessfully planned a military campaign against the Turks. Within the Church, Gregory effected a certain shift of power from the local churches to the Roman or Apostolic See. Less than a century later, however, no less an authority than the immensely influential Bernard of Clairvaux forcibly distinguished between the authority of the pope and that of the papal collaborators in Rome: 'the murmuring of the churches' would not stop, he warned, 'unless the Roman Curia ceased to give judgement in untried cases and in the absence of the accused, simply as its members happen to wish' (*Epistola*, 48). Writing in 1139 to Innocent II (pope 1130–43), Bernard was fearlessly forthright:

Justice is perishing in the Church . . . episcopal authority is being treated with utter contempt, so long as no bishop is in a position to avenge promptly injuries done to God, or is allowed to punish illicit acts of any kind even in his own diocese. Cases are referred to you and to the Roman Curia. You reverse, so it is said, what has been rightly done; you confirm what has been wrongly done. Shameless and contentious people from among the clergy, even men expelled from monasteries run off to you. On their return they boast and bluster to the effect that they have found protectors, when in fact they ought to have felt the punishment of an avenger . . . everywhere the bishops are despised and put to shame; and the fact that their right judgements meet with contempt derogates most gravely from your authority also. (*Epistola*, 178)

The unique dignity of the papal office made this falsely functioning centralism intolerable for Bernard. It was harming bishops, demoralizing clergy and religious, and scandalizing the laity. Shortly before he died in 1153, Bernard finished a treatise (*On Consideration*), addressed to Eugenius II (pope 1145–53), like Bernard a Cistercian and the first Cistercian to occupy the Chair of Peter. Bernard spoke the truth to his much-loved former student. With pernicious people deliberately and with impunity injuring others by appealing to papal legates and to Rome, justice was not being done: 'to have appealed wrongly and also with impunity is an encouragement to groundless appeals ... it is allowable to appeal, not in order to oppress others, but only if you are yourself oppressed' (3. 2. 7). Eugenius himself was 'the successor of Peter, not of Constantine'; he should remember that Peter knew 'nothing of going about at any time bedizened with jewels and silks, decked with gold, riding upon a white horse, escorted by soldiery, surrounded by attendants acclaiming him aloud' (ibid. 4. 3. 6).

Some decades later the Fourth Lateran Council, held in 1215 under Innocent III (pope 1198–1216) and attended by more than a thousand bishops, laid down healthy provisions for hearings:

> He who is the object of an inquiry should be present at the process, and, unless absent through contumacy, should have the various headings of the inquiry explained to him, so as to allow him the possibility of defending himself. As well, he is to be informed not only of what the various witnesses have accused him of but also of the names of those witnesses. (*Constitutions*, 8)

Church law, which eventually brought the Code of Canon Law for the Western Church (1983) and the Code of Canons of the Oriental Churches (1990), aimed to protect rights as well as foster good order throughout the Catholic Church. However, right to the end of the twentieth century various offices of the Roman Curia have continued the practice of receiving and acting on secret denunciations. Regularly the 'objects' of inquiries are not given the names of their delators. The problem Bernard put his finger on is far from solved. Nor, for that matter, are the conflicts between secular rulers and popes.

From 1157 the German king and emperor, Frederick I or 'Barbarossa' (emperor 1155–90), insisted on the expression 'holy empire' (*sacrum imperium*) as a counterpart to the 'holy Church' or spiritual jurisdiction of the popes and so gave rise to the title 'Holy Roman Emperor'. (This title, held by a succession of German rulers, by Charles V (emperor 1519–56), and Hapsburg rulers, was abolished by Napoleon I in 1806.) Barbarossa took offence at claims that the *sacrum imperium* was a papal gift and insisted on it being a free crown governed by Roman law. Before 1179 he had supported three antipopes and led the German bishops into a schism that lasted seventeen years. Aggressive and grandiose, he wanted to emulate Charlemagne whom he had canonized or declared a saint by Paschal III, one of the three antipopes he had set up. Eventually, joined by Philip II (king of France 1180–1223) and Richard I, called Cœur-de-Lion (king of England 1189–99), Barbarossa took a large army on the Third Crusade (1189–92) to recover the Holy Land from the Muslims. He led his troops across the Dardanelles, only to die in Southern Asia Minor, drowned when crossing a river.[14] The split Barbarossa caused within the Church did not last long. But within three centuries other rulers were to help trigger long-standing divisions in Christianity.

The Wounds of the Church

Any stock-taking of the pre-Columbus Church must include some account of several 'wounds'—to borrow an expression used by Innocent IV (pope 1243–54) in his opening homily at the First Council of Lyons (1245) and by Antonio Rosmini-Serbati (1797–1855) for the title of his book on ecclesiastical reform, *The Five Wounds of the Church*. We name three such wounds from the pre-1492 Church: the exile of popes in Avignon and the strife over antipopes; the persecution of Jews and heretics; deteriorating relations with Muslims.

Within the body of Christian believers, the recurrent presence of antipopes down to 1449 (all faithfully listed along with the popes in an appendix to the *Oxford Dictionary of the Christian Church*) weakened Catholic life and continued to hamper attempts at reunion with the Orthodox Church. Matters were exacerbated by 'the Babylonian Captivity', a phrase applied by Francesco Petrarch (1304–74) and later writers to the exile of popes in Avignon from 1309 to 1377.

Clement V (pope 1305–14), a member of an important French family, started these seventy years of papal exile from Rome by fixing his residence at Avignon in 1309. Generally subservient to the interests of the greedy and unscrupulous Philip IV, called the Fair (French king 1285–1314), Clement encouraged scholarship but harmed the papacy by selling ecclesiastical positions and imposing heavy taxes. Encouraged by revelations she received after the death of her husband in 1341, St Bridget of Sweden (*c.*1303–73) campaigned for the reform of Church life and the return of the papacy from Avignon to Rome. In 1349 Bridget took up residence in Rome but

[14] On this crusade and related matters see J. Gillingham, *Richard I* (New Haven, Conn.: Yale University Press, 1999).

died before the 'Babylonian Captivity' ended. Eventually Gregory XI (pope 1370–8), seemingly encouraged by St Catherine of Siena (*c.*1347–80), transferred the papacy from Avignon back to Rome. His premature death occasioned 'the Great Schism', a period of thirty-nine years that saw Western Christendom divided between eight popes and antipopes and ended only when the Council of Constance elected Martin V (pope 1417–31).

Persecutions of Jews and heretics inflicted a second wound on the life of the Church. Wrongly encouraged by certain NT texts (e.g. Matt. 27: 24–5; 1 Thess. 2: 14–16), from the fourth century some Christian writers indulged in anti-Jewish polemics. Thus St John Chrysostom (d. 407), while still a presbyter in Antioch, preached eight sermons to stop Christians from attending synagogues and following Jewish practices. His sharp rhetoric cast a long shadow on Christian–Jewish relations. Collectively accused of being 'Christ-killers' and deicides ('God-killers'), from the eleventh century Jews suffered violent attacks; in some cases whole communities were wiped out. Bernard of Clairvaux raised his voice in protest against such crimes, addressing a notorious anti-Semite, the monk Raoul, in the language John 8: 44 used of the devil: 'I suppose that it is enough for you to be as your master. He was a murderer from the beginning, a liar, and the father of lies' (*Epistola*, 365). Bernard saw faith as always a matter of persuasion and never of compulsion, and so rejected forced conversions of Jews or others. Nevertheless, dreadful legends about Jews murdering children, poisoning water supplies, and desecrating the Eucharist fostered killings and expulsions. Jewish people were expelled from England (1290), France (1394), Spain (1492), and Portugal (1496). The Fourth Lateran Council had helped to trigger evil results. Its 1215 decree on Jews excluded them from public employment, confined them to ghettos, and required them to wear yellow stars in public.

In Medieval Europe struggles with heretics, unlike the persecutions of the Jews, often involved armed conflicts—a hint of terrible religious wars to come with the Reformation. Several sects (in France, Germany, and Italy), which admitted to membership only the morally and doctrinally pure, were dubbed 'Cathars (the pure)'. The most significant of such groups, named 'Albigensians' after Albi, their centre in Southern France, understood redemption as the soul's liberation from the flesh, dismissed matter as evil, and hence rejected Christ's incarnation, the sacraments, and the resurrection of the body. Its adherents were divided into the perfect, who did not marry and lived a very austere existence, and ordinary believers who led normal lives until they came to be in danger of death (DH 800–2; ND 19–21).

Pope Innocent III organized a series of preaching missions (1203–8) among the Albigensians and other Cathars; for this campaign he enlisted the help of Dominic and his followers. When a papal legate was assassinated in 1208, Innocent authorized an anti-Albigensian Crusade, which led to the notorious Massacre of Béziers on 22 July 1209. Both sides committed atrocities, and fighting continued sporadically until the Treaty of Paris in 1229 signalled the victory of the Northern (Catholic) forces. Alongside its strong religious dimension, the Albigensian conflict was also connected with independence movements in that part of France. But one cannot overlook the way this crusade put into practice the teaching of the Third Lateran Council (1179); its canon 27 urged the use of force by secular authorities against heresy.[15] Pope Gregory IX, c.1233, set up ecclesiastical tribunals to detect and prosecute the Albingensian heresy, with the inquisitors drawn mainly from the Dominican and Franciscan Orders. At the height of this Inquisition in Southern France, each year perhaps three persons were burnt at the stake for heresy.[16]

In 1174 a rich citizen of Lyons, (Peter) Valdes (d. before 1219) distributed his wealth among the poor and began preaching in southern France. By frequently attacking worldly corruption in the Church, he and his followers provoked constant friction. After efforts failed to win them back, in 1182 or 1183 they were excommunicated and expelled from Lyons. Their rejection of any kind of violence, refusal to take oaths, preaching without official approval, and questioning of the validity of sacraments administered by unworthy priests made the rift too wide to heal. When Innocent III launched the Crusade against the Albigensians, that also affected the Waldensian bases in southern France. Many Waldensians migrated to Spain, Germany, Bohemia, Poland, Savoy, and Piedmont. Eventually those who did not return to the Catholic Church looked for contacts

---

[15] See *The History of the Albigensian Crusade: Peter of Les Vaux-de-Cernay's Historia Albigensis*, trans. W. A. and M. D. Sibly (Woodbridge: Boydell & Brewer, 1998).

[16] See 'Inquisition, the', *The Oxford Dictionary of the Christian Church*, 836–7. In recent years scholarly research into the records of the Inquisition in Spain, Italy, and elsewhere has shown how the inquisitors sometimes or even often acted with an enlightenment and tolerance that purveyors of popular legends continue to ignore; see A. Hamilton, 'Rewriting the Black Legend', *Times Literary Supplement*, 28 January 2000, 29.

with the Protestant Reformation, and some adopted Calvinist confessions of faith and ecclesiastical structures.[17]

Relations with Muslims that worsened from the eleventh century must be named as a third wound in the Catholic Church. Early in the eighth century the forces of Islam crossed from North Africa and conquered Spain. The new Muslim rulers normally tolerated Christians (and Jews) as 'people of the book', even if some episodes of persecution occurred. From 850 to 859 fifty Christians were killed in Cordoba, but some of them had rashly provoked martyrdom by entering a crowded mosque to preach Jesus Christ. For centuries tolerance usually prevailed between Muslims, Christians, and Jews, especially in such major cultural centres as Cordoba. An outstanding Arabic philosopher and polymath, Averroes (1126–98) was born and lived there. His commentaries on Aristotle exercised a considerable influence on Christian thinkers in Paris and elsewhere. The Jewish philosopher Moses Maimonides (1138–1204) was also born in Cordoba and eventually settled in Old Cairo. Writing in both Hebrew and Arabic, he influenced such Christians as Thomas Aquinas by his principal treatise, the *Guide for the Perplexed*, which aimed to synthesize divine revelation with the findings of human reason produced by Aristotle. The gradual reconquest of Spain by Christian principalities and the Crusades, however, changed relations with Muslims and Jews.

The preaching of Peter the Hermit encouraged the First Crusade (proclaimed in 1095),[18] the start of a series of expeditions undertaken by Western Christian forces to 'liberate' the Holy Land from Islamic domination and keep it under Christian control. Military threats to Constantinople and the Eastern Empire, growth of population in the West, ambitions of political leaders, and a fresh devotion to the earthly life of Jesus and to the places where he lived and died joined in motivating these military-style pilgrimages. The Fifth Crusade ended in 1270 with the death of the French king, St Louis IX. This is normally considered the final crusade, even if Christian expeditions against the Turks continued in

---

[17] On the Waldensians see G. Audisio, *The Waldensian Dissent: Persecution and Survival* (Cambridge: Cambridge University Press, 1999). On conflict with the Waldensians and related issues, see A. Ferreiro (ed.), *The Devil, Heresy & Witchcraft in the Middle Ages: Essays in Honor of Jeffrey B. Russell* (Leiden: Brill, 1998); see also DH 790–7, 809, 913; ND 403, 640, 1301, 1411, 1504, 1703, 1802.

[18] See J. Philipps (ed.), *The First Crusade: Origins and Impact* (Manchester: Manchester University Press, 1997); J. Riley-Smith (ed.), *The Oxford Illustrated History of the Crusades* (Oxford: Oxford University Press, 1995).

later centuries. The crusades fired the imagination of writers and painters, as well as increasing cultural contacts. But they had lasting evil effects on Christian–Muslim relations, as well as on relations between Eastern and Western Christians. When the Crusaders captured Jerusalem in July 1099, they killed around ten thousand Muslims, as well as many Jews. This barbaric slaughter sent shock waves around the Mediterranean world. Christian minorities in Muslim countries experienced hardships that they had not known before. In 1204, when the Fourth Crusade switched to Constantinople from its original objective (Egypt), the Crusaders sacked the city and set up the Latin Empire and patriarchate; they achieved only a temporary reunion between the Eastern and Western Churches. The long-term effect of the Fourth Crusade was to seal more or less the schism between Rome and Constantinople and weaken the Eastern Empire against Muslim inroads.

A few years later, in 1236, Christian forces reconquered Cordoba. When Granada, the last Spanish territory held by the Muslims, surrendered in 1492, the new Christian Spain of Ferdinand and Isabella failed to incorporate its Muslim minority, as well as expelling its Jewish population. A few years earlier (1478), Ferdinand and Isabella had set up the Spanish Inquisition, an efficient instrument of ecclesiastical and civil control. Not long before, the Ottoman Empire, founded around 1300 in Turkey, had captured (Christian) Constantinople in 1453. By the end of the sixteenth century the Ottoman power extended from Hungary, through the Balkans and Greece to Egypt. This Muslim expansion into Europe, at least by sea, was dealt a crushing blow by the naval forces of the Christian League at the battle of Lepanto (North of the Gulf of Corinth) in 1571. By that time the expeditions of Christopher Columbus (1451–1506) to the West Indies, Central America, and South America had changed the direction of world and Catholic history.

FROM COLUMBUS TO JOHN PAUL II

Those who set out to trace the history of Catholicism from 1492 until 2000 have so much to summarize that it becomes dangerously easy to bypass or even simply avoid important questions and changes. The principle guiding our choices and emphases remains the same. We will be looking for what was distinctively, although not necessarily uniquely, Catholic in those centuries. In other words, we will ask: what has 'being

Catholic' meant at different times and in different places in that past? That could open the way to appreciate how the experience of the ages has shaped the Catholic Church we see today. These were centuries deeply marked by religious persecutions and wars. Rather than move along apportioning the blame, we will attempt to understand the processes involved. In general, faith entered so deeply into the lives and consciousness of most Catholics (and others) that they simply took it for granted that their shared religion necessarily underpinned their common social and political existence. Real differences of faith were seen as socially and politically intolerable. To organize themes, we will look in order at the expansion of Europe, the Reformation, the new learning, and the coming of the world Church.

Whatever we achieve in the closing section of this chapter, we certainly do not want to give the impression that the present Catholic Church and the pontificate of John Paul II have been the natural culmination of a whole set of attractive, progressive forces at work for centuries. Both in individual lives and in the Catholic Church at large, God often writes with crooked lines.

The Expansion of Europe

The discoveries initiated by Columbus in 1492 revealed the existence of millions of human beings in societies that had gone on for many centuries without the slightest chance of hearing about Jesus Christ and joining the Church. The arrival of Europeans in the Americas raised with new rigour the issue of universal participation in the benefits of Christ's redemption. How could he have been the Saviour for the indigenous peoples of the Americas? How could they have shared in his redemptive grace without even hearing his name?[19]

Europeans had not lost a sense of many people living in Africa and Asia—beyond the borders of their 'Christendom'.[20] When Genghis Khan was elected chief of the Mongol tribes in 1206, this election triggered a series of events that led to the world becoming one. He created an empire that devoured China and penetrated into Europe. At the same time, routes

---

[19] In *Salvation outside the Church?* (London: Geoffrey Chapman, 1992), Frank Sullivan describes well how Columbus's discovery raised questions about the salvation of those who had for long centuries remained without any contact with the Christian message.

[20] See S. H. Moffett, *A History of Christianity in Asia*, i. *Beginnings to 1500* (San Francisco: Harper, 1992).

opened up in the opposite direction. The Venetian traveller, Marco Polo (c.1254–1324) visited China in 1271–5 and knew the court of Kublai Khan, Genghis's grandson and successor. Marco Polo's account of his travels gives the earliest European description of the Far East. His tales of the wealth of 'Cathay' fascinated later generations, including a Genoese navigator, Christopher Columbus, who thought he could reach Asia by sailing westward. Without the events Genghis Khan set in train, the New World might have remained undiscovered by the West for longer, perhaps much longer.

The start of the Western Age of Discovery predates, however, Columbus's crossing of the Atlantic. Portuguese navigators such as Prince Henry the Navigator (1394–1460), a maritime and mathematical pioneer, promoted the exploration and colonization of the Canaries and the Azores. Under his patronage Portuguese seamen sailed well down the West coast of Africa. In 1487 the Portuguese Bartolomeu Dias (d. 1500) became the first European captain in modern times to round the Cape of Good Hope and so open up new sea routes to India and beyond.[21] Within a few years of these Portuguese voyages and Columbus's discovery, Europeans began to circumnavigate the world, to name it with European names ('Africa', 'America', 'Asia', and 'Australia'), and to map it. Western and Christian domination was on the way.

Alexander VI (pope 1492–1503) divided the New World between Spain and Portugal, giving their kings sovereign power over the lands that their subjects were discovering and making them responsible for evangelizing the people of those lands. The Portuguese rulers developed an empire in Africa, America, and the Far East, and sent Catholic missionaries around the world. Apart from Angola, Mozambique, and such small enclaves as East Timor and Goa, the major lasting result of this evangelization and colonization remains Brazil, currently the largest Catholic nation in the world; its population of over 170 million people is still predominantly Catholic.

Under Emperor Charles V, king of Spain from 1516 to 1556, the Spanish Empire spread through America. In 1521 Mexico fell to Hernando Cortes (1485–1547), and in 1530 Peru was conquered by Francisco Pizarro (c.1475–1541). Dominicans, Franciscans, and other missionaries arrived shortly

---

[21] Herodotus, a Greek historian who died before 420 BC, tells of travellers sailing around Africa (*History*, 4. 42).

after the violent invasions and massacres committed by the *conquistadores*, and preached the Christian message, sometimes with methods that failed to respect the freedom and religious sensitivities of the Aztecs of Mexico, the Incas of Peru, Mayas, and other American Indians. Catholicism was established everywhere in Central and Southern America, and some groups, notably the Mexicans, often embraced the new faith with enthusiasm. But the Indian societies were ravaged by violent invaders in search of gold and devastated by small-pox, other diseases, and alcoholism. The Indian population of Spanish-ruled America declined by at least 75 per cent in the first hundred years of that rule. The collapse of the local population led the *conquistadores* to begin importing black slaves from Africa. Some religious leaders and writers, such as Bartolomé de Las Casas (1474–1566), denounced the crimes committed in the name of Spain and Christianity. Significantly this courageous Dominican also served (1542–50) as bishop of Chiapas, a poor diocese in Southern Mexico where in the 1990s the Indian population hit world headlines over their struggle for civil and religious rights.

By 1620 thirty-six bishoprics and countless parishes in Central and South America served the Spanish settlers, Indian converts, and other groups, with everything under the control of two viceroys: one in Peru and the other in New Spain (Mexico). Through the viceroys the running of the colonial state and the organization of the church depended upon Madrid. The papacy had no control, for example, over the appointment of bishops.

One group that maintained its freedom from royal control was the Jesuits, who both in Old and New Spain insisted on their primary obedience being to their superior general resident in Rome and through him to the pope. Besides developing colleges in the towns, they spread out among the Indian populations where their frontier missionary work put into practice the entirely peaceful evangelization methods advocated by Las Casas. They sometimes succeeded in a remarkable way—as with the Guarani Indians of Paraguay. From 1603 they began settlements or 'Reductions', which combined agricultural work, various crafts, and worship that included much music. With the help of brothers (non-ordained members of the Order), some of them ex-soldiers who had survived European wars before joining the Society of Jesus, the Jesuit missionaries trained the Guaranis to defend themselves effectively against slave traders. The 1767 expulsion of Jesuits from Spanish America largely brought to an end a glorious chapter in missionary work. The ten settlements of the

Chiquitos mission, in what became Bolivia, survived the 1767 disaster somewhat better. There the Jesuit mix of education, agriculture, and liturgical celebration even more skilfully integrated the Indian language and culture with Christianity.

A few Jesuits, such as St Peter Claver (1580–1654), ministered to a very different group: the African slaves imported in ever-increasing numbers into Brazil, Cuba, Venezuela, and other lands of the Portuguese and Spanish Empires. In particular, the slaves provided labour for the sugar plantations. Adrian Hastings describes the work of Claver and his colleagues:

Alonso de Sandoval . . . and his assistant, Pedro Claver, worked indefatigably in the docks of Cartagena where thousands of blacks were unloaded every year, often more dead than alive after their fearful Atlantic crossing. With a group of black interpreters picked to cope with the range of African languages needed, Sandoval and Claver ministered to the slaves materially and spiritually without stopping for more than 50 years. In his book [*De instauranda Aethiopum salute*] Sandoval denounced the abominable treatment of the slaves and listed the African peoples and languages they represented, while appealing to other Jesuits to join him in this work. He and Claver were undoubtedly two of the most heroically dedicated and saintly men religious history, even Jesuit history, can record.[22]

But these two heroic priests enjoyed little back-up. Many Jesuits and others ministered to the Indians, but the population of black slaves, often much worse treated, were totally subjected to their white owners. The black population came to accept Christianity but sometimes with a West African mix, as in the Afro-Brazilian cults. Catholic Brazil became the last country in the world to abolish officially slavery—only in 1888.

Out in Asia heroic missionaries such as St Francis Xavier (1506–52), 'the Apostle of the Indies', reached India, Sri Lanka, Malacca, the Molucca Islands, and Japan. One of the first Europeans ever to visit Japan, he created flourishing Catholic communities there. Sadly, fear of foreign invasions triggered savage persecutions from the end of the sixteenth century. In the first half of the seventeenth century thousands of Christians suffered death for their faith, until in 1640 Japan was closed to all foreigners and Christianity itself proscribed. When these restrictions were lifted in the second half of the nineteenth century, Catholic missionaries

---

[22] A. Hastings, 'Latin America', in A. Hastings (ed.), *A World History of Christianity* (London: Cassell, 1999), 347.

discovered many hidden Christians, who had secretly kept and handed on the faith. Xavier himself had died on an island south of Canton, while waiting to enter China.

Within a few years of his death, however, other Jesuits entered China—in particular, the Italian Matteo Ricci (1552–1610), whose learning in mathematics, astronomy, and languages allowed him to preach the Christian message. The German Jesuit Adam Schall (1591–1666) helped reform the Chinese calendar (officially adopted after 1644). By this and other astronomical achievements (such as the prediction of an eclipse in 1629), the way was opened for a Flemish Jesuit, Ferdinand Verbiest (1623–88), to be nominated president of the Chinese Imperial Board of Astronomy. This appointment by the Chinese ruling dynasty embodied the highpoint of a missionary endeavour that not only combined faith with human learning but also adapted Christian ceremonies to the local culture. Sadly the success of this latter adaptation gave rise to a violent controversy over 'the Chinese rites'. Clement XI (pope 1700–21) condemned such adaptations, and Benedict XIV (pope 1740–58) even required missionaries to take oaths against them. Eventually twentieth-century popes and the Second Vatican Council (1962–5) were to encourage adaptation to various cultures and the full role of the local clergy.

This full role came slowly in many places: for instance, in the Philippines. Evangelization by Dominican, Franciscan, and other missionaries followed the start of Spanish rule in 1565. Even though the majority of Filipinos had been baptized by the end of the eighteenth century, the indigenous clergy remained in inferior positions. It was only in 1905 that the first Filipino bishop was appointed. Pope Pius XI, however, vigorously encouraged local leadership. In 1926 he personally consecrated six Chinese bishops; in 1936 he appointed the first Japanese archbishop of Tokyo.

In West Africa the horrors of the slave trade continued until the 1860s. By that time Catholic, Protestant, and Anglican missionaries had begun serious evangelization of Africa south of the Sahara. In Italy, post-Napoleonic France, and elsewhere a new enthusiasm grew to promote missions. Such religious congregations with a specifically African focus as the Holy Ghost Fathers, the Society of African Missions, the White Fathers, and the Verona Fathers came into existence. Through the twentieth century, with dedication and help of African laymen and women, Catholicism grew enormously in Africa. Despite the wounds of colonialism and recurrent wars, by the year 2000, 175 million out of 350 million Christians in Africa were Catholics. The first two African Catholics to become bishops of dioceses were appointed in 1939. By the year 1990 there were over 350 such African bishops, many of them vitally concerned with the task of indigenizing or inculturating Catholic rituals in their regions.[23]

A last wave of Catholic missionary expansion that should be recalled involves North America, Oceania, and other parts of the world. From the nineteenth century congregations of religious women began playing a major role in bringing Catholicism to such countries as Canada, the United States, and Australia,—among others. Along with numerous male religious and priests, Irish Sisters of Charity, Marist Sisters, Presentation Sisters, Religious of the Sacred Heart, Sisters of Mercy, and many other nuns founded schools and hospitals around the world. They came from France, Germany, Ireland, Italy, and other European countries. The missionary activity of Mary Aikenhead (1787–1858), St Frances Xavier Cabrini (1850–1917), St Rose Philippine Duchesne (1769–1852), Catherine Elizabeth McAuley (1778–1841), Nano Nagle (1718–84), and their associates played a key part in creating world Catholicism. All this expansion of European Catholicism had hardly started before fierce problems arose at home in Europe itself—with the sixteenth-century Protestant Reformation.

The Reformation

At least since the Council of Vienne (1311–12) a cry for 'reform in head and members' was heard in the Church, as her life at various levels had become marked by many grave abuses. The situation was aggravated by the 'Babylonian Captivity' of the papacy in Avignon (1309–77), the Great Western Schism (1378–1417, a period when eight popes and antipopes divided Western Christianity), and the Black Death or bubonic plague which suddenly arrived in 1346 and killed at least a quarter of the European population. It is estimated, for example, that one-third to one-half of the population of England died in 1348–9. Across Europe the Black Death killed up to twenty million people; Europe did not reach its pre-1348 level again until the sixteenth century began.[24] The most

---

[23] See A. Hastings, *The Church in Africa 1450–1950* (Oxford: Oxford University Press, 1994); B. Sundkler and C. Steed, *A History of the Church in Africa* (Cambridge: Cambridge University Press, 2000).

[24] See N. F. Cantor, *In the Wake of the Plague: The Black Death and the World It Made* (New York: Free Press, 2001).

generous priests, monks, and friars suffered disproportionately, since they tried to help the sick and dying. This loss of the best religious leadership also played its part in demoralizing church and society. The scandalous lives of such Renaissance popes as Alexander VI, who secured his own election largely through bribes and devoted much of his papal energies to furthering the position of his children, made reformation a crying need.[25]

Judgements over the health or sickness of the Catholic Church in various countries still vary enormously. What, for example, was the situation like in England on the eve of the Reformation? Was the official church there well organized and meeting the spiritual needs of ordinary people? Eamon Duffy and others have drastically revised the conventional picture of a dysfunctional Catholicism in radical need of reform. But the debate still continues about the state of English faith before Henry VIII (king of England 1509–47) triggered the break with the papacy.[26] The vigour of sixteenth-century Catholicism in Spain has come to be more widely recognized. Cardinal Ximénez de Cisneros (1436–1517) reformed the religious orders and encouraged learning. Among other contributions to the new learning, he commissioned the first polyglot bible of modern times, a six-volume work with parallel texts in Hebrew, Greek, and Latin. The monarchy controlled ecclesiastical affairs, insisted on a uniform religious-political orthodoxy, and helped make Spain an intensely religious society. Scholarship flourished, with Dominican theologians and philosophers leading the way. One of them, Francisco de Vitoria (c.1485–1546) developed a theory of international law that has proved lastingly important. Dominicans, Franciscans, and Jesuits provided an army of missionaries for the evangelization of the New World. Mystics such as St John of the Cross (1542–91), St Teresa of Avila (1515–82), and St Ignatius

[25] See H. J. Hillerbrand (ed.), *The Oxford Encyclopedia of the Reformation* (Oxford: Oxford University Press, 1996). For an overview see S. F. Hughes, 'Sixteenth Century: An Overview', in A. Hastings *et al.* (eds.), *The Oxford Companion to Christian Thought* (Oxford: Oxford University Press, 2000), 668–74.

[26] E. Duffy, *The Stripping of the Altars* (New Haven, Conn.: Yale University Press, 1992); id., *The Voices of Morebath: Reformation and Rebellion in an English Village* (New Haven: Yale University Press, 2001). See also E. J. Carlson (ed.), *Religion and the English People 1500–1640: New Voices, New Perspectives*, Sixteenth Century Essays and Studies, 45 (Kirksville, Mo.: Thomas Jefferson University Press, 1998); T. Cooper, *Last Generation of Catholic Clergy* (Woodbridge: Boydell & Brewer, 1999); K. Hylson-Smith, *Christianity in England from Roman Times to the Reformation*, ii. *From 1066–1384* (London: SCM Press, 2000); C. Marsh, *Popular Religion in Sixteenth-Century England: Holding Their Peace* (New York: St Martin's Press, 1998); J. Shinners and W. J. Dohar, *Pastors and the Care of Souls in Medieval England* (South Bend, Ind.: University of Notre Dame Press, 1998).

Loyola (1491–1556) left their enduring mark on the world through their work and writings.

The start of the Protestant Reformation, often simply and better called the Reformation, is traditionally dated to 1517, when Martin Luther (1483–1546) produced his ninety-five theses in protest against the scandalous sale of indulgences and other abuses of papal and clerical power. The official church granted 'indulgences' or remissions of punishment in purgatory for sinners who had repented of their sins but who not yet fully satisfied for the harm they had caused. In 1517, on the authority of Pope Leo X, indulgences were being sold to raise money from the German faithful to help pay for the building of the new St Peter's Basilica in Rome. Luther felt outraged not only at this squalid practice but also at the whole idea that church leaders could exercise control over the fate of human beings in the afterlife. Intensely concerned with our being justified through Christ ('Where do I find a gracious God who will heal the wounds of guilt-stricken conscience?'), Luther argued for justification through divine grace alone (*sola gratia*), by faith alone (*sola fide*), and not by good works. He understood the Bible (and not human traditions) to be the only authoritative rule of faith (*sola scriptura*), and spread knowledge of the scriptures by translating the Bible into German. He also introduced the vernacular for the celebration of the Eucharist, demanded that lay people should receive Communion under both kinds, defended the right of the clergy to marry, and opposed papal authority. Luther spread his ideas through preaching, pamphlets, and hymns in German, some of which (e.g. 'A mighty fortress is our God') are sung today by many different Christians, including Catholics.

Among the plethora of Protestant groups that emerged at the Reformation some were extreme, even anarchical, but others were committed to clear ideas and precise ecclesiastical order. Jean Calvin (1509–64) promoted this style of Reformation in France, Switzerland, and elsewhere. In his commentaries on the scriptures and even more in his *Institutes* (first edition 1536), he showed himself a more rigorous theologian than Luther and more aware of the importance of organization.[27] Presbyterianism, the form of church government initiated by Calvin, is distinguished, on the one hand, from episcopalianism or the rule of bishops and, on the other hand, from congregationalism or the rule of the local congregation, which

---

[27] See B. Cottret, *Calvin: a Biography* (Edinburgh: T. & T. Clark, 2000).

one finds, for instance, among Baptist Christians. Presbyterianism involves rule through a series of courts, up to the General Assembly—with the representative ministers and elders participating after being elected.

Undoubtedly nationalism and economic interests helped the cause of the Reformation. But it was often a deeply felt religious movement that aimed to purify church life and base Christian existence on the scriptures. Luther and Calvin expressed complementary emphases of perennial theological importance. If Luther's call for reform was more oriented towards human beings who hear and believe God's word, Calvin looked to the majesty of God who elects the predestined and gives them the grace of obedient faith. In the twentieth century the Second Vatican Council was to acknowledge frankly 'that continued reformation' to which Christ always calls his Church (*Unitatis Redintegratio*, 6)—a confession that converged with the Reformers' sense of the enduring power of sin that constantly threatens our communion with God.

Nevertheless, despite a Catholic respect for Calvin, Luther, and other leading Reformers that grew through the twentieth century, some lines must be drawn: for instance, against Luther's notion of the human will being simply 'captive' to evil. In *De Libero Arbitrio* of 1524, Erasmus of Rotterdam (*c.*1469–1536), while respecting the sovereignty of God's grace and action, defended the free will of human beings. Erasmus's 1509 work, *Laus Stultitiae* (*The Praise of Folly*), had fiercely satirized the scandalous abuses he saw in the life of monasteries and of the Church at large. His edition of the NT in Greek (1516) proved not only a landmark for biblical scholarship but also witnessed to his desire to base Christian life on the scriptures. But like the bishops at the reforming Council of Trent (1545–63), Erasmus did not agree that sin had so corrupted human beings that they could not freely exercise their wills in response to the initiative of God's gifts. Nor did he accept division in Christendom as the price of badly needed reform.

Meeting over three periods for a total of eighteen years, the Council of Trent remains the longest council in the history of the Church. Held in the Northern Italian city of Trent, this council can in many ways be seen as the culmination of a movement of Catholic renewal that predated Luther rather than simply responded to the Protestant Reformation.[28] The first

---

[28] See R. Bireley, *The Refashioning of Catholicism 1450–1700* (Basingstoke: Macmillan, 1999); M. A. Mullett, *The Catholic Reformation* (London: Routledge, 1999); J. W. O'Malley, *Trent and*

eight sessions (1545–7) did, however, treat such major themes raised by the Reformers as the relationship between scripture and tradition, original sin, justification, and the sacraments. Tensions between Emperor Charles V and the Pope led to a suspension of the Council, which eventually resumed for a second period (1551–2). The achievements of sessions nine to fourteen included decrees on the Eucharist and on the sacraments of penance and extreme unction (now called the anointing of the sick). After the new French king, Henry II, joined forces with some German princes who defeated Charles V and even threatened to overrun Trent, the Council was once again adjourned; it finally met again for a third period (1562–3). Its sessions fifteen to twenty-five defined doctrines about the Eucharist, the sacraments of orders and matrimony, and purgatory. Disciplinary measures covered such items as the 'form' of marriage, indulgences, the need for an index of prohibited books, and a range of Church reforms. Trent brought a certain uniformity to Western or Latin Catholics, with the standard missal for Mass, the standard breviary (or book for daily prayer by priests and others), and (eventually with the Sixto-Clementine Bible of 1592) the standard (Latin) text of the scriptures. Through its careful restatement and/or reformation of a whole range of beliefs and practices, the Council of Trent reshaped Catholicism certainly up to the end of the eighteenth century and even into the twentieth century.

The Council symbolized and sealed a parting of the ways between Catholics and Protestants. In a prophetic mode Protestants had denounced the worldliness and downright corruptions of Catholicism, but at the cost of reducing the sacramental mediation (of God's grace and the Holy Spirit) to baptism and the Eucharist. By maintaining a full sacramental system, the Catholic Church continued to touch and bless with the divine presence all dimensions of life. In the eighteenth century Dr Samuel Johnson (1709–84) expressed this difference. Old, ill, and saddened by the thought of dying, he declared in the last summer of his life: 'A good man of a timorous disposition, in great doubt of his acceptance with God, and pretty credulous, may be glad to be of a church where there are so many helps to get to heaven. I would be a Papist, if I could.

All That: Renaming Catholicism and the Early Modern Age (Cambridge, Mass.: Harvard University Press, 2000); R. Po-Chia Hsia (ed.), *The German People and the Reformation* (Ithaca, NY: Cornell University Press, 1988); id., *The World of Catholic Renewal 1540–1770* (Cambridge: Cambridge University Press, 1998).

I have fear enough; but an obstinate rationality prevents me.'[29] In Paul Tillich's terms, Dr Johnson yearned for 'the Catholic substance'.

Even before the Council of Trent closed in 1563, the religious map of Europe was being redrawn. When Elizabeth I (1533–1603) succeeded to the throne in 1558, England definitively ceased to be in communion with the bishop of Rome. The Church of England emerged as an attractive 'middle way' between Catholicism and Protestantism (especially in its Calvinist form). Through St Peter Canisius (1521–97) and others, Jesuits became deeply involved in the struggle to save Austria, England, Germany, Poland, Scotland, and other countries for the one Catholic Church.[30] The political and military dimensions of religious differences culminated in the Thirty Years War (1618–48), which weakened Spain, enormously strengthened France, and devastated Germany. Hostilities ended in 1648 with two treaties constituting the Peace of Westphalia that endorsed the principle of 'cuius regio eius religio', which could be roughly translated as 'the government of a state determines its religious adherence'. At the same time, this peace settlement extended protection to most religious minorities (whether Protestant in Catholic states or vice versa) already in existence. Innocent X (pope 1644–55) denounced the treaties of Westphalia in a papal bull, but was universally ignored.

The New Learning

Just as reform movements predated Luther's protests, so too did the growth of new learning and new thinking. Fifteenth-century Florence, universities across Europe, religious orders, and individuals such as Johannes Gutenberg (d. 1468) fostered a literacy and learning that changed the world in which Catholics lived and thought. In the second century AD printing had begun in China, but geographical separation and, later, the opposition of Islam prevented the invention from reaching Europe. In 1450 Gutenberg, a Mainz blacksmith, created a movable typeface of identical letters and invented what we know as the printing press. His masterpiece was the Forty-Two-Line Bible of 1455. Presses spread across Europe. Before the start of the sixteenth century over 28,000 editions of books had been printed. A vast new reading public grew up. As there was no copyright, pirated editions boosted sales.

---

[29] *Boswell's Life of Johnson*, Everyman paperback (London: Dent, 1960), ii. 519.
[30] See J. W. O'Malley, *The First Jesuits* (Cambridge, Mass.: Harvard University Press, 1993).

Translations into modern languages spread the classical texts from ancient Greece and Rome. With its annual book fairs around Easter and in the early autumn, Frankfurt encouraged a booming publishing trade. Mass literacy was on the way. In the year 2000 many recalled Gutenberg's invention of the moveable typeface and dubbed him 'the man of the second millennium'. To celebrate his contribution to the spread of learning, some preachers used to invoke the memory of Gutenberg by opening their sermons with the words of John 1: 6–7: 'There was a man sent from God, whose name was John. He came for testimony, to bear witness to the light.' A still-popular Christmas carol, 'Hark the Herald Angels Sing', uses a tune Felix Mendelssohn (1809–47) wrote for the 1840 Leipzig celebrations of Gutenberg.

Gutenberg made possible the new humanism of such figures as Erasmus and his witty and courageous friend, St Thomas More (1477–1535). Benedictines, Dominicans, and other older religious orders played an active role in the spread of literacy and learning. But from the sixteenth century, Jesuits became the schoolmasters of Europe and the New World, delivering a classical education to generations of students. In 1551 the Roman College had opened, to be eventually renamed the Gregorian University, the mother of Jesuit colleges and universities around the world.[31] Other new religious institutes came on the scene to spread education. Mary Ward (1585–1645), a pioneer of an active, missionary ministry for religious women, founded the Institute of the Blessed Virgin Mary. In three branches it continues its educational work today. In 1680 St Jean Baptiste de La Salle founded the Brothers of the Christian Schools, also known as the De La Salle Christian Brothers. Other male and female religious congregations founded in the nineteenth century, such as the Faithful Companions of Jesus, the Society of the Sacred Heart, the Irish Christian Brothers, the Marist Brothers of the Schools, the Society of St Francis de Sales (commonly known as the Salesians) and various Franciscan Sisters continue to dedicate themselves to the ministry of education.

In the post-Gutenberg world, Catholics and others had many things to learn and to question. The new learning, no less than the discovery of other continents and the Reformation, challenged old certainties. Was monarchy God's chosen form of government, so that it would always be

---

[31] See J. W. O'Malley *et al.* (eds.), *The Jesuits: Culture, Science and the Arts 1540–1773* (Toronto: University of Toronto Press, 1999).

sinful to rebel against a monarch?[32] Or could one agree with Juan Mariana (1536–1624) in justifying in certain circumstances the killing of tyrants? Was St Robert Bellarmine (1542–1621) correct in opposing the views of James I of England (1566–1625) on the Divine Rights of Kings, and in holding that popes enjoyed only indirect, not direct, power in temporal matters? Should or could the state be used to enforce church requirements? When Mary Tudor succeeded to the throne of England in 1553, she attempted to reverse the Reformation and restore the Catholic religion. Heresy trials claimed around 400 victims in the five years of her reign. When this Catholic revival ended in 1558 and Elizabeth I came to the throne, it took a hundred years to reach another total of 400 men and women executed, this time for their Catholic faith.

Around Europe, particularly in Northern Europe but not in Spain (where the Spanish Inquisition rejected the persecution of witches), trials of witches increased from the late fourteenth century and peaked in the late sixteenth and early seventeenth centuries. Ordinary Catholics, Protestants, and Anglicans denounced their female neighbours whom they suspected of indulging in diabolic magic, especially by harming or even killing children. Widespread infant mortality fostered such suspicions. In pre-industrial Europe 20–30 per cent of all children died in the first year of life; only half of all children survived to 5 years of age. Over the centuries around 50,000 were executed for alleged witchcraft. Friedrich von Spee (1591–1635), a composer of hymns and pastoral poetry, was appointed confessor to women accused of witchcraft and quickly realized the insanity of the popular hysteria over witches. This Jesuit had, nevertheless, to accompany around 200 innocent victims to the stake. His attack on witchcraft trials, *Cautio criminalis*, helped to bring their suppression in some places. Spee himself died in Trier when ministering to plague-stricken soldiers during the Thirty Years War.[33]

More than a century later, over in North America Charles Carroll (1737–1832) became the only Catholic among the fifty-five signatories of the American Declaration of Independence (1776). During the colonial era Catholics had been almost everywhere a despised and victimized minority. Along with his cousin, Archbishop John Carroll (1736–1815),

[32] See P. K. Monod, *The Power of Kings: Monarchy and Religion in Europe 1589–1715* (New Haven, Conn.: Yale University Press, 1999).

[33] See R. Briggs, *Witches and Neighbours* (London: Penguin, 1998); and 'Witchcraft', *Oxford Dictionary of the Christian Church*, 1757–8.

the first Catholic bishop in the United States and the founder of George-town University, Charles Carroll came to symbolize American religious freedom and a sense that the Catholic faith could and should be reconciled with the best features of the new, democratic political order.

Across the Atlantic the European union of altar and throne, which reached back to Emperor Constantine and was widely considered the happy norm for Catholic life, came to a grinding halt when the furies raged in the French Revolution. A well-educated parish clergy had led the people in the practice of the Catholic faith. Inspired by the work of St Vincent de Paul (1581–1660) and St Louise de Marillac (1591–1660), religious men and women dedicated themselves to the care of the sick and the poor. The Reign of Terror (1793–4) targeted clergy and religious along with aristocrats, while the revolutionary government slaughtered devout peasant masses in the Vendée. When Napoleon had Pius VI (pope 1775–99) carried off as a prisoner to France, he took the Catholic Church to the edge. The troubles of the French Revolution unhinged papal power and prestige, and reduced the Catholic Church in France to its weakest state in over a thousand years. But the ministry of the Curé of Ars, St Jean-Baptiste Marie Vianney (1786–1859), Lourdes as a place of pilgrimage for millions since the 1858 visions of St Bernadette Soubirous (1844–79), and the remarkable flowering of devotion to the Sacred Heart of Jesus symbolize the dramatic resurgence of Catholicism in post-Napoleonic France and beyond.

The nineteenth-century Pius IX, despite some attractive features of his reign, epitomizes the resistance to better insights of modern reason. Opposed to freedom of speech and religion, he used public executions in an attempt to maintain public order right up to 1870, when the papal states fell and the forces of united Italy entered Rome. Although the nineteenth century saw the emancipation of Jews in most countries, in 1850 Pio Nono had reinstated in the city the closed ghetto for Jews and introduced anti-Jewish legislation. At a time when slavery was being abolished, he argued that it could be reconciled with divine revelation and the natural law. Pio Nono died in 1878, exactly one century before the election of John Paul II, a pope who rejected the death penalty, repeatedly asked pardon for the wrongs Catholics have committed against Jews, and worked hard to further dialogue between the Catholic Church and other Christian communities. During the pontificate of Pio Nono, John Paul II would have been gaoled in Castel San Angelo for saying, writing, and doing such things. At the end of the twentieth century his international impact depended in part on something Pio Nono could not imagine: namely, being freed in 1870 from the burden and limitation of governing a sovereign country, the papal states.

Both before and after Pio Nono, Catholics and other Christians faced a serious challenge from the Enlightenment, the first major intellectual movement in the Western world to develop outside the control of the Catholic Church (and of Christianity in general) for well over a thousand years. It started in seventeenth-century Europe (and spread to North America), resisted authority and tradition, championed human rights, encouraged empirical methods in scientific research, and aimed at deciding issues through the use of reason alone.[34] Many figures of the Enlightenment rejected miracles and special divine revelation, and could be strongly opposed to traditional Christianity. The First Vatican Council (1869/70) defended a proper collaboration between faith (the response to divine revelation) and reason (DH 3015–19; ND 131–5). The theological and philosophical debate with those who upheld the autonomy of human reason eventually led to the Second Vatican Council's Pastoral Constitution on the Church in the Modern World (*Gaudium et Spes*) and John Paul II's 1998 encyclical on faith and reason, *Fides et Ratio*. But, quite apart from these and earlier official responses, the frightful tragedies of modern times have robbed of much of its appeal the brave new world of the secular Enlightenment. In any case desanitized versions of the Enlightenment have made it clear that such heroes as David Hume (1711–76) and even Immanuel Kant (1724–1804) excluded blacks from the equality and freedoms they championed. The rights of 'man' did not always include even the rights of (white) women.[35]

The second half of this chapter, from the discoveries initiated by Christopher Columbus in 1492 until the twentieth century, has describe various overlapping movements that have deeply configured contemporary Catholicism (and indeed Christianity at large): the expansion of Europe into the Americas, Asia, Africa, and Oceania; the changes associated with the Protestant Reformation and the Council of Trent; the new

---

[34] See J. I. Israel, *Radical Enlightenment: Philosophy and the Making of Modernity 1650–1750* (Oxford: Oxford University Press, 2001).

[35] See J. Shaw, 'The Late Seventeenth and Eighteenth Centuries', in R. Harries and H. Mayr-Harting (eds.), *Christianity: Two Thousand Years* (Oxford: Oxford University Press, 2001), 162–91, at 178–86.

learning facilitated by Johannes Gutenberg's invention of the printing press (1450); the American Declaration of Independence (1776), the shock of the French Revolution (1789), and the challenge of the Enlightenment.

The Coming of the World Church

How then can we sum up the situation of Catholicism at the end of the twentieth century, one marked by the immense and murderous catastrophes of two World Wars? It proved a bloodstained century, with 55 million being killed or starving to death during the Second World War (1939–45). One act of wilful murder stands out, the Shoah. Adolf Hitler (1889–1945) and his collaborators systematically exterminated nearly six million European Jews, one million of them children. Along with Nazism, the Communism of Joseph Stalin (1879–1953) and of Mao Tse-Tung (1893–1976) marked the century until, at least in Europe, this ideology officially ended when the Berlin Wall came down in November 1989. The sudden collapse of the Soviet Union was perhaps the most surprising event in the entire century.

Dramatic changes affected the twentieth-century story of Catholicism. In 1900 almost two-thirds of the world's Catholics lived in Europe and North America; by 1993 three-quarters of them lived in Latin America, Africa, and Asia. An even more startling demographic change is the fact that, by the time the world population passed the 6 billion mark in October 1999, more than half the Catholics who have ever existed lived in the twentieth century.

Another way of expressing the shift is to recall the conclave of cardinals who elected Paul VI (pope 1963–78); 65 per cent of those cardinals were Europeans and more than a third were Italians. By the time of the 1978 conclave that elected John Paul II, the Italian cardinals were down to a quarter and those from Western Europe down to less than a half. Beyond question, the Italians and Europeans were still over-represented in 1978. But a clear demographic change had begun in the college of cardinals, and it was no accident that in electing John Paul II, they chose the first non-Italian pope in more than four hundred years.

He himself as a Polish bishop had attended Vatican II, the first Ecumenical Council to show the universality of the Catholic Church. Even so the Council manifested a trend rather than an achieved reality. For example, only 311 of the 2,600 Council Fathers came from Africa; of these 311, only 60 were Africans. Nevertheless, that Council revealed how, within the Catholic Church and beyond, the old days of European hegemony were drawing to a close.

It is worth recalling how, when the Council opened in October 1962, the Cuban missile crisis had brought the USA and the Soviet Union to the brink of a nuclear war. John XXIII (pope 1958–63), who had called the Council, played a key role in defusing that crisis. A few months later he published his plea for a new world order, *Pacem in Terris* ('Peace on Earth'). When he died in June 1963, some units of the Russian navy flew their flags at half-mast. In October 1965, a few weeks after the fourth session of the Council opened, Paul VI flew to New York to address a message of peace ('Never again war!') to the United Nations—being the first pope ever to speak to that body which represents the world. Popes John and Paul did their part in giving the Council a message for all humankind—something dramatically continued by Pope John Paul II.

The Council had a double aim: an *aggiornamento* (updating) of the Church's own life, worship, and teaching; and new relationships with other Christian communities, with Jews, with Muslims, and with the members of other world religions. The first and last of the sixteen documents issued by the Council express the double aim. Through *Sacrosanctum Concilium* (4 December 1963) the bishops endorsed the reform of worship through (1) a return to earlier and simpler forms and (2) the use of the vernacular or local language. The last and longest conciliar text, *Gaudium et Spes* (7 December 1965), spelled out the bishops' ideals and values for Christian and human life towards the end of the second millennium. That same day Paul VI and the Orthodox patriarch of Constantinople issued a joint declaration, expressing their regret for nine centuries of division and hopes for future reconciliation. Through ceremonies held simultaneously in the Vatican and at the patriarch's residence in Istanbul they lifted the mutual excommunications between the Orthodox and the Catholic churches. The following day the Council, the greatest event in the lives of twentieth-century Catholics, ended with a solemn liturgy.

The Council[36] has affected the lives of Catholics around the world in many ways: through the new rites used for the administration of baptism and the other sacraments, through closer relations with other Christians, through the encouragement given to new forms of life consecrated to prayer and apostolic activity, through changes in the training of candidates for the

---

[36] On Vatican II see R. Latourelle (ed.), *Vatican II: Assessment and Perspectives*, 3 vols. (Mahwah, NY: Paulist Press, 1989).

FIG. 6. Pope John XXIII is joined by 2,600 bishops and cardinals on 12 October 1962 at the opening of the second Vatican Council: the most significant event in twentieth-century Catholic history. (Topham Picturepoint.)

ministry, and through other larger and smaller changes. Many of the new directions are reflected in the 1983 Code of Canon Law (for the Western Church) and the 1990 Code of Canons of the Oriental Churches (for the Eastern Church). The Council also opened the door to developments on a scale hardly imaginable to earlier Catholics. Let us mention a few examples.

First, the papacy. By continuing and enormously expanding the practice of Paul VI, John Paul II made the papacy a world presence not least by visiting almost every major nation and many smaller nations around the globe. By April 2002 he had been out of Italy ninety-five times on 'apostolic pilgrimages', which often included stops in several countries. Second, since the closing of Vatican II in 1965, the Catholic Church has experienced the rise of Catholic feminism, the work of various liberation theologians (who frequently looked back to Las Casas for their inspiration), and fresh attempts at dialogue with the great religions of Asia. In the closing chapters of this book we will come back to these and other present trends and challenges.

The opening chapters of this book inevitably tracked matters chronologically: the first millennium of Catholicism and then its second. The five chapters that follow will take up Catholic doctrinal teaching, using the general councils of the Church as major signposts. Here too we can present matters more or less chronologically. The main exception to a chronological order comes at once in Ch. 3: its account of Catholic understanding of revelation, the scriptures, and tradition will be heavily shaped by modern teaching. Chapter 4 presents the trinitarian and christological doctrines as substantially developed by the first seven councils (from Nicaea I in 325 to Nicaea II in 787). Chapters 5 and 6 examine Catholic teaching first on creation and human sin, and then on the new life of grace and glory—developed, in particular, by Augustine of Hippo (354–430), Thomas Aquinas, and the Council of Trent. Chapter 7 takes up the seven sacraments, which were in a special way expounded by the Council of Trent and the Second Vatican Council (with the subsequent liturgical changes it prompted). In Ch. 8 we turn to the Church, her structure, and her mission—major themes at Vatican I and Vatican II. We now summarize the Catholic understanding of divine revelation and its consequences in the inspired scriptures and living tradition. Let us once again insist that we will be setting out what is distinctively, but not necessarily uniquely, Catholic.

3

Revelation, Tradition, and Scripture

Long ago God spoke to our ancestors in many and various ways by the prophets, but in these last days he has spoken to us by a Son.

(Hebrews 1: 1–2)

Jesus Christ...by his whole presence and self-manifestation, by words and deeds, by signs and miracles, but especially by his death and glorious resurrection from the dead, and finally by the sending of the Spirit of truth—completes and perfects revelation, and confirms it with the divine witness.

(Vatican II, *Dei Verbum*, 4)

All scripture is inspired by God and is useful for teaching, for reproof, for correction, and for training in righteousness.

(2 Timothy 3: 16).

Before setting out any doctrines about God, human beings, the sacraments, the Church, and the rest, we must spell out the way Catholic teaching understands the divine revelation, the response of human faith, the tradition that hands on belief in God, and the scriptures that are inspired by the Holy Spirit. The interpretation of the foundational realities of revelation, faith, tradition, and scripture persistently shapes and colours the way particular doctrines are understood.

DIVINE REVELATION

Revelation or 'taking away the veil' indicates the disclosure, freely brought about by God's loving initiative, of what was previously unknown, the primary theme of the Second Vatican Council's Constitution on Divine

Revelation of 1965, *Dei Verbum* ('the Word of God'). This classic document understands such disclosure to be primarily God's self-revelation, which invites the personal response of faith, and to be secondarily the communication of truths about God and human beings that would otherwise remain unknown. Since the time of the Enlightenment, the truths of revelation had been frequently contrasted with those of reason, the latter understood as accessible to human intelligence without any special divine communication being strictly necessary. This distinction between truths of revelation and those of reason and the view of revelation as being primarily information or 'propositional' truths disclosed by God characterized, albeit not totally, the teaching of the First Vatican Council (1869–70) in its Dogmatic Constitution on the Catholic Faith, *Dei Filius* ('the Son of God') (DH 3004–45; ND 113–40). The response of faith was accordingly presented as primarily an assent of the human intelligence to these supernatural truths, an assent (1) justified by the authority of God who reveals the truths, and (2) made possible by the help of the Holy Spirit. Such a propositional view of revelation takes second place in *Dei Verbum*, which recognizes revelation to be first the personal manifestation of the divine Mystery (upper case) and second the disclosure of divine mysteries (lower case) that were previously hidden from human knowledge and understanding. In revelation we primarily meet God and not divinely authorized truths. This understanding of God's self-manifestation entails presenting human faith as a matter of a *total* human response to the divine self-revelation. Far from being predominantly or even exclusively the mind accepting revealed truths, faith is the 'obedient' response of the whole person with the help of the Holy Spirit—head, heart, and actions—to the self-manifestation of God (*Dei Verbum*, 5).

Three Qualities of Revelation

Vatican II's Constitution on Divine Revelation understands revelation to be essentially 'sacramental', in the sense of coming through something that is done (e.g. the immersion in water or the pouring of water in baptism) and something that is said (e.g. the formula 'I baptize you in the name of the Father and of the Son and of the Holy Spirit'). Like the sacraments the divine self-revelation occurs through an interplay of deeds and words: for instance, through the words of the prophets illuminating and explaining the events or deeds of Israel's history.

The sacramental view of revelation taken by *Dei Verbum* also involves acknowledging its salvific character. The self-revelation of God changes and even transforms human beings who hear the divine word and let themselves be opened to recognize God's self-manifestation in their history. The OT prophets, in particular, appreciated that the divine words, so far from being merely informative statements, powerfully bring about results. God's word is like rain that causes germination, 'giving seed to the sower and bread to the eater' (Isa. 55: 10). One appreciates then how and why the opening chapter of *Dei Verbum* uses the history of revelation and salvation history interchangeably; God's revelatory and salvific activity may be distinguishable but are never separable. They belong together as the two sides of the same divine reality: God's loving self-communication. When Christ 'completes and perfects' the divine self-manifestation, he reveals that 'God is with us to liberate us from the darkness of sin and death and raise us up to eternal life' (*Dei Verbum*, 4). In language highlighted by John's Gospel, Christ is the saving 'Life' of the world precisely because he is the revealing 'Light' of the world, and vice versa. This interplay of the light and life we receive from Christ was expressed well over a thousand years ago by Christians in the Eastern Mediterranean; they carved on the tombs of their beloved dead two Greek words together: '*phōs* (light)' and '*zōē* (life)'. *Phōs* ran down the inscription and intersected in the letter 'omega' with *zōē* which ran across. The central position of omega brings Christ to mind, inasmuch as he shares the divine title of being the Alpha and the Omega, the first and last letters of the Greek alphabet, which apply to Christ as the beginning and the end of all things (Rev. 22: 13).

Vatican II presents revelation not only as God's sacramental and salvific self-revelation but also as utterly Christ-centred. In his incarnation, life, death, resurrection, and co-sending (with God the Father) of the Holy Spirit, Christ forms the climax of the divine self-revelation (*Dei Verbum*, 4, 17). In the words of John's Gospel: 'the Word became flesh and lived among us, and we have seen his glory, the glory of the Father's only Son ... No one has ever seen God. It is God the only Son, who is close to the Father's heart, who has made him known' (John 1: 14, 18). Christ is simultaneously the Revealer (or, with the Holy Spirit, the primary agent of divine self-revelation), the Revelation (or the visible, incarnate 'process' of divine self-revelation), and, with the Father and the Holy Spirit, the primary 'content' of revelation.

In one sense the whole Christ-event was and remains the fullness and completion of divine revelation. Having spoken and acted through the visible presence of his incarnate Son (and the mission of the Spirit), God had and has nothing greater to say, nothing more to reveal, and no other agent of revelation who could be compared with, let alone match, Christ. In that sense the historical revelation through Christ is full, unparalleled, and unsurpassable in principle; to use the language of the Letter to the Hebrews, this saving revelation has happened 'once and for all' (Heb. 7: 27; 9: 12; 10: 10). God can and will call up subordinate mediators of revelation, but they can and will never be like Christ either in kind or degree. His divine identity puts him qualitatively beyond any possible 'rival' in the work of revelation (and salvation).

But in another sense, we do not yet enjoy the fullness and completion of revelation. The final vision of God is still to come. As St John puts it, 'Beloved, we are God's children now; what we will be has not yet been revealed. What we know is this: when he [God] is revealed, we will be like him, for we will see him as he is' (1 John 3: 2). As we wait in hope for this complete, saving revelation, we see and know 'dimly' and not yet fully. Looking forward to the fullness of God's self-manifestation that will complete our redemption, St Paul writes: 'Now we see in a mirror dimly, but then face to face. Now I know in part: then I shall understand fully, even as I have been fully understood' (1 Cor. 13: 12). It is at their peril that Christian believers fail to follow the lead of John and Paul and acknowledge that in one very significant sense we do not yet have the fullness or completion of the divine revelation, that 'glorious manifest-ation of our Lord, Jesus Christ' (*Dei Verbum*, 4) still to come. The 'not yet' of this future manifestation qualifies the revelation 'already' achieved through Christ and the Holy Spirit. In his 1998 encyclical letter *Fides et Ratio* ('Faith and Reason') Pope John Paul II quoted St Paul in support of his statement about 'that fullness of truth which will appear with the final revelation of God' (no. 2). This fullness of truth and revelation will come only in the future.

Foundational and Dependent Revelation

Furthermore, we should recall here how *Dei Verbum* also portrays revela-tion as an ongoing reality which is ever being actualized and constantly invites human faith: 'The "obedience of faith" (Rom. 16: 26) ... must be given to the God who reveals' (no. 5). People are called, in one generation after another, to accept in faith the divine self-manifestation that was completed with Jesus and his first disciples. *Dei Verbum* associates revelation as it happened then with revelation as it happens now (in the Church) in these terms: 'God, who spoke in the past, continues to converse with the spouse of his beloved Son' (no. 8). Vatican II's Constitution on the Sacred Liturgy, *Sacrosanctum Concilium* ('the Sacred Council'), apropos of the various ways Christ is present in the Church's public worship, acknowledges that 'it is he himself who speaks when the holy scriptures are read in the Church'; in the context of worship 'Christ is still proclaiming his gospel' (nos. 7, 33). Other documents of Vatican II and the teaching of Pope John Paul II, most notably his 1979 Apostolic Exhortation on Catechesis in Our Time, *Catechesi Tradendae* ('Handing on Catechesis') and his 1980 encyclical letter *Dives in Misericordia* ('Rich in Mercy'), portray revelation as also being a present reality which is repeatedly actualized here and now. Just as faith is a present event, so too is the light of divine self-revelation that comes through the Eucharist, the other sacraments, preaching, reading the scriptures, public and private prayer, and many other channels that summon forth faith.

In using 'revelation' of what repeatedly happens now, John Paul II was not alleging that God reveals new truths and so enlarges the original foundational divine self-manifestation conveyed by Christ and his first followers. Those who still think of revelation as being primarily propositional truths can easily spring to that false conclusion. What the Pope wanted to underline in speaking of revelation in the present was God's living and enlightening voice speaking now and calling human beings to respond, also here and now, with faith. John Paul II was certainly not alleging that there is or could be an 'increase' in the content of the essential truths revealed once and for all through Jesus and the Holy Spirit.

In short, modern Catholic teaching has portrayed God's revelation not only as reaching its unsurpassable climax in the past (with Jesus Christ) but also as a present and future event. We can express this triple time reference by distinguishing 'foundational' revelation, which took place back there and then in the first century AD, from 'dependent' revelation, which is ceaselessly actualized now for those who hear God's revealing word, and from 'eschatological' (final) revelation, which will be the definitive self-revelation of God at the end of history. These terms, especially the first and the second, call for a little more explanation.

Without using our terminology, traditional Catholic theology spoke of foundational revelation 'ending with the death of the last apostle'. This language pointed to a truth: aided by the Holy Spirit, the apostles and other early followers of Jesus took decades to discern, interpret, and express their experience of Jesus in his life, death, and resurrection. In fact, they spent a lifetime plumbing and proclaiming the meaning of what they had experienced in the crucified and risen Jesus. Collectively and individually they gave themselves to interpreting and applying the meaning, truth, and value of their total experience of Jesus and his Spirit. Understood this way, the period of foundational revelation covered not only the climactic events (Jesus' life, death, and resurrection, with the coming of the Spirit), but also the decades when the apostles and their associates assimilated these events, proclaimed the good news about Jesus, fully founded the Church for all peoples, and wrote the inspired books of the NT. During those years the apostles were not receiving new truths, as if Christ had failed to complete revelation by all that he did, said, and suffered. Rather they were being led by the Holy Spirit to express, interpret normatively, and apply what they had directly experienced of the fullness of revelation in the person of Christ. Thus the activity of the Spirit through the apostolic age also entered into foundational revelation—in its phase of immediate assimilation. That age belonged to the revealing and redemptive Christ-event and normatively did so in a way which would not be true of any later stage in Christian history.

When the apostolic age closed—roughly speaking at the end of the first century—there would be no more founding of the Church and writing of inspired scriptures. The period of foundational revelation, in which the activity of the original witnesses brought about the visible Church and completed the written word of God, was finished. Through the great tradition (which includes the scriptures, the sacraments, preaching, and teaching) launched by the apostolic Church, later generations could share 'dependently' in the saving self-communication of God mediated through the climactic and unrepeatable events surrounding Jesus and his apostles. Without using our term 'dependent' revelation, the prologue of *Dei Verbum* cites 1 John 1: 2–3 to indicate how till the end of time all later generations of Christian believers will be invited to accept and depend upon the witness of those who announced what they had personally experienced of the full divine revelation in Christ: 'We proclaim to you the eternal life which was with the Father and was made manifest to us.'

We remarked above on the way some still resist talk of (dependent) revelation occurring here and now. The problem may be a verbal one: namely, a sense that revelation always happened (or happens) dramatically—through supernatural visions, divine oracles, and other special phenomena. But divine self-revelation *also* took place (foundational revelation) and continues to take place (dependent revelation) in ordinary ways and is not limited to extraordinary events and remarkable episodes.

Before moving on from this account of divine revelation, one should recall that not only *Dei Verbum* but also some of the other fifteen documents from the Second Vatican Council fill out what revelation entails. The last and longest document from the Council, the Pastoral Constitution on the Church in the Modern World, *Gaudium et Spes* ('Joy and Hope') of 7 December 1965, for example, adds some important themes: above all, the way that divine revelation also throws light on the human condition. The disclosure of the mystery of God illuminates such basic and painful 'enigmas' as those of suffering and death; the revelation brought by Christ manifests to human beings what they are and what they are to become. Christ lifts the veil on both God and the human condition; the disclosure of God simultaneously reveals the origin, nature, and destiny of human beings (*Gaudium et Spes*, 10, 22, 41).[1]

Vatican II also had important things to teach about God's saving revelation to all peoples. That issue, which is more crucial than ever, will be treated in the final chapter of this book.

TRADITION

After its opening chapter on divine revelation, *Dei Verbum* moves in its second chapter to treat tradition, to be understood both as the process of 'handing on' (tradition as act) and the living heritage that is handed on (tradition as content)—with both the process and the heritage being located within the Church community. The dynamic of tradition, both as act and content, is already very much at work in the history of Israel, when the Jewish people hand on the memory of their sufferings and the powerful disclosure of God, who delivered them from slavery in Egypt

[1] For more on Vatican II's teaching on revelation, see G. O'Collins, *Retrieving Fundamental Theology* (Mahwah, NJ: Paulist Press, 1993), 48–97.

and brought them home from exile in Babylon. Parents must pass on to their children the marvellous story of the saving acts of God (Deut. 6: 20–5; 26: 5–10), which justify the loving loyalty to 'the Lord, our God' which is the heart of the law (Deut. 6: 4–9).

With the outpouring of the Holy Spirit, the invisible bearer of tradition, the whole Church, and not simply her authoritative leaders, has been empowered to transmit her memory, experience, and expression of the foundational self-revelation of God that was completed with Christ and the NT community. Thus 'tradition' involves the present 'Church in her doctrine, life, and worship' transmitting to every generation '*all* that she herself is, *all* that she believes' (*Dei Verbum*, 8; italics added). This total view of tradition is significant for the question of scripture and tradition: that is to say, the relationship between the written and inspired word of God and the *larger* reality of the whole Church in her 'transmitting' role.

Tradition as process (or act) and as living heritage (or content), after being quietly endorsed for well over a thousand years, was severely tested by the sixteenth-century Reformation's principle of 'scripture alone' (*sola scriptura*). Faced with this challenge, the Council of Trent in its fourth session of April 1546 taught that the 'gospel', which is roughly equivalent to 'revelation', is 'the source of all saving truth and rule of conduct', and is 'contained' not only in the 'written books' but also in the 'unwritten traditions which have come down to us' (DH 1501; ND 210). Even though the Council had spoken of only *one source*, 'the gospel' in the singular, this teaching through its language of the gospel being 'contained' in 'written books' and 'unwritten traditions', led many Catholics to develop the 'two-source theory', according to which some revealed truths could be contained in tradition and not in scripture.

The documents of Vatican II and, in particular, *Dei Verbum*, although they do not expressly set out to pronounce on this long-standing two-source theory, in effect rule it out—not least by understanding revelation primarily as the living self-communication of God (*Dei Verbum*, 2–6), rather than as a body of revealed propositions or propositional truths contained in the Bible or other sources. Moreover, in highlighting the process of tradition (singular) rather than individual traditions (or particular teachings and practices), *Dei Verbum* insists on the way that tradition and scripture are united in their origin (revelation), function, and goal (ibid. 9). Being so strictly united in their origin, function, and goal, scripture and tradition cannot be treated as if they were two sources, and certainly not as if they were two separate sources.

Other important items in Vatican II's teaching on tradition include the way *Dei Verbum*, while acknowledging only scripture as 'the word of God', recognizes the role of tradition in actualizing and clarifying revelation (ibid. 8)—a striking example of how tradition and scripture dynamically function together to serve the life of faith. What is at stake here is also the sense of all human beings and not simply Catholic Christians being essentially 'traditional'. The various societies that make up humanity all receive an immensely rich cultural heritage from their past; experiencing together multifaceted reality, they can receive and find the truth about God and themselves in a never-ending dialogue between the tradition they have inherited and the experiences they meet. The divine self-revelation is actualized for human beings who are through and through 'traditional' beings.

Secondly, Vatican II's documents on ecumenism (*Unitatis Redintegratio*, 14–17) and on the Eastern Churches (*Orientalium Ecclesiarum*, 5–6) expressed the way Tradition (upper case) or the patrimony as a whole is passed on through particular traditions (lower case). Yves Congar (1904–95), a notable theological expert at Vatican II, championed the distinction between the Tradition and the traditions. Along with some outstanding Protestant theologians such as Gerhard Ebeling (b. 1912) and philosophers such as Hans-Georg Gadamer (1900–2002), Congar also encouraged many Protestants to recognize that an exclusive appeal to scripture alone is not possible. Scripture has its uniquely powerful role in judging and reforming specific traditions, but the Tradition of the Church is the essential setting for appropriating and understanding revelation. Let us put this point another way. The Bible as the inspired record of Christian origins provides all believers with the mirror and test of their self-identity, and official teachers of the Catholic Church are called to stand 'under' the written word of God and 'serve' it (*Dei Verbum*, 10). Nevertheless, the inspired scriptures do not interpret themselves; they are read and applied by a living community with its authoritative leaders.

SCRIPTURE

Four out of the six chapters of *Dei Verbum* deal with the inspired scriptures, but the document first expounds revelation and tradition—a way of showing how they are 'prior' and 'broader' realities. Despite its high doctrine of biblical inspiration, Catholic Christianity is primarily a religion of the word, not of the book. God's living word, handed on and constantly reactualized in the worship, teaching, and whole life of the community, takes a certain precedence over the inspired writings.

The Formation of the Biblical Record

The Bible should not and cannot be simply identified with revelation. As a living, interpersonal event, revelation takes place or happens. God initiates, at particular times and places and to particular persons, some form of self-communication. The divine initiative achieves its goal and revelation occurs when human beings respond in faith to the divine self-communication they experience.

As such, the scriptures are not a living, interpersonal event. They are written *records* which, after the history of divine revelation had begun and under the inspiration of the Holy Spirit, came into existence through the work of some believers at various stages in the foundational history of God's people. This is to say, Catholics (and other Christians) believe that God's Spirit prompted certain people to set certain things down in writing. Thus the scriptures differ from revelation in the way that written documents differ from interpersonal events that took place and take place. It makes perfectly good sense to say with exasperation, 'I left my copy of the Bible behind in the London Underground.' But we would have a good deal of explaining to do if either of us were to say to a friend, 'I left revelation behind in the Underground.'

In the history of the Bible's composition, the gift of revelation and the special inspiration to write the scriptures were not only distinguishable but also separable. This is another way of illustrating the difference with which we are concerned. Either directly or through such mediators as the prophets and, above all, Jesus himself, revelation was offered to *all* the people. The gift of God's saving self-communication was held out to everyone. The special impulse to write the scriptures was a charism given only to those who under the guidance of the Holy Spirit composed or helped to compose the sacred texts. To be sure, the scriptures were intended for everyone. But the charism of inspiration was given only to some persons.

Even in the case of the sacred writers themselves revelation and the charism of inspiration did not coincide. Opening themselves in faith to the divine self-manifestation and remembering the revelatory events (e.g. the deliverance from Egyptian captivity) and words (e.g. the divine messages through the prophets) of the past was one thing. Being guided by the Holy Spirit to set down certain things in writing, i.e. the gift of biblical inspiration, was another. God's self-revelation impinged on the entire life of the sacred writers. In cases that we know of, the charism of inspiration functioned only in limited periods of their lives. Thus divine revelation operated in Paul's life before and after his call/conversion around AD 36. Around AD 50 he wrote his first (inspired) letter that has been preserved for us, 1 Thessalonians, and then composed his other letters in the 50s and into the early 60s. The divine self-communication affected the whole of Paul's life, the charism of inspiration only the last decade or so of his apostolic activity.

Reflection on the *content* of the Bible offers another angle on the distinction between revelation and the inspired work of the sacred authors. The Bible witnesses to and interprets various persons, events, and words that mediated the divine self-revelation. The Letter to the Hebrews opens by acknowledging the incarnate Son of God as the qualitatively superior climax in a long series of mediators of revelation (Heb. 1: 1–2). A wide variety of events manifested God's loving designs for human salvation: from the call of Abraham and Sarah, the exodus, births of royal children, the Babylonian exile, through to the crucifixion and resurrection of Jesus, with the outpouring of the Spirit. Prophetic utterances, parables, creeds (e.g. Deut. 26: 5–9; Rom. 1: 3–4), hymns (e.g. Phil. 2: 6–11), kerygmatic summaries (e.g. 1 Cor. 15: 3–5), and, supremely, the words of Jesus himself serve to disclose the truth of God and human beings. When we read the scriptures with an eye for the persons, events, and words that convey and witness to the divine self-revelation, we will have much to find.

At the same time, however, the Bible also records matters that are not so closely connected with revelation. The language of human love and courtship fashions the Song of Solomon, which—paradoxically for a scriptural book—contains no explicit religious message. Alongside many lofty prescriptions to guide the worship and life of Israel as a holy people, Leviticus includes numerous regulations about wine and food, about the sick and diseased (in particular, lepers), about sexual relations, and many matters that can hardly be derived from some special divine revelation. This book, which was written under the inspiration of the Spirit and took its final form in the sixth or fifth century B C, contains pages of rituals and laws, which usually look as if they come from old human customs rather than from some divine disclosure. The Book of Proverbs records the moral and religious instruction that professional teachers offered Jewish youth after the Babylonian exile. The wisdom of the ages seemed based on the lessons of common human experience, and is in part (Prov. 22: 17–24: 22) modelled upon the *Instruction of Amenemope*, an Egyptian book of wisdom. Where religious faith supports Proverbs' view of an upright human life, Ecclesiastes seems to use reason alone to explore the meaning of human existence and the (limited) value of our life which ends in the oblivion of death.

Whole sections of the Bible speak more of the human condition and less directly of divine revelation. The fact that the inspiration of the Holy Spirit operated in the writing of some book does not automatically point to a high 'amount' of divine self-disclosure showing through that book. Some of what the inspired Bible records can seem a long way from God's saving self-communication. See, for instance, the story of a concubine's murder and the subsequent revenge of the Benjamites (Judg. 19: 1–20: 48) or Saul's visit to the witch of Endor (1 Sam. 28: 1–25). Under the special impulse of biblical inspiration, the sacred writers have recorded such stories of human failures, sins, and atrocities—episodes that show how people failed to respond to God's overtures but which have little to witness positively and directly about divine revelation itself. In brief, an inspired record is one thing; its revelatory content is another.

Using the Bible

In distinguishing between revelation and biblical inspiration, we have so far been directing attention to the formation of the scriptures in the past. What does the relationship between revelation and inspiration look like, if we turn to the role of scriptures in the life of Catholics and other Christians today?

First of all, experience witnesses to the way biblical texts can communicate divine revelation. Inspired texts continually prove themselves to be 'inspiring', and bring people into living contact with God. The Holy Spirit who guided the writing of the Bible continues to guide the reading of the Bible. Passages from the prophets and the psalms, words of Jesus from the Gospels, and reflections from Paul's letters can let the truth of and from God shine forth. These scriptural texts may repeatedly bring us fresh light; we can hear God's voice speaking to us through these words. What was long ago written under the impulse of the Holy Spirit can become inspiring and illuminating for us today. As Vatican II repeats from St Ambrose of Milan, when we read the scriptures, we listen to God (*Dei Verbum*, 25).

It is also a fact of Christian experience that less 'promising' parts of the Bible may also enjoy such a revealing impact. At first glance some scriptural texts seem 'primitive' (such as Saul's visit to the witch of Endor), 'boring' (such as the genealogies in 1 Chr. 1–9), or filled with a hatred that is incompatible with the revelation of the divine love. Such passages may act as negative 'foils', which express the true nature of divine revelation and an appropriate response to it. Saul's nocturnal visit to the witch of Endor is at least an inspired cautionary tale: we should not try to enter into contact that way with the other world. Some exiled Israelites did cry out for savage vengeance on their Babylonian and Edomite enemies (Ps. 137: 7–9). Their prayer, which faithfully records their desire for revenge, works to illuminate God's loving concern for all (Jonah 4: 11) and Jesus' prayer that his executioners be forgiven (Luke 23: 34). As regards the biblical genealogies, they may not always say much to most people in the North-Atlantic world. But for some other cultures, to lack ancestors is to suffer diminishment in one's personal identity; within the biblical setting the genealogies recall how God guides human history and, in particular, prepares for the birth of Jesus himself.

In short, experience shows how any biblical text can lead people to know the deep truth of God and of the human condition. Normally the 'great' sections of the scriptures have this revelatory impact, and trigger what we have called 'dependent' revelation. But some thoroughly 'unpromising' scriptural texts can initiate or renew a luminous knowledge of God. This point has more relevance nowadays for many Catholics and others who share the same lectionaries, since the prescribed readings for the Sunday and weekday Eucharist include a much broader selection from the Bible than was the case before Vatican II.

Here we should add that, like other texts, once biblical texts reached their final form and began circulating, they started to have their own history as people in different situations read, interpreted, and applied them. Whether it is a psalm, a letter by St Paul, a poem, a novel, or a political constitution, a text can mean and communicate to readers more than its author(s) ever consciously knew or intended when writing in a particular situation for a specific audience. Changes of context strikingly show how texts can express further ranges of meaning. We will make something more of Matthew 26: 52 ('Those who take the sword will perish by the sword') when we proclaim the verse in one of the war cemeteries at Verdun than when we study it in the library of Rome's Biblical Institute. There is a plus value to all published texts, and especially to scriptural texts when appropriated in the new and challenging contexts of church and world history.[2]

Having acknowledged the revelatory power of the scriptures, we should also recall some limits and qualifications. The Bible was not and is not the only means for receiving divine revelation. *Before* the Jewish scriptures came to be written, God had already initiated the special revealing and saving history of the chosen people. Christians acknowledged in Jesus the climax of that revelatory and salvific history at least two decades before the first book of what would be called the NT (1 Thessalonians) came to be written. Even after the biblical canon (of which more later) was formed, not only contact with the scriptures but also an immense range of other means can mediate the divine self-communication, even to the point of radically changing lives. It was a night spent in reading St Teresa of Avila's autobiography that moved St Edith Stein (1891–1942) towards Christian faith and, eventually, martyrdom. The means for conveying God's revelation need not, at least initially, have anything directly to do with the scriptures. In the concluding chapter of this book, we will face the question of divine revelation reaching non-Christians who do not read or hear the Bible. God's word reaches them by means other than the inspired scriptures of Christianity. We should also note another limit in the Bible's revelatory impact. Sadly one can read and study the scriptures without being open to the Holy Spirit whose inspired guidance led to the writing of the sacred books (*Dei Verbum*, 12). A merely scholarly knowledge of the Bible may yield little or no personal knowledge of God, and in fact block the Bible from becoming a vehicle for revelation.

To sum up. As an inspired text, the Bible illuminates for millions the deepest reality of God and human beings; it is indispensable for Christian existence, both collectively and individually. The 1993 document from the Pontifical Biblical Commission, *The Interpretation of the Bible in the*

---

[2] For two examples of such plus value, see G. O'Collins, *Fundamental Theology* (Mahwah, NJ: Paulist Press, 1986), 254–6.

Church, fills out beautifully what *Dei Verbum* taught about the light that all Catholics and other Christians should constantly draw from the inspired scriptures.[3] Nevertheless, revelation or the living word of God remains a larger reality and is not limited to the Bible and its immediate impact. One cannot and should not simply identify revelation with the scriptures. God's living word is not confined to a written text, even an inspired one. This fact legitimates the order in which *Dei Verbum* handles matters. The greater reality of revelation is clarified (ch. 1) before the document turns to tradition (ch. 2) and the inspired scriptures (chs. 3–6).

At the same time, however, we are justified in calling the scriptures the written 'word of God' (*Dei Verbum*, 9). First, unlike any other religious texts available for Christian and, in the case of the Jewish scriptures, Jewish use, they were written under the special guidance of the Holy Spirit. In a unique way that came to an end with the foundation of the Church in the first century, God was involved in the composition of these texts.[4] Second, all the scriptures have some relationship to *foundational* revelation—to those persons, events, and words that mediated God's salvific self-communication that reached its decisive climax with Christ and his first followers. Even in the case of those books and sections of the Bible which focus less vividly and immediately on the divine revelation, some link can be found. Thus the love poems that make up the Song of Solomon relate themselves to the history of revelation and salvation by invoking key personages and places in that history (e.g. Solomon, David, and Jerusalem). The male protagonist of these poems suggests Israel's faithful, divine Husband (e.g. Hos. 2: 14–23). Third, in the post-apostolic period of dependent revelation any section of the scriptures may become for believers the living word of God. The revelatory and salvific scope of John's Gospel can be applied to the Bible: 'These things are written that you may believe that Jesus is the Christ, the Son of God, and that through

---

[3] See also O'Collins, '*Dei Verbum* and Exegesis', *Fundamental Theology*, 136–49.

[4] To speak of divine 'involvement' is certainly not to reduce inspiration to verbal dictation, as if the inspired writers heard a heavenly voice dictating the words that they were to transcribe. Christian art sometimes reflects this reduction of the inspired writers to the status of being mere copyists. In the Pazzi chapel of the Church of Santa Croce in Florence, for instance, Luca della Robbia beautifully represents the evangelists. An eagle has arrived from heaven to hold a text for John to copy down; a lion performs the same service for Mark. Here wonderful art can be very misleading. In producing the scriptures, God and human beings collaborated; the inspired writers were genuinely and fully active in using their own talents. God's 'inspiring' work does not entail reducing the sacred writers to being mere secretaries who copied down faithfully what they were told. See O'Collins, *Fundamental Theology*, 230–1.

believing you may have life in his name' (John 20: 31). Our 'believing' is the completion of, and our 'life' the consequence of, God's self-revelation.[5]

Saving Truth

Biblical inspiration has sometimes been misunderstood as simply synonymous with 'inerrancy' or immunity from error—a view that creates impossible difficulties for those who cherish the Bible. One should prefer positive talk here (truth rather than immunity from error) and, even more importantly, appreciate that truth is a result or consequence of inspiration. Despite a mechanical view of inspiration that highlighted the role of the Holy Spirit as 'principal author' and hardly allowed for the sacred writers being genuine human authors (DH 3293; ND 227), Pope Leo XIII in his 1893 encyclical *Providentissimus Deus* clarified the distinction between biblical inspiration and truth: the Bible is inspired, *and therefore* it is true (DH 3292; ND 226). But is the Bible always and necessarily true? And what does one mean here by 'truth'?

Errors and inconsistencies have been seen to abound in the scriptures. The account of the world's creation being completed in a week (Gen. 1: 1–2; 3) looks incompatible with the findings of cosmology and the theory of evolution. The Psalms and other OT books reflect in places the view that the earth is a flat disc and the sky above is a solid vault supported by columns at the ends of the earth. Particular books have their special puzzles. How could Jonah have survived three days in the belly of the whale, not to mention the puzzle about his passage into and out of the great fish?

Add too the fact the Bible gives us conflicting accounts of the same episode. How did the Israelites elude their Egyptian pursuers? In describing the escape through the Red Sea, Exodus 14–15 offers three versions. Moses stretched out his hand and—as in the Cecil B. de Mille scenario—the waters piled up like walls to let the Israelites pass through. Then the waters flooded back over the Egyptians (Exod. 14: 16, 21*a*, 22, 27*a*, 28). In a second version, an east wind proved decisive. It dried up the sea for the Israelites, while the Egyptian chariots got stuck. Then God stopped the Egyptians with a glance and threw them into the sea (Exod. 14: 21*b*, 25–6). Finally, an angel of the Lord and the column of cloud no longer went in front of the Israelites, but behind them. As a result the pursuing Egyptians

---

[5] On reading the scriptures with openness and faith, see G. O'Collins and D. Kendall, *The Bible for Theology* (Mahwah, NJ: Paulist Press, 1997).

could no longer see their quarry, who thus happily escaped (Exod. 14: 19–20). Then who killed Goliath—David or Elhanan (1 Sam. 17; 2 Sam. 21: 19)? Did the site of the Jerusalem Temple cost David 50 shekels of silver or 600 shekels of gold (2 Sam. 24: 24; 1 Chr. 21: 25)? In short, factual inconsistencies and errors of a historical, geographical, and scientific nature turn up frequently in the scriptures.

Worse than that, various moral and religious errors appear in the Bible. The books of Job and Ecclesiastes denied life after death. Could God really have given Saul and his followers the command to kill every human being and animal in the city of Amalek (1 Sam. 15: 3)? St Paul and other early Christians apparently expected the world and its history to be terminated speedily with the second coming of Jesus and the definitive arrival of God's kingdom (e.g. 1 Thess. 4: 15–5: 11).

Faced with such evident factual, moral, and religious errors, those who put the case for biblical truth frequently recall three interconnected points: the *intentions* of the sacred authors, their *presuppositions*, and their *modes of expression*. Thus the authors of the opening chapters of Genesis could be defended. They intended to teach a number of religious truths about the power and goodness of the Creator God, about the sinfulness of human beings, and so forth; they did not intend to teach some doctrine of cosmogony and cosmology. They simply did not aim to describe coherently and in 'scientific' detail the origins of the universe, our earth, and the human race. In recalling the second coming of Jesus, Paul did not intend to communicate a timetable of its arrival but to encourage a full and urgent commitment to Christian life. In sum, it is unfair to accuse biblical or any other writers of falling into error by ignoring the difference between the points they really wished to communicate and those that lay outside any such intentions.

Second, some biblical authors show that they shared with their contemporaries certain false notions about cosmology and astronomy. But their acceptance of a flat earth, for instance, remained at the level of their presuppositions; it was not the theme of their direct teaching. The Bible was not artificially protected against geographical, cosmological, and astronomical errors to be found in the presuppositions of the sacred authors. Similarly the view that genuine human life ends at death formed a presupposition for the drama of Job and not the direct teaching of that book. At a time when death was believed to end all, how could an innocent person interpret and cope with massive suffering? Job did not debate with his friends whether or not there is life after death, but whether undeserved suffering can be reconciled with the existence of an all-good and all-powerful God.

Third, Pope Pius XII in a 1943 encyclical letter pointed out how alleged errors are often simply no more than legitimate modes of expression used by biblical writers:

In many cases in which the sacred authors are accused of some historical inaccuracy or some inexact recording of certain events, on examination it turns out to be nothing else than those customary forms of expression or narrative style which were current among people of that time, and were in fact quite legitimately and commonly used.

(*Divino Afflante Spiritu*; DH 3830; ND 226; trans. corrected)

Modern historians would be expected to scrutinize the evidence and settle the issues. Just how did the Israelites escape their pursuers? Who really killed Goliath? How much did David pay for the Temple site? But the kind of religious history represented by the Books of Exodus, Samuel, Kings, and Chronicles did not need to tidy up inconsistencies and settle disputed details. Admittedly, the honesty of Hebrew historiography put it in a class by itself in the Middle Eastern world. It recorded King David's shameful sins of adultery and murder, along with other failures on the part of leaders and people. It showed itself clearly superior to the stereotyped and empty glorification of monarchs found in the records of other nations. Nevertheless, the religious significance of events mattered more to the Hebrew historians than any 'merely' material exactitude. They felt no overwhelming curiosity that would have pushed them into clarifying the record when various traditions reported conflicting details.

In the case of the Book of Jonah, asking about the prophet's survival inside the fish overlooks the work's literary genre. The book is a piece of fiction, an extended parable about God's mercy towards everyone and keeps its religious punch for the last few verses. Any question about its truth or error will be decided by one's assessment of that religious message. To read Jonah as if it were a historical work lands one in absurd questions about the storyteller's details. Was Nineveh, for instance, really such a huge city that it took three days to cross (Jonah 3: 3)?

Likewise we save ourselves from unnecessary and silly trouble by recognizing the kind of literature we face in Genesis. The early chapters of that book reflect on the nature of God and the nature of human beings;

they are not attempting to give an account of the prehistorical origins of the human race. If we ignore that fact, hopeless puzzles turn up. When, for example, Cain murdered Abel and was about to be sent away as 'a fugitive and a wanderer on earth', God 'put a mark on Cain, so that no one who came upon him would kill him'. So Cain left Eden for the land of Nod, 'knew his wife, and she conceived and bore Enoch' (Gen. 4: 14–17). We would mistreat this story if we started asking: where did these others come from who might have threatened Cain's life? For that matter where did Cain's wife come from, if Adam and Eve were the parents of all the living? We must recognize that Genesis does not purport to be a detailed version of human origins.

Doubtless, respect for the intentions, presuppositions, and modes of expression used by the sacred authors goes a long way towards mitigating the force of many difficulties about biblical truth. All this concerns the human authors of the Bible.[6] St Augustine of Hippo makes a similar point apropos of the divine intention when inspiring the writing of the sacred texts. The inspiration from the Holy Spirit had a religious purpose and did not as such aim to further secular truth: 'We do not read in the Gospel that the Lord said, "I shall send you the Paraclete who will teach you about the movements of the sun and the moon." He wished to make Christians, not mathematicians.'[7] Nevertheless, more needs to be said—not to mount a fully successful rescue operation but to elucidate the truth of the scriptures. What has been said so far concerns the intentions, presuppositions, and literary styles found in one biblical book after another. What if we stand back and view the Bible as a whole? What is the truth of the Bible in general?

Adrian Hastings rightly points out how human society depends on 'the basic sense of correspondence between what is asserted and reality'; this notion of truth 'grounds order and justice as much as science

---

[6] 'Fundamentalist' interpretation, along with its proper respect for central truths of divine revelation and for the uniquely sacred quality of the inspired Bible, neglects the intentions of the human authors, the literary forms in which they wrote, and the whole historical formation of the scriptural texts. By ignoring the historical and human factors involved in the making of the Bible, such a naive approach creates many false problems, especially over questions of biblical truth.

[7] *Contra Felicem Manichaeum* 1.10. In 1633, when censuring Galileo Galilei for his heliocentrism, the Roman Holy Office (now the Congregation for the Doctrine of the Faith) forgot Augustine's guideline for interpreting the scriptures; see the 1992 observations by Pope John Paul II on the Galileo case in ND 184a–c.

and history'.[8] This basic and common way of understanding truth assesses propositions about the ownership of property, perpetrators of crimes, chemical elements, and past events by their correspondence with the available data. How does this correspondence version of truth fit the Bible? We would grievously mistreat the scriptural texts if we tried to reduce them all to a mere set of informative propositions whose sole function was to make factual judgements that correspond to reality. The Bible is much more than a catalogue of propositions which are to be tested for their correspondence to the data. To be sure, the scriptures do contain many true statements that correspond to the 'facts', but they also contain many items that cannot be tested in this way. Questions in the biblical text, like questions elsewhere, may be helpful and meaningful, but as such questions do not make assertions, cannot correspond to the data, and hence may not be assessed as 'true' or 'false'. To ask a question does not involve saying anything true or false. Furthermore, exhortations abound in the Bible. Such language may evoke and/or change attitudes, but in themselves exhortations cannot be true or false. Likewise laws, whether recorded in the Bible or elsewhere, can be just, clear, demanding, or impossibly burdensome, but precisely as such a law cannot be true or false.

In brief, we may not reduce the scriptures to a set of infallibly true propositions. All the verses of the Bible are inspired or written under the special guidance of the Holy Spirit. But that is not to say that all the verses of the Bible make factual claims or communicate truth in propositions that can or must be checked for their correspondence with the 'facts' and declared to be true.

We do better here to recall what biblical 'truth' (*emet* in Hebrew and *aletheia* in Greek) purports to be. Biblical versions of truth, if not utterly different from that common understanding of truth just described above, have their own special accents. They tend to be interpersonal, less one-sidedly intellectual, oriented towards transformation and action, progressive and essentially Christocentric. In both the OT and the NT the language of truth, whether writers use *emet*, *aletheia*, or equivalent terms, locks into the people's experience of a highly personal God. In the OT God is shown through word and deed to be 'true'—that is to say, constantly trustworthy and reliable. 'The Lord your God is God, the faithful God who maintains

---

[8] A. Hastings, 'Truth', in A. Hastings *et al.* (eds.), *The Oxford Companion to Christian Thought* (Oxford: Oxford University Press, 2000), 718.

covenant of loyalty with those who love him and keep his commandments, to a thousand generations' (Deut. 7: 9). By their fidelity to the covenant, the people should prove themselves to be loyally conformed to the divine reality and so persons of 'truth' (e.g. Exod. 18: 21). In the NT the God who remains utterly faithful and true (Rom. 3: 1–7) is fully revealed through the person of his Son. 'The truth is in Jesus' (Eph. 4: 21); 'grace and truth have come through Jesus Christ' (John 1: 17). The powerful presence of Christ and the Holy Spirit enables believers to 'do what is true' (John 3: 21) and to 'belong to the truth' (John 18: 37). The truth that will 'make them free' (John 8: 32) does much more than conform their minds to reality; it transforms their entire person. This rapid account of 'truth' in the OT and NT allows us to suggest four interrelated considerations.

First, biblical truth is progressive, in the sense that the biblical record shows the divine pedagogy (*Dei Verbum*, 15) at work in guiding people towards a truer knowledge of God and of the human condition. As a record written under the inspiration of the Holy Spirit, the Bible faithfully recalls, for instance, a 'savage' view of God that made the Israelites attribute to God a command to wipe out all the inhabitants of the city of Amalek (1 Sam. 15: 3). They needed to be guided by the great prophets to an appreciation of God's tender mercy towards everyone.

Second, to recognize biblical truth as progressive means looking for that truth in the complete Bible. The truth is to be found in the whole canon of scriptures. In *this* sense the truth of the Bible is coextensive with inspiration. The whole Bible is both inspired and (therefore) true.

Third, biblical truth is primarily a person; for Catholics and other Christians it is the person of Jesus Christ. He is the Truth (upper case) attested prophetically in the OT and apostolically in the NT. Biblical writings point to him and participate in his truth. Ultimately the Bible does not convey a set of distinct truths but has only one truth to state, the personal disclosure of God in Jesus. In his 1920 encyclical *Spiritus Paraclitus*, Pope Benedict XV wrote: 'All the pages of the Old and the New Testament lead toward Christ as the centre.'[9] A twelfth-century Augustinian canon, Hugh of Saint Victor, shared a similar christological vision: 'All divine Scripture speaks of Christ and finds its fulfilment in Christ, because it forms only one book, the book of life which is Christ.'[10] Many

---

[9] *Enchiridion Biblicum* (Bologna: Dehoniane, 1993), 486–7.
[10] *De Arca Noe morali*, 2. 8–9.

others could be cited who endorsed a similar Christocentric view of the scriptures—not only early Christian writers and later Catholic teachers but also such leading figures of the sixteenth-century Protestant Reformation as Martin Luther and William Tyndale.

Here we should warn against letting such a healthy Christocentrism lapse into a rigid Christomonism, which forcibly finds references to Christ everywhere in the OT. Many OT writings do record words and deeds that prepared for Christ's coming, and various persons in the OT prefigure him. But that does not mean forcing everything into a promise-fulfilment mould. Many passages in the OT, for instance in Wisdom literature, are connected with Christ rather remotely, and sometimes only in the sense that they shed light on the human condition which the Word of God was to assume at the incarnation.

Fourth, the scriptures create and illuminate situations in which God speaks to us, so that we are enabled to see and practise the truth. Here if anywhere the truth will be known by living in it. Biblical truth is to be experienced and expressed in action even more than it is to be seen and affirmed in our judgements. The Second Vatican Council hoped to see every group within the whole Catholic Church enlivened by the Bible and its truth (*Dei Verbum*, 21–6). It was not surprising to find John Paul II's apostolic exhortation *Ecclesia in America*, which drew together the work of the 1997 synod of bishops from North, South, and Central America, warmly endorsing a prayerful reading of the Bible, not only for all Catholics but also for 'all Christians' (no. 31).

The Canon of Scripture

Four paragraphs above we wrote of looking for biblical truth in 'the whole canon of scriptures'—still a controversial Roman Catholic claim, even though such ecumenical translations as *The Oxford Annotated Bible* reflect the way the situation has changed since the sixteenth-century Reformation. Let us take up matters point by point.

One can describe the biblical canon as a closed list of inspired books that provide in a fixed, written form an authoritative standard for Christian belief and practice. 'Canonization', the recognition of the sacred books, presupposes and goes beyond inspiration or the special guidance of the Holy Spirit in the actual composition of the scriptures. In the OT period inspired writings came into existence centuries before there was any question of a canon, be it a Jewish or Christian one. The exercise of the gift of inspiration preceded in time the later process of 'canonization'. In that process the inspired books were recognized as such by the post-apostolic Church. Catholics acknowledge in a decree from the Council of Trent (DH 1501–4; ND 210–13) a definitive act of recognition that clearly established the biblical canon. In solemnly defining the canon, Trent confirmed the decision of the fifteenth-century Council of Florence (DH 1334–5), which had been based on earlier teaching of popes and Church councils, as far back as the local Council of Laodicea (*c.* AD 365). Much earlier, as we saw in Ch. 1, second-century Christians such as Irenaeus upheld the enduring authority of the Jewish scriptures against Marcion and recognized as normative the four Gospels against Gnostic attempts to introduce new 'gospels'. Even that early, a canon or list of scriptures was beginning to take shape. In his *Festal Epistle* of 367, Athanasius of Alexandria eventually provided the first full list of the twenty-seven books of the NT.

What principles guided bishops, councils, and theologians over the centuries when they recognized *these* books and not *those* (e.g. the *Epistle of Barnabas* and 1–2 *Clement*) as belonging to their closed list of inspired and sacred books? Apostolic origin, orthodoxy, and liturgical use seem to have governed Christian recognition of the inspired writings.

First, there was the historical criterion of apostolic origin. The canonical writings came from the period of foundational revelation, which climaxed with the coming of Christ and the post-Pentecost activity of the first-century Church. Apostolic origin was often taken strictly, as if all the books which now constitute the NT canon were written by the apostles (the Twelve and St Paul) or by one of their close associates (e.g. Mark as Peter's collaborator or Luke as Paul's). In such terms the apostles authoritatively recognized the Jewish scriptures (which they inherited) and the new works (which they or their associates wrote for the emerging Christian communities). Nowadays such a strict version of apostolic origin no longer works. Very few scholars would agree, for example, that Paul wrote Hebrews or that Peter was the author of 2 Peter.

Nevertheless, in a broader sense this first criterion still carries weight in distinguishing canonical from non-canonical writings. Only those works which witnessed to Christ prophetically (the Jewish scriptures) or apostolically (the first-century Christian scriptures) could enter the canon. These writings formed an inspired record from believers who experienced the foundational revelation that ended with the apostolic age. Only persons who shared in the events that climaxed with the coming of the Holy Spirit and the foundation of the Church were in a position to express through inspired scriptures their written testimony to those experiences. Such later writings as the Chalcedonian Definition, the works of Thomas Aquinas, or the documents of the Second Vatican Council can be true, even infallibly true. But they all belonged to the period of dependent revelation, could not as such witness to the experiences of the period of foundational revelation, and emerged at a time when the charism of biblical revelation had ceased. Seen in this way, the criterion of apostolic origin still works to accredit canonical writings.

Second, there was the theological criterion of conformity to the essential message, 'the purity of the Gospel' (the Council of Trent), or 'the Catholic faith that comes to us from the apostles' (the First Eucharistic Prayer or Roman Canon). Since it failed to match adequately this test of orthodoxy, *The Shepherd of Hermas*, which in any case seems to date from the middle of the second century and so could not be of apostolic origin, was eventually excluded from the canon after enjoying canonical respect in Greek-speaking churches of the second and third century. The Book of Revelation, after widespread rejection by Greek-speaking Christians, who also doubted its apostolic authorship, came to take its place in the canon when its orthodox content was sufficiently recognized.

To be sure, there was and is a certain circularity involved in this second criterion. Since certain writings fitted their understanding of Christian faith, believers judged them to be orthodox, accepted them into their canon, and then proceeded to use them to test orthodoxy. Nevertheless, these scriptures which were truly written under the special guidance of the Holy Spirit never simply mirrored what the Church community actually was, but in fact challenged Christians by picturing what they should be. In calling believers and actually leading them to a truly transformed life, the scriptures established their orthodoxy by vindicating themselves in practice.

Third, constant usage, particularly in public worship, also secured for inspired writings their place in the definitive canon of the Christian Bible. The 'law' of praying the scriptures supported the 'law' of believing them to belong in the canon of inspired scriptures. This process may resemble but is not identical with the 'canonization' of such classical authors as Cervantes, Dante, Goethe, Homer, Plato, and Shakespeare. In both cases readers more or less quickly came to acknowledge the permanent value of the given writings. Yet the two processes are not on a par. First, classics are drawn not just from the beginning of a given literature (e.g. Homer) but also from the later history of that literature (e.g. Plato, Shakespeare, and Goethe). The inspired books of the biblical canon all come from the origins of Christianity. The charism of biblical inspiration ceased with the age of foundational revelation; classics can appear at any stage in the story of a particular literature. Second, the beauty of their language and related literary qualities establish the classics of world literature. Their continuing relevance for belief and worship guided the recognition of the books of the Bible. Literary considerations played and play at best a secondary role. When the gifted and cultured Augustine of Hippo first encountered the scriptures of Christianity, he found them to be primitive and 'barbarous' writings (*Confessions*, 3: 5).

Before leaving the question of the canon, we need to say something about its closed and authoritative nature. We wrote above of the canon as a 'closed list'. Since the charism of inspiration ended with the first century or foundational period of Christianity, there could be no later instances of inspired writings. The closed nature of the canon followed from the normative and closed nature of the apostolic age and its special charisms. Just as the members of the apostolic Church participated in the unique, once-and-for-all character of the coming of Christ, so too did their sacred writings, both those they produced themselves and those they took over from their Jewish forebears. The inspired books shared thus in the unrepeatable role of the apostles and their associates. Second, unless the canon is closed and not open to modification, it cannot function as a canon— that is, as a truly and fully normative standard for Christian belief, worship, and practice. Precisely as constituting a canon, these books, although they were frequently written to meet particular needs and serve particular occasions (e.g. most of the letters of St Paul), were and are, nevertheless, acknowledged as an adequate version of Christianity. Otherwise, they could hardly be an authoritative norm for Christian faith and life.

The consequences of this position on the canon follow clearly. On the one hand, to exclude some writings and thus *reduce* the canon (as Marcion and others have done) would be to tamper with the richness of the Church's foundational record of God's self-communication, to minimize the diversity in the OT and NT experience and witness, and ultimately to challenge the divine fullness of Christ's person and work. On the other hand, to increase the canon by adding later writings, as the ancient Gnostics did with their new gospels and other writings, challenges the complete and unrepeatable quality of what Christ revealed and did— personally and through his apostolic witnesses.

Concretely what are the canonical books of the Catholic Bible? *The Oxford Annotated Bible* prints, first, thirty-nine books of the OT, then seven books (plus sections of books) under the heading of the 'Apocryphal/Deuterocanonical' books (works composed or translated into Greek some time after 200 BC), and then the twenty-seven books of the NT. 'Deuterocanonical' is the Catholic name for those seven books (Tobit, Judith, Wisdom, Sirach or Ecclesiasticus, Baruch, and 1 and 2 Maccabees) plus further portions of other books, found in the Greek or Septuagint version of the OT but not in the canon of Hebrew scriptures that emerged in the second century AD. Protestants have normally called these writings the 'Apocrypha' ('hidden' or 'not genuine'), and often not included them in their Bibles. Some of the apocryphal/deuterocanonical works (e.g. Judith, Wisdom, and 2 Maccabees) were composed in Greek; others (e.g. Baruch and 1 Maccabees) were originally written in Hebrew but only the Greek translation is extant. Tobit was originally written in Hebrew or Aramaic, but apart from some fragments in those languages, only the Greek version remains. Composed in Hebrew before 180 BC, Sirach was rendered into Greek fifty years later; since 1900 two-thirds of the original Hebrew text has been recovered.

When Catholics and Orthodox speak of the 'deuterocanonical' ('of the second canon') books of the Bible, they do not intend a negative judgement, as if these books were automatically less important or less inspired. The term refers rather to the fact that debates preceded their securing a permanent place in the canon. St Jerome, for instance, advocated excluding these books and following the Hebrew canon of scriptures. The Council of Laodicea likewise does not include the deuterocanonical books on its list of sacred writings. But fourth- and fifth-century documents from popes do so (see DH 179, 213; ND 201–3). 'Deuterocanonical' can also be seen to refer to the fact that the books in question were composed (or translated into Greek) at the end of the OT period: that is to say, *after* the composition of the other OT books.

Catholic acceptance of the seven deuterocanonical books (and the further portions of other OT books) can be justified on the basis of the three criteria indicated above: apostolic origin, orthodox content, and liturgical usage. The NT authors, by regularly following the Septuagint version of the scriptures, show how in general that version was the primary Bible for first-century Christians. In particular, at times the NT authors echo or quote deuterocanonical books and make no distinction between the authority of those books and the other scriptures they inherited from their Jewish background. Second, down through the centuries Catholics have found the deuterocanonical books illuminating for their faith and practice: e.g. the moral instruction to be drawn from Sirach and Tobit. Third, Catholic worship has been enriched by the deuterocanonical works: for instance, the Prayer of Azariah incorporated into Daniel 3. From a Catholic point of view we are glad to see the deuterocanonical books included in such a major ecumenical work as *The Oxford Annotated Bible*, which follows Martin Luther's practice of printing them as a separate section between the OT and the NT writings. Specifically Catholic bibles, such as *The New Jerusalem Bible*, follow not only the content but also the ordering of the Septuagint—a tradition that represents a seldom-noted convergence with the Greek Orthodox Church. The Greek Orthodox go even further than most Catholics by recognizing as inspired the entire text of the Septuagint, including those books that are translations from an original Hebrew or Aramaic.

Finally, we examine the question of authority. Since authority is primarily invested in persons, the authority of the canonical scriptures for life and practice derives from God, supremely revealed in Jesus Christ. Thus the normative quality of the scriptures reaches back through the authority of the apostolic tradition to Christ himself. These inspired writings, in recording and interpreting for all future generations the experiences of the Jewish people, of the apostolic leaders, and of all those who shared directly in the events of foundational revelation, speak with an authoritative voice because they express the prophetic and apostolic witness that was ultimately legitimized by the person of Christ.

Sometimes the authority of the scriptures is presented as self-authenticating. Over the centuries Christians have experienced the scriptures as a source of faith and life. The Bible has proved itself to be religiously effective and hence authoritative. Clearly there is much truth in this way of expressing the authority of the scriptures. Nevertheless, one must also point beyond the human experience of the biblical text to the Holy Spirit, the personal authority who has made that experience possible.

The divine authority that stands behind the Bible must not be isolated from the personal faith of those who freely open themselves to the scriptures and expect to find in them light and life. The biblical witness questions its readers, points their way to the truth, and enables them to live in fidelity to the foundational self-communication of God in Christ. It is not that the Bible will clearly provide authoritative answers to all new questions that arise in the life of the world and the Church. But attentive openness to the biblical witness will provide the setting in which answers can emerge.

Some books of the Bible prove more enlightening and authoritative, inasmuch as they treat religious questions and revelation more directly than others. The Second Vatican Council pointed towards this kind of variation: 'Among all the scriptures, even those of the New Testament, the Gospels deservedly have a special place, because they are the principal witness to the life and teaching of the incarnate Word, our Saviour' (*Dei Verbum*, 18). One could say that all books of the Bible are canonical and authoritative, but some are more canonical and authoritative than others. Our next chapter will take up the heart of the matter, the revelation of the tripersonal God through the coming of Jesus Christ.[11]

---

[11] The basic documents for this chapter are Vatican II's Dogmatic Constitution on Divine Revelation (*Dei Verbum*) of 1965 and the Pontifical Biblical Commission's *The Interpretation of the Bible in the Church* of 1993 (many different editions of both documents are available). *The Oxford Companion to Christian Thought* contains relevant articles on 'Apocrypha, Jewish'; 'Bible, Its Authority and Interpretation'; 'Faith'; 'New Testament'; 'Old Testament'; 'Revelation'; 'Tradition'; and 'Truth'. The 1997 (3rd) edition of *The Oxford Dictionary of the Christian Church* contains relevant articles on 'Apocrypha'; 'Bible'; 'Canon of Scripture'; 'Faith'; 'Revelation'; and 'Tradition'. In R. E. Brown *et al.* (eds.), *The New Jerome Biblical Commentary* (Englewood Cliffs, NJ: Prentice Hall, 1990), one finds two helpful articles: R. E. Brown and R. F. Collins, 'Canonicity' (pp. 1034–54), and R. F. Collins, 'Inspiration' (pp. 1023–33). All three reference books provide further bibliography along with each of these articles.

4

The Tripersonal God and the Incarnate Son

To the King of the ages, immortal, invisible, the only God, be honour and glory forever and ever. Amen.   (1 Timothy 1: 17)

[Being] beyond the reach of the human mind, incomprehensible, and invisible, [God] made himself visible, comprehensible, and knowable, so that those who accept and see him may possess life.

(St Irenaeus, *Adversus Haereses*, 4. 20. 5)

The first disciples of Jesus faced the great question of early Christianity: how should his life, death, and resurrection (together with the outpouring of the Holy Spirit) revise their inherited Jewish faith in one God? After experiencing the forgiveness of sins, the fresh life given with baptism, the celebration of the Eucharist within a new community, the gifts of the Holy Spirit, and a vivid hope of sharing in Jesus' resurrection from the dead, what were they now to believe and think of God?

One might use modern language to ask: why, how, when, and where did this new question about God arise for the disciples of Jesus? The short answer is: with, in, and through the resurrection of the crucified Jesus and the outpouring of the Holy Spirit. The long answer is this chapter on the doctrine of the tripersonal God and the doctrine of Christ. Even more than in the chapters that follow, what is distinctively Catholic about these doctrines is in no way alleged to be uniquely Catholic.

JEWISH MONOTHEISM

Since the trinitarian faith of early Christianity was to identify YHWH as the Father of our Lord Jesus Christ (Eph. 1: 3, 17), we need to recall the antecedent Jewish faith in God. What was the story and shape of that faith? Here, as much as anywhere, we will see how Christian faith does not replace Israel's faith but develops and expands it.

The Story of Faith

Jewish faith grew through a long history of personal and collective encounters with God: from such shadowy figures as Abraham, Sarah, Melchizedek, and others who belong to the patriarchal period (that lasted down to around 1200 BC), who are gratefully remembered in the NT (e.g. Rom. 4: 1–25; Heb. 5–7), and two of whom (Abraham and Melchizedek) are recalled in the First Eucharistic Prayer or Roman Canon, down to Mary, Joseph, Elizabeth, Zachariah, Simeon, and Anna—those holy Jewish men and women who people Luke's account of Jesus' conception and birth (Luke 1–2). From these chapters of Luke's Gospel, Catholics and other Christians have drawn some very Jewish prayers that have constantly nourished their life with God: the *Magnificat* (from the words of Mary), the *Benedictus* (from Zachariah), the *Nunc Dimittis* (from Simeon)—not to mention the *Gloria* inspired by the angelic praise when Christ was born (Luke 2: 14) and the *Ave Maria* or *Hail Mary,* inspired words addressed to Mary by the angel Gabriel and by Elizabeth (Luke 1: 28, 42).

Dramatic moments punctuated the long Jewish story. When calling Abraham and Sarah to leave their home and take on a pilgrim existence, God promised them special blessings: 'I will make you a great nation . . . In you all the families of the earth will be blessed' (Gen. 12: 1, 3). God appeared to Moses in the 'flame of fire' that came out of a blazing bush on a mountain in the wilderness, presenting himself as 'the God of Abraham, the God of Isaac, and the God of Jacob' and revealing the divine name of YHWH, interpreted as 'I am who I am'. God commissioned Moses to liberate the descendants of Abraham and Sarah, the chosen people, from captivity in Egypt (Exod. 3: 1–4: 17). Their deliverance involved not only forty years of wandering in the desert but also God's covenant at Mount Sinai, pre-eminent among the seven covenants gratefully recalled by Ben Sira (Sir. 44–7).

Around 1000 B C with King David a Jewish monarchy emerged, and the historical books offer connected and often overlapping narratives of Israel's story, narratives consistently determined by a sense of God's constant involvement with the descendants of Abraham and Sarah. The anointing of David, for instance, was understood to bring upon him permanently the powerful presence of God's spirit (1 Sam. 16: 1–13). YHWH shaped the identity and functions of his visible representative, the king who became God's 'son' on the day of his installation (Ps. 2: 7).

Traditionally ascribed to David, the psalms formed the hymnal of ancient Israel and seem to have been mostly composed to accompany acts of worship in the magnificent Temple constructed in Jerusalem by David's son and successor, King Solomon. The psalms reflected the people's deeply personal experience of God, as they joyfully praised YHWH, asked for help in time in trouble, expressed confidence in the divine power, and, both collectively and individually, poured out their hearts to their God. The psalms would become the prayerbook for Catholic Christianity, used day after day by communities and individuals in their public and private worship. If the ancient axiom *lex orandi lex credendi* (the law of prayer is the law of belief) applies anywhere, it applies to the way in which for two thousand years the psalms have shaped and interpreted the Catholic sense of who and what God is. Those who daily pray the psalms should not need to be persuaded that what primarily matters is knowing (and experiencing) God with the heart rather than merely knowing about God with the mind. Such personal knowledge of God slips easily into committing oneself to God in faith.

Jews, Catholics, and other Christians have found the psalms maintaining their basic religious identity as creatures bound in an intimate relationship to their Creator and Lord. These prayers have constantly served to purify false images of God and eradicate the idolatry that seeks to manipulate the divine for one's immediate advantage and forgets the need for moral and spiritual renewal. In a psalm traditionally attributed to David, after the prophet Nathan reproached him for his sins of adultery and murder, the psalmist declares: 'My sacrifice, O God, is a broken spirit; a broken and contrite heart, O God, you will not despise' (Ps. 51: 17). 'The God of the psalms' is the shortest and best answer to the question: who is God for the OT?

Over the centuries Catholics have learned more of God from praying the psalms than from studying the teachings of general councils of the

Church.[1] Philosophical precision shaped these teachings, as when the Fourth Lateran Council confessed 'the one true God' to be 'eternal, immense [i.e. being unmeasured and unmeasurable], unchangeable, incomprehensible, almighty, ineffable', and 'entirely simple' (DH 800; ND 19). To this list the First Vatican Council added a few such attributes as God being 'infinite in intellect, will, and all perfection' (DH 3001; ND 327). These precise adjectives can keep errors at bay. More importantly, the boundlessly intense nature of these attributes (God as being in-finite, immense and un-changeable, and therefore for us in-comprehensible, and in-effable) respects the mysterious otherness of the divine Being who largely transcends human knowing.

The story of faith also included all that the prophets communicated about God and the way human beings should live before God. First, in the greatest prophetic communications the divine holiness and glory figured centrally. Thus on the occasion of the call in the Temple of the prophet Isaiah (active *c.*742–*c.*701 BC), heavenly creatures proclaimed: 'Holy, holy, holy is the Lord of hosts; the whole earth is full of his glory' (Isa. 6: 3). (As the *Sanctus*[2] or *Trisagion*, this thrice-holy acclaim of God has passed into the worship of Catholics and other Christians.) A prophet to the Jewish exiles after the capture and destruction of Jerusalem in 587 BC, Ezekiel nineteen times extolled 'the glory of the Lord' (e.g. Ezek. 10: 3–4), the glorious and overpowering majesty of God that would return to the restored or Second Temple (Ezek. 43: 1–12). Second, during the exile in Babylon the anonymous author of Second Isaiah (Isa. 40–55), joyfully announced that God their Saviour would bring the exiles home. He revered God as not only the Lord of history but also the Creator of the universe (e.g. Isa. 40: 12–31; 44: 24), 'the Holy One of Israel' (Isa. 41: 16, 20). Third, for some centuries, in worshipping one God, Israel may have practised only monolatry ('worship of one God') without necessarily denying the existence of lesser deities and being explicitly monotheist. By the time of Second Isaiah, however, Israel's monotheism clearly entailed rejecting the reality of any other gods (Isa. 43: 10–13; 44: 8; 45: 21–2). This anonymous prophet witnessed to genuine monotheism, the

---

[1] Until recently only a small minority of Catholics and other Christians could read, much less be moved to study the teachings of the councils. Yet, indirectly, through worshipping together and living their faith, most Christians absorbed those teachings.

[2] After the preface of every eucharistic prayer, the Sanctus introduces the hymn of praise that follows.

belief in one (and only one), personal, all-powerful, all-knowing, and all-loving God, who is the Creator and Lord of everyone and everything and yet exists distinct from and 'beyond' the whole universe. Fourth, at a time of cruel suffering for the Jewish exiles, Second Isaiah confidently proclaimed God not only as Creator, Saviour, and Lord of all history for the chosen people, but also as the One whom all nations should worship and in whom *all* can find salvation (Isa. 45: 22–5).

This final point recalls the promise to Abraham and Sarah: in them '*all* the families of the earth' would be blessed (Gen. 12: 3). What precedes that promise in the text of Genesis is the covenant with Noah, which shares the divine promise and law with all human beings and, indeed, with all non-human creatures (Gen. 9: 1–17). This universal covenant interprets Noah's three sons as the ancestors for all nations. The divine covenant with this Hebrew patriarch enjoys universal, cosmic extension. The Book of Jonah, probably written in the fifth century BC and so some decades after Second Isaiah, witnesses powerfully to the divine love for all people. God's merciful forgiveness extends to all human beings. The NT was to endorse God's loving concern for all peoples (e.g. Acts 14: 15–17; 17: 22–8), a truth that many Catholics and other Christians were often to forget down the centuries.

Images of God

We saw in Ch. 1 how Irenaeus opposed the errors of Marcion, who rejected the Creator God of the OT as a mere 'demiurge' and cruel deity, not to be identified with the 'Father' of Jesus Christ. Against such aberrations Irenaeus championed the Jewish scriptures and their doctrine of God. Eventually the fourth-century Nicene-Constantinopolitan Creed was to target Marcionite error with its confession of '*one* God, *Father* almighty, maker of heaven and earth'. The Jewish Creator God (and Lord of history) is identical with the *Father* of our Lord Jesus Christ. Before moving to the NT doctrine of God, let us recall some significant ideas and images that Catholics (and other Christians) draw from the OT.

Their religious experience led the Israelites to develop an image of God that combined in a remarkable way *majestic transcendence* and *loving closeness*. Although initially associated partly with sanctuaries and other such places, YHWH was experienced as going beyond the limits of *space*. The God of the patriarchs not only encountered them in Haran, Canaan, and Egypt, but also transcended the usual national boundaries—bringing

Israel on its exodus 'from the land of Egypt, the Philistines from Caphtor, and the Syrians from Kir' (Amos 9: 7). Unlike the gods of other oriental nations, Israel's deity was not identified in space as the sun or another heavenly body. The sun, the moon, and the stars belonged among the things created by God (Gen. 1: 14–18). YHWH also went beyond the limits of *time*. Other Middle Eastern gods issued from chaos and various myths proclaimed their birth. Israel's God, however, was known to be simply and always there, 'the first and the last' (Isa. 44: 6), the God who 'in the beginning created the heavens and the earth' (Gen. 1: 1). The Israelites admitted neither a theogony nor an ageing process for their God.

The divine holiness expresses the awesome and mysterious 'otherness' of God experienced by the Israelites. In particular, they refrained from pronouncing the personal name YHWH believed to have been revealed to Moses (Exod. 3: 13–15). In place of this tetragrammaton (word of four letters), they said 'Adonai (Lord)' when the scriptures introduced the sacred name. The Greek translation (Septuagint) of the OT showed a similar reverence by rendering YHWH as 'Kyrios (Lord)'. About 6,800 times the OT names God as 'Lord', but neither in the sense of lording it over his people nor of being coldly distant from them.

Besides knowing God to be 'apart' and 'beyond', the Israelites knew God to be 'near', with them, and even 'within' them. Moses put the question to the people: 'what other great nation has a god so near to it as the Lord (Adonai) our God is whenever we call to him?' (Deut. 4: 7). Psalm 139 witnessed to the way God is everywhere and with everyone, knowing the psalmist's every deed and thought and being with him from the moment of conception. In *The Hound of Heaven*, a poem cherished by generations of Catholics and other Christians, Francis Thompson (1859–1907) translated into modern terms this psalm's sense of God being always closely present to every person. Jeremiah spoke of 'a new covenant', which would be written by God on human hearts and that would enable everyone to know God (Jer. 31: 31–4). Ezekiel announced that, when God's own 'spirit' had been put within them (Ezek. 37: 14; 36: 26–7), the people would know that God had spoken and acted.

Gender language also reflected a striking blend of 'otherness' and 'closeness' in the image Israel had drawn from its experience of God. On the one hand, YHWH is utterly beyond the sexual activities typically attributed to ancient deities. The sense that God is literally neither male nor female and transcends any creaturely representations stood behind the

OT prohibition of visible divine images made of stone, metal, or wood. The prophet Hosea witnessed to this sense of divine transcendence when God spoke through him: 'I am God and no man, the Holy One in your midst' (Hos. 11: 9). But, on the other hand, Hosea and other prophets used vivid verbal images in talking of God as a husband who revealed a wounded but tender love when his people acted like a harlot. God wished to enjoy a second honeymoon that would repeat the desert experience when the people were first liberated from Egypt: 'I will now allure her, and bring her into the wilderness, and speak tenderly to her' (Hos. 2: 14).

Along with their language of God as 'lover/husband', the OT authors witnessed to what they knew of a divine tenderness that even goes beyond that of human mothers (e.g. Isa. 49: 15; Sir. 4: 10). On occasions they also named or addressed God as 'Father' and consistently as a tender, caring Father. This talk of YHWH as Father was doubtless kept to a minimum by the other verbal image of God as Husband to the people (e.g. Isa. 54: 4–8; Jer. 2: 2; Ezek. 16: 1–63). Another obvious reason for the OT rarely applying to God the metaphor of Father was that such usage might easily suggest the 'natural', procreative activity attributed to Baal, Asherah, and other gods and goddesses of the Near East. Far from being that kind of biological or physical parent, YHWH did not even have a consort. The divine fatherhood (and the Israelites' corresponding filial status) was understood to result from the free divine choice and activity in the history of salvation. It was above all the deliverance from Egypt that made them God's sons and daughters (e.g. Hos. 11: 1). No other OT writer excelled Hosea in portraying the loving, parental care of God towards his chosen but rebellious children: 'It was I who taught Ephraim to walk, I took them up in my arms . . . I led them with cords of human kindness, with bands of love. I was to them like those who lift children to their cheeks. I bent down to them and fed them' (Hos. 11: 3–4).

The name of God as 'Father', although occurring in a variety of historical, prophetic, and sapiential texts, turns up barely more than twenty times in the entire OT. The name will come into its own with the fullness of revelation through Jesus' life, death, and resurrection, along with the birth of the Church in the power of the Holy Spirit. So too will three personifications of the divine creative, revealing, and saving activity to be found in the OT: Wisdom, Word, and Spirit.

Although it reworked some older material, the Book of Proverbs seems to date from the late sixth or early fifth century BC. As a personification of

God's activity, Lady Wisdom fills the first nine chapters, setting before her hearers a choice: either folly and disaster or fear of God and life. Her role in creation is developed in the famous description of her primordial relationship to God: 'The Lord created me at the beginning of his work, the first of his acts of long ago. Ages ago I was set up, at the first, before the beginning of the earth. When there were no depths I was brought forth...I was beside him like a master worker' (Prov. 8: 22–4, 30). Proverbs 9: 1–6 depicts Wisdom as building her house and inviting the simple to join her feast of food and wine that symbolize the doctrine and virtue that come from God. Lady Wisdom's house and banquet would provide language for the NT and post-NT interpretation of Jesus, divine Wisdom in person. The most extensive treatment of Wisdom comes in a book originally written in Hebrew *c.*180 BC, Sirach. Here Wisdom proclaims her divine origin: 'I came forth from the mouth of the Most High' (Sir. 24: 3). She 'holds sway over all the earth, and over every people and nation' (Sir. 24: 6). By divine choice Wisdom dwells in Israel and finds her home in Jerusalem. But such a choice does not mean that Wisdom is absent elsewhere in the world; rather she is present to the whole human race. The Book of Wisdom, probably written shortly before Jesus' birth and hence the last of the OT books, describes Lady Wisdom lyrically as a beautiful reflection or emanation of God's glory (Wis. 7: 25–8: 1). The unity between Wisdom and God reaches a climax when YHWH's saving deeds in the people's deliverance from captivity in Egypt are attributed to her (Wis. 10: 15–18). The identification between God and Wisdom becomes closer than ever.[3]

By expressly identifying Jesus with the divine Wisdom, as did St Paul (1 Cor 1: 24), Justin Martyr, and many other writers of the early centuries, Christians made a decisive leap in taking this personification to be a distinct divine person. Like Lady Wisdom, the Son of God was acknowledged to be active in the creation and conservation of the universe (e.g. 1 Cor. 8: 6; Col. 1: 16–17; Heb. 1: 1–2). The first Christians knew that Jesus had brought them, through his death and resurrection, the *new creation* of

---

[3] On Wisdom see R. E. Murphy, *The Tree of Life: An Exploration of Biblical Wisdom Literature* (New York: Doubleday, 1990). Many scholars have rightly seen Wisdom themes (taken e.g. from Sirach 24) in John's Gospel, particularly in the Prologue and in ch. 6. Without denying the presence of those themes, we want to note, however, that John did not start 'In the beginning was Wisdom ...', does not confess 'Wisdom became flesh and dwelt amongst us', and, in fact, never uses the term 'Wisdom'.

graced life, the historical culmination of God's redemptive activity for human beings and their world. As agent of this *new* creation, the incarnate Son of God must also be, so they recognized, the divine agent for the *original* creation of all things. Likewise, being the central protagonist of salvation history, he was also seen to be active in the unfolding of that history prior to the incarnation (e.g. 1 Cor. 10: 4; John 12: 4).

The Logos or Word of God converged with Wisdom as another OT divine personification that foreshadowed the distinct existence of a second person in God. Like Lady Wisdom, the Word was understood to be with God and powerfully creative from the beginning (Gen. 1: 1–2: 4; Isa. 55: 10–11). The psalms, in particular, celebrated the creative and conserving Word of God (e.g. Ps. 33: 8–9). Sirach appreciated how the divine Word operates to conserve creation: by God's Word 'all things hold together' (Sir. 43: 26)—language that will be applied to Christ by Colossians 1: 17.

'Spirit' shows up frequently (nearly 400 times) in the OT as a third way of articulating the creative, revelatory, and redemptive activity of God. When dealing with the divine 'spirit' (Hebrew *ruah*; Greek *pneuma*), the OT highlighted its power as wind, as the breath of life, and as the divine inspiration that comes upon prophets. At creation 'the spirit' of God hovered over the surface of the water (Gen. 1: 2). Occasionally the prophetic books tell of prophets being empowered to speak God's word (e.g. Isa. 61: 1; Ezek. 2: 1–2). Such examples of the 'spirit' empowering human beings to speak God's word indicate how in pre-Christian Judaism 'spirit', 'word', and 'wisdom' were almost synonymous ways of speaking of God's manifest and powerful activity in the world. The psalms use 'spirit' (or 'breath'), 'word', and 'wisdom' as equivalent parallels: 'By the *word* of the Lord the heavens were made, and all their host by the *breath* of his mouth' (Ps. 33: 6). The work of creation can be expressed in terms of God's 'word' or in terms of the divine 'spirit', as Judith's thanksgiving to God also illustrates: 'Let all your creatures serve you, for you spoke, and they were made. You sent forth your spirit, and they were created' (Judith 16: 14). 'Spirit' likewise parallels 'wisdom' (e.g. Wis. 9: 17), even to the point of their being identified (e.g. Isa. 11: 2). In short, like 'wisdom' and 'word', the divine 'spirit' was a third way of articulating and even personifying God's activity in and revelation to the world.

The NT and post-NT Christian language for the one God, now acknowledged to be tripersonal, flowed from the Jewish scriptures. The doctrine of the Trinity was deeply Jewish in its origins. Of course, the

Jewish, monotheistic faith and its language were deeply modified in the light of Jesus' life, death, and resurrection (together with the outpouring of the Holy Spirit). Nevertheless, naming God as 'Father', 'Son' (Word and Wisdom), and 'Spirit' found its roots in the OT. There 'wisdom', 'word', and 'spirit' (or 'holy spirit'—only in Ps. 51: 13 and three other passages) functioned, frequently synonymously, to acknowledge God's nearness to the world and to the chosen people—a nearness that did not, however, compromise the divine transcendence or that holy otherness that sets God beyond all other beings.

THE CHRISTIAN GOD

It was Jesus who personally triggered the development from Jewish to Christian monotheism, or belief in one God now distinguished into three persons. Jesus' preaching and activity raised the question of his identity (who was he?), along with the closely related but distinct question: who did he think he was? The historical data, found above all in the Gospels of Matthew, Mark, and Luke, support the conclusion that, at least implicitly,[4] Jesus claimed an authority and identity on a par with God. One can understand why some religious leaders would reject Jesus' claims as blasphemous and incompatible with their strict monotheism. In what follows we want, first of all, (1) to sum up what Jesus implied about himself through what he said and did; then (2) we will move to what NT believers and writers had to say about him as the Church developed. In sorting out the differences between (1) and (2), we will use the approach and the criteria indicated above in Ch. 1, n. 2.

Jesus and the Kingdom of God

Nothing is more certain about Jesus than that he preached the kingdom or royal reign of God. He announced this decisive deliverance from evil and new age of salvation as already present and operative but not yet completed. His parables, miracles, table fellowship with sinners, and other

---

[4] 'Implicitly' is utterly central to our argument here. Jesus did not go around *explicitly* proclaiming 'I am consubstantial with the Father,' or 'I am the second person of the Trinity.' Of course, centuries of reflection and debate transpired before Christians settled on such language as their common orthodox teaching about the identity and significance of Jesus. But there was a starting-point for the development of such teaching in Jesus' self-evaluation that his words and deeds implied.

works belonged integrally to his message of the present and coming kingdom. They were powerful signs that the final age of salvation was already beginning. Jesus himself was inseparably connected with the inbreaking of the divine kingdom. With his personal presence, the rule of God had come and was coming.

At times Jesus expressed his mission in prophetic (e.g. Mark 6: 4; Luke 13: 33) and messianic (e.g. Matt. 11: 2–6) terms. But did he conceive of himself as being *merely* a righteous prophet or the anointed (*merely* human) agent of God's final salvation? Or did he lay claim, at least by implication, to being more than human and someone with a unique relationship to the God whom he characteristically called 'Abba' or 'Father'?

A startling, if mainly implicit, claim to more than human authority emerged from various aspects of Jesus' ministry for the kingdom: his freedom in changing and radically reinterpreting the law given by God to his people; his forgiving sins through his words and actions; his taking over the Temple in Jerusalem; his favourite self-designation as 'Son of man', in particular to claim for himself the divine prerogative of sitting in judgement on all people at the end.[5] Repeatedly Jesus testified to himself as decisive for human beings' final relationship to God; their future salvation, so he stated, depended on their present relationship to him (e.g. Luke 12: 8–9). When preaching his message of 'my' or 'your' '(heavenly) Father', Jesus at times showed that he understood himself to stand in a special, even unique, relationship to God (e.g. Matt. 11: 25–7).[6] Hence in evaluating Jesus' self-claims, we also need to reflect on the testimony to his filial consciousness.

Some scholars argue for a Jesus who was only a prophet-like holy man, or at most a charismatic healer and exorcist. Was Jesus just a wandering Galilean teacher of wisdom and wonder-worker who made no claims, not even implicit claims, to divine status but whose followers gradually and

---

[5] For a fuller presentation of these and other aspects of Jesus' ministry, see S. T. Davis, 'Was Jesus Mad, Bad, or God?', in S. Davis, D. Kendall, and G. O'Collins (eds.), *The Incarnation* (Oxford: Oxford University Press, 2002), 221–45; N. T. Wright, 'Jesus' Self-Understanding', ibid. 47–61; C. A. Evans, 'Jesus' Self-Designation "The Son of Man" and the Recognition of his Divinity', in S. Davis, D. Kendall, and G. O'Collins (eds.), *The Trinity* (Oxford: Oxford University Press, 1999), 29–47; G. O'Collins, *Christology* (Oxford: Oxford University Press, 1995), 47–81; C. Tuckett, *Christology and the New Testament: Jesus and his Earliest Followers* (Edinburgh: Edinburgh University Press, 2001).

[6] See O'Collins, *Christology*, 113–35.

mistakenly elevated him to divine status? One who purported to be only the son (lower case) of God and was changed into the Son (upper case) of God? Was there then such a doctrinal development that took decades to transform the man Jesus into the God Christ and climaxed with the clear endorsement of Jesus' divinity by John's Gospel?[7] This thesis of such a gradual, first-century development must face at least two major challenges.

First, we summarized above the reasons for recognizing that Jesus himself had already made some astounding claims about who he was and what he was doing, claims that set him dramatically apart from other charismatic holy men of ancient Galilee and account for the fact that powerful religious leaders of his time found Jesus so disturbing that they joined forces with Pontius Pilate to have him put to death. The more one plays down or even explains away Jesus' claims about himself, the more difficult it becomes to understand why anyone would have decided to do away with such a relatively inoffensive teacher and healer. It is not that we want to maintain that the *only* reason for upholding Jesus' divine identity (in relationship to the Father through the Spirit) is that he understood himself to have and, at least implicitly, claimed to have such a divine identity-in-relationship. Nevertheless, the post-Easter image of Jesus was partly supported by the earthly Jesus' own self-image. His filial consciousness and further (largely implicit) claims about himself remain the permanent point of departure for confessing his identity—a confession that rests upon and is filled out by many other factors such as the Church's ongoing experience of faith in Christ being supported by the Holy Spirit. In her common worship the members of the Church have both remembered Jesus' life and claims and experienced his presence.

To be sure, all the points listed above about Jesus' claims need to be argued out in close detail. Here we insist only on one item: in general, implicit claims need not be 'low', in the sense of concerned only with relatively unimportant matters. An implicit claim can be dramatically 'high' or concerned with extremely important matters, even those that bear on our final salvation. In short, the distinction between 'implicit' and blatantly 'explicit' claims has nothing to do with the seriousness of what is

---

[7] For an example of such a thesis see G. Vermes, *The Changing Faces of Jesus* (London: Penguin Press, 2000); see the review of this book by G. O'Collins in *The Tablet*, 1 July 2000, 895–6. On Jesus and responses to his identity and work, see M. Bockmuehl (ed.), *The Cambridge Companion to Jesus* (Cambridge: Cambridge University Press, 2001); D. Ford and M. Higton (eds.), *Jesus* (Oxford: Oxford University Press, 2002).

being claimed—in this case, Jesus' personal divine status. Implicit claims differ from explicit ones merely through the manner in which they are made: indirectly and by implication rather than directly and expressly. From NT times believers' experience of the risen Christ's redeeming activity as the Son of God has underpinned their faith in him, but has done so together with the memory of his personal sense of filiation implied and expressed in his activity for the divine kingdom.

Second, Paul's letters prove a thorn in the side of any thesis about Christians only gradually developing their belief in Jesus' divinity. Around 230 times his letters, which date from AD 50 to around 62, call the crucified and risen Jesus 'Lord', applying to him a name used for God nearly 7,000 times in the OT: *Adonai* in the Hebrew texts and *Kyrios* in their Greek translation, the version normally read by the earliest Christians. In the first century 'Lord' also had a range of merely human meanings, sometimes being simply a courteous form of address ('sir'). But in the scriptures that Paul inherited the title was frequently a way of speaking to or of YHWH. How then was Jesus understood when the apostle set 'the Lord Jesus Christ' side by side with 'God our Father' as the source of 'grace and peace'—that is to say, of integral salvation? Over and over again in the opening greetings of his letters Paul described Jesus that way. In doing so he distinguished a divine 'Lord' from any merely human one.

An astonishing affirmation came from the apostle when he expanded the classic Jewish confession of the true God, the Shema (Deut. 6: 4–9; 11: 13–21; Num. 15: 37–41), and set Jesus as the 'one Lord' alongside 'one God, the Father'. Paul never paused to argue for this Christian confession of monotheism that included Jesus (1 Cor. 8: 6). He obviously presumed that the Christians of Corinth to whom he was writing agreed with him: Jesus was and is the divine Lord (and the pre-existent agent of creation, 'through whom all things exist') to be included within their confession of the one God. Equally astonishing was a hymn that Paul composed or, more likely, took over from early Christian worship (Phil. 2: 6–11). There the apostle attributed to Jesus 'equality with God', as well as the right to bear the divine name of 'Lord' and so receive adoration from the whole universe. The language of that hymn echoed a key confession of the one, universal God from Isaiah 45: 22–3.

Both as regards 'Lord' and other such titles as 'Son of God', the meaning of Paul's language is to be gleaned from its context. But there is no great difficulty in doing that. English speakers know the difference between calling God 'my dearest Lord' and addressing a judge as 'my Lord', just as Italians know the difference between using 'Signore' in prayer and speaking to a respectable-looking stranger as 'Signore'. Paul made clear the difference between calling Christians adopted 'sons and daughters of God' and confessing Jesus as the pre-existent Son of God sent into the world for our salvation (e.g. Rom. 8: 3–4; Gal. 4: 4–7).[8] The evidence from Paul and other NT writers makes it clear that very soon after Jesus' resurrection from the dead Christians proclaimed him to be not just a wonderful human being vindicated by God but the only Son of God and their divine Lord.[9]

Obviously anyone can argue that Paul and other NT Christians were mistaken in acknowledging Jesus' divinity. But such a thesis also involves one in holding that from the earliest decades of Christianity countless men and women have been committing idolatry by giving divine worship to a person who was and is merely human.

The Tripersonal God

When experiencing the risen Jesus as the one who made it possible for them to join him in praying to God as 'Abba', NT Christians knew themselves to enjoy their adopted status as sons and daughters through the Holy Spirit whom they had received (Rom. 8: 14–17; Gal. 4: 4–7). They prayed the 'Our Father', identifying and worshipping God as 'the Father of our Lord Jesus Christ' (e.g. Rom. 15: 6). Thus Christians, while continuing to be monotheistic by maintaining faith in one God (e.g. Gal. 3: 20), the same God for Jews and Gentiles alike (Rom. 3: 29–30), now included in their new form of monotheism Christ the Son of God and the Holy Spirit (*Pneuma*). Thus Christian faith became 'christological' and 'pneumatological'.

At some point in the first century Christian communities stopped baptizing simply 'in the name of Jesus' (e.g. Acts 2: 38; 10: 48) and began baptizing 'in the name [singular] of the Father and of the Son and of the Holy Spirit' (Matt. 28: 19). This tripartite formula did not offer anything like the later, full-blown doctrine of God as three in one and one

[8] On Jesus as the Son of God see O'Collins, *Christology*, 113–35, as (divine) Lord, ibid. 136–43, and as personally and eternally pre-existent, ibid. 237–44. On his pre-existence see also G. O'Collins, *Incarnation* (London: Continuum, 2002), 13–25.
[9] On Jesus' resurrection see S. Davis, D. Kendall, and G. O'Collins (eds.), *The Resurrection* (Oxford: Oxford University Press, 1997).

in three. Admittedly it suggested a certain unity ('the name'), distinction, and equality between 'the Father', 'the Son', and 'the Holy Spirit'; yet the formula did not clarify such matters as their interrelatedness. It provided, nevertheless, a foundation and starting-point for confessing and expounding the Trinity.

More than twenty years before Matthew's Gospel was completed (around AD 80), Paul had concluded a letter with a trinitarian benediction: 'the grace of our Lord Jesus Christ, the love of God [the Father], and the fellowship of the Holy Spirit be with you all' (2 Cor. 13: 13). As with the baptismal formula from Matthew, Paul maintained the Holy Spirit in the third place, but changed the order of the first two figures, named them differently ('Lord Jesus Christ' instead of 'the Son', and 'God' instead of 'the Father'), and spoke not of their 'name' but of 'grace', 'love', and 'fellowship', associated respectively with the first, second, and third figure. In an earlier letter Paul spoke in a different order and more succinctly of 'Spirit', 'Lord', and 'God' (an order that reversed the first and third figures in Matthew's baptismal formula), and insisted that spiritual gifts come from the same divine source and should contribute to the common good: 'there are varieties of gifts, but the same Spirit; and there are varieties of service, but the same Lord; and there are varieties of working, but it is the same God who inspires them all in every one' (1 Cor. 12: 4–6).

Paul's teaching on the Father, Son, and Spirit never became abstract or philosophical. It remained firmly situated within the context of the salvation that the baptized experienced within their common history. Through the indwelling *Spirit*, they constituted the one body of *Christ* (e.g. 1 Cor. 6: 19; 12: 12–27) and the one family of *God the Father* (e.g. 2 Cor. 6: 18). The apostle witnesses to this soteriological or saving view of faith in the 'tripersonal' God, from whom the baptized receive their adoption, their ongoing guidance, and their future inheritance:

For all who are led by *the Spirit of God* are sons (and daughters) of *God*. For you did receive a spirit of slavery to fall back into fear, but you have received a *Spirit* of adoption. When we cry '*Abba! Father!*', it is that very *Spirit* bearing witness with our spirit that we are sons (and daughters) of *God*, and if sons (and daughters), then heirs of *God* and joint heirs with *Christ*. (Rom. 8: 14–17)

A further striking, 'trinitarian' passage from Paul, one that follows the order of Matthew's baptismal formula (by speaking of 'God [the Father]', 'his Son', and 'the Spirit of his Son'), closely associates God's 'sending' the

Son with the sending of the Spirit (Gal. 4: 4–7).[10] Nevertheless, while intimately relating 'Son' and 'Spirit', neither Paul nor any other NT writer identify them. Jesus was conceived through the power of the Spirit (Matt. 1: 20; Luke 1: 35)—a statement that cannot be reversed. It was the Word, not the Spirit, that became flesh (John 1: 14). It was the Son, and not the Spirit, who was sent 'in the likeness of sinful flesh' to deal with sin (Rom. 8: 3) and who was not 'spared' but 'given up for us all' (Rom. 8: 32). Through his resurrection Christ, and not the Spirit, became the 'firstborn' of a new eschatological family (Rom. 8: 29) and 'the first fruits of those who have fallen asleep' (1 Cor. 15: 20). It is the indwelling Spirit that helps us pray 'Abba' and witnesses to Christ (Rom. 8: 15–16; 1 Cor. 12: 3), and not an indwelling Christ who makes us pray like that and witnesses to the Spirit. Finally, unlike the Spirit, it is the crucified and resurrected Christ who at the end will subject all things to his Father (1 Cor. 15: 24–8). The NT's story of Christ's mission, conception, death, resurrection, and its aftermath distinguishes him from the Holy Spirit.[11]

The writing of the NT was not completed before debates about Christ and the Trinity started. Paul's letters set the terms of one enduring challenge. The apostle wrote of Christ as being both Son of God and 'born of a woman' (Gal. 4: 4), or as both Son of God and 'descended from David' (Rom. 1: 3). How could believers interpret and relate these parallel affirmations about Christ's divine sonship and his humanity without tampering with the integrity of either element? Heterodox solutions reduced or simply sacrificed either Christ's divinity or his humanity. The Ebionites, a label that covers a number of early Christians of Jewish background, dropped his divinity, while the Docetic (i.e. human only in appearance) tendency questioned the genuine bodily and historical reality of Jesus. Since they dismissed his body as being only apparent, i.e. really 'heavenly', Docetists in effect excluded Christ's true incarnation and death. To eliminate every link between the evil demiurge (or creator of the material universe) and Jesus the Saviour, Marcion attributed to the latter a merely heavenly body. In the early centuries of Christianity, and especially in the fourth, the major challenge came, however, from those who, like the Ebionites, sacrificed Christ's divinity in the name of faith in the one God.

---

[10] See G. D. Fee, 'Paul and the Trinity: The Experience of Christ and the Spirit for Paul's Understanding of God', in Davis, Kendall, and O'Collins (eds.), *The Trinity* 49–72.

[11] On the NT's distinction between Christ and the Holy Spirit, see further O'Collins, *Christology*, 146–51.

The second half of this chapter will track some of the important ways in which Christians in general and Catholics in particular have developed teaching about Christ and the tripersonal God.

The Councils

Chapter 1 traced the developments in Christology and trinitarian teaching that ran from the First Council of Nicaea (325), through the Council of Chalcedon (451) and down to the Second Council of Nicaea (787). Nicaea I defended the true divinity of the Son who is 'generated', but not created, by the Father and shares such essential divine attributes as eternal existence. Constantinople I (381), as well as upholding the divinity of the Holy Spirit, rejected the teaching of Apollinarius of Laodicaea and so maintained that the Son had assumed a full humanity, including a rational soul. By defending the use of *Theotokos* (Mother of God) as a title for Mary, the Council of Ephesus (431) underlined the unity of Christ's humanity and divinity: his being human is not *separated* from his being divine. Twenty years later the Council of Chalcedon added that Christ is *one person* in *two natures*, with his humanity and divinity remaining distinct and not being confused. In passing let us underline the importance of Chalcedon's language of 'distinct but not separate', a principle that applies beyond teaching on Christ to such matters as the writing of the inspired scriptures (where the input of the human writers and the Holy Spirit is distinguishable but not separable) and, as we shall see, to the nature of the Church. The three general councils that followed Chalcedon added some significant footnotes to its doctrine, most notably when Constantinople III (680/1) taught that Christ enjoys two wills, a human will and a divine will which, while distinct, have always operated together in perfect harmony.

Unlike the doctrine of, and terminology for, the one person of the incarnate Son of God in two natures (or Christ 'in himself'), the redemption (or Christ 'for us') did not provoke theological debate and teaching from the first seven councils of the Church. All parties simply took for granted that it was only through Christ that human beings could be saved, and that the purpose of everything from his incarnation to this final coming was, as the creeds stated, 'for us and for our salvation'. One enduring result of this lopsided development has been that, whereas theology and official teaching have tended to watch carefully talk about

Christ 'in himself', talk about Christ 'for us' has at times suffered from harmful imprecision—as we will illustrate below. The councils left open (1) the question of how redemption is to be understood, as well as (2) the task of developing reflection on the Trinity in the light of the Nicene-Constantinopolitan Creed. Let us look first at (2).

God the Father

From the outset Christian believers have tried to explore faithfully the unity, diversity, and relationships between Father, Son, and Holy Spirit. St Augustine of Hippo played a key role in this development. He has often been contrasted with the Cappadocians (St Basil, St Gregory of Nazianzus, and St Gregory of Nyssa) on the grounds that whereas they started their trinitarian theology with the three persons (and then moved to the one shared essence), he began with the unity of the divine being in one essence or substance and then moved to the three persons. This stereotype has frequently been expressed through the captions 'Eastern' and 'Western' trinitarian doctrine. The truth here is somewhat different, as we will see from two comparisons used by Augustine.

After dedicating the early books of his masterpiece, *De Trinitate*, to what the scriptures witness about the divine persons, Augustine takes up the interpersonal relationship of paternity and filiation to develop the model of trinitarian love (*De Trinitate*, 8. 8. 12). The Father is the Lover, the Son the Beloved, and the Holy Spirit the mutual Love that passes between Father and Son. Eastern Christians have at times criticized this analogy for depersonalizing the Holy Spirit or at least for not allowing the identity of a distinct person to come through clearly. After all, in the I–Thou relationship, the mutual gift of love that two persons bestow on each other is not a third person, or at least does not emerge as an activity that defines a person distinct from the I and the Thou. However, no matter what limits finite creatures may suffer from in their mutual love, the case is different with God, who *is* love (1 John 4: 8, 16). Within the divine life, the Holy Spirit is the Love (uppercase) that the Father and the Son bestow on each other.

In the *De Trinitate* Augustine went on to exploit the human soul and its highest faculties as the best available analogy for the Trinity. He was encouraged to do so by the biblical understanding that human beings are made in God's image and likeness (Gen. 1: 26–7). Augustine's trinitarian theology could also draw support from the way the NT hints that the generation of the Son (e.g. Matt. 11: 27—'no one knows the Son except the Father') and the procession of the Holy Spirit (e.g. Rom. 5: 5—'God's love has been poured into our hearts through the Holy Spirit') are sometimes mirrored in the two basic activities of the human spirit: knowing and loving. In any case, by interpreting the Son as the Word coming from the divine Mind, Irenaeus, Tertullian, Athanasius, and others prepared the way to expound the generation of the Son in terms of the Father's act of thought. Augustine himself contributed the theme of the Holy Spirit as the fruit and reality of mutual love. In the scheme of the mind's being, the mind's knowledge of itself, and the mind's love for itself Augustine found an image of the Trinity: the Father as Being, the Son as Consciousness, and the Spirit as Love (*De Trinitate*, 9. 2. 2). Augustine brought further refinements into this model of the Trinity with the scheme that he preferred: the human memory (with knowledge coming through memory), intelligence (or understanding), and willing (ibid. 9. 8; 10. 10, 14–16; 11. 11, 17–19). The psychological analogy attends to the way in which the interior word arises as a kind of 'brain child' and thus through an act that can be compared with generation. The eternal Word or Son of God is distinct from and yet identical with the generating Father. Similarly the divine act of love gives rise to its eternal fruit, the Holy Spirit.

Augustine's psychological analogy of self-presence, self-knowledge, and self-love has proved enduringly influential. It avoids any risk of tritheism or falling into the error of holding three gods. But does it encourage a modalist view of God—that is to say, one that understands the names of 'Father', 'Son', and 'Holy Spirit' to refer merely to three modes or manners in which a monopersonal God exists, acts, and is revealed? Does this analogy, taken from a human being's cognitive and affective powers, 'save' the divine unity but 'lose' the divine threeness? How can the divine knowing and willing illuminate the existence in God of three persons and not be taken to be merely the interior soliloquy of only one person?

It can be argued that the inner life of the Trinity is so mysterious that any analogy will almost certainly run the risk of some error. It is better to edge towards a modalism that preserves monotheism than fall into vulgar tritheism. Furthermore, in Book 15 of *De Trinitate* Augustine highlighted again the love analogy in an attempt to interpret the Trinity. The Holy Spirit is the Gift of mutual love between Father and Son—a theme already developed much earlier in *De Trinitate* (5. 11–12). Centuries later Richard of St Victor (d. 1173) was to argue that mutual love, to be perfect, must be love shared with a third person. In God, we find not just an I–Thou relationship or reciprocal love but also the Holy Spirit as the 'Co-beloved'. There is a movement from self-love (the Father) to mutual love (the Father and the Son) to shared love (the Father, Son, and Holy Spirit). This interpretation of God as absolute communion of love takes a little further Augustine's trinitarian theology of love.

By the time of Richard of St Victor, two changes in the doctrine of God were beginning to break in: representations of the first person of the Trinity and a trend towards 'rationalism'.

For a thousand years Christians had reverently avoided representing the Father and so respected the mystery of One who, both within the godhead and beyond, is the sublime Source of all life and did not 'come on mission' for the salvation of the world, as did the Son and the Spirit. During the first millennium something similar had also happened in the case of the Son. Christian artists pictured him as largely bypassing pain, unconquered by death, and already reigning from the cross. But then, as we saw early in Ch. 2, eleventh-century developments in devotion and art furthered a deep sense of Jesus in his loving, suffering, human existence. Christian artists finally found the courage to represent more directly the crucifixion and Jesus' agonizing death. Parallel to this fresh sense of the human, suffering Christ, one also finds a fresh sensibility to his divinity and place in the Trinity. The strong Christ of trinitarian life belongs to a renewed appreci-ation of the tripersonal God that began in the tenth century, led to the institution of the Feast of the Holy Trinity in 1334, and was reflected in art—not least in the new willingness to portray God the Father.

The greatest of all medieval poets, Dante Alighieri (d. 1321), lent his weight to this popular appreciation of faith in the tripersonal God but did so with an image that remains discreet. At the end of his *Paradiso*, Dante envisioned God as utterly active, with 'spinning' or 'circling' symbolizing the completely actualized divine perfection; in the divine spinnings, the Holy Spirit 'proceeds from' or is 'breathed by' both Father and Son: 'In the profound and clear ground of the lofty light there appeared to me three spinnings (circlings) of three colours and of the same extent. The One seemed reflected by the Other as rainbow by rainbow, and the Third seemed fire breathed forth equally from the One and the Other' (Canto 33. 115–20). As elsewhere in the *Paradiso*, spinning symbolizes completely actualized thought and perfection.

A century later, around 1411, St Andrew Roublev painted the most popular contemporary image of the Trinity, which is now found in the Tretiakov Gallery in Moscow. It presents the three 'angels' who visited Abraham and Sarah (Gen. 18: 1–15). A divine unity and harmony pervades the composition, in which the three figures sit around the one table and are entirely referred to each other in a continuous dialogue of love. The Roublev icon (like the tradition that led up to it) is one of the few representations of the Trinity in which the Holy Spirit has a human face, albeit in angelic style. But it is not the only one in which God the Father has a human face.

At least from the early twelfth century, Western iconography was developing the 'Throne of Grace', undoubtedly the most important representation of the Trinity in the West. Turning up for centuries in a painted or carved form, it shows the Father holding the cross with the Son dead on it (or the Father simply holding the body of the Son) with the Holy Spirit as a dove hovering over them. One cross links the three figures; their unity is also expressed by their being turned towards each other. Frequently, as in the sublime version by El Greco exhibited in the Prado (Madrid), the dead body of the Son already hints at the luminosity of his coming resurrection. Many visitors to Santa Maria Novella in Florence have seen and marvelled at the *Throne of Grace* painted shortly before Masaccio died in 1428; in this version the Father exists mysteriously outside the space (and time) of our human world.

Some Western paintings of the Trinity that show the Father in a human form have chosen other moments in the whole story of God's work for our salvation: for instance, the childhood of Jesus, his baptism, or his final glory. Thus Bartolomé Murillo (1617–82) in the *Heavenly and Earthly Trinities* shows the Child Jesus standing on a higher level than Mary and Joseph and receiving their adoration. God the Father looks down and the Spirit as a radiant dove hovers above Jesus' head. Going beyond the voice from heaven ('You are my beloved Son') reported by the Gospels, the *Baptism of Christ* by Giovanni Bellini (d. 1516) adds the figure of the Father riding on some clouds right above the Holy Spirit, a glorious dove descending on Jesus. Titian (d. 1576) in his *Trinity in Glory* depicts all humanity drawn heavenward towards the Father and the Son, who are seated facing one another with the radiant Spirit hovering as a dove between them.[12]

---

[12] On these and other works see D. Brown, 'The Trinity in Art', in Davis, Kendall, and O'Collins (eds.), *The Trinity*, 329–56.

Some Christians prefer that the Father never be represented in images, and that we content ourselves with the heavenly voice reported by the Gospels at Jesus' baptism and transfiguration. Others, in fact many others, find their life of prayer encouraged by the icon of Roublev (from the East) and/or the best versions of the Throne of Grace (from the West). In both cases they see not only the Son but also the Father and the Spirit revealed in the work of human redemption. The *Throne of Grace* shows this clearly. Roublev's painting finds its centre in the chalice on a table. The table brings to mind the Last Supper celebrated just before Christ's death and resurrection, while the chalice hints at the cup of the passion (Mark 10: 38–9). Thus both the *Throne of Grace* and Roublev's icon point to the dying and rising of Christ as *the* climactic moment when the Trinity is revealed. Even with such a preference for the *Throne of Grace* and Roublev, we must recognize how Murillo, Bellini, Titian, and other artists also tie the presentations of the tripersonal God into events in the history of human salvation: the childhood of Jesus, his baptism, his post-resurrection glory, and so forth. Christian art[13] did much better than academic theology, which emerged from the twelfth century (see Ch. 2) and eventually allowed the question of God to be raised speculatively and in isolation from the historical revelation of the tripersonal God.

Debates with François-Marie Arouet (better known as Voltaire) (1694–1778), Denis Diderot (1713–84), and other figures of the Enlightenment (see Ch. 2) unfortunately pushed many apologists for mainstream Christian faith into arguing about God on 'merely' rational grounds, bracketing off the special history of the people of God, marginalizing the person of Jesus Christ, and developing what they called 'natural theology'. They turned God into a hypothesis for justifying the existence of the world—a procedure that eventually led to atheism as the hypothesis seemed to become less necessary. The apologists should have listened more to Blaise Pascal (1623–62), who deeply experienced and championed the God of Abraham, Isaac, and Jacob, the God and Father of Jesus Christ. Great mathematician and physicist that he was, Pascal rightly refused to raise the question of God except in terms of that history which climaxed with Jesus' life, death, and resurrection, with the coming of the Spirit.[14] Pascal's

---

[13] See V. N. Lazarev, *The Russian Icon: From its Origins to the Sixteenth Century* (Collegeville, Minn.: Liturgical Press, 1997); J. Pelikan, *The Illustrated Jesus Through the Centuries* (New Haven, Conn.: Yale University Press, 1997).

[14] See M. J. Buckley, *At the Origins of Modern Atheism* (New Haven: Yale University Press, 1987).

conviction here followed what we saw (in Ch. 2) about those popular devotions developed by medieval Dominicans and Franciscans: the rosary, the Christmas crib, and the Stations of the Cross. Such devotions implied that we know God through the history of Jesus, taken in its totality—in what went before his death and resurrection and in what has came after.

Sometimes Thomas Aquinas is accused of encouraging the separation of speculative reason and historical revelation. Beyond question, he examined what it means to call God the absolutely perfect, timeless, spaceless, and unchanging Being. He presented God as the ultimate, ungrounded Ground of all reality, One who sustains and moves everything. Far from talking of one reality alongside other realities, Aquinas insisted on God as *the* Reality that comprehends, grounds, and determines all other realities. The humbling consequence of such doctrine is that we cannot possess or dispose of God with our minds or in any other fashion. As regards Aquinas's arguments for the existence of God, the 'five ways' that he developed in the *Summa Theologiae* (I q. 2 a.3), they do not purport to be independent proofs of God's existence, still less to replace belief. Rather they emerge from a prior faith in and experience of God, and aim at illustrating the reasonableness of that faith and at introducing a theological inquiry grounded in revelation. Aquinas highlighted the mutual clarification that faith and reason can bring to each other.

Admittedly Aquinas divided his treatment of God into two parts: God as one ('De Deo Uno', *ST* I qq. 1–26) and God as three ('De Deo Trino', *ST* I qq. 27–43). He introduced this distinction for pedagogical reasons. Unfortunately many later Catholic scholars treated the oneness of God in the mode of philosophical reason, and introduced revelation and theology only when they had to speak of the Trinity. They forgot the constant need to lead God-talk back to the scriptures and the inspired account of the divine self-communication in the history of revelation and salvation. They often attempted to define the divine attributes independently of the tripersonal God made known in and through the biblical story. But any Christian and Catholic account of God should depend primarily on the tripersonal God, fully revealed in the history of Jesus.

Unquestionably the order and beauty of nature manifest God and the divine creative activity. The psalmist sings a long hymn to God, the creator of the earth and provider for all its inhabitants (Ps. 104: 1–35). Another psalm sees God's glory in the phenomena of the universe: 'the heavens are telling the glory of God; and the firmament proclaims his handiwork'

(Ps. 19: 1). But the psalms, far from leaving history behind, constantly locate themselves within the story of God's saving and revealing activity. Psalm 19, for instance, presses on to praise the revelation of the divine will in the law that was communicated through Moses (Ps. 19: 7–14). The Book of Wisdom recognizes that God can be known, apart from revelation, through the good and beautiful things we see (Wis. 13: 1–9). But the same book gives this passage a full setting in God's historical dealings with Israel: for instance, by a long section on King Solomon's quest for wisdom (Wis. 7: 1–8: 21), by meditating on figures in the biblical story who led up to Abraham and Sarah (Wis. 10: 1–11: 4), and by a long comparison between the Israelites and the Egyptians (Wis. 11: 5–19: 22). St Paul echoes the Book of Wisdom when declaring that nature shows forth God's eternal power and divine nature (Rom. 1: 19–20), but the apostle never loses sight of the divine self-communication in biblical history and the 'trinitarian' face of the history of Jesus.

As the second millennium slipped into the third, a wealth of publications on the Trinity has witnessed to a widespread desire to rehabilitate belief in the tripersonal God as the deep truth at the very heart of Catholic and all Christian faith. A healthy reaction has set in against the modern, Western situation in which trinitarian faith seemed to have been reduced to little more than a logical puzzle for experts. In a slim volume, *The Trinity*, which originally appeared in 1967, Karl Rahner (1904–84) who was arguably the outstanding Catholic theologian of the twentieth century, complained that faith in the Trinity was marginal in the lives of Christians. However, when nine years later he himself published a 450-page introduction to Christian faith, he had hardly anything to say about the Trinity![15] Such examples of neglect of the Trinity could be easily multiplied. In such a situation it was understandable, if highly regrettable, that finding the trinitarian mystery irretrievable and even intolerable, some writers have opted for 'one God' and jettisoned 'three persons'.

Public worship, however, has always maintained the centrality of the Trinity. The Nicene-Constantinopolitan Creed that churches across the world use at the Eucharist constantly reminds Christians of their trinitarian faith and does so by recalling the history of salvation—from creation to the end of the world. The celebration of baptism, along with the now

---

[15] *Foundations of Christian Faith: An Introduction to the Idea of Christianity* (New York: Crossroad, 1978; German original 1976).

more frequent renewal of baptismal vows, also recalls to the attention of believers the trinitarian faith at the heart of their lives. The Eucharist opens 'in the name of the Father, and of the Son, and of the Holy Spirit', and closes (as do normal Christian blessings) with a blessing in the name of the Trinity. The content of the eucharistic prayers, both in the East and in the West, is repeatedly trinitarian. The short doxology, 'Glory be to the Father and to the Son and to the Holy Spirit', and the 'long' doxology, 'Glory to God in the Highest', address the tripersonal God. The collects, or variable prayers, in the divine office and in other liturgical ceremonies, above all in the Eucharist, end by invoking the Trinity. In short, where many theological writers have failed to be trinitarian in focus, liturgical texts have clearly maintained that the Trinity is the message of salvation. For Catholics and other Christians the 'law' of public worship has never ceased to indicate the central 'law' of belief, faith in the tripersonal God.

When encouraging Catholics to prepare well for the Holy Year of 2000 and the coming third millennium, John Paul II swept aside suggestions about seven years of preparation, one for each of the seven sacraments. In his 1994 apostolic letter *Tertio Millennio Adveniente* ('The Third Millennium Approaching'), he went to the trinitarian heart of the matter by inviting all Christians to dedicate in a special way 1997 to Jesus Christ, 1998 to the Holy Spirit, and 1999 to God the Father.

Those who wish to know what Catholics believe about the Trinity in general, and God the Father in particular, could well be advised to attend some church services, preferably in both the Eastern and Western rites. By listening carefully to the prayers and hymns and by contemplating the icons and other images, they will have a closer chance of appreciating what their faith in the tripersonal God means in the great scheme of things to rank-and-file believers.

Chapter 9 will reflect on the moral consequences of faith in the Trinity. We devote the rest of this chapter to the Holy Spirit and to some questions about Christ 'in himself' and 'for us'.

The Holy Spirit

We quoted above Dante's words about 'the Third' as 'fire breathed forth *equally* from the One and the Other'. He was following Thomas Aquinas and classic medieval theology about the Holy Spirit 'proceeding from' or 'being breathed equally by the Father *and the Son* (Filioque)'. Here we reach a point that has divided Western and Eastern Christianity. How are the Father and the Son related in and to the emergence of the Spirit?

Along the lines of his image of the Trinity as spring/river/canal, Tertullian wrote of the Spirit being 'from the Father through the Son' (*Adversus Praxean*, 4). In the two following centuries we find this language of the Spirit proceeding 'from the Father through the Son' in the works of such writers as Hilary of Poitiers, Gregory of Nyssa, and Cyril of Alexandria. In the fourth century Marius Victorinus drew on such passages as Jesus' words in John 16: 14 ('He [the Spirit of truth] will glorify me because he will take what is mine and declare it to you') to reach the conclusion that the Son, together with the Father, 'produced' the Holy Spirit. Victorinus' much publicized conversion to Christianity and resignation of his post as a famous rhetor in 362 (after which he dedicated himself to theological writing) played a role in Augustine's own decision to seek Christian baptism in 386.

Subsequently Augustine himself wrote of the Father endowing the Son with the *capacity* to produce the Spirit. Hence, it is in a primordial or 'original' sense that the Spirit proceeds from the Father. For Augustine to deny this procession from the Father and the Son, 'as from one principle' would be to violate the divine unity (*De Trinitate*, 5. 14). Some later Christian art in the West did in fact violate the divine unity by representing the Spirit being breathed equally and simultaneously from the *separate* mouths of the Father and the Son. But, in Augustine's view of the Trinity, the Spirit proceeds from the Father through the Son, with the Son being considered the agent of the Father in this procession by equally producing the divine Spirit. What the Son does here, according to Augustine, happens 'through the gift of the Father' and not independently, just as the Son's divinity is derived by generation from the Father. Being and acting in such a 'derivative' way does not exclude being equal in divinity and in the production of the Spirit.

In general, the Greek theologians of the Christian East found no difficulty in saying that the Spirit proceeds from the Father through the Son, the Son being considered the Father's instrument or agent. But it remained axiomatic that the Father alone is the ultimate source or fountainhead of deity and that both the Son and the Spirit derive from him, the former by generation and the latter by procession. For Eastern theologians, however, the *Filioque*, or 'from the Father and the Son', suggested a fundamental difference over the mystery of the triune divinity—an unacceptable view of the Son being equal in the production of the Father. Hence, they normally rejected the Augustinian idea of the Son forming with the Father a single co-principle for the procession of the Spirit. They detected here a double origin for the Spirit that contradicts the divine unity.

Distinguishing between the Spirit's mission in history for human salvation and the 'procession' of the Spirit within the eternal life of God, Eastern theologians have continued to appeal to John 15: 26: 'When the Advocate comes, whom *I will send* to you *from the Father*, the Spirit of truth *who proceeds from the Father*, he will testify on my behalf.' This perspective insists that only the Father is the ultimate source and fountainhead of divinity, from whom the Son and the Spirit derive—the former by generation and the latter by procession. Yet it is worth remarking that the original, unexpanded form of the Nicene-Constantinopolitan Creed did not state that the Spirit proceeds from the Father *alone*. In confessing that the Spirit proceeds from the Father, it refers to One who has this name precisely because of the generation of the Son. In effect, the creed confesses that the Spirit proceeds 'from the Father of the Son'.

Here one can undoubtedly indulge unsubtle polarities and even downright caricatures, whether it be about the procession of the Holy Spirit in particular or about the whole doctrine of the Trinity in general, as if all the problems and differences were to go back, for instance, to the Greeks beginning with the reality of the divine persons and Augustine and other Latins with the unity of the divine nature. But one should respect the fear that Eastern Christians have about neglecting or subordinating the Spirit. They remain strongly trinitarian in their faith because they experience the life and living witness of the Spirit in the Church. Their worship and life have been deeply configured by the role of the Holy Spirit, and they have found that role threatened by those who declare the Spirit to have proceeded 'also from the Son'. We need to ask: how trinitarian have we Western Catholics been? The Eastern problems with the Western understanding of the procession of the Holy Spirit spring from concerns about the subordination (1) of the Spirit to the Son in the life of Christians, and (2) of the doctrine of the Spirit (Pneumatology) to the doctrine of Christ (Christology) in official teaching and the work of theologians. In the Christocentric theology of the West, which at times has seemed to indulge 'Christomonism' or a unilateral stress on Christ's being and work, the

Spirit becomes exclusively the Spirit of Christ (almost a mere function of the risen Christ) rather than the Spirit of God the Father.[16] Such medieval and later mystics as St Hildegard of Bingen (1098–1179) and St Ignatius Loyola (1491–1556) maintained, however, a proper balance in their trinitarian images that featured and cherished the distinct place of the Holy Spirit both within the life of God and in the story of salvation. We find exemplified here the power of mystical experience to receive and communicate the full scope of the tripersonal God's self-revelation.[17]

When Augustine wrote his *De Trinitate* and other works in which he expounded the Trinity, the Western church had not yet unilaterally added to the Nicene-Constantinopolitan Creed, the words about the Spirit proceeding from the Father 'and the Son'—the *Filioque* addition that since the time of Patriarch Photius of Constantinople (see the end of Ch. 1) has contributed to the separation between Eastern and Western Christianity. We say 'contributed', since the division arose and continued also because of a wide range of political, cultural, and ecclesial factors. Theological differences over the *Filioque* and its interpretation never operated alone and as the only cause. The *Filioque*, a term expressing what came to be called the 'double' procession of the Holy Spirit, may have already been interpolated into the text of the Creed at the Third Synod of Toledo in 589. It had undoubtedly been added in 675 at the Fourth Synod of Braga. After being widely used in the West from around 800 when the Creed began to be chanted at Mass, the addition was eventually adopted also in Rome when Emperor Henry II in 1013 ordered the Latin church everywhere to add the *Filioque*. In the historical context of Toledo III and Braga IV, the *Filioque* addition appears to have been introduced to support orthodox trinitarian doctrine against recurrent 'modalist' denials of personal distinctions within God. A strong view on the Son's role in the eternal procession of the Spirit helped to clarify that the 'Son' and the 'Spirit' are distinct persons and not mere modes or manners in which a monopersonal God acts and is revealed in history.

---

[16] See Y. Congar, *I Believe in the Holy Spirit*, i (London: Geoffrey Chapman, 1983), 157, 159–60. Congar recognizes the element of truth in the criticism of some Orthodox theologians: Western Christians, in general, and Catholics, in particular, have played down both the personal identity of the Spirit within the mystery of God and the Spirit's active role in the history of salvation.

[17] See S. M. Burgess, *The Holy Spirit: Medieval Roman Catholic and Reformation Traditions* (Peabody, Mass.: Hendrickson, 1997). Burgess also pays proper attention to the way John Calvin rightly championed the 'internal testimony' of the Holy Spirit.

After the mutual excommunications of 1054, the Council of Florence (1438–45) proved the most serious effort to heal the split between Eastern and Western Christianity. The official representatives of the Orthodox Christians included even Joseph, the patriarch of Constantinople. The 1439 Decree for the Greeks, while defending as legitimate the addition of the *Filioque*, also accepted the more dynamic, Eastern formula according to which the Spirit 'proceeds from the Father through the Son' (DH 1300–2; ND 322–4). Hence the Council did not insist on the *Filioque* being added when the Nicene-Constantinopolitan Creed was recited or sung. Motivated partly by the fear of Turkish conquest and the threat to Constantinople (which fell to the Turks in 1453), the agreements with Greeks and others achieved at the Council of Florence did not prove long-lasting. But through the Union of Brest (1595–6) millions of Slavs joined the Catholic Church, with the Council of Florence as a platform, just as other Eastern groups were to do later.

The debate over the unilateral, Western addition of the *Filioque* was replayed down through the centuries, as were attempts to heal the split. On occasions Pope Paul VI and Pope John Paul II recited the Creed without this addition. In January 1964, Paul VI and Athenagoras (1886–1972), the patriarch of Constantinople, met in Jerusalem, the first meeting between a pope and a patriarch of Constantinople since Eugenius IV (pope 1431–47) met Patriarch Joseph during the Council of Florence. At Pentecost 1986 John Paul II published one of his longest encyclicals *Dominum et Vivificantem*, aimed at giving a very full and appreciative account of the Holy Spirit, and so helping to heal the division between Orthodox and Catholic Christianity. During a sermon preached in St Peter's Basilica on 29 June 1995 in the presence of Bartholomew I, the ecumenical patriarch of Constantinople, the Pope dramatically requested a clarification on the Greek and Latin traditions regarding the procession of the Holy Spirit. He did not want the traditional Latin addition of the *Filioque* (or the Spirit somehow also proceeding from the Son) to obscure any harmony over the Nicene-Constantinopolitan Creed of 381. Three months later the Pontifical Council for Promoting Christian Unity published such a clarification regarding the procession of the Holy Spirit. The document emphasized that the Father is the 'origin' or 'source' both of the Son and of the Holy Spirit (ND 339, 938). In the introduction to its September 2000 declaration, *Dominus Jesus*, the Congregation for the Doctrine of the Faith followed the example of Paul VI and John Paul II by quoting the whole of the Creed but without the *Filioque*. This was tantamount to admitting that the 'double' procession of the Holy Spirit does not belong to the essentials of faith.

The doctrine of the Holy Spirit has its crucial importance in relations between the Orthodox and Catholics. But, especially under the pontificate of John Paul II, teaching on the role of the Spirit in the spiritual lives of the adherents of the great world religions has been prominent. In his 1990 encyclical *Redemptoris missio*, John Paul II wrote of the universal presence and activity of the Spirit, which 'affect not only individuals' but also 'cultures and religions' (ND 1166–75, at 1172). We will return to this question in our final chapter.

The Incarnate Son

What remains for this chapter is the formidable task of filling out some themes which we judge to belong to Catholic (and other) teaching on Jesus Christ. One could dedicate pages to the personal pre-existence of the Incarnate Son in eternal relationship to the Father and the Spirit, or to an event that inaugurates the trinitarian story of Jesus: the virginal conception which took place through the power of the Spirit and revealed, in particular, the divine origin of Christ as the Son of God. Then one might take up the question of the sinless life of the incarnate Son of God, the knowledge he enjoyed in his human mind (see what was reported from Aquinas in Ch. 2), his freedom, and other aspects of his earthly story. Since one of us has already treated these and related issues in several books,[18] we have decided to limit ourselves to two central issues: the possibility of continuing to use the language of 'one person in two natures', and possible interpretations of Christ's work as redeemer.

1. The teaching of the Council of Chalcedon (AD 451) about the one person or subsistence (*hypostasis*) of Christ in two natures has remained normative for mainstream Christianity. *Hypostasis* as signifying one individual had and has a wider application than 'person' as signifying a rational individual. Every person is a *hypostasis* but not every *hypostasis* (e.g. an individual dog or tree) is a person. One might sum up the contribution of Chalcedonian teaching by saying that the incarnate

---

[18] See e.g. O'Collins, *Christology*, 237–44, 254–78. That book also indicates what would happen if Christ were only human or were only divine; it is decisive for Christian faith that he is both human and divine (ibid. 154–8, 228, 230–1).

Word of God is only one individual (person) but has two 'things', his divine and human natures. He is one 'who' but has two 'whats'. The 'oneness' we acknowledge with reference to the person, the 'twoness' with reference to the natures (see Ch. 1 above).

Hence the incarnate Son of God is and was a human being (or better has and had a human nature), but is not a human person. Let us expand this vital point, especially for readers who may jump at once to the conclusion that if he was/is not a human person, he cannot have been a 'real' human being. The Son of God took on or assumed all the natural endowments of a complete human being, but did not become a human person. In addition to the characteristics of divinity that he already possessed from eternity, the Word of God acquired around 5 BC (when Mary conceived Jesus) all the essential characteristics of a fully authentic human being. That made him and continues to make him a genuine human being. His loving 'descent' from heaven 'altered' him by adding the human nature through which he could operate visibly and humanly. But his humanity did not and does not have the independence that would constitute a second (human) person alongside the divine person of the Word of God.

If in the incarnation, the Son of God had, so to speak, 'teamed up with' an already existing person, he could not truly have 'become flesh' (John 1: 14) or assumed the full human condition (Phil. 2: 7–8). What would have resulted would have been a very special, even uniquely special, relationship between two individuals: a divine subject (the person of the Son of God) and a human subject (the person of the Son of Mary), who was very intimately related to the Son of God but not strictly identical with him. Any such 'two-sons' view in effect excludes a genuine incarnation and pictures Christ as a kind of temple of the divine Word or as a person filled with the divine Spirit. Such a Christ might differ in degree from others so graced by God, but not in kind.

As has normally been the case with general councils of the Church, the Council of Chalcedon used the terms 'natures' and 'person' or 'subsistence', without stopping to define them. What is two in Christ it called the 'natures', what (or rather who) is 'one' it called the person or subsistence. Instead of being the proper work of an ecumenical council, the analysis and definition of terms belong rather to philosophers and theologians.

Prosopon, after initially indicating a mask worn by an actor on stage to signify some character, began to denote the visible manifestation or 'face' of someone, or—one might say, someone's public 'persona'. Without too

FIG. 7. Birds and a rabbit join two little angels in worshipping the Christ Child in this Chinese nativity scene from 1947. (The Art Archive/Missions Etrangères Paris/Dagli Orti.)

much trouble, through the third into the fifth century *prosopon* (in Greek) and *persona* (in Latin) came to indicate an individual human being, while often maintaining the overtones of such an individual as visibly manifested.

For centuries, however, as we pointed out in Ch. 1, *hypostasis* was dogged by controversy, in particular when translated into Latin as *substantia* or 'that which stands under'. To begin with, *hypostasis* could, among other things, denote either (*a*) an essence or (common) substance in the Latin sense, or (*b*) an individuating principle. The ambiguity for Romans in the meaning of the Greek *hypostasis* emerged in a furiously indignant letter from St Jerome (d. 420) to Pope Damasus. About thirty years of age, Jerome was then living among some hermits in the Middle East. He had met some Greek-speaking Christians who shocked him by their terminology for the Trinity: '[They] are trying to extort from me, a Roman Christian, their unheard-of formula of "three hypostases" . . . I ask them what "three hypostases" are supposed to mean. They reply, "three persons subsisting". I reply that this is my belief. They are not satisfied with the meaning; they demand the term' (*Epistola*, 15. 3). Less than a century later, however, by endorsing the teaching of Chalcedon, St Leo the Great and Latin Christians did just what had outraged Jerome: they accepted *hypostasis* as meaning a subsistent subject rather than the basic essence or substance.

The Chalcedonian definition obviously took the two 'natures' as equivalent to (*a*) 'divinity' and 'humanity', (*b*) being 'truly God' and 'truly man', or (*c*) being as God *homoousios* (of the same substance/essence) with the Father and as man *homoousios* (of the same substance/essence) with us. In the case of 'consubstantiality' with the Father, the Council had in mind a numerically identical substance or being. Here it understood 'same' in the sense of 'identical' or 'one and the same'; there is only one divine substance, essence, or nature. But in the case of 'consubstantiality' with us human beings, the Council used the term in a generic sense. There are innumerable instances of the human substance or being. We share the 'same' substance with Christ, but we do not share an 'identical' substance with him. Our being is not 'one and the same' substance with his.

By supplying right at the heart of its particular contribution to teaching on Christ three sets of equivalents for 'two natures' (see *a–c* above), Chalcedon refrained from rigidly imposing just one way of speaking about the duality in Christ. The principal churches in both East and

West accepted the language of 'one person in two natures', but some groups of Christians would not do so and at times suffered for not endorsing the complete Chalcedonian teaching. Better relations between Christian communities in the twentieth century led to agreements about faith in Jesus Christ that followed Chalcedon but, out of respect for certain religious and cultural sensitivities, avoided some of the Council's terminology. Thus the May 1973 christological declaration signed by the (Oriental Orthodox) Coptic pope, Shenouda III of Egypt, and Pope Paul VI officially set at rest one cause of the schism that arose in the fifth century when some Christians in Egypt and elsewhere refused to accept the language of 'two natures'. The 1973 declaration, recalled in Ch. 1, avoided that language, but said what is functionally the equivalent by confessing Jesus as 'perfect God with respect to his divinity, perfect man with respect to his humanity'. The declaration went on to say: 'in him are preserved all the properties of the divinity and all the properties of the humanity together in a real, perfect, indivisible and inseparable union' (ND 671a). Thus the declaration could say what Chalcedon taught by using the God–man and divinity–humanity language (*a* and *b* above).

But how well have the characteristic terms from Chalcedon, 'person' and 'natures', worn over fifteen centuries? The overwhelming majority of Christian teachers repeated the Council's language about the 'two natures' of Christ. At times they forgot the infinite qualitative difference between the uncreated divine nature and the created human nature, falling into the mistake of treating the two natures as if they were two of the same kind or two more or less equal species of the same genus, 'nature'.

Some modern authors claim that this term has changed or enlarged its meaning too much to be any longer serviceable. In short, what people in the twenty-first century mean by 'nature' is not what the bishops at Chalcedon meant in the fifth century. Unquestionably 'nature' is used in a variety of ways nowadays: as denoting, for example, scenery and the countryside (e.g. 'I love walking in the woods and getting back to nature'), or as denoting the universe (e.g. 'the laws of nature apply everywhere'). But modern languages also still use 'nature' in the sense of the essential features or properties of something, a usage that stands in continuity with Chalcedon's teaching about 'the character proper to each nature' of Christ (DH 302; ND 615) and finds an echo in the 1973 joint declaration, which speaks of 'all the properties' of the divinity and the humanity. The problem is not so much with Chalcedon's two-nature talk (which remains useful and intelligible), but with its teaching of one 'person'.[19]

In the third century Tertullian had written of 'three persons in one substance' to account for the unity and threeness of God. 'Person' pointed to the distinctive identity of the Father, Son, and Holy Spirit—an identity in a dynamic relationship derived from the one source (the Father), as suggested by Tertullian's trinitarian images of the fountain, the river, and the canal or the root, the shoot, and the fruit. Augustine, as we saw above, conceived of the relations between the three divine persons in terms of the psychological analogy of human memory, understanding, and will. At the same time, he recognized 'the great poverty from which our language suffers'. 'The formula of three persons', he pointed out, 'has been coined not in order to give a complete explanation by means of it, but in order that we might not be obliged to remain silent' (*De Trinitate*, 5. 10). Up to the time of Augustine, Christians developed their thinking about 'person' in order to frame their doctrine of the Trinity. By the time of Chalcedon, the challenge for teaching and terminology concerned rather the one subject or person, who is Jesus Christ.

More than half a century after Chalcedon, Boethius (d. *c*.524), in a work entitled *On the Person and Two Natures of Christ*, defined 'person' as 'an individual substance of rational nature' (no. 3). This influential account of 'person' highlighted the individuality and rationality of the reality that is the centre of action and attribution. Boethius' rational individual is the 'someone' who acts and who is also the subject to whom we attribute things. This definition had nothing as such to say about the loving freedom, interrelatedness, and dignity of persons.

Thomas Aquinas added some footnotes, as it were, to Boethius' notion of person—in particular, about the supreme value of personhood. What proved more challenging was the way René Descartes (1596–1650) furthered the notion of person as a unique subject of consciousness and self-consciousness. More than a century later, a concern for freedom and morality prompted Immanuel Kant (1726–1804) to stress 'person' as the subject of freedom, a moral end in itself and never a means to an end—a view that recalls Aquinas's stress on the unique dignity of persons. Their different justification for this dignity, however, kept Aquinas and Kant

---

[19] On the development in the notion of 'person' and an initial bibliography, see H. S. Pyper, 'Person', in *The Oxford Companion to Christian Thought*, 532–3.

significantly apart. Where Aquinas based personal dignity on God, who regards human beings 'with the greatest respect' (*Summa contra Gentiles*, 3. 112), Kant argued that the very nature of persons 'marks them out as ends in themselves' and beings to be treated always with dignity and 'never simply as means' (*Groundwork of the Metaphysics of Morals*, 65–6). The philosophical input from Descartes, Kant, and John Locke (1632–1704) led to the emergence of a (but not the) typically modern notion of person as the subject of self-awareness and freedom—in brief, person as the self-sufficient ego or the conscious and autonomous self ('I think and am free; therefore I am a person').

From Chalcedon and Boethius to Aquinas, there is a good deal of common ground in the notion of 'person' as a rational, subsisting, individual subject. But has usage in modern times broken completely with fourth-, fifth-, and sixth-century usage of *prosopon* and *hypostasis?* Not altogether. Nowadays many highlight the interrelatedness of persons and stress how persons are interpersonal. This insight reaches back through Richard of St Victor's reflections on the communion of love (see above) to the Capaddocian Fathers in the fourth century (Basil the Great, Gregory of Nazianzus, and Gregory of Nyssa). Their teaching on the Trinity, which paved the way for the fuller version of the Nicene Creed professed at Constantinople I and endorsed at Chalcedon, shows a strong sense of persons being interpersonal and in communion. Their understanding of *hypostasis* and *prosopon* anticipated something of a modern stress on the interrelatedness of persons.

Much more problematic is the widespread identification of persons with minds. One could say that such a modern equation does no more than push Chalcedon's teaching on Christ's 'rational soul' (DH 301; ND 614) to an extreme. If so, it does this in a way that would be excluded by Chalcedon. If to be a person is to be a mind or conscious self, then Christ's human mind entails his being a distinct human person. With such a move, we would be endorsing something excluded by Chalcedon: two distinct (even separate) persons, one human (corresponding to the human mind) and one divine (corresponding to the divine mind) in Christ. This is not to deny that being 'minded' should belong essentially to any account of what it is to be a person or what a person has. We are challenging the simple equation: to be a mind is to be a person, and vice versa. Such an equation, when pushed further, would mean that the absence or loss of normal consciousness would involve the absence or loss of personal status.

Then unborn children, as well as adults who are asleep or in a coma, would not enjoy the status, dignity, and rights of persons.

All in all, medieval and modern themes about persons as interrelated, 'minded', free, and supremely valuable beings move beyond the conceptuality of Chalcedon and its times. Nevertheless, the objection that those who still follow Chalcedon in declaring Christ to be 'one person' have kept the word without noticing that it has simply changed its meaning is not on target. Despite the many centuries of development that the term has undergone, there are still some common elements between the use of 'person' in the fifth century and the twenty-first century: as a rational individual that is the centre of action and attribution and exists in relationship (in Christ's case, primarily to the Father and the Spirit). That justifies retaining the Chalcedonian formula of 'one person in two natures', so long as we challenge some of the ways in which 'person' is understood and used in the modern world: for instance, as a mind or as a conscious, autonomous self who aims to live a self-sufficient (or should we simply say 'selfish'?) existence. Such modern notions invite scrutiny and criticisms. Some prefer to speak of Christ as one 'subject' or 'individual'. The drawback here, however, is that personal language is the best and highest language we have. When we name Christ as one 'person', there is a sense of dignity and value automatically involved that may be lacking with the language of 'subject' or 'individual'. The latter language can even be compatible with treating people as 'non-persons'—something that happened to Christ in his passion and death but which his dedicated followers could never bear to happen to him or to any other person.

2. While never giving Christ the title 'Redeemer', the NT calls him 'our redemption' (1 Cor. 1: 30) and sixteen times names him 'Saviour' (e.g. Luke 2: 11). His redemptive activity, which can be summarized as (*a*) deliverance from evil, (*b*) expiating or cleansing from sin, and (*c*) reconciling through love, marks the whole story of Jesus from his incarnation, through his ministry, to his resurrection from the dead, the sending of the Spirit, and the final coming in glory.

Apropos of (*a*), NT and post-NT Christians understand Christ's redemptive activity to break the curse of death and the power of sin, so that death has now been turned into a passage from the dominion of sin into eternal, utterly satisfying life. The viciously cruel crucifixion of Jesus, while symbolizing the weakness and failure of suffering, has become the means of human redemption. By dying and rising, Jesus has overcome all sin and evil and effected a new exodus from bondage. To celebrate this deliverance, Christian liturgies have taken over songs with which Moses and Miriam led the Jewish people in praising God for their victorious liberation from bondage (Exod. 15: 1–21). The manumission of slaves in Greco-Roman society and the ransoming of prisoners of war also shaped the original setting in which Christians proclaimed Christ as having 'bought' or 'liberated' those who were captive. St Paul writes of the human race being, along with the whole creation, 'in bondage to decay' and 'groaning' for redemption (Rom. 8: 18–23), of Jews being slaves to the law (Gal. 4: 1–7), and of Gentiles being enslaved to 'gods' and 'elemental spirits' (Gal. 4: 8–9). Christ redeemed or 'bought' us out of such a situation.

At times the NT authors speak of Christ 'buying' us at 'a price' (1 Cor. 6: 20), 'ransoming' us with his 'precious blood' (1 Pet. 1: 18–19), and 'giving his life as a ransom for many' (Mark 10: 45). But nowhere does the NT speak of this 'price' or 'ransom' being paid to someone (e.g. God) or to something (e.g. the law). Some Christians have expanded the content of this metaphor for redemption, taking 'ransom' as if it literally described some kind of transaction, even with a specific price paid to someone. Those who have failed to observe the limits of the metaphor at times even spoke of human beings as in the possession of the devil, whose 'rights' of ownership were 'respected' by the price of Jesus' blood being paid to release them from bondage.[20] For the NT, however, the act of redemption was 'costly', in the sense that it cost Christ his life. The beneficiaries of this redeeming action became free (e.g. Gal. 5: 1) or, by coming under Christ's sovereignty, 'slaves' to him (e.g. Rom. 1: 1). Nowhere does the NT accept or imply that Satan has any rights over human beings. The metaphor of 'redemption' represents Christ as effecting a deliverance and not as literally paying a price to anyone. St Anselm of Canterbury (d. 1109) vigorously objected to any talk of the devil's rights, and through *Cur Deus Homo* established 'satisfaction' as a long-standing term for Christ's saving work when understood as expiation.

Concerning (*b*), 'every sin', Anselm argues, 'must be followed either by satisfaction or by punishment' (*Cur Deus Homo*, 1. 15). God does not wish to punish but to see the good project of creation 'completed' (ibid. 2. 5).

---

[20] In the fifth century St Gregory of Nazianzus vigorously protested against the whole idea of redemption as a price paid to the devil (*Oratio*, 45. 22), but for the time being this protest failed to carry the day.

Satisfaction, Anselm explains, requires from human beings not only that they should stop sinning and seek pardon but also that they do something over and above their existing obligations: a work of supererogation that will satisfy for the offence. However, since all sin offends the 'honour' of the infinite God, the reparation must have infinite value—something of which finite human beings are incapable. Moreover, they have nothing extra to offer God, since they already owe God everything. Thus Anselm concludes to the 'necessity' of the incarnation. Only the *God*-man can offer something of infinite value; the personal union with the incarnate Son confers such value on the human acts of Christ. Only the God-*man* has something to offer: being without sin, Christ is exempt from the need to undergo death and hence can freely offer the gift of his life as a work of reparation for the whole human race. Anselm illustrates the redemptive 'cash value' of Christ being in himself both divine and human.

Anselm laid a fresh stress on the humanity and the human freedom of Christ, who spontaneously acts as our representative and in no way is to be construed as a penal substitute who passively endures suffering to appease the anger of a 'vindictive' God. Anselm's theory of satisfaction may be vulnerable on other grounds,[21] but it still retains its grandeur and fascination.[22] Some prefer to express the expiatory dimension of salvation in terms that more closely follow the Letter to the Hebrews: Christ the great high priest and victim offered a unique sacrifice that once and for all purified a sinful world and brought a new and final covenant relationship between God and human beings.

Sadly such language has been misconstrued, especially from the late Middle Ages, to mean that Jesus was a penal substitute, who was personally burdened with the sins of humanity, judged, condemned, and deservedly punished in our place. Through his death he 'satisfied' the divine justice and propitiated an angry God. Thus Anselm's theory about Jesus offering satisfaction or reparation to meet the requirements of commutative justice and set right a moral order damaged by sin acquired, quite contrary to Anselm's explicit statements, elements of punishment and vindictive justice. Such penal additions to Anselm's theology of satisfaction turn up, briefly and in passing, when the Council of Trent expounds the sacrifice of the Mass (DH 1743; ND 1548), and at greater length in the

---

[21] See O'Collins, *Christology*, 200–1.

[22] See P. Gilbert *et al.* (eds.), *Cur Deus Homo*, Studia Anselmiana, 128 (Rome: S. Anselmo, 1999).

writings of Luther and Calvin. Catholic preachers such as J. B. Bossuet (d. 1704) and L. Bourdaloue (d. 1704) went as least as far as the Protestant Reformers in vividly picturing God's vengeance and anger being appeased at the expense of the crucified Son. As a victim of divine justice, Christ was even held to suffer the pains of the damned! Themes from this penal substitutionary view linger on in the works of Hans Urs von Balthasar, Wolfhart Pannenberg, and some other modern theologians.[23]

Many Catholics and other Christians now reject this language as entailing an unacceptable vision of God, supported by misinterpretations of the scapegoat ceremony on the Jewish Day of Expiation, of the fourth suffering servant son (Isa. 52: 13–53: 12), of Jesus' cry of abandonment on the cross, and of some dramatic passages from Paul's letters (e.g. 2 Cor. 5: 21; Gal. 3: 13). Victimized by human violence and not by a vindictive God, the non-violent Christ, through his self-sacrificing death as our representative (not penal substitute), removed the defilement of sin and restored a disturbed moral order.

With respect to (*c*), one must insist that the NT never speaks of redemption altering God's attitudes towards human beings and reconciling God to the world. The sending or coming of God's Son and the Spirit presupposes God's loving forgiveness (e.g. Luke 15: 11–32). Through Christ and the Spirit, God brings about redemptive reconciliation by renewing us; it is our resistance to God that needs to be changed. Both John (e.g. John 3: 16; 1 John 4: 10) and Paul (e.g. Rom. 8: 6–11; 2 Cor 5: 18–21) bear eloquent witness to the loving initiative of God the Father in the whole story of the redemptive reconciliation of human beings and their world.

The language of loving self-sacrifice expresses the costly self-giving of Christ who let himself be victimized by the powers of this world. Over and over again the Synoptic Gospels show us how he valued every individual, and not simply the man of great wealth (Mark 10: 21), as unique and irreplaceable. Through love Christ made himself vulnerable, and his loving self-sacrifice produced life and growth; this sacrifice brought a renewed communion between human beings and the tripersonal God.[24] Through a sacrifice that comprises Christ's incarnation, life, death, and resurrection, along with the coming of the Holy Spirit, human beings were made fit to enter a new, loving fellowship with the all-holy God. Here

---

[23] See B. Sesboüé, *Jésus-Christ l'unique médiateur*, i (Paris: Desclée, 1988), 67–79, 360–5.

[24] In presenting Christ's passion as a 'meritorious sacrifice', Thomas Aquinas stresses how, from beginning to end, it was inspired by love (*ST* III q.48 a.3.)

the root of the term proves illuminating: by Christ's *sacri-ficium* or 'holy making', men and women have been made holy. His 'sacri-fice' enables them to join him in entering the very sanctuary of God (Heb. 9: 11–12, 24) and enjoy the heavenly 'banquet' (e.g. Matt. 8: 11).

In short, love seems the primary, albeit not exclusive, key for interpreting salvation. Those who prefer this key follow the lead of Dante's story of human redemption in his *Comedy*. His masterpiece ends by celebrating the divine love that 'moves the sun and the other stars'.

This chapter has ended by summarizing what we as two Catholics understand to be an appropriate way of interpreting Christ's redemptive activity. But do all human beings need redemption? And is Christ the unique (that is to say, unparalleled in fact and in principle) Saviour of all men and women of all times and places? The first question finds its response in what we say about universal sinfulness in our next chapter. The second question will be addressed in our final chapter.

5

The Human Condition: Created and Sinful

If someone wishes to see God, who is invisible in nature and in no way visible, he understands and knows him from his works . . . Through the incarnation of the Word, the universal providence and its leader and creator, the Word of God himself, have been made known. For he became man that we might become divine; and he revealed himself through a body that we might receive an idea of the invisible Father; and he endured insults from men that we might inherit incorruption.

(St Athanasius, *De Incarnatione*, 54)

Certain new theologians dispute original sin, which is the only part of Christian theology which can really be proved. Some . . . in their almost too fastidious spirituality, admit divine sinlessness, which they cannot see even in their dreams. But they essentially deny human sin, which they can see in the street.

(G. K. Chesterton, *Orthodoxy*, ch. 2)

Intelligent and perceptive books on the human condition, especially in its Western setting, have not been lacking in recent years. Such sociologists as Robert Bellah and Anthony Giddens have offered their account of the modern situation.[1] Some philosophers have described in striking terms our current state.[2] Cosmologists have fascinated the general public with

---

[1] R. Bellah *et al.*, *Habits of the Heart: Individualism and Commitment in American Life* (Berkeley, Calif.: University of California Press, 1985); id., *The Good Society* (New York: Knopf, 1992); A. Giddens, *The Consequences of Modernity* (Palo Alto, Calif.: Stanford University Press, 1990).

[2] See Alastair MacIntyre, *After Virtue: A Study in Moral Theory* (Notre Dame, Ind.: University of Notre Dame Press, 2nd edn. 1984); Charles Taylor, *A Catholic Modernity* (Oxford: Oxford University Press, 1999).

their findings and theories about a universe that began in an initial fireball of radiation. But let us go beyond sociologists, philosophers, and cosmologists and ask in the light of Christian faith: what can we say about the existence and nature of the whole cosmos in general and of the human condition in particular? Where does the world come from? These questions challenge scientists and believers alike, but the latter have to deal with further, thorny issues. How can we understand the relationship between creator and creature? Does this relationship limit creaturely freedom? Sin and human weakness, while raising doubts about the goodness of God's creation, also call into question the extent to which humanity can shape and give meaning to its own existence.

In responding to these questions, this chapter will set out Catholic beliefs about creation and sin, beliefs also endorsed by many other Christians. Such doctrines constitute a common heritage that stems from Paul, John, Irenaeus, Augustine of Hippo, and other ancient writers. They developed a theology of creation and sin, which served as a foundation for their faith in the Trinity and in the redemption effected by Christ and his Spirit.

CREATOR AND CREATION

As early as the second century, Irenaeus stated that the Christian profession of faith should begin with 'God the Creator, who made the heaven and the earth, and all things that are therein', and should demonstrate that 'there is nothing either above him or after him; and that, influenced by no one but of his own free will, he created all things, since he is the only God, the only Lord, the only Creator, the only Father, alone containing all things, and himself commanding all things into existence'. The urgent need to combat the Gnostics' dismissal of material creation as defective and as the work of an inferior 'divine power' stimulated Irenaeus to present a Christian understanding of the entire cosmos: it is God's own creation (*Adversus Haereses*, 2. 1. 1).

In 325, the First Council of Nicaea articulated the Church's belief in God, the 'maker of all things, visible and invisible' (DH 125; ND 7). The First Council of Constantinople I (381) expanded this profession of faith to call the one and true God 'maker of heaven and earth, of all things visible and invisible' (DH 150; ND 12). This specified in greater detail how God alone is the source of all things, without exception. These two councils did no more than sum up what the Bible and early Christian writers had been saying about creation.

Creation, God's First Word

The NT inherits, rather than develops for itself, a theology of creation. By introducing the agency of the Son, it does, however, reinterpret the OT view of created existence. Let us see the details. The Exodus experience and God's self-manifestation at Mount Sinai had shaped the history and self-identity of God's chosen people. In understanding the way in which God had prepared a people for himself, the Israelites looked back to the stories of the patriarchs (Abraham, Isaac, and Jacob), their wives (Sarah, Rebecca, Leah, and Rachel), and their families (Gen. 12–50). The Lord who led his people out of Egypt was the God who had guided Abram out of Ur and made him 'Ab-raham', the 'Father of a people'.

Around the time of King David, the 'Yahwist' theological tradition (the one that named God 'YHWH') looked even further back and expressed its belief that God's paternal guidance spanned all time and history (Gen. 2–3). Just as David ruled over God's chosen people, so YHWH was the sovereign of the whole universe. At the time of the Babylonian captivity in the sixth century BC, the 'Priestly' tradition explored more deeply God's creative relation with things. When creating, God calls things into being and redeems them from 'primordial chaos'.[3] God's creative work can be only good—so concludes the first page of the Bible (Gen. 1: 3–2: 4a). Existence results from the very first word that comes from God, a word he addresses to his creatures before any other. It is the word that sustains all the other words that God subsequently directs toward his creation.

Through their encounter with Greek thought in the third and second century BC, OT authors reconstrued creation from an original chaos as God's making things *out of nothing* (2 Macc. 7: 28) and not merely, like a world architect, rearranging things that pre-exist. By means of his deliberate command—free from any internal necessity or external pressure—

---

[3] Hebrew had no equivalent for 'nothing' and 'nothingness', concepts that come from Greek classical culture. Although the biblical authors had to make do with the idea of 'primordial chaos', they knew that God's creative action belongs to God and God alone. No creature can ever 'make' something the way God does—a conviction reflected by the fact that *bara*, a word for the effortless (creative and salvific) work of God is used, in its forty-seven occurrences in the OT, almost exclusively for divine actions. On creation see K. Ward, *Religion and Creation* (Oxford: Clarendon, 1996).

God brings into existence and sustains everything: 'Whenever you hide your face, they are dismayed; whenever you take away their breath, they die and return to their dust' (Ps. 104: 29). Were God to 'hide his face', his creation would revert to the 'pit', that is, to non-existence (Ps. 143: 7). Creation, therefore, includes that relatedness between God and creatures, whereby the latter continually depend on the former for their existence. Thus the whole world belongs to God and reveals God's glory. The Psalms respond with praise and admiration: 'The heavens are telling the glory of God; and the firmament proclaims his handiwork' (Ps. 19: 1).

Irenaeus grasped the fact that defining existence as *creation* implies faith in God as *Pantocrator*, the all-powerful and utterly free creator and the one source of everything that exists. By insisting on God's utter transcendence ('nothing above him') and complete liberty in creating the world 'of his own free will', Irenaeus opposed Stoic pantheism and, even more, Gnostic views of divine emanations. Stoic philosophy did not hold God to be a personal being; it saw the universe permeated by reason, a divine fire that kept everything in existence. For such a philosophical outlook there could be no foundational relationship between creatures and the transcendent creator, such as Irenaeus taught. Gnostic schemes of thought varied, but they usually included speculations about 'aeons', a series of emanations from the supreme being. The lowest one of these, a 'demiurge' (Greek 'craftsman'), fashioned the world, a dismal place in which darkness imprisons the divine light and redemption means escaping from that darkness through special knowledge. Against such speculations, Irenaeus insisted on 'the only God' (and hence no divine aeons or emanations) and 'the only creator' (and hence no lower demiurge) who freely made all things and made them good. As well as upholding the goodness of God's entire creation, both spiritual and material, Irenaeus also acknowledged the christological dimension of creation: Christ is the one and only mediator between God and creation.[4]

As we saw in Ch. 4, NT writers recognized the role of the Son in God's creative work (e.g. John 1: 3; 1 Cor. 8: 6). All things were created 'through' the Son and 'for' the Son (Col. 1: 16). The 'only Father' has, in Irenaeus' image, 'two hands', his Son and his Spirit through whom he creates (*Adversus Haereses*, 4. 40. 1). Here Irenaeus prepared the way for the Nicene confession of the eternal, uncreated Son as being the one 'through whom

---

[4] Gnostic thought continues to return in various guises. Modern information technology and its cyberspace, for instance, take people into a notional environment of 'virtual reality' and can diminish their sense of physical objects being embodied in real places.

all things were made' (DH 125–6; ND 7–8), and for the trinitarian teaching developed by the Cappadocians and Augustine: all divine activity 'ad extra' (on the outside), starting from creation, is shared in common by the three persons of the Trinity.

Justin, an older contemporary of Irenaeus, had already drawn some important consequences for a theology of creation that involved the Son: above all, the notion of the 'seeds of the Word' or *semina Verbi* that have been implanted everywhere (see Ch. 1). No place and, even more importantly, no human person is 'outside' the presence of the creative Word and his 'seeds'. Many centuries later, the Second Vatican Council drew on Justin for the theme of the 'seeds of the Word' in its 1965 decree on missionary activity, *Ad Gentes*. The key second footnote of that decree quoted Irenaeus about the Word/Son, through whom all things were made, who is always present to the entire human race and to all creation, and who reveals the Father to all in accordance with the divine plan.

Thus Justin and Irenaeus established some enduring lines for distinctively Catholic teaching about creation. Against recurring attempts to explain the cosmos in terms either of pantheism or of necessary emanations from God, that teaching was to uphold the sovereign divine freedom which through creation brought about a reality different from God and yet in a constant relationship of dependence upon God.[5] God has freely and directly created all that exists; creation radically differs from God (who necessarily exists) and yet totally depends on God. God is intrinsically present in the entire created world (divine immanence), while being radically 'beyond' and 'above' it (divine transcendence). The products of creation are in God (Acts 17: 28), participate in being that belongs preeminently to God, but are not parts of God. Furthermore, created reality—in particular, material reality—is good and not something defective or evil. The incarnation made this clear: the Word through whom 'all things were made' became 'flesh' (John 1: 14), a text repeatedly cited by Irenaeus against the Gnostics and in support of the visible goodness of creation.

A Unique Creation

Both OT theology and Greek culture took for granted the centrality of human existence in the great scheme of things. Instead of grounding

---

[5] Thus the First Vatican Council (1869/70) was to reject philosophical outlooks that supported pantheism or refurbished theories about the emanation of the universe from the divine substance (DH 3002–3, 3021–5; ND 412–18).

matters, as the Greeks did, in the universal qualities of being as one, good, true, and beautiful, the chosen people of God drew their view of the human condition from faith in God as lord of history and creator of the world, with humanity as the climax of God's creative work. The Israelites thought that animals are connected to the ground and, unlike human beings, only indirectly related to God (Gen. 1: 24–5). The Bible opens with two distinct accounts of the 'beginning', both of which drive home the same point: the human being is the 'only creature on earth which God willed for itself' (Vatican II, *Gaudium et Spes*, 24).

Human existence, according to biblical revelation, consists in relationships—between human beings and nature, among human beings themselves, and between human beings and God. The older Yahwist account of creation (Gen. 2) portrays God placing man in the garden and providing for all his needs. The later Priestly tradition (Gen. 1) shows God preparing the 'house' and then bringing in the human tenants: 'male and female' (Gen. 1: 27). The garden and the house belong to the divine proprietor, while humanity can only be God's steward and mouthpiece. Communication is both vertical (between God and humanity) and horizontal (among human beings themselves). The older Yahwist account of creation dwells on the fact that man needs a partner, while the later Priestly version shows God creating humankind as a community. It is to humanity as a whole that God delivers the injunction: 'Be fruitful and multiply, and fill the earth and subdue it' (Gen. 1: 28).

Human creation can respond to and collaborate with the creator— something clearly implied when God says: 'Let us make man in our image, according to our likeness' (Gen. 1: 26). The Bible speaks of one reality that is simultaneously 'image' and 'likeness'. Irenaeus and other early Christian writers developed, however, a basic distinction: the image is permanent, while the likeness is subject to change. Whatever human beings are as God's image, they are and cannot not be: if they were to cease to be God's image, they could no longer be human. The image therefore is the heart of human existence. The likeness is the image in action: it develops; it can progress and regress; it can even disappear through sin. Likeness implies a tension that lasts a whole lifetime.

Through sin those who are created in God's image wish to shape their own being, regardless of God's plan. The fundamental tragedy of sin is that, although persons remain in God's image, they exhibit something fully opposed to what they are and continue to be. We return below to the theme of sin.

The sense of human beings as created in the divine image understands human existence as manifesting God's glory on earth. Unfortunately, Western Christianity has frequently opted for an essentialist reading of what a human being is and lost sight of the aesthetic dimension. It has dwelt upon the triad, memory, understanding, and love, which show how the soul reflects its creator and trinitarian prototype. Eastern Christianity, however, has followed Irenaeus and subsequent writers: humanity is created in God's image and called to participate in God's own being. The theology of the image remains for Eastern Christians fundamental for their reflection on humanity.

God is the prototype, since Genesis proclaims that humanity is created in God's own image. Humanity is the image that understands itself in God's own light and can find its fulfilment only in God. In the third and fourth centuries, the Alexandrian school of theology maintained that only the soul could be the image, since both God and the soul are spiritual in nature; at best, the body somehow participates in what pertains to the soul. The Antiochene school, however, dwelt on the biblical datum that God made the whole human being in the divine image.

Although this might seem a highly technical point, it has far-reaching resonances. Modern philosophy and neurological sciences still heatedly debate what specifically constitutes the human being: is it the self? Is it the brain or some part of it—i.e. the 'hardware', the grey matter which forms the two lobes? Is it the cortex, that controls the two lobes of the brain and links brain activity with bodily operations? Or is it the mind, the 'software' that makes the brain function and operate?[6]

God creates humankind *in the Word*, argued St Athanasius of Alexandria, and so we are created according to the Logos. Here Athanasius introduced an interesting pun: the human is *logikos*, which means both 'rational' and

---

[6] The bibliography on this subject is immense. Here are some examples: G. Basti, *Il Rapporto Mente-Corpo nella Filosofia e nella Scienza* (Bologna: Edizioni Studio Dominicano, 1991); J. C. Eccles, *How the Self Controls the Brain* (Berlin: Springer-Verlag, 1994); id., *Evolution of the Brain: Creation of the Self* (London: Routledge, 1991); A. Kenny, *The Metaphysics of Mind* (Oxford: Oxford University Press, 1989); J. Kim, *Philosophy of Mind* (Boulder, Colo.: Westview Press, 1998); K. R. Popper and J. C. Eccles, *The Self and Its Brain: An Argument for Interactionism* (New York: Routledge, 1984); C. Söling, *Das Gehirn-Seele-Problem: Neurobiologie und theologische Anthropologie* (Paderborn: Schöningh, 1995); F. J. Valera *et al.*, *The Embodied Mind. Cognitive Science and Human Experience* (Cambridge, Mass.: MIT Press, 1992).

'made according to the Logos'. The Letter to the Colossians presented Christ as being the image of the invisible Father, the firstborn over the original creation and the firstborn of the second creation, the resurrection (1: 15, 18). Hence, human beings cannot truly understand what they are unless they do so in the light of Christ. Since God created us in Christ, Athanasius argued, we must be images (lower case) of the perfect Image (upper case) of the Father, Christ himself. Humankind can reach a full knowledge of itself only through, with, and in Christ.[7] 'The Word of God came in his own person', Athanasius concluded, 'so that, as he was the Image of the Father, he could create afresh man after the image' (*De Incarnatione*, 13. 7).

Although all sides agreed that the believer's existence should be 'in Christ', the Alexandrian school stressed the 'spiritual' dimension of human existence according to the prototype, the Word of God manifested to us in Jesus Christ. The Antiochene school, however, held that human persons in their totality, soul and body, are created in the image of Christ and thus should assimilate their existence to the Word made flesh. For the Alexandrian school, the ideal was the Word at the right hand of the Father, while for the Antiochene school the model was Christ who fulfilled the Father's will while he was in the flesh.

Irenaeus blessed God for the incarnation: it enabled human beings to understand the original dignity with which the Father had created them in the beginning: 'For in no other way could we have learned the things of God, unless our Master, existing as the Word, had become man. For no other being had the power of revealing to us the things of the Father, except his own proper Word' (*Adversus Haereses*, 5. 1. 1). It was only through Christ that we could grasp the dignity and task given us through creation.

Two centuries after Irenaeus, Basil of Caesarea reflected on the intimate relationship between the Son and the Father, to whom belongs the unique glory and majesty of the one God. Basil stated an important theological principle: 'the honour paid to the image passes on to the prototype' (*De Spiritu Sancto*, 45). Applied to the interpersonal relations between human beings, Basil's principle illustrates how mutual respect among humans ultimately stems from the respect due to the creator, the source of the dignity that belongs to every individual. Basil's brother, Gregory of Nyssa, turned to the language of painting to portray humankind as God created it:

---

[7] See the concluding doxology of all eucharistic prayers, both East and West: 'through him [Christ], with him, in him ... '.

As painters transfer human forms to their pictures by means of certain colours, laying on their copy the proper and corresponding tints, so that the beauty of the original may be accurately transferred to the likeness, so I would have you understand that our Maker also, painting the portrait to resemble his own beauty, by the addition of virtues, as it were with colours, shows in us his own sovereignty (*De Hominis Opificio*, 5. 1).

In line with the Alexandrian school, Gregory of Nyssa stressed the spiritual dimension of the created image. Gregory distinguished between archetype and prototype, with both terms referring to the divine Word. As archetype, the Word is the modelling source, while as prototype it is a model to be imitated. Only on the spiritual level can humans imitate a prototype, whose essence is divine and incomprehensible (ibid. 11. 3).

Gregory sums up 'the greatness of man' as consisting 'not in his likeness to the created world but in his being in the image of the creator's nature' (ibid. 16. 2). At the same time, as the bridge between 'the divine and incorporeal nature' and 'the irrational life of animals' (ibid. 16. 9), human beings have a responsibility towards the natural world. We will develop below a fuller basis for this responsibility: the interconnectedness of all created things through their common origin, history, and goal.

Stewardship of Creation

The Genesis theme of men and women created in the divine image expresses not only humanity's inherent dignity but also the mission that issues from it. Gregory of Nyssa appreciated how humanity's unique relationship with God goes beyond the merely static beauty of a divine portrait: there are also the virtues that reveal in us God's sovereignty, the attributes that show how we human images imitate the divine prototype. Human images of God manifest the divine rule on earth and have the unique mission of being God's stewards there, continuing and completing God's creative work by presiding in the divine name over the rest of creation. A psalm celebrates the wonderful share in his own dignity that God has granted human beings by giving them authority over the rest of creation: 'You have given them dominion over the works of your hands; you have put all things under their feet, all sheep and oxen, and also the beasts of the field, the birds of the air, and the fish of the sea' (Ps. 8: 6–8). The Yahwist tradition of creation pictures God expressing this human dominion by bringing to the first man all the 'animals of the field' and 'birds of the air' so that he might give them their names (Gen. 2: 19–20).

In his commentary on Genesis, Claus Westermann shows how the Priestly tradition reinterprets the dominion God gives human beings over the animal world (Gen. 1: 28). At the beginning, God places human beings under a strictly vegetarian regime: seed-yielding plants and the fruit of trees (Gen. 1: 29). When the Yahwist account of the flood story ends, the Priestly tradition take up the story and tells of the covenant that God establishes with humanity (and with all creation) through the persons of Noah and his descendants. Here the Bible introduces for the first time a divine permission to eat animal flesh (Gen. 9: 2–3). According to Westermann, this concession from God takes into account the tension stemming from the flood: 'animals are delivered into the hands of humans'.[8] At the same time, the Priestly tradition prohibits eating flesh with blood (Gen. 9: 4), as Leviticus 17: 10–11 will do.

Thus, from the outset, the Bible introduces norms meant to regulate the way human beings preside over the rest of creation. God, the common source of all beings, is the origin of humanity's dominion over the rest of his creatures. All come from God, even if only human beings can hear and respond to God: it is only through Adam, Eve, Noah, and others in the Genesis story that the created universe can hear its creator and find words and actions with which to respond. Only human beings enjoy self-consciousness, and it is only through human beings that the created world is aware of the divine self-communication and can respond appropriately. To borrow Francis of Assisi's language, humanity is to raise its voice and enter into communion with God, on behalf of 'brother sun' and 'sister moon'.

In this history of creation, God remains the one and only Lord, because nothing exists unless God constantly keeps it in existence and does not let it slip back into nothingness. That includes human stewardship as well. As Thomas Aquinas points out, we human stewards of God can never create energy or anything else out of nothing; we can only transform or convert what we have been given.[9] We can only be God's co-workers and collaborators; at best, our dignity lies in the fact that God calls us to be his 'co-creators'.[10]

---

[8] C. Westermann, *Genesis 1–11. A Commentary* (Minneapolis: Augsburg, 1984), 462–3.

[9] Aquinas states that when we make something, change occurs only in terms of 'motion according to quantity, quality, and place' (*ST* I q. 45 a. 2 ad 2); there is a fundamental difference between God's creative activity and the 'making' activity of creatures.

[10] Philip Hefner identifies the human person as a 'created co-creator': *The Human Factor. Evolution, Culture and Religion* (Minneapolis: Fortress, 1995), 35–6.

The fundamental interconnectedness of all creation means that it has only one *history*, which finds in God its source and goal. While the human contribution brings about the birth of *culture*, it gives rise to two conflicting forces which, in the flood story of Genesis, come to a head: the one that seeks God and the other that constructs a world which allows no place for the creator. We shall see how human sin turns work into toil, and life into a burdensome struggle that battles against thorns and thistles and ekes out an existence from the soil (Gen. 3: 17–19). The flood account strikingly portrays the close link between human sin on the one hand, and creation and culture on the other (Gen. 6: 5–8: 22). Described earlier as 'good' (Gen. 1: 31), the very earth has become 'corrupt' through human violence and aberration (Gen. 6: 11–12).

A new age opens after the flood; through the covenant with Noah, God's blessing reaches out to all creatures, both human and non-human (Gen. 9: 1–17). In Noah and his entourage, creation rediscovers its life-giving relation with its maker and readdresses itself to him. The rainbow in the sky is to be, in perpetuity, the symbol of a cosmic covenant with God (Gen. 9: 12–17). While creation and human culture are purified through the flood (in which Christians will see baptism prefigured) and reorient themselves to their creator, God restores the communion he intended from the beginning, and renews his original mission to humanity: 'Be fruitful and multiply, and fill the earth' (Gen. 9: 1; see 1: 28).

A striking recognition of God as the creator and sustainer of everything is expressed in St Paul's hope for fulfilment. He puts human beings and nature together in a common history, characterized by the interplay of two diverse forces: *one* is 'bondage to decay', and the *other* is 'eager longing' for the glorious transformation to come (Rom. 8: 18–25). Human existence is a lifelong pilgrimage towards God, the fullness of being and *final goal* of all creation. When the 'new heaven' and the 'new earth' come to pass (Rev. 21: 1), the whole of creation will be freed from imperfection and made new by the glory of God.

But describing human stewardship and the interconnectedness of all creation, in its origin, history, and goal, is one thing. Assessing humanity's intervention in God's creation throughout the centuries is a different matter. What has Christian and, in particular, Catholic handling of God's creation looked like over the last two thousand years?[11]

[11] See D. Christiansen and W. Grayer (eds.), *'And God Saw That It Was Good': Catholic Theology and the Environment* (Washington, DC: United States Catholic Conference, 1996).

ECOLOGY: MINDING OUR 'HOME'
AND HERITAGE

Since the 1960s, many people have realized that our planet does not possess endless resources and cannot continue to be a life-giving environment unless human beings quickly become much more responsible and ecologically sensitive stewards of the created world. In an epoch-making address delivered to the American Association for the Advancement of Science in 1966, Lynn White placed the burden of the global environmental crisis squarely on the shoulders of Christianity. He singled out Catholic and Evangelical theology as major forces that have shaped Western environmental attitudes. 'By destroying pagan animism', White stated, 'Christianity made it possible to exploit nature in a mood of indifference to the feelings of natural objects.'[12] As a result, White insisted, humanity lost its ability to contemplate nature as God's handiwork, and deemed it less and less worthy of respect. The teaching of Genesis 1: 26–7 about God's making humanity in the divine image, White argued, has been misused to reinforce the idea that human beings can act like 'gods' and behave in any way they like. Such a reading has gone along with a habitual misrepresentation of the mission to multiply and exercise *dominion* over all things (Gen. 1: 28). Humanity, White concluded, has turned things into mere objects, resources to be exploited and squandered at will.

Despite criticisms directed at White's cry of alarm, his fears of an impending ecological disaster seem justified. Although environmental concerns feature on current international agenda, little has been done to safeguard our earth. But did White read correctly the texts of Genesis and later Christian tradition?

The Catholic tradition, as White admitted, has produced a Francis of Assisi, 'the greatest spiritual revolutionary in Western history', who proposed 'an alternative Christian view of nature and man's relation to it'.[13] In his *Canticle of Brother Sun* (also called the *Canticle of the Creatures*), Francis praised God as revealed in the natural world and expressed love for all creatures. The monastic tradition, initiated centuries earlier by Bene-

---

[12] Lynn White, 'The Historical Roots of Our Ecological Crisis', *Science*, 155 (10 March 1967), 1205; id., 'Continuing the Conversation', in I. G. Barbour (ed.), *Western Man and Environmental Ethics: Attitudes toward Nature and Technology* (Menlo Park, Calif.: Addison-Wesley, 1973), 55–64.

[13] 'The Historical Roots of Our Ecological Crisis', 1207.

dict of Norcia, saw God's glory in the whole cosmos, and invited human beings to 'pray and work' in response. The Benedictine tradition, followed by innumerable men and women, cultivated the earth and fostered agricultural customs that respected the local eco-cycle. They encouraged their contemporaries to marvel at God's glory in creation, and express thanksgiving in work, prayer, and song. Such a tradition looks quite incompatible with the innumerable ways in which humanity has abused its God-given 'home': from the unnatural fodder that has spread mad cow disease to uncontrolled deforestation and the squandering of fossil fuels.

Sadly, Catholics have often forgotten the Benedictine and Franciscan traditions that might have helped them fulfil their God-given mission to care for the earth and carry forward God's creative work. In neglecting and destroying nature, Catholics, like millions of others, have been neglecting and destroying themselves and their environment. Human beings have so often forgotten that they form the self-conscious, responsible part of created, interconnected nature. What message might encourage an eco-logical consciousness and responsibility? The themes of (*a*) stewardship' and (*b*) 'the sixth day' suggest two ways of responding to the current ecological crisis.

(*a*) Stewardship implies a relation on three different levels: towards God first, and then towards the present and the future creation. As God's representatives on earth, human beings can govern in God's name only if they deepen and develop a personal relationship with the creator. Such a relationship, therefore, means recognizing that the earth can never be one's personal possession: it is God's gift to humanity and to infra-human creation as a whole. Economic progress should not mean, for example, that one-fifth of the world's population continues to use four-fifths of the planet's resources and condemns millions to perennial poverty. In 1965 the Second Vatican Council called attention to such a 'wretched' state of affairs:

At the very time when the development of economic life could mitigate social inequalities (provided that it be guided and coordinated in a reasonable and human way), it is often made to aggravate them; in some places, it even results in a decline of the social status of the underprivileged and in contempt for the poor. While an immense number of people still lack the absolute necessities of life, some, even in less advanced areas, live in luxury or squander wealth. Extravagance and wretchedness exist side by side. While a few enjoy very great power of choice, the majority are deprived of almost all possibility of acting on their own initiative and responsibility, and often subsist in living and working conditions unworthy of the human person.   (*Gaudium et Spes*, 63)

Besides calling for a Franciscan-style of sharing brotherhood that works here and now for the good of all, stewardship towards God's creation implies a third relationship: towards those created beings that will exist in times to come. A right use of creation remembers the human and non-human 'neighbours' that form the future generations to whom we will bequeath the planet we have inherited. The OT prophets dreamed of a future harmony for the whole of nature, a time when 'the wolf shall live with the lamb, and the leopard shall lie down with the kid, and the calf and the lion and the fatling together, and a little child shall lead them' (Isa. 11: 6; see Ezek. 47: 1–12). What would Isaiah and Ezekiel have made of a world in which human ravages threaten to wipe out wolves, leopards, and lions, and have already destroyed hundreds of species?

(*b*) In terms of the first chapter of Genesis, humanity's mission is to situate itself fully in the 'sixth day of creation', and co-operate with the God who has been at work on all the earlier days. Such teamwork continues what until then has been God's task alone, and will attain its goal on the 'seventh day' of 'rest', when God will be manifested as the Lord of all creation. In the meantime humanity is called to preserve its eco-system and not turn the world into an ecological time-bomb, ready to explode at any time. Thus we can reach the Lord's seventh day and share in the final 'banquet', when God will be 'all in all' (1 Cor. 15: 28). Irenaeus contemplated humanity as made in the image of the uncreated, tripersonal God and progressing under divine guidance towards the 'seventh' day:

Man, a created and organized being, is rendered after the image and likeness of the uncreated God,—the Father planning everything well and giving his commands, the Son carrying these into execution and performing the work of creating, and the Spirit nourishing and increasing [what is made], but man making progress day by day, and ascending towards the perfect, that is, approximating to the uncreated One. (*Adversus Haereses*, 4. 38. 3)

A Coda: Science and Religion

Lynn White's ecological concerns signal a shift that has occurred in the relationship between natural science and Christian (and, specifically,

Catholic) faith in God as creator. This science has given rise to modern technologies that utilize, and sometimes ravage, created realities. Nowadays tensions and challenges concern practice; from Galileo's time to the nineteenth century they arose mainly from theoretical knowledge.

In 1633 the Roman Inquisition condemned Galileo Galilei (1564–1642) for endorsing the system first proposed by Nicolaus Copernicus (1473–1543), the Polish astronomer who had argued that the earth moves around the sun and not vice versa. The condemnation of Galileo still symbolizes the enduring image of an official church refusing to accept new discoveries and trying to curb scientific freedom. The negative stand of many Christians towards the theory of evolution proposed by Charles Darwin (1809–82) further reinforced the image of an anti-scientific church. The evolutionary process, which Darwin detected in biological development and which later science extended in all directions, highlighted the need for the appropriate interpretation of biblical texts, as discussed in Ch. 3 above. In the twentieth century scientific discoveries and technological advances developed in a spectacular fashion. Along with that growth, many came to question the conviction, widely held in the nineteenth and early twentieth centuries, that science alone could answer ultimate questions about meaning and value. Scientists of the calibre of the Nobel prize-winner, Ilya Prigogine (b. 1917), have turned to philosophical and theological issues, while astrophysicists such as Stephen Hawking (b. 1942) and Roger Penrose (b. 1931) speculate on the ultimate nature of time. On its own, scientific progress may prove dehumanizing and extremely dangerous to the whole human race and its environment (e.g. through nuclear weapons and the abuse of energy sources that has led to global warming).

For many people, the priest-paleontologist Pierre Teilhard de Chardin (1881–1955) has symbolized the end of the old antagonisms between science and religion.[14] Far from finding the evolution of the species in conflict with revealed truth, Teilhard acknowledged the wisdom and power of God who through the laws implanted in creation arranged for a marvellous development from within—from the biosphere (with its

---

[14] In recent years John Polkinghorne and some other scientists turned Anglican priests have symbolized for many people the end of old antagonisms between science and religion. A particle physicist, Polkinghorne resigned his professorship at Cambridge University in 1979, was ordained to the ministry, and went on to write a number of significant books on matters involving science and religion. In March 2002 he received the Templeton Prize for wedding scientific thought and Christian faith.

many forms of life), to the noosphere (with its presence of thinking beings), and on to the pneumatosphere (the universe brought through the Holy Spirit or *Pneuma*), and our final destiny in God through Christ. Everything evolves from within, except for human souls which are created immediately by God (DH 1007, 3896; ND 419, 1007). Here, the teaching of the Church recognizes that every single human being is directly related to the creator—a relationship that is not mediated either through other persons or through the evolutionary process itself.

God is truth. Whether found in the religious sphere or in that of science, all truth is based in God and can never be opposed to itself (*Gaudium et Spes*, 36). Pope John Paul II made this point, with reference to the Galileo case, in a 1992 address to the Pontifical Academy of Sciences (ND 173). Previously, at a 1983 symposium of scientists commemorating Galileo's work, the Pope had endorsed a new dialogue between the official church and science (ND 164–76c). In a message he addressed on 1 June 1988 to the Director of the Vatican Observatory, John Paul II stated: 'What is critically important is that each discipline (science and theology) should continue to enrich, nourish, and challenge the other to be more fully what it can be and to contribute to our vision of who we are and what we are becoming.'[15] At the same time, ecological threats and, as we shall see in a later chapter, various developments in medical science have created many challenges for Catholic and other Christian thinkers and leaders.

SIN IN HISTORY

Irenaeus' optimistic picture of humanity, made in 'the image and likeness of God' and 'ascending towards the perfect', had to come to terms with sin. Irenaeus introduced, for the first time in the Christian tradition, a

[15] 'Message of John Paul II', in R. J. Russell *et al.* (eds.), *John Paul II. On Science and Religion: Reflections on the New View from Rome* (Notre Dame, Ind.: University of Notre Dame, 1990), M7. That same message contained a striking set of questions as to the way findings of modern science may enrich our understanding of some Christian beliefs: 'Might contemporary cosmology have something to offer to our reflections on creation? Does an evolutionary perspective bring any light to bear upon theological anthropology, the meaning of the human person as *imago Dei*, the problem of Christology—and even upon the development of doctrine itself? What, if any, are the eschatological implications of contemporary cosmology, especially in the light of the vast future of the universe? Can theological method fruitfully appropriate insights from scientific methodology and the philosophy of science?' (ND 176c). On the science–religion debate, see J. F. Haught, *God After Darwin: A Theology of Evolution* (Boulder, Colo.: Westview Press, 2000).

distinction between image and likeness: 'image' is what we always are, while 'likeness' is what we can become and/or lose through sin. To develop his view of sin and its consequences, Irenaeus drew on Genesis and on Paul's Letter to the Romans. Presenting Christ as the second or last Adam, Irenaeus showed how Christ has reconciled with God the first Adam's sinful descendants, has recapitulated human history, and leads all creation to immortal glory. To understand human sin, Irenaeus was not content to reflect on the symbol of Israel's captivity in Egypt, but went back to the very beginning when Adam and Eve chose an existence contrary to God.

From the Beginning... Sin

The richly symbolic language of the opening chapters of Genesis pictures God as creating all things 'good', with humanity forming the climax of God's creative work. 'The man' and 'the woman' of Genesis 2 transgressed the divine command, ate the forbidden fruit, and lost both their innocent relationship with one another and their trusting relationship with God. The story vividly portrays their loss of innocence and urge to redress their self-image: 'The eyes of both were opened, and they knew that they were naked; and they sewed fig leaves together, and made loincloths for themselves' (Gen. 3: 7). They now 'knew' through their experience the difference between 'good' and 'evil' (Gen. 3: 5). In their guilt they tried to hide 'themselves from the presence of the Lord God' (Gen. 3: 8). Those who hoped that eating the forbidden fruit would make them even more 'like God' (Gen. 3: 5) now anxiously try to get away from God. Sin has disrupted their basic relationship with their divine Lord.

The story of the first sin brilliantly presents what everyman and everywoman do: their instinct is to put the blame on someone else. The man blames the woman and even God: 'the woman whom you gave to be with me, she gave me fruit from the tree' (Gen. 3: 11). The woman blames the crafty serpent who tempted her: 'the serpent tricked me, and I ate' (Gen. 3: 13). But the man and the woman have deliberately disobeyed the divine will and must suffer the consequences.

The Genesis story picturesquely tells what follows the sinful loss of their first innocence, when the man and the woman were unashamedly naked (Gen. 2: 25)—in a guiltless relationship to one another and to God, which traditional language was to call 'original justice'. The biblical text appeals to an ancient explanation for the pain of childbirth, when God says to the woman: 'I will greatly increase your pangs in childbearing; in pain you

FIG. 8. An etching by Albrecht Dürer (d. 1528) shows our 'first parents' deceived by evil and about to fall into sin by eating the forbidden fruit. (Harris Museum and Art Gallery, Preston/ Bridgeman Art Library.)

shall bring forth children' (Gen. 3: 16). In place of an ideal relationship of joyful equality and mutual dependence intended by the creator (Gen. 2: 18–23), the woman finds herself 'ruled over' by her husband (Gen. 3: 16) and named by him 'Eve' (Gen. 3: 20). Where pain now characterizes the woman's experience of giving life through childbearing, something similar holds true of the man. His work in cultivating the garden should have been normal and natural (Gen. 2: 15), but sin turns work into distressing toil (Gen. 3: 17–19). In bringing life, in this case by gaining bread from the ground and its crops, the man too will have to suffer pain. In language that is as fresh as ever, the Genesis story drives home the point: far from enhancing their life, sin leaves the man and the woman less than what they should really be, and ushers in destructive consequences.

The most distressing consequence concerns death. Fashioned from dust (Gen. 2: 7), the man and the woman are by nature mortal; their death should have been like that of Abraham, who was to die surrounded by his family in 'ripe old age'—a death that peacefully completes a life spent in faithful obedience to God (Gen. 25: 1–11).[16] But disobedience to God has changed the experience of death for sinful human beings; death has become a troubling, inexorable fate (Gen. 3: 19), a distressing sign of sin. Flanked by suffering and pain, death signals the radical change sin has brought to the human condition.

Having made a decision unworthy of those created in the divine image (Gen. 1: 26–7), the man and the woman are banished from the garden of Eden into a foreign place. Cherubim and a flaming sword now guard the entrance to the garden and 'the way to the tree of life' (Gen. 3: 24). Other books of the Bible will use exile and suffering in a foreign land to symbolize sin and the lot of sinners: Jesus' parable of the lost son, for example, pictures the dissolute sinner as leaving his parental home for 'a distant country' (Luke 15: 13). The last book of the Bible will portray final damnation as 'the second death' to which the damned will be banished (Rev. 20: 10, 14) and final redemption as entering a heavenly Jerusalem and receiving God's abundant blessings from the 'tree of life'. For humanity, paradise regained will mean re-entering the garden and being given access to the final 'tree of life', watered by the river of life coming from the Lamb (Rev. 22: 1–2).

---

[16] According to the Yahwist tradition, physical death is humanity's return to dust and the handing back of life's breath to God. The OT expresses a firm belief in afterlife only in post-exilic times.

The Genesis story sees the disobedience of Adam and Eve as initiating an avalanche of sins. Cain murders his brother; this fratricide paves the way for a terrifying increase of violence and the unbridled revenge killings practised by Cain's descendant, Lamech (Gen. 4: 8, 23–4). Violence also brings a breach of boundaries between heaven and earth. 'Beings of the heavenly court' take human wives even though their offspring remain mortal and do not become semi-divine (Gen. 6: 1–4). Whatever the source of this fragment of mythology, lustful practices contribute to the steady advance of sin that degrades the human condition. Once called 'good' (Gen. 1: 31), the earth itself is now corrupted through the wicked deeds of human beings (Gen. 6: 11–13). In their colourful way, the opening chapters of Genesis show human beings opting against God and one another. Evil decisions coalesce and shape a whole situation of sin, which needs 'cleansing' to allow for a new beginning (Gen. 9: 1–7).

Although God's judgement takes the form of a catastrophic flood, the merciful love of God still operates. Earlier in the Genesis story, God provides garments of skin to replace the flimsy clothing of fig leaves, and fittingly dresses up the man and the woman after they sin (Gen. 3: 21). He puts a 'mark' on the first murderer, so that no one would kill Cain (Gen. 4: 15). Then, the Bible uses Babylonian traditions of prehistoric floods to highlight God's faithful mercy that sharply contrasts with the stubbornness and the sinful inclinations of the human heart. At the flood, God respects human freedom and offers all people the option of avoiding the impending doom. He then rescues Noah and a remnant of human beings and animals: they are the ones who have taken up God's offer (Gen. 6: 5–8: 22).

Notwithstanding the new beginning marked by God's covenant with Noah, the history of sin continues. The story of the tower of Babel expresses an arrogant attempt to overreach human limitations (Gen. 11: 1–9). The attempt ends in an insuperable breakdown in human communications: the people are scattered over the face of the earth and their one language is broken up into many. The biblical text takes an old legend about the origin of the different language groups and uses it to symbolize proud desires to procure fame and security, something that quickly proves self-destructive (Gen. 11: 4).

Genesis thus illustrates how sin advances gradually, steadily, and inexorably. It has a 'history': the sum of many individual, free, and concrete choices that coalesce to alienate humanity from God. Unlike the man and the woman of Gen. 3, sin cannot be blamed on 'the serpent' or some other obnoxious source. Humanity chooses to become 'like God' and to experience existentially ('to know') the difference between good and evil (Gen. 3: 5). The avalanche effect of sin, before and after the flood, continues to account for the progressive separation sin brings between the creator and humankind. The sum of so many single evil options forms a wedge that pushes God and humanity further apart. The cherubim with the flaming swords at the garden's door (Gen. 3: 24) symbolize the need for repentance, conversion, and purification. Only thus can humanity again receive access to its creator.

The opening chapters of Genesis present the sinfulness that emerged at humanity's origins and left an enduring legacy of evil in options against God, oneself, other human beings, and created nature. Catholic Christianity came to express that heritage in terms of inherited 'original' sin and deliberate personal sin.

Original Sin

Christians have always understood baptism as the means by which God frees human beings from sin, brings them a rebirth, and through the Holy Spirit makes them new creations in Christ (Rom. 6–8). In ancient Christian catacombs, numerous tombstones indicate the length of this new existence, showing the exact number of days, months, and years the person lived after being baptized.

In the course of the second century, or perhaps even earlier, Christians started baptizing children and infants, as well as continuing to baptize adults. From the third century, Catholic theology had to come to terms with an issue that is still controversial today: does baptism always remit sins, even in the case of infant baptism? Adults become sinners, and obviously do so through their own free choice. But what about infants and children who have not yet reached the age of reason and are too young to have consented to sin? If baptism always remits sin, what could that sin be in the case of infants? In this way reflection on 'original sin' developed out of established practice and came to a head in the late fourth century, in the controversy between Augustine of Hippo and the disciples of Pelagius.

Pelagius and his followers, as we saw in Ch. 1, highlighted the power of human freedom and encouraged an ascetical life. For the Pelagians, as they came to be known, Adam's sin had not interiorly harmed his descendants and, in particular, had left intact their natural use of free will. Hence human beings could achieve salvation through their own sustained efforts.[17] But babies, they argued, are born quite sinless and so their baptism serves only to insert them into the Church.

Before setting out the teaching on original sin developed by Augustine and others, we must first summarize the drift of a key passage from Paul: Romans 5: 12–21. The apostle, who sees all human beings to be enslaved to sin and death, ascribes this universal misery not only to Adam as humanity's first parent but also to all human beings, since they ratify their present, ungraced state by their own personal sins. Paul considers Adam the initial cause of humanity's sinful and mortal condition: through him 'sin entered into the world' (Rom. 5: 12*a*) and death was its direct consequence (Rom. 5: 12*b*). Then Paul adds the conclusion that 'death spread to all, because all sinned' (Rom. 5: 12*c–d*). Paul considers Adam a historical figure like the rest of us, and we all sin through the bad exercise of our human freedom. In the wake of Adam's evil influence, we continued promoting a universal situation of slavery to sin and death.

But where Adam initiated and headed the age of universal sin and death, Christ heads the age of grace and life that God offers to all (Rom. 5: 14). Paul is concerned with something greater than the mere remission of sins: he deals with the full inheritance that will be ours in Christ at the end of time. Paul repeatedly insists in Romans 5 that Christ's benefits prove incomparably greater than all the harm caused by Adam and his descendants. Christ gives life in a superabundant way, which far surpasses the deadly impact of sin. Thus, in dealing with the history of sin, the apostle compares and contrasts what has come from Adam and what comes from Christ; it is only in and through Christ that anyone can be justified. Lastly we should add that Paul does not address some of the questions that Augustine and the Pelagians were to raise in the fourth century: sin's transmission from one generation to the next, the particular question of infant baptism, and children's need to be delivered from an inherited sinfulness.[18]

Long before Augustine, Tertullian (d. *c.*225) and Cyprian (d. 258)— both of Carthage in North Africa—tried to explain the Church's baptismal practice. They believed that we are all born into this world carrying a

---

[17] Over the centuries Pelagianism has surfaced again and again: e.g. under modern forms of secular humanism, which, while reducing 'salvation' to this-worldly success, understands such success as a goal to be reached by one's work and efforts.

[18] See J. A. Fitzmyer, *Romans*, Anchor Bible 33 (New York: Doubleday, 1993), 405–28.

'wound', or bearing a 'wounded inheritance'. Since this 'inherited sin' does not result from any deliberate act of our own will against God, it can never bar our way to God's mercy. When writing about baptism, Cyprian distinguished the effects of baptism. First and foremost, baptism restores humanity to full communion with God the Father in Christ and through the Holy Spirit; its secondary effect is to remit sin: 'the Father sent the Son to preserve us and give us life, in order that he might restore us' (*De Opere et Eleemosynis*, 1).

Augustine resisted the Pelagians on two grounds.[19] First, the long-standing practice of baptizing infants and doing so for the remission of sins meant that infants come into the world in some kind of inherited sinful state. Second, since God sent his Son to save the whole of humanity, everyone must somehow be under the reign of sin and consequently in need of baptism. Without being baptized into the life of Christ, no one could have access to God. Given that everyone needs salvation, then baptism must be required of and available to all human beings, including children. Since baptism is necessary for salvation, Augustine had to conclude that those children who died without baptism could not inherit eternal life, and suffered what he called 'the lightest possible condemnation', the nature of which he could not 'define' (*Contra Iulianum*, 5. 44). He also drew the conclusion that refusing to baptize a child constituted an act of injustice and cruelty towards that child (*De Gratia Christi et de Peccato Originali*, 2. 5. 5). Children and babies, as well as adults, have the right to be 'born from water and the Spirit', so that they may enter the kingdom of God (John 3: 5).

Unable to read the NT easily in the original Greek, both Augustine and before him Ambrosiaster (an otherwise unknown fourth-century writer who commented on Paul's letters and was for long confused with St Ambrose of Milan) understood the Old Latin translation of Romans 5: 12*d*—'in whom all sinned'—to mean that we are all born sinners 'in Adam'. Being incorporated in advance in Adam, all men and women have already sinned en bloc in the very person of Adam. When discussing Romans 5: 12*c* ('death spread to all'), Augustine interpreted 'death' as bodily death. The classical philosophy of his day encouraged Augustine to understand death simply as a threat and imperfection: it has to be God's punishment and a direct consequence of Adam's sin.

---

[19] On the mindset of Pelagius and his followers, see Peter Brown, *Augustine of Hippo: A Biography* (Berkeley, Calif.: University of California Press, new edn. 2000), 462–4.

Challenged by the Pelagians, Augustine led the other bishops at the Sixteenth Council of Carthage (AD 418) in upholding the following positions: first, physical death is the direct consequence of sin; second, the universal and constant Catholic tradition is that of baptizing children 'for the remission of sins'; and, third, whoever dies in 'original sin'—i.e. without receiving baptism—is condemned to eternal damnation (DH 222–4; ND 501–2). Even though incapable of committing personal sins, children have inherited from Adam 'original sin, which must be expiated by the bath of regeneration' (DH 223; ND 502).

In their present state, Augustine insisted, human beings suffer greatly from the consequences of Adam's sin; their created condition of freedom is deeply impaired, though not destroyed. Against Pelagius and his followers Augustine rightly asserted that, whatever belongs to our human condition, cannot be a matter of individual choice and that, at all times, human beings truly need God's grace to participate in Christ's redemption. Augustine understood too that in challenging the reality of original sin the Pelagians called into question the meaning of baptism itself, and of our rebirth in Christ as the necessary requirement for salvation.

Although earlier theology had formulated original sin as a statement about the uniqueness of Christ's mediation and his redemption of humanity, after Augustine and the Pelagian controversy it became more an assertion about the corrupt nature of our human condition. Irenaeus had shown how in Christ we should understand our existence as created in the image of God; Augustine and the Sixteenth Council of Carthage added: only in Christ do we come to the newness of life and to a full communion with God. In Christ, we can come to know and welcome God's original plan for humanity and, in the same Christ, we can more than recover the treasures lost through sin.

The official Catholic teaching on original sin, as developed in the fifth and sixth centuries, expressed the sinful condition of all human beings: we may be free, but we are all born sinners. The Second Council of Orange (AD 529) was to condemn Pelagius posthumously for holding that through Adam's sin 'the freedom of the soul remained unharmed'; Adam's 'fall' damaged all his descendants and, in particular, their 'freedom of the soul' (DH 371–2; ND 504–5). They are all born deprived of the life of grace that they ought to have possessed and would have possessed but for Adam's sin. Bodily death continued to be considered the primary sign and conse-quence of original sin (ibid.). Thus official teaching emphasized the need for spiritual rebirth through baptism: the fullness of life and grace is no natural right or personal achievement, but God's free gift through Christ. Hence 'original sin' refers not only to our human solidarity in sin but also to our call to a new, supernatural life in Christ. Far from being merely a depressing statement about the wounded or deficient nature of our inherited human condition, the doctrine of original sin underlines humanity's need for Christ's grace: there is no way to true fulfilment and eternal life except through him.

In the Middle Ages, Catholic teaching and theology added only a few footnotes to the teaching on original sin that came down from the patristic period. In a letter of 1201, Pope Innocent III distinguished personal sin from original sin. Unlike personal sin, original sin is simply inherited and does not involve any deliberate offence against God. Consequently, in the case of infants, who are not yet capable of personal conversion, original sin can be 'forgiven' through baptism alone. Innocent added that, whereas those infants who die in the state of original sin will not enjoy the beatific vision, hell is a punishment reserved for those (adults) who have sinned deliberately against God (DH 780; ND 506). The Pope thus settled an issue, raised already by Augustine: do unbaptized infants merit hell? Medieval theologians proposed the existence of 'limbo', appealing to later teaching that had been falsely attributed to the Sixteenth Council of Carthage (DH 224), and that spoke of 'a certain middle place', which was neither heaven nor hell. We return in a later chapter to the question of the final destiny of the unbaptized.

The sixteenth-century leaders of the Protestant Reformation reopened the issue of original sin, but at the other extreme from any Pelagian optimistic minimalizing of the damage caused by Adam's fall. Martin Luther, John Calvin, and other Reformers looked pessimistically at the human condition. While Augustine spoke of a *massa alienata* or *damnata* in humanity's 'one body' condemned in sin, as opposed to the *massa candida* or purified body (*Sermo* 293), Reformed theology first interpreted Augustine's *massa damnata* as a *massa perditionis* or body condemned to eternal punishment. Adam's sin had a maximal effect, inasmuch as it had totally corrupted human beings and completely destroyed their freedom. Luther, in particular, identified human concupiscence or disordered desire as the presence of original sin in us; he understood concupiscence to be a direct consequence of Adam's fall and an irresistible inclination to sin which persists even after baptism. The Reformers knew that justification uniquely belongs to Christ; consequently salvation comes through faith alone (*sola fide*). Humanity's role in the process of justification can only be passive and receptive.

In its fifth session (1546) the Council of Trent produced a decree on original sin that, while largely reaffirming earlier teaching, added some important insights and emphases. The grace of justification can be understood only in relational terms: it is God's gift to humanity, while the process of conversion constitutes the human response to that same gift. Trent, while refusing to interpret original sin as a constitutive element of our human condition, made five points. First, through the merits of Christ baptism truly remits the guilt of original sin and makes the baptized 'the beloved children of God'. Second, baptism restores the 'holiness and justice' lost through sin.[20] Third, original sin is transmitted through 'propagation', something the Council refused to specify further. Fourth, concupiscence remains in the baptized as an 'inclination to sin'; even though concupiscence 'comes from [Adam's] sin and inclines to [personal] sin', it is not 'sin in the true and proper sense'. Fifth, Trent understood 'death' as referring to the 'captivity in the power of . . . the devil' that draws upon itself 'the wrath and indignation of God' (DH 1510–15; ND 507–12). Consequently, the effect of original sin is spiritual rather than bodily death.

The emphasis of this official Catholic teaching on original sin was positive rather than negative: it stresses 'the grace of our Lord Jesus Christ' rather than the depravity of human beings. Original sin allows us to understand that evil cannot be a power or an actual *being* that exists on some kind of par with God; evil is the direct result of some action (a *doing*) on the part of God's creatures, whether angelic or human. Catholic teaching also indicates that evil does not necessarily characterize our universe: although sin and evil can lord it over history, the final say always belongs to God. Such teaching reflects the *Exultet*, a hymn of praise sung during the Easter Vigil, which goes back to the time of St Augustine and calls original sin the 'happy fault' that merited for us such a Saviour.

The twentieth century brought new support and challenges for the doctrine of original sin. Writers such as G. K. Chesterton (1874–1936) and Reinhold Niebuhr (1892–1971) commented that original sin is probably

---

[20] The Council of Trent, *Decree on Original Sin* (DH 1511, 1515; ND 508, 512). Trent chose the words 'holiness and justice' as biblical concepts that could express God's gift to humanity before the fall.

the most credible and even obvious article of Christian belief. When born into this world, babies are normally welcomed with love but also inherit a sinful situation for which they are not personally responsible. At least partly, they are at the mercy of a legacy of evil that stretches back to the beginning of human history. The doctrine of original sin supplies a plausible account for a situation that every newcomer on the human scene must face. Second, a modern sense of human solidarity in doing good and in committing evil encourages a more comprehensive understanding of original sin. We experience this solidarity for good (in the new life brought by Jesus Christ) and for evil (in a stubborn propensity to sin that the baptized must confront even after the deepest personal conversion). Third, polygenism, the view that the human race does not derive from an original pair of ancestors but from many, seems to threaten the doctrine of original sin and its transmission to all the descendants of 'Adam and Eve'. In a 1950 encyclical, *Humani Generis*, Pope Pius XII warned that polygenism may not be clearly reconcilable with belief in original sin and its transmission (DH 3897; ND 420). Some Christians turn to the Bible to take a stand for monogenism against polygenism. But this is a thoroughly modern problem: neither the authors of Genesis nor Paul could have taken a position on something they knew nothing about. While theology discusses the possibility of polygenism, some molecular biologists entertain the idea that our race may derive not from many, but from one original couple.[21]

Infant baptism continues to be questioned. Many argue that only adolescents or adults can decide whether or not to become Christians and be baptized. Augustine, the pastor, felt it his duty to 'labour on behalf of those children who, though under the protection of parents, are left more destitute and wretched than orphans'. He was speaking about believers' unbaptized children, babies who were still 'unable to demand

---

[21] *Homo sapiens sapiens* emerged in Africa. Molecular biology and mitochondrial DNA testing suggest a hypothesis, popularly known as the 'Lucky Mother' or the 'African Eve'. Relying solely on maternal lineage, organelle genetics point to one phylogeny (one biological strain), so that all modern human mitochondria would have originated from an 'Eve' who lived in Africa somewhere more than 100,000 years ago. See R. L. Cann, M. Stoneking, and A. C. Wilson, 'Mitochondrial DNA and Human Evolution', *Nature*, 325 (1987), 31–6; A. C. Wilson and R. L. Cann, 'The Recent African Genesis of Humans', *Scientific American*, 266 (1992), 68–73; A. G. Thorne and M. H. Wolpoff, 'The Multiregional Evolution of Humans', ibid. 76–83; F. J. Ayala, 'The Myth of Eve: Molecular Biology and Human Origins', *Science*, 270 (1995), 1930–6.

for themselves' the grace of Christ that their parents 'denied them' (*De Peccatorum Meritis*, 3. 13. 22). In response to Pelagius, Augustine wrote: 'Let him grant that Jesus is Jesus even to infants ... He shall, indeed, save his people; and among his people surely there are infants ... In infants, too, there are original sins, on account of which he can be Jesus, that is, Saviour, even unto them' (*De Nuptiis et Concupiscentia*, 2. 35. 60). When parents baptize their children, they show their own faith that baptism brings the one meaningful existence they know. By choosing not to baptize their offspring, believers may be questioning the truth that Jesus Christ is 'the way, the truth and the life' for all (John 14: 6).

Personal Sin

Where Paul's Letter to the Romans stands behind the development of the doctrine of original sin, Catholic views on personal sin draw heavily on the OT scriptures. The last section of this chapter completes our outline of the human condition. Having examined sinfulness in its inherited form, we now summarize Catholic thinking about the sinfulness that results from personal freedom. Some questions, however, will need to be delayed for later chapters on grace, the sacraments, and moral theology.[22]

Prophets and Wise Men

God's covenant with Noah recalls the conviction that human beings have been created in the divine 'image' (Gen. 9: 6). Yet the biblical narrative rarely loses sight of the sinful failures and even slavery to evil that plague humankind. The Ten Commandments sum up various duties towards God and neighbour (Exod. 20: 2–17; Deut. 5: 6–21). The Deuteronomic version, in particular, goes on to insist that obedience to these commandments will bring real welfare and rich blessings (Deut. 6: 1–3). The divine commandments spell out the conditions of human well-being, but they also hint at persistent iniquity. Human beings lapse into idolatry by setting up false gods. They murder other people, commit adultery, steal, and bear false witness. The OT repeatedly condemns these and other sins as rebellion against the Lord, as foolishness, and as infidelity to the covenant relationship with God.

The great OT prophets, in particular, denounce human crimes and offences. In the name of God, Isaiah inveighs against the people's religious

---

[22] For a summary of the issues and a bibliography on sin, see 'Sin', *Oxford Dictionary of the Christian Church*, 1505.

superficiality (Isa. 1: 10–20); they must learn to 'rescue the oppressed, defend the orphan, and plead for the widow' (Isa. 1: 17). Amos warns Israel against trampling on the poor, pushing aside the needy, and taking bribes (Amos 5: 11–12). Through the prophet Hosea, God indicts Israel. Sin brings suffering and death to the whole of creation: 'Swearing, lying and murder, and stealing and adultery break out; bloodshed follows bloodshed. Therefore the land mourns, and all who live in it languish; together with the wild animals and the birds of the air, even the fish of the sea are perishing' (Hos. 4: 2–3). Israel must learn again to 'seek' God and 'live' (Amos 5: 4). Sin repudiates God's offer of life and love.

Personal responsibility for sin is by no means absent in the Genesis story: Adam, Eve, and Cain, for example, are pictured as personally culpable. The free exercise of personal responsibility ultimately accounts for the heinous nature of sin and the outrageous disruption it brings about in God's order of creation. However, Jeremiah (31: 27–30) and, even more clearly, Ezekiel (18: 1–4) underscore individual responsibility. Human beings are prone to blame others (e.g. parents or ancestors), instead of recognizing their personal guilt that brings misfortune. God is not powerless or deaf; it is the contamination of sin that wrecks people's lives (Isa. 59: 1–21). Sins are free choices made from the heart; God wants to change wicked human hearts and turn sinners into obedient people (Ezek. 11: 19–21).

Psalm 51, the *Miserere*, understood as King David's prayer after his sins of adultery and murder (2 Sam. 11: 1–27), sums up OT thought on the evil of sin. In the first place, sin is a personal offence against God: 'Against you, you alone, have I sinned, and done what is evil in your sight' (Ps. 51: 4). Terrible injustice has been committed against Uriah the Hittite, Bathsheba's husband, but the fundamental evil of sin consists in the ruptured relationship with God. Sin is a clear sign of the absence of true wisdom and of a joyless heart (Ps. 51: 6). The *Miserere*, with the parable of the prodigal son (Luke 15: 11–32), has shaped profoundly the way Catholics (and many other Christians) understand sin—not as a merely ethical evil, let alone a regrettable mistake, but as a personal offence against a loving God for which one must take responsibility and ask forgiveness. Like David in the *Miserere* the prodigal acknowledges his sins to be first and foremost an offence against God ('I have sinned against heaven') and only then an offence against his father (Luke 15: 18, 21).

Indebted to the OT and the Jewish sense of sin, Western Catholic priests and others recite the *Miserere* every Friday at morning prayer.

That psalm (and, behind it, the story of David's adultery and murder) and Jesus' parable of the prodigal son have also moulded the way Catholics (and other Christians) react to their sins. In recognizing their guilt and asking pardon of God, they follow a middle path between (*a*) a pathological scrupulosity, which compulsively detects sin where none exists or tortures itself over past sins long forgiven by God, and (*b*) a laxity, which refuses to accept one's culpability and dismisses even grave sins as minor 'mistakes' or blemishes on one's record caused by unfortunate circumstances and/or the failure of others.

Before leaving the OT, let us add a word about the Wisdom of Solomon, the most theological of all the deuterocanonical works (see Ch. 3). Written only a few years before the birth of Jesus, it pictures poignantly the reasoning of sensual and ungodly sinners (Wis. 1: 16–2: 24). They think of themselves as being 'born by mere chance' and of death as the end of their existence. Life has no meaning for them, and they give themselves to sensual satisfaction—even at terrible cost to others. Wisdom allows us to listen in to their talk and thoughts: 'Let us oppress the righteous poor man; let us not spare the widow or regard the grey hairs of the aged. But let our might be our law of right' (Wis. 2: 10–11). The OT prophets also denounce the oppression of the helpless, righteous people. But the Book of Wisdom goes further in depicting dramatically the way in which wicked sinners urge each other to live frivolously and persecute mercilessly. Their wickedness has blinded them; their sin clouds and corrupts their reasoning; they know neither God nor 'the secret purposes of God' (Wis. 2: 21–2).

The New Testament and Beyond

Jesus and his first followers keep up the Jewish teaching on sin while adding some new accents. Jesus saw that sin comes from within a person (e.g. Mark 7: 20–3; Matt. 5: 27–8). Like the author of Wisdom, he knew that something goes wrong in the human mind and heart even before sinners commit evil actions. Jesus upheld the Ten Commandments (Mark 12: 19) and followed the prophets in stigmatizing social injustice, especially the failure to act justly and lovingly towards those in terrible need (Luke 16: 19–31). Jesus went so far, according to one tradition, as to make the Final Judgement depend simply on our practical concern for the hungry, the sick, prisoners, homeless persons, and others in great need (Matt. 25: 31–46). Jesus broke new ground by linking together the command to love

God and love our neighbour (Mark 12: 28–34). This was to turn all sins into failures to follow the love-command.

The NT authors normally do not add much to the OT teachings on sin. James, for example, stigmatizes abuses committed by the wealthy (2: 1–7; 4: 13–17; 5: 1–6). Yet many of these warnings not only have their background in the OT prophetic and wisdom traditions but also echo sayings of Jesus about the dangers of wealth. But the Johannine literature and the Pauline letters introduce new themes when writing about sin.

The striking Christocentrism of John entails representing sin as choosing darkness, hatred, and falsity, rather than light, love, and truth. Thus sin becomes a refusal to 'come' to Christ and believe in him. This very Christocentric perspective on faith and sin also includes introducing its counterpoint, the devil, 'a murderer from the beginning' and 'the father of lies' (John 8: 44). Sinners are 'children of the devil' (1 John 3: 8). Even more than John, Paul almost personifies sin itself. Sin is a cosmic force of evil that enters into human beings through their submission to it. Along with death, its fearful consequence and expression, sin has exercised dominion over human beings and made them its slaves (Rom. 5–8). Believers cease to be slaves of sin when they become God's slaves (Rom. 6: 15–23). Another strong emphasis from Paul is his teaching that 'all have sinned' (Rom. 3: 23), Jews by offending against God's written law and Gentiles by not following what they could know through the visible things God has made and through the law written in their hearts (Rom. 1: 18–3: 20).

In many ways, Paul illustrates how sin threatens the life of the Church, especially when believers turn back to the lifestyle of their 'old self' that they have renounced at baptism (Rom. 6: 6; see Eph. 4: 22; Col. 3: 9). Sin can manifest itself as instability in the profession of faith, or the acceptance of a 'different gospel' (Gal. 1: 6). Believers can become 'lazy', 'faint-hearted', 'weak' (1 Thess. 5: 14), envious, and quarrelsome (1 Cor. 1–4). They can bring civil cases against each other 'before the unrighteous', rather than turn for help to 'the saints' (1 Cor. 6: 1). Paul enjoins Christians to 'deliver to Satan for the destruction of the flesh' anyone guilty of illicit sexual relationships (1 Cor. 5: 1–5). Some of the Corinthian Christians abuse the eucharistic assemblies (1 Cor. 11: 17–30), or accept 'false apostles, deceitful workmen', who disguise themselves as 'apostles of Christ' (2 Cor. 11: 13). Paul admits that he is afraid to visit the Corinthians a third time, since he may encounter 'quarrelling, jealousy, anger, selfishness, slander, gossip, conceit, and disorder' (2 Cor. 12: 20).

Post-NT Christian teaching clarified biblical thinking on sin and, as we saw above, articulated the doctrine of original sin. The Church of the second and third centuries, as we shall see in Ch. 7 when dealing with the sacrament of reconciliation, specified those sins that could never be remitted: adultery, wilful murder, and idolatry (or apostasy).

St Augustine developed three definitions of sin. First, sin is 'anything done, said or desired against the eternal law' (*Contra Faustum*, 22. 27), a definition that in reverse order prompted many writers to call sin any thought, word, or deed against the will of God.[23] Augustine explained eternal law as 'the divine order or will of God, which requires the preservation of natural order, and forbids its violation' (ibid.). Speaking of sin as disobedience to the *will of God* (rather than 'against the natural law'), Augustine made it clear that sin is no mere breach of an impersonal law but a personal act of rebellion disrupting our relationship with God.

Augustine's second conception of sin centred around an egoistic love of self, associated with a deep unwillingness to love God. Quoting Sirach 10: 13 as 'Pride is the beginning of sin', Augustine asked: 'And what is pride but the craving for undue exaltation? And this is undue exaltation, when the soul abandons him to whom it ought to cleave as its end, and becomes a kind of end to itself' (*De Civitate Dei*, 14. 13). Augustine distinguished between two cities moulded by two distinct loves: 'The earthly by the love of self, even to the contempt of God; the heavenly by the love of God, even to the contempt of self. The former, in a word, glories in itself, the latter in the Lord' (ibid. 14. 28).

Third, Augustine also defined sin as a 'turning away from God and turning toward creatures' (*De Libero Arbitrio*, 2. 53). Sin, as 'aversion' or turning away from the contemplation of God and 'conversion' or turning to creatures, brings about 'a disorder and a perversity', because sinners distance themselves from the creator, the highest good in person, and turn towards inferior, created realities (*Ad Simplicianum*, 1. 2. 18). Augustine considered such a lapse of the will to be evil, 'because it is contrary to the order of nature, and an abandonment' of the good 'which has supreme being for some other thing which has a lesser [good]' (*De Civitate Dei*, 12. 8). Augustine's Platonist background supported this third version of sin: on the hierarchical scale of existence, the sinner freely decides to move downwards rather than upwards. Augustine underscored the fact that sin

---

[23] Thomas Aquinas e.g. cites this definition in *ST* I-II q. 71 a. 6.

proceeds from a deliberate and free decision on the creature's part to discard God's plan and determine one's own actions; the creature turns to selfishness as opposed to interdependence and interconnectedness, two fundamental characteristics of God's creation (see *De Civitate Dei*, 14. 11).

The Catholic tradition has often oscillated between the legal and the relational understanding of sin (Augustine's first two definitions): sin is a decision against God's law or the disruption of the creature's relationship with the creator. Those who explain sin as contrary to the divine will or the 'eternal law' can appeal to Vatican II's declaration on religious liberty, *Dignitatis Humanae*. It calls 'the supreme norm of human life' the 'divine law itself—eternal, objective, and universal—whereby God orders, directs and governs the whole world and the ways of the human community with a wise and loving plan' (no. 3). Vatican II understands here 'the divine law' as equivalent to what has often been called 'the natural law', an objective moral order intended by God for all human beings and their world. Hence *Gaudium et Spes* took sin to be an obstacle that bars the way to God's plan being actualized for humanity: Jesus, it declared, came to free humanity from the bondage of sin which 'has diminished the human being, blocking the path to fulfilment' (no. 13).

In the wake of Vatican II, Catholic teaching explored in greater depth the personal and relational implications of sin (Augustine's second definition). In a 1984 apostolic exhortation John Paul II defined sin as 'the radical cause of all wounds and divisions between people, and in the first place between people and God' (*Reconciliation and Penance*, 4). The *Catechism of the Catholic Church* summed up the Church's tradition as follows: 'the sinner wounds God's honour and love, his own human dignity as one called to be a son of God, and the spiritual well-being of the church, of which each Christian ought to be a living stone' (no. 1487).

We should note two further significant pieces of Catholic teaching on sin: the distinction between 'mortal' and 'venial' sin, and the growing awareness of 'social' sin. On the basis of the NT distinction between sins that 'exclude from the kingdom of God' (e.g. 1 Cor. 6: 9–10) and those that do not do so (Jas. 3: 2; 1 John 1: 8; 5: 16–17), the Church has consistently distinguished 'mortal' from 'venial' sins. Mortal or 'deadly' sins involve (*a*) a deliberate and radical turning away from God that comes (*b*) through clear knowledge and (*c*) full consent (*d*) in a truly serious matter (see DH 1537, 1444, 1680–2; ND 1626, 1938, 1945). Mortal sin, hence, turns us into 'enemies of God' and entails the loss of sanctifying grace and the risk of eternal damnation (DH 1680; ND 1626). Venial or 'excusable' sins, through which 'we are not excluded from the grace of God', truly harm our relationship with God and with others, but do not entail a direct, fundamental choice against God (ibid.). Thomas Aquinas was the first to systematize the distinction between 'mortal' and 'venial' sin (*Summa contra Gentiles*, 3. 139; *ST* I-II q. 88 a. 1). Together with the 1973 rite for the sacrament of reconciliation, the 1983 Code of Canon Law and the 1990 Code of Canons for the Oriental Churches (the two official legal codes for the Western and Eastern Catholic Church, respectively) converge in speaking of 'grave' sins and 'venial' sins, and in dropping the term 'mortal' sins. The *Catechism of the Catholic Church* (1992) uses, however, both 'mortal' and 'grave' when explaining the forgiveness of sins in the sacrament of reconciliation. Which terminology will eventually prevail, 'mortal' or 'grave', is a very minor issue when compared with the harm sins do to human beings in their relationships with God, with one another, with themselves, and with their world.

While the language of 'mortal' or 'grave' sin, as distinguished from 'venial' sin, has a long history, teaching about 'social' sin and 'sinful structures' of society has emerged more forcefully and explicitly in modern times. Since Leo XIII's 1891 encyclical, *Rerum Novarum*, popes led the way in developing Catholic teaching on the rights and obligations of different members of society in their relationship to the common good, both national and international. The Second Vatican Council encouraged at every level justice in the social order (*Gaudium et Spes*, 9, 63–93), and in the Decree on the Apostolate of Lay People called on Catholics to participate actively in social causes (*Apostolicam Actuositatem*, 7, 8, 13). Social justice, international solidarity, and human rights became constant themes of John Paul II's teachings. In a 1987 encyclical, *Sollicitudo Rei Socialis*, he used the concepts of 'social sin' and 'structures of sin'—language already found in his 1984 apostolic exhortation, *Reconciliation and Penance*.

John Paul II underlined the fact that 'sin, in the proper sense, is always a personal act, since it is an act of freedom on the part of an individual person and not properly of a group or community'. Then, he added that 'to speak of social sin means . . . to recognize that, by virtue of human solidarity which is as mysterious and intangible as it is real and concrete, each individual's sin in some way affects others'. To the 'ascending' solidarity that is 'the profound and magnificent mystery of the communion of saints', there corresponds another perverse, 'descending' solidarity:

a 'communion of sin, whereby a soul that lowers itself through sin drags down with itself the church and, in some way, the whole world'. Thus John Paul II revived Augustine's third definition of sin and, without watering down personal accountability, he also highlighted the 'structures of sin' that result from many individual sins (*Reconciliation and Penance*, 16; ND 2067b–c). In his *Sollicitudo Rei Socialis* (no. 46), John Paul II drew the following conclusion:

The principal obstacle to be overcome on the way to authentic liberation is sin and the structures produced by sin as it multiplies and spreads. The freedom with which Christ has set us free (cf. Gal. 5: 1) encourages us to become the servants of all. Thus the process of development and liberation takes concrete shape in the exercise of solidarity, that is to say in the love and service of neighbour, especially of the poorest.

From the start of his pontificate, John Paul II constantly recalled the diverse forces that diminish our freedom and subject us to futility.[24] Our existence urgently needs God's gift of grace. To that we now turn.

[24] See e.g. the 1979 encyclical *Redemptor hominis*, 8 (ND 517).

6

The Life of Grace and the Hope of Glory

> By grace you have been saved through faith, and this is not your own doing: it is the gift of God. (Ephesians 2: 8)

> I am filled with his love and his beauty, and I am sated with divine delight and sweetness. I share in the light, I participate also in the glory, and my face shines like my Beloved's, and all my members become bearers of light. Then I finally become more beautiful than those who are beautiful, wealthier than those who are wealthy, and more than all the mighty I am mighty and greater than kings, and much more precious than all that is visible, not only more than the world or the men of the world, but also more than heaven and all the angels of heaven, for I possess the creator of the whole universe to whom is due glory and honour, now and forever. Amen.

> (Simeon the New Theologian, *Hymn of Divine Love*, 16)

According to the Christian Good News, the Father shares his 'grace' with men and women of all times, calling them to a complete union with the tripersonal God and with one another. What is the life of grace freely given to us now through Christ, and what is our hope of glorious fulfilment at the end? This chapter aims to set out Catholic teaching on the present communion with God in the risen Christ and through the Holy Spirit, and on the consummation of this graced life in the final kingdom beyond death.

THE LIFE OF GRACE

The Catholic doctrine of grace has emerged from two great controversies, the first being the crisis provoked by Pelagius (d. after 413), whose stress on self-sufficient human freedom and commitment underplayed the need for God's grace and represented human beings as capable of achieving salvation largely through their own resources. More than a thousand years later, leaders of the Protestant Reformation highlighted the damage done to human nature by original sin and presented human beings as intrinsically incapable of any good actions. The Council of Trent (1545–63) had to face the question: how does justification through Christ's grace save and change human beings? Besides explaining the teaching on grace as it emerged from the fifth- and sixteenth-century crises, we also need to show the differing aspects highlighted by the Christian West and East (both Orthodox and Catholic) in their understanding of the new life of grace.

The Pelagian Crisis

From NT times Christian believers understood grace as a totally gratuitous gift of God, the unmerited favour of being saved in Christ through faith. As St Paul put it, 'since all have sinned and fall short of the glory of God, they are now justified by his grace as a gift, through the redemption that is in Christ Jesus, whom God put forward as a sacrifice of atonement by his blood, effective through faith' (Rom. 3: 23–5). The divine initiative of love stood behind the whole process: 'God, who is rich in mercy, out of the great love with which he loved us even when we were dead through our trespasses, made us alive together with Christ—by grace you have been saved—and raised us up with him' (Eph. 2: 4–6). The early Church experienced the fullness of Christ's grace as a new birth (John 1: 13; 3: 3; 1 Pet. 1: 3–5) and as the divine love poured 'into our hearts' through the gift of the Holy Spirit (Rom. 5: 5). The Spirit prompted the prayer of 'Abba' or 'Father', which showed believers to be adopted children of God and to be brothers and sisters of the risen Christ (Rom. 8: 12–17; Gal. 4: 5–7).

One might sum up what grace meant to the early Christians as the new life that had its source in the crucified and risen Christ and its immediate cause in the Holy Spirit. This twofold relationship to the Son and the Spirit transformed fully those who were justified and constituted them 'adopted' sons and daughters of the Father. In that way the gift of grace, accepted in faith, meant and means an intimate sharing in the life of the tripersonal God. At the same time, God's free self-gift calls for a personal response through a life worthy of God's children.

Until the late fourth century the doctrine of grace, or being 'made holy' through Christ in the Holy Spirit, was more or less universally accepted.

As we saw in Ch. 1, Pelagius challenged this tradition.[1] Against Pelagius and Pelagianism, St Augustine of Hippo led two hundred bishops at the Sixteenth Council of Carthage (held in 418) to condemn the view that the freedom of human beings has not been weakened by inherited sin, and that they can achieve salvation through their own sustained efforts (see also Ch. 5). Appealing to such Gospel texts as 'apart from me you can do nothing' (John 15: 5), this regional but highly significant council insisted on our absolute need for divine grace (DH 225–30; ND 1901–6).

The struggle to understand the interaction between divine grace and human freedom continued during Augustine's lifetime and beyond his death in 430. Some monks in southern France, including St John Cassian of Marseilles (d. 435) and St Vincent of Lérins (d. before 450), developed the view that human beings can make their first step towards God without the help of divine grace. While accepting that grace is indispensable for salvation and thus rejecting Pelagianism, those who developed Semi-Pelagianism (as it came to be called in the late sixteenth century) did so in opposition to the severe version of predestination that Augustine proposed in his old age. The Pelagian controversy provoked him into making some extreme assertions about God's primary role in the life of grace: from the 'mass of sin' or the sinful human race (see Ch. 5) God elects only some persons for eternal salvation. Anxious to tip the balance in the opposite direction, the Semi-Pelagians failed to acknowledge the sovereign efficacy of divine grace, right from our first steps towards salvation. Semi-Pelagianism was condemned at the Second Council of Orange in 529, which insisted that it is 'the illumination and inspiration of the Holy Spirit' that makes it possible and easy to open oneself in faith to 'the saving message of the Gospel' (DH 377; ND 1919). Somehow forgotten for many centuries, the teaching of this council emerged again at the end of the sixteenth century; thereafter, it helped to fashion the teaching on faith as developed by the First and Second Vatican Councils. In particular, Vatican II appealed to the Second Council of Orange when insisting that, before human beings can exercise faith, they must 'have the grace of God to move and assist' them (*Dei Verbum*, 5).

The Christian East and West

The Second Letter of Peter states that God's 'divine power has given us everything needed for life and piety' and called us 'to his own glory and

---

[1] See B. R. Rees, *Pelagius: Life and Letters* (Woodbridge: Boydell & Brewer, 1998).

goodness'. These gifts constitute God's 'promises' to humankind: a divine call to 'escape from the corruption that is in the world through lust' and to become 'participants of the divine nature (*physis*)' (2 Pet. 1: 3–4). This striking picture of grace as sharing in the very being or nature of God appears in what is arguably the last NT work to be written. The Christian East and West have read this passage in different contexts. While the East characteristically starts with eternal life as the origin of everything, the West often approaches God as the source of freedom for individual human persons. The East dwells on the whole 'economy' or history of relations between God and creatures, while the West insists on the individual's response to God. A theology of grace, according to the Eastern tradition, follows St Athanasius and other early Christian writers in understanding grace within the wider perspective of God's glory and the divinization of humanity. The Western tradition often studies in detail the human actions that respond to God's call.

Despite their different starting-points and emphases, both East and West know the life of grace to be the effect of Christ's redemption. But while the West often understands redemption to result from the events of Holy Thursday, Good Friday, and Easter Sunday, the East holds that the redemption of humanity comes from the whole story of Christ's life on earth, which starts with the incarnation and ends with the sending of the Spirit at Pentecost. In line with Paul and Irenaeus, the East interprets Christ's life among us within the totality of God's plan and his relationship with the whole of history, humankind, and the world.

Eastern theology has hardly developed a theology of original sin. Adam's 'happy fault' is a simple accident, though with far-reaching consequences. The East emphasizes God's unchanging will that creates, calls, and restores humankind through the gradual recapitulation of all things in Christ. Under the guidance of the Holy Spirit, creation itself joins human beings in yearning for completion; the Spirit transforms those groans of pain into prayer and a gradual becoming like God (Rom. 8: 14–30). Through the Spirit, humanity—created in the image of God—will be fully restored to its original beauty.

While the West interprets grace as a conversion process, the Christian East understands conversion as the full liberation of the whole of creation, so as to manifest once more the glory God intended for his creatures from the beginning of time. Divinization, *the* master theme of Eastern theology, goes beyond the Western understanding of sanctification. While the latter is generally considered God's direct action on human beings, deification implies both God's and humanity's contribution in one dynamic process. When human beings progressively participate in God's own being through the action of the indwelling Spirit, their divine likeness—born anew in baptism after being lost through sin—becomes steadily more similar to the prototype who is Christ, the 'Image of the invisible God, the firstborn over all creation' (Col. 1: 15). Just as Athanasius had done in the fourth century, the East continues to insist on the believers' need to conform to Christ and be images (lower case) of the Image (upper case) of God.

According to the Christian East, Western theology has often taken the life of grace to be a theology about humanity rather than about the Holy Spirit's sanctifying action within us. However, nowadays many Catholics and other Christians in the West have become fascinated by the beauty of the Eastern view of grace, since it highlights the indwelling of the Spirit and our deification through a personal relationship with the tripersonal God. Communion with the Trinity, the triune interaction that St Andrew Roublev (d. 1430) magnificently conveyed in his world-famous icon, is the goal of our lifelong quest for God. Maintaining the biblical understanding of humanity as created in God's image, the Christian East interprets sanctification as the communication of divine 'energies', which beautify and complete God's original creation.[2]

The differing outlooks between Eastern and Western Christians on the nature of grace mean that the East often finds it hard to grasp and follow such distinctions in Western theology as 'created' and 'uncreated' grace, and that the West may look at Eastern theology as being too contemplative and mystical. But John Paul II wanted to see both Christian traditions integrated, as being 'the two lungs' of the one Church.[3] Apropos of the life of grace, he cited Simeon the New Theologian (949–1022), a

---

[2] The theology of grace in terms of 'divine energies' was developed by St Maximus the Confessor and became the cornerstone of Eastern monastic spirituality thanks to John of Sinai (known as St John Climacus) and St Simeon the New Theologian. St Gregory Palamas and the tradition of Mount Athos developed extensively this theology. It spread widely through the efforts of important saints of the Russian Church, such as Paisy Velichkovsky (the person behind the *Philocalia* and the anonymous *The Way of the Pilgrim*), John of Cronstadt, Seraphim of Sarov, and Theophan the Recluse.

[3] 'The Church needs to learn to breathe again with its two lungs—its Eastern one and its Western one': John Paul II to the Roman Curia on 28 June 1985. In his 1987 encyclical *Redemptoris Mater* he referred to the Second Council of Nicaea (787) and yearned after the day 'when the Church can begin once more to breathe fully with her *two lungs*, the East and the

prominent figure of the Byzantine tradition, in order to extol the Holy Spirit's action in the believer:

I see the beauty of your grace, I contemplate its radiance and reflect the light; I am taken up by your ineffable splendour; I am led out of myself, while reflecting on myself; I see how I was and what I have become. O prodigy! I am alert, I am full of respect for myself, of reverence and fear, as before you yourself; I do not know what to do, because I am overcome by timidity; I do not know where to sit down, to what I should come near, where to rest these members that belong to you; for what undertaking, for what work I should use these astounding divine marvels.[4]

Medieval Theology: The Image

Just as the Eastern and Western traditions developed distinct readings of the theology of grace, the High Middle Ages in the West construed in two ways human beings as images of God. The scholastic theologians explained the believer's life of faith as a spiritual movement through which the human image journeys to become a fully fledged likeness of God in Christ. Or else they borrowed from Augustine's trinitarian theology: everything human and spiritual reflects the soul's triadic constitution. Since the human soul comprises memory, intellect, and will, the process of graced conversion follows the same pattern and consists of knowing, understanding, and loving.[5]

Bonaventure exemplifies the first approach: individuals embark on their journey towards God by looking for footprints or clues (*vestigia*) of God within creation itself. These stimulate the human image to recognize the nature of its very being, so that it feels the call to imitate the prototype. The person thus enters a process of love, meant to enhance the likeness and render it all the more similar to God. Bonaventure wrote:

Since it happens that God is contemplated not only outside us and within us, but also above us: outside through vestige, within through image, and above through

West' (no. 34; see also his 1996 encyclical *Ut unum sint*, 54). Speaking to the Roman Curia (21 December 1996), the Pope identified the Church's need to breathe fully with her *two lungs* as one of the main challenges for Christianity's third millennium. On 30 November 1992 (St Andrew's feast day, the patronal feast of the Patriarchate of Constantinople), Bartholomew I mentioned the 'fundamental ecclesiological truth' of the 'two lungs' in an address to Cardinal Edward Cassidy (see *Ekklesia* 1 (1–15 January 1993) 14).

[4] Simeon the New Theologian, *Hymns*, 2. 19–27, as quoted during a general audience by John Paul II on 13 September 2000, in his reflection on 'The Christian as inspired by the Spirit'; see G. A. Maloney (ed.), *Hymns of Divine Love by St. Symeon the New Theologian* (Denville, NJ: Dimension, 1999), 17.

[5] See Augustine, *De Trinitate*, 11. 9–11.

the light of Eternal Truth, since 'our mind itself is formed immediately by Truth Itself'; those who have been exercised in the first manner, have entered already into *the entrance-hall* before the tabernacle; but those in the second have entered into *the holies*; moreover those in the third enter with the supreme Pontiff into the *Holy of Holies*; where above the ark are the Cherubim of glory overshadowing the propitiatory; through which we understand two manners or steps of contemplating the invisible and eternal things of God, of which one hovers around the things essential to God, but the other around the things proper to the persons.[6]

Bonaventure's theme of light recalls the theology of Pseudo-Dionysius (lived *c*. AD 500): it stresses the soul's lifelong journey towards God's unapproachable light and the process by means of which the soul gradually purifies itself, as it approaches its divine beloved.

Those medieval authors who illustrated the life of grace by drawing on an Augustinian-style triadic scheme did so in differing ways. Bernard of Clairvaux and his Cistercians accentuated the will and dwelt primarily on the role of divine and human love within the life of grace. The Victorines, the scholars of the abbey of St Victor in Paris, considered the intellect to be the primary seat of the divine image, and cosmic contemplation the image's golden way to God. Bonaventure and later Franciscan theology tried to work out a compromise between these two traditions, and thus harmonize the affective and the intellectual approach to God. Medieval spirituality could therefore understand the life of grace as an ongoing conversion which, after the initial turning away from evil towards God (the *via purgativa*), enters a process of enlightening imitation (the *via illuminativa*), and moves towards full union with God (the *via unitiva*).[7]

Linking some elements of Neoplatonic philosophy with Christian mysticism, Meister Eckhart (*c*.1260–1327) emphasized grace as the source of the true life that comes from God: 'The work of grace is to make the soul quick and amenable to all divine works, for grace flows from the divine spring and is a likeness of God and tastes of God and makes the soul

---

[6] Bonaventure, *The Journey of the Mind into God*, 5. 1. This translation has been prepared by *The Franciscan Archive* (a WWW Resource on St Francis and Franciscanism), with a particular emphasis on preserving the metaphors used by Bonaventure.

[7] Many Western schools of spirituality adopt a triple access to God: the way of purification, the way of imitation, and the way of contemplative union. The second approach gave us the fifteenth-century classic attributed to Thomas à Kempis, *The Imitation of Christ*, while the third way inspired the anonymous *The Cloud of Unknowing*, usually dated to the close of the fourteenth century. This triple access to God provides a profound hermeneutic of Ignatius Loyola's *Spiritual Exercises* (16th cent.).

like God.'[8] Usually Eckhart referred to the highest dimension of the human soul as the small spark of God: 'a transcending light and an image of the divine nature and created by God'.[9] Eckhart translated the three traditional ways (purgative, illuminative, unitive) into four steps that could account for the soul's journey towards God:

The soul takes four steps into God. The first is that fear, hope, and desire grow in her. Again she moves on, and then fear and hope and desire are quite cut off. At the third stage she comes to a forgetfulness of all temporal things. At the fourth stage she enters into God where she will eternally dwell, reigning with God in eternity, and then she will never again think of temporal things and of herself, being fused with God and God with her. And what she then does, she does in God.[10]

Summing up the believer's journey in this world, Meister Eckhart moved directly to prayer: 'May God help us take these steps here [i.e. on earth] and (thus) die, that we may rejoice in Him in eternity. Amen.'[11]

The Reformation and Beyond

By the late Middle Ages some theologians, such as Jean de Mirecourt (taught in Paris between 1344 and 1347, and died sometime after 1349) and Gabriel Biel (*c*.1420–95), so stressed God's omnipotence and sovereign freedom that the issue of predestination once again came to the fore: God saves whomsoever he wants and can seem arbitrary in choosing the elect. Endless calamities, such as war, disease, and the Black Death (or bubonic plague), questioned humanity's power to shape and give meaning to life. Once earthly existence turned out to be so insecure, individuals saw that they could count only on the divine stability of the life to come. Four-teenth- and fifteenth-century popular spirituality implored God's mercy and tried by all possible ways and means to lay hold of the Kingdom of God 'by force' (Matt. 11: 12). Devotions mushroomed, and the urge to accumulate merits through meritorious actions could not be contained. These developments stimulated further a widespread feeling of insecurity that radically challenged faith in baptism and its salutary effects. If individuals could not be sure of the very life they were leading, could they ever be sure of the life to come?

---

[8] M. O. C. Walshe, *Meister Eckhart. Sermons and Treatises* (London: Watkins, 1981), ii. 241.
[9] Ibid. (1979), i. 244. [10] Ibid. ii. 259–60. [11] Ibid. 260.

We must recall also the revitalization of cultural, political, and religious life brought by the Renaissance, a loosely defined but powerful movement that arose in fourteenth-century Italy and emerged in France, England, and Germany in the second half of the fifteenth century. Dante Alighieri (1265–1321), Lorenzo Valla (*c.*1406–57), Pico de la Mirandola (1463–94), and other leading writers showed a profound understanding of human nature and dignity; this encouraged the retrieval of Platonic thought in fifteenth-century Florence. The positive evaluation of the human condition and destiny remains permanently visible in many works of Renaissance art. Valla, for instance, explored the interplay of divine foreknowledge and human freeedom in the context of the mystery of predestination or our being elected for salvation through the eternal foreknowledge and will of God. When writing in the sixteenth century on human freedom, both Erasmus of Rotterdam and Martin Luther referred to Valla's seminal work.

An Augustinian Friar, Luther inherited from the current Augustinian theology both a sense of God's sovereign freedom in granting grace, and a radical pessimism about the bondage to evil of human beings. In the controversy with Erasmus who emphasized the significance of human freedom, Luther published in 1525 *The Bondage of the Will.* He argued:

If God's grace is wanting, if it is taken away from that small power [of free will], what can it [the human will] do? It is ineffective, you say, and can do nothing good. So it will not do what God or his grace wills. Why? Because we have [now] taken God's grace away from it, and what the grace of God does not do is not good. Hence it follows that *free-will* without God's grace is not free at all, but is the permanent prisoner and bondslave of evil, since it cannot turn itself to good.[12]

The Reformers reinterpreted Augustine's understanding of humanity as a *massa damnata* (a condemned body) as a *massa perditionis* (a body that is lost). Calvin explained 'natural corruption' as follows: 'All man's faculties are, on account of the depravity of nature, so vitiated and corrupted that in all his actions persistent disorder and intemperance threaten because these inclinations cannot be separated from such lack of restraint.' He summed up his position as follows: 'We teach that all human desires are evil, and

---

[12] M. Luther, *The Bondage of the Will*, trans. J. I. Packer and O. R. Johnston (Grand Rapids, Mich.: Revell, 1998), 104. The Word of God, Calvin believed, 'cannot penetrate into our minds unless the Spirit, as the inner teacher, through his illumination makes entry for it'. Only then can Christ 'engraft us into his body so that we become partakers of every good' (*Institutes of the Christian Religion* (Philadelphia: Westminster, 1960), i. 582).

charge them with sin—not in that they are natural, but because they are inordinate.'[13] Through sin, not only had humanity's God-given likeness been lost, but also it had become hopelessly corrupt and no longer an image of God. Since the human will is utterly under the sway of sin and cannot do anything good, salvation comes exclusively through God's action.

According to the major Reformers, original sin (see Ch. 5 above) had so deeply damaged our human nature that we remain steeped in sinfulness and commit sin in every action. Luther and Calvin used strong, even lurid, language about our depravity. But there is room for a generous reading that seems closer to what they intended and, for that matter, to what Catholic saints and some outstanding biblical figures (e.g. Isa. 6: 1–7) have sometimes said about their own human weakness and wickedness. The closer we draw to God in our spiritual lives, the more we will become aware of and even terrified by the overwhelming divine holiness that rises infinitely above our tainted and limited nature. How then can God's justifying grace reach us sinners? Luther preached that Christ's righteousness is legally ascribed or imputed (rather than imparted) to us. Internally we remain sinners but externally we are 'acquitted' by God through faith in Christ's redeeming merits.

Sadly a solemn Catholic response to Luther came late and appeared a year after his death, when the Council of Trent produced its decree on justification in 1547 (DH 1520–83; ND 1924–83). The bishops, gathered at Trent, did not choose between Augustine's more pessimistic and Aquinas's more optimistic interpretation of the human condition but highlighted the gratuitousness and relational character of God's grace. Trent's decree therefore agreed with Luther and other Protestant Reformers by acknowledging the utter primacy of divine grace, love, and saving power in the whole process of justification. Even if human beings can 'reject' the illumination of the Holy Spirit, by their own free will they cannot 'take one step towards justice in God's sight'. They must always be 'awakened and assisted by divine grace, if they are to repent of their sins and be reborn through baptism' (DH 1525–6; ND 1929–30). The righteousness that makes human beings acceptable to God comes through faith in Christ and not through any human works. When human beings accept divine grace, they do so through the gift of God.

---

[13] J. Calvin, *Institutes of the Christian Religion*, i. 604.

The Tridentine decree on justification differed from the teaching of Luther and other Reformers in three ways. First of all, the grace received through baptism intrinsically transforms or regenerates sinners through the power of the Holy Spirit. Justification brings not only 'the remission of sins' but also an interior 'sanctification and renewal through the voluntary reception of grace' (DH 1528; ND 1932). In spite of the 'depravity' of the human condition, every person remains free to accept fully God's gifts of faith and grace; through baptism, God truly justifies the believer. Second, the justified can and should observe the commandments. They can grow in justifying grace, and through the strength imparted by Christ perform good works that merit for them eternal life. The Council of Trent described as follows the life of the justified: 'Jesus Christ himself continuously infuses strength into the justified, as the head into the members ... and the vine into the branches...; this strength always *precedes*, *accompanies*, and *follows* their good works which, without it, could in no way be pleasing to God and meritorious' (DH 1546; ND 1947; italics ours); traditional theology consequently refers to this gift of God as 'prevenient grace'. What the Council of Trent taught here corresponds to what, in Ch. 1, we saw Augustine enunciating: when God crowns our merits, he in fact is crowning his gifts. Third, this positive result of Christ's justifying grace means that human beings do not remain in permanent bondage to sin. Even before justification human beings' free will, while weakened and distorted, was in no way 'extinct' (DH 1521, 1555; ND 1925, 1955). After justification they can freely co-operate with God's grace and do not necessarily 'sin in all their works' (DH 1539; ND 1940). They can live out to the full their communion of mind, heart, and will with God.

These last paragraphs set out perhaps too starkly the differences between differing views of grace that emerged at the Reformation. Although often seen as mutually exclusive, the Catholic and Lutheran approaches, for example, may be interpreted as complementing rather than contradicting each other. Despite important differences in terminology and emphases, a consensus is possible. In 1967 the international Catholic–Lutheran theological dialogue began. Three decades later, its 'Joint Declaration on the Doctrine of Justification', which contains forty-four common statements covering basic tenets regarding justification, was accepted by the Catholic Church and the World Lutheran Federation and signed in Augsburg on 31 October 1999. Some differences still remain: for instance, about the interplay between divine grace and human freedom.

Before leaving the Council of Trent's decree on justification, the most important piece of official Catholic teaching on God's grace, two items call for mention. First, biblical quotations and references pervade the text; it clearly intends to take its stand on what God revealed in Christ about the life of grace—a revelation recorded and interpreted by the scriptures. Second, one chapter of the decree reflects a revived influence of Thomas Aquinas, which began around 1500. In the fourteenth and fifteenth centuries Catholic theological life had declined, secondary issues took the limelight, and Aquinas's writings were widely neglected. Cardinal Thomas Cajetan (1469–1534) and others made Aquinas once again a leading authority in the Catholic church; the *Summa Theologiae* became the standard textbook for theological students. Hence it is not surprising to find the Council of Trent following Aquinas in listing various 'causes' of justification: namely its final, efficient, meritorious, instrumental, and formal causes (DH 1529; ND 1932). Trent picked up this Aristotelian-style language, but it almost never reflected Thomas in assigning our redemption to the 'efficacy of Christ's death *and resurrection*' (DH 1534; ND 1936; emphasis ours). Usually Trent's decree on justification appealed only to 'the merits' of Christ's passion (DH 1529–30; ND 1932–3).

After the time of Trent, some Catholic circles persisted in thinking about grace in three less than fruitful ways. First, the perennial challenge of reconciling God's dominion and human free will roused strong debates between the Jesuit and Dominican orders on the 'aids' that divine grace gives to human freedom. A Spanish Jesuit, Luis de Molina (1535–1600), developed a new theory about the relationship between freedom and grace. In giving grace, God knows and takes into account the decisions that human beings would freely make in any situation in which they might be placed. Molina called this divine foreknowledge 'middle' know-ledge, because it is more than a knowledge of mere possibilities but less than a vision of actual future events. Dominicans, in particular Domingo Bañez (1528–1604), strongly opposed Molinism. In emphasizing God's sovereign freedom, Bañez spoke of divine concurrence in human action as 'physical pre-motion', an idea that does not seem to leave space for true human freedom. Between 1598 and 1609, an official commission, De Auxiliis, met in Rome but failed to resolve the issue. Pope Paul V put an end to the discussion and explicitly forbade Jesuits to brand Dominicans as Calvinists and the Dominicans to call Jesuits Pelagians. Since the 1970s Alvin Plantinga (b. 1932) and others have revived interest in and stirred up fresh debate about the theory of Molina.[14] This is a fascinating example of some modern heirs of the Protestant Reformation, who are outstanding philosophers, making common ground with Catholic thinkers.[15]

A few decades later Cornelius Jansen (1585–1638), bishop of Ypres, revived some pessimistic ideas from Augustine about the human condition and destiny. Jansen tipped the balance towards God's sovereign and seemingly arbitrary action by claiming that divine grace irresistibly determines our decisions and that Christ died not for all but only for the predestined. Pope Innocent X in 1653 condemned some of Jansen's extreme ideas (DH 2001–5; ND 1989), and this was done again in 1656 and 1690. Despite their stress on the power of God's grace, Jansenists preached a strict morality and encouraged a scrupulous approach to the reception of the sacraments. They understood Holy Communion to be the reward for virtue rather than 'bread for the wayfarer'. Jansenist scrupulosity cast a long shadow, even well into the twentieth century among many French, Irish, and other Western Catholics. It was not until the 1992 *Catechism of the Catholic Church* that an official document provided a helpful working approach to the mysterious interplay between divine election and human freedom. It did so on the basis of God's eternal existence being present to all moments of time: 'To God, all moments of time are present in their immediacy. When therefore he establishes his eternal plan of *predestination*, he includes in it each person's free response to his grace' (no. 600). Predestination, consequently, is more of a reflection on the presence of God's love in all history, rather than an authoritarian exercise of God's will by means of which he arbitrarily prefers one person to another, and predestines the elect to heaven and the reprobate to hell.

A second less-than-happy feature of post-Tridentine reflection on grace was the widespread tendency among Western Catholics to speak of grace as if it were a 'thing'. This unfortunate language, which had already emerged by the late Middle Ages, lost sight of the relational and historical dimensions of God's grace, so important in Patristic theology, and persisted down to the twentieth century in manuals of theology. Going beyond a somewhat useful distinction between 'habitual' grace (or grace

---

[14] See T. P. Flint, *Divine Providence: The Molinist Account* (Ithaca, NY: Cornell University Press, 1998).

[15] Their rediscovery of the power of Thomas Aquinas's thought has also brought some brilliant Protestant Christians into debate among themselves and with their Catholic counterparts.

as a relationship continuing through time) and 'actual' grace (or the divine help given for a particular human act),[16] such theology focused attention on the created reality and particular effects of grace rather than on the personal indwelling of the Holy Spirit.

A distinction made by Thomas Aquinas and other medieval theologians between the natural and supernatural orders, or between what is due to our created nature and what derives from the free gifts of divine love, supported a third limit in post-Tridentine Catholic thinking about grace. In the area of faith and reason, the First Vatican Council (1869–70) distinguished between 'natural' knowledge of God and 'supernatural' revelation. In the light of what St Paul says in the first chapter of his Letter to the Romans, it contrasted the 'way' to 'know' God that comes through the 'natural light of human reason' with 'another, supernatural way', due to divine revelation (DH 3004–5; ND 113–14). To be sure, the Council distinguished, without separating, the natural and the supernatural 'ways' or orders. But one lacked a firm statement that God not only wishes to save all human beings but also has already, through the Holy Spirit, made Christ's saving grace effectively present in the lives of all human beings without exception. We owe such teaching to the Second Vatican Council's *Gaudium et Spes* (the Pastoral Constitution on the Church in the Modern World, 22) and the 1979 encyclical of John Paul II (*Redemptor Hominis*, 13). Through Christ's saving grace and the coming of the Holy Spirit the world has already been 'supernaturalized'—that is to say, 'Christified' and 'spiritualized'. The 'natural' order is a mere abstraction: the one and only order is the one created by God (as we have seen in Ch. 5), the real order of divine grace. In an outstanding fashion, Henri de Lubac (1896–1991) and Karl Rahner (1904–84) helped prepare for Vatican II's teaching by making it clear that all human beings live in a world of grace.[17]

Various forces conspired to renew Western Catholic thinking about grace by restoring a sense of the indwelling of the Holy Spirit and our personal union with the crucified and risen Christ. The highly personal devotion to the 'heart' of Jesus, which was encouraged by the visions of St Margaret Mary Alacoque (1647–90) and pervaded Western Catholicism from the nineteenth century, Pope St Pius X's encouragement to

---

[16] See E. Yarnold, *The Second Gift. A Study of Grace* (London: St Paul, 1974), 50–76.

[17] The major study that unravelled the issue of the 'two orders' was H. de Lubac, *Sûrnaturel. Études historiques* (Paris: Montaigne, 1946), trans. R. Haughton as *The Mystery of the Supernatural* (London: Geoffrey Chapman, 1967).

receive Holy Communion frequently and to make one's First Communion at an earlier age (instructions issued in 1905 and 1910, respectively), and the image of the Church as the body of Christ, which climaxed with Pius XII's 1943 encyclical, *Mystici Corporis*, prompted a sense of grace entailing a loving relationship with Christ. Pope Leo XIII's 1897 encyclical, *Divinum Illud*, initiated among Western Catholics a 'rehabilitation' of the role of the Holy Spirit in their lives as graced by God. Yves Congar documented the story of this rehabilitation,[18] signalled officially in the documents of the Second Vatican Council (e.g. *Lumen Gentium*, 4; *Unitatis Redintegratio*, 15) and more fully expressed by John Paul II in his encyclical *Dominum et Vivificantem*. Although not often interpreted this way, we can read his first three encyclicals, *Redemptor Hominis* of 1979, *Dives in Misericordia* of 1980, and *Dominum et Vivificantem* of 1986 as being a trinitarian teaching on the life of grace—meditating on the Son, the Father, and the Holy Spirit, respectively. Divine 'self-communication', a recurrent theme in *Dominum et Vivificantem*, highlights the way the life of grace entails first and foremost a personal relationship with the tripersonal God. It almost suggests glossing the cherished Eastern term for the grace of God, 'divinization', as 'trinification'.

This last paragraph has highlighted individual contributions to the renewed appreciation of the life of grace, reflected by Vatican II and by earlier and later papal documents. But from the end of the nineteenth century various movements also helped revive a more personal insight into the life of grace: the liturgical, biblical, patristic, and ecumenical movements. The official liturgy of the Church, both East and West, enshrines a prayerful sense of the grace of God, 'without whom nothing is holy and nothing is strong' (Collect for the seventeenth Sunday of the year), and with whom we can live now and reach our eternal home in the life to come. The biblical movement let more and more Catholics recognize the radically personal nature of God's dealings with sinful and graced men and women that the scriptures record and interpret. A renewed contact with Irenaeus, Origen, Athanasius of Alexandria, the Cappadocians, Augustine of Hippo, and other writers from the early centuries of Christianity also reinvigorated a personal sense of God's grace. Nothing if not biblical, these authors vividly expressed what the forgiveness of sins and a graced

---

[18] Y. Congar, *I believe in the Holy Spirit*, trans. D. Smith, 3 vols. (London: Geoffrey Chapman, 1983).

union with the tripersonal God involve. In particular, the study of such Greek Fathers as Athanasius and the Cappadocians encouraged further contacts with the Christian East, both Orthodox and Catholic.

To Western Catholics and other Christians who want to deepen their understanding of what the grace of God means, we offer these pieces of advice: listen to and reflect upon liturgical texts, especially those in use at the Eucharist, baptism, and the sacrament of reconciliation. Then prayerfully read the scriptures and the ancient Fathers, before sharing in an Eastern liturgy. Let what you hear, see, and smell lead you into the mystery of God's self-giving. In that best of all ways you will grasp the new life into which God desires to usher the whole human family. Finally, surrender any suspicion that God's gift of grace encroaches on human freedom. It is wrong to take divine grace and human freedom as opposed or even in inverse proportion, as if more grace entailed less freedom. The lives of luminously saintly men and women shows that the truth is quite the opposite: free self-determination grows in direct proportion with their nearness to and graced union with God.[19] It is sin, not grace, that curtails our freedom and harms our life.

CHRIST AS FULFILMENT

A graced existence, as we have seen, means the indwelling of the Holy Spirit, adoption through Christ as God's sons and daughters, and participation in the divine life. If that is the life of grace now, what can we say about the coming life of glory that grace initiates? The history of God's gracious self-communication began with the creation of the cosmos and human beings (see Ch. 5). It culminated in Christ's resurrection from the dead and the outpouring of the Holy Spirit (Ch. 4). It is moving now to its consummation, the *parousia* or final coming of Christ that will bring, through the glorified Christ, the ultimate self-gift of God to human beings and the transfiguration of the cosmos.

This summary of the fulfilment that Catholics and other Christians hope for makes it clear how everything centres on Christ, 'the Alpha and the Omega, the first and the last, the beginning and the end' (Rev. 22: 13). The origin of all things (e.g. John 1: 13) he is also the 'Eschatos', the future

---

[19] See K. Rahner, 'Grace and Freedom', in id. *et al.* (eds.), *Sacramentum Mundi* (6 vols., London: Burns & Oates, 1968–70), ii. 424–7.

and final One. In this provisional period between his resurrection from the dead and the end, the risen Christ is overcoming hostile forces and will abolish death, 'the last enemy' (1 Cor. 15: 20–8). The Holy Spirit is at work in and for humanity and the created universe, while everyone and everything waits to be freed for the glory to come (Rom. 8: 18–25).

By the time of Christ, the Pharisees, the Qumran community, and other Jewish groups believed in afterlife, a general resurrection from the dead, and a general judgement on the 'Day of the Lord', with eternal reward or punishment to follow when God brought the history of the world to its end. Faith in these 'last things' shifted for Christians, inasmuch as they held that Jesus' personal resurrection had initiated the general resurrection (1 Cor. 15: 20, 23), and that he himself would be the judgement of God in person (Matt. 25: 31–46). The day of God's final and decisive intervention in judgement was now reinterpreted as Christ's final and decisive intervention.

The Awaited One: A Common Hope

St Paul's First Letter to the Thessalonians, generally agreed to be the oldest document in the NT and to have been written around AD 50, shows how the apostle and the Christians to whom he wrote were living with a vivid hope that Jesus Christ would come soon and gather them all to himself. When this was to occur was not known. 'The Day of the Lord' would 'come like a thief in the night' (1 Thess. 5: 2). Nevertheless it would be soon, even in the lifetime of the apostle himself (1 Thess. 4: 13–5: 3). A few years later, when closing his First Letter to the Corinthians, Paul quoted an early Christian prayer, apparently used even by Greek-speaking communities in its original Aramaic form: 'Marana tha!' or 'Come, O Lord!' (1 Cor. 16: 22). Many years later the Revelation of John, which would become the last book of the Bible, closed with the same prayer in Greek, 'Come, Lord Jesus!' (Rev. 22: 20).

New Testament Christians expected that the Lord's coming was to bring the general resurrection of the dead, the doomsday of judgement for all, glorious salvation for the elect, the damnation of the reprobate, and the transfiguration of the world. Various elements fed these vivid hopes of an imminent end and/or coloured the way they expressed it: images from the OT prophetic and apocalyptic books, dramatic scenarios from inter-testamental literature (which were written around the time of Jesus but never became canonical books of either the OT or the NT), urgent words of Jesus (derived from him, even if adapted and expanded by the early Christians) about living in expectation of the end, Jesus' own resurrection from the dead (the beginning of the general resurrection, as already mentioned), and the experience of a new existence through the forgiveness of sins and the outpouring of the Holy Spirit. The anxiously awaited coming of the Lord would both change the present situation and reveal new things. The First Letter of Peter spoke of an inheritance 'kept in heaven', the 'salvation in readiness which will be revealed at the end of time' (1 Pet. 1: 4–5). Paul highlighted the glorious resurrection at the end (1 Cor. 15: 20–8) and the fullness of knowledge to come: 'Now we see in a mirror, dimly, but then we will see face to face. Now I know only in part; then I will know fully' (1 Cor. 13: 12). Or else the apostle drew together the glorious consummation of salvation and what is still to be revealed (Rom. 8: 18).

Paul himself had to adjust his end-time expectations. When writing 1 Thessalonians he anticipated being one of those 'left alive until the Lord comes' (1 Thess. 4: 15). But when he wrote 2 Corinthians (2 Cor. 4: 16–5: 5) and Philippians (1: 20–4), he had apparently 'reconciled himself' to being dead before the Lord's final coming. Another, more significant shift took place in the apostle's thinking. At the start he envisaged the final resurrection affecting the Christian community, whether dead or still alive (1 Thess. 4: 15–18). His mature masterpiece expected a resurrection that would encompass not only Christians and other human beings but also the whole created universe (Rom. 8: 18–25; 11: 25–6).

Some twentieth-century scripture scholars made much of the difficulty NT Christians experienced in adjusting their expectations and recognizing that the Lord's final coming might be indefinitely delayed. It was even argued that Luke wrote his Gospel and the Acts of the Apostles to help early Christians to cope with the embarrassing delay in the end of all things. What strikes many other scholars, however, is rather the ease with which NT Christians adjusted to the delay in the timetable. Paul, or someone writing in his name, had to take the Thessalonians to task about thinking that doomsday had already arrived: 'As to the coming of our Lord Jesus Christ and our being gathered together to him, we beg you ... not to be quickly shaken in mind or alarmed ... to the effect that the day of the Lord is already here' (2 Thess. 1: 1–2). The last Gospel to be written had to take into account that, although the apostolic generation had almost died out, the Lord had not yet come (John 21: 20–3). The delay in the arrival of the Lord's day posed a serious difficulty for what is probably the last NT book to be written. Irreligious scoffers were anticipated to come 'in these last days' and to say: 'Where is the promise of his coming? For ever since our ancestors died, all things continue as they were from the beginning of creation!' (2 Pet. 3: 3–4). The author of the letter countered by insisting that God does not measure time as mortal human beings do. The delay reveals the divine patience and desire that sinners should repent.

Even after an intense expectation of the Lord's imminent coming died down, for hundreds of years a communitarian dimension continued to shape Christian attitudes towards death, judgement, heaven, and hell. The general resurrection of the dead and the coming of the Lord to judge all people (Matt. 13: 47–50; 25: 31–46) could be pictured only as eminently social events. The ancient symbols of faith professed a communal belief in the coming of the Lord 'to judge the living and the dead', 'the resurrection of the body' (or of 'the flesh', or of 'the dead'), and the 'life everlasting' (or 'the life of the world to come') (ND 1–13). The resurrection of the dead, the judgement, and the life to come concerned everyone. A social, ecclesial dimension surrounded even such clearly individual episodes as martyrdom and the request of prayers for the deceased.

As presented by Luke, the death of the protomartyr, St Stephen, took place in a public, social setting and brought about serious consequences for the Christian and Jewish communities in Jerusalem (Acts 6: 8–8: 8). The writings of St Ignatius of Antioch (d. *c.*107) and St Justin (d. *c.*165), which preceded their martyrdom, and the publicity attested by the acts of such martyrs as St Polycarp (d. *c.*155), Sts Perpetua and Felicitas (d. 202), and St Cyprian (d. 258) made their deaths not only heroic, personal sacrifices but also personal testimonies before the world (see Mark 13: 9–11).[20]

At least from the end of the second century, as attested by the tomb inscriptions of Abercius, bishop of Hierapolis in Phrygia (in modern Turkey), Christians prayed for the dead, and at least from the third century celebrated the Eucharist for them (and with them, as much as possible: that is, beside the deceased's resting place). In Ch. 1 we recalled

---

[20] Through the efforts of St Antony of Egypt (d. 356) and others, religious life developed as a surrogate for martyrdom. St Basil of Caesarea (d. 379) in the East and St Benedict of Nursia (d. 547) in the West gave a stable configuration to this new form of Christian existence, which meant anticipating in community here and now the communion with the risen Lord that is to come beyond death.

Monica on her deathbed asking her two sons to remember her at the altar of God. Believers knew that their dead, although dying in God's friendship, still needed to have their personal sins expiated or cleansed and to grow spiritually before reaching the vision of God. Such prayers for the dead, far from being mere individual practices on behalf of deceased individuals, belonged in the wider setting of the 'communion of saints', an article found in the Apostles' Creed and primarily denoting a fellowship in Christian life with the saints and all the baptized faithful, both still living or already dead.[21] Christians, faced with the death of a relative or close friend, believed that they had not lost their link with the deceased, and maintained through prayer their communion with the dear departed. Inevitably, praying for the dead became a typical feature of eucharistic liturgies both in the East and in the West.

Whether by violent martyrdom or by 'natural' causes, death means the definitive end of an individual's life and a final personal encounter with God. Along with their lively sense of the ecclesial and social dimension of death, ancient Christians also acknowledged its individual aspect. They recalled some stories from Jesus that depicted the death of such individuals as the rich fool (Luke 12: 16–21), a 'rich man', and the poor 'Lazarus' (Luke 16: 19–31). The individual subject's moment of death concerned NT and later Christians. Nevertheless, the social context of death and life beyond death remained primary: Jesus himself had set the social tone. Some Sadducees presented Jesus with a puzzling case for faith in the resurrection, a woman who in obedience to the Law married successively seven brothers: 'at the resurrection, when they rise from the dead, whose wife will she be, since all seven had married her?' Jesus refused to be drawn on this *individual* case, but insisted on what the resurrection will bring to *all* the elect; a transformed, 'angelic' life with God that leaves behind any marital unions (Mark 12: 18–27). Jesus' parable of the five foolish and five prudent girls at a wedding celebration put entry into God's final kingdom in a clearly social setting. When the bridegroom came, 'those who were ready went in with him to the marriage feast, and the door was shut' (Matt. 25: 1–13).

Only a few official documents on the final destiny of Christians and other human beings have come down from the first millennium. Let us recall two documents which exemplify the communitarian and even

---

[21] J. N. D. Kelly, *Early Christian Creeds*, 3rd edn. (London: Longmans, 1972), 388–97.

cosmic mentality that continued to characterize Christian teaching and thinking about the shape of things to come. One challenge to mainstream Christian teaching on human destiny came from those who claimed that the punishment of hell is not eternal but only temporary, or, in other words, is a period of purgation to be followed by the general restoration of all damned human beings and demons to their former state (*apokatasta-sis*). A provincial council held at Constantinople in 543 condemned those who held 'that the punishment of the demons and of wicked human beings is temporary, and that it will have an end at some time or that there will be a complete restoration (*apokatastasis*) of demons and wicked men' (DH 411; ND 2301). Later in this chapter we will examine hell and its eternity. Here we want only to highlight the 'social' way church leaders approached the issue. So far from considering the possible deliverance of this or that individual 'soul' from hell, which some later legends attributed to the mercy and power of the Virgin Mary, these sixth-century official Christian teachers faced the question of the general restoration of the damned to their original state.

Our second example comes from a profession of faith approved by the Eleventh Council of Toledo in 675. The bishops confessed a true resurrection of the body for all the dead, and added: 'We do not believe that we shall rise in an ethereal body or, in any other body, as some foolishly imagine, but in that body in which we live, exist, and move' (DH 540; ND 2303). This seventh-century council took a stand against deviant versions of what lies in store for us—errors that had been around, particularly in Gnostic circles, since the second century. Irenaeus, Tertullian, and other Christians of the second and third centuries set their face against the Gnostics who downplayed matter, overemphasized the spiritual, and interpreted redemption as the human spirit escaping from the bonds of the material creation, understood as intrinsically evil, to the world of light. These writers insisted on a true resurrection of the flesh, and repudiated any reduction of it to the rising of a mere ethereal body. The Eleventh Council of Toledo coupled such over-spiritualized views of the resurrection with the error of expecting resurrection in some 'other body': we will rise, the Council insisted, in that same body in which we have lived. Centuries earlier Irenaeus had struggled with the bodily continuity which he knew must be upheld if risen human beings were to remain personally identical with what they had been. He asked: 'With what body will the dead rise? Certainly with the same body in which they died, otherwise those who rise will not be the same persons who previously died' (*Adversus Haereses*, 5. 13. 1).

The challenge can be stated baldly: in what sense must we rise with the *same* body? What counts here as bodily sameness? Does it mean a numerically identical body? If so, what can that entail? It may be best to speak of 'embodied histories' being raised. In resurrection God will bring to new, transformed life, the total embodied histories of all those who have lived and died. However, we translate Irenaeus' insistence on the resurrection 'with the same body', Gnostic-style tampering with resurrection hope has been around since the second century. Caroline Walker Bynum brilliantly documents the persistent resistance of Christians to recurrent attempts to over-spiritualize the reality of bodily resurrection which normally involved reducing the personal continuity between risen persons and their prior, earthly existence.[22] The majority of Christians rejected any notion of 'ethereal' bodies and any tampering with bodily (and hence personal) continuity between the deceased and the risen, however difficult it might be to envisage what such continuity might be like.

What comes through the debates and teaching on the resurrection from the time of Irenaeus and in later centuries is the concern with the general resurrection or resurrection of 'all the dead'. What primarily concerned believers for the first millennium was the risen destiny for everyone or for the embodied histories of all those who have died before the final coming of the Lord.

The Last Things

The arrival of the second millennium brought a sea-change in Christian sensibility, at least in Western Europe. A passionate devotion to the human Jesus (as friend and lover), deep personal friendships, the lofty ideals of courtly love, and a renewed interest in the Song of Songs showed up in the writings of St Anselm of Canterbury (*c*.1033–1109), Peter Abelard (1079–1142), St Hildegard of Bingen (1098–1179), St Bernard of Clairvaux (1090–1153), and other mystics. All this heralded a new sensibility which flourished with St Francis (1181/2–1226), St Clare (1193/4–1253), and the popular piety inspired by the Franciscan movement; it has left its lasting witness not only in writing but also in fresh developments in liturgy, painting, sculpture, and Gothic architecture.

[22] C. W. Bynum, *The Resurrection of the Body in Western Christianity* (New York: Columbia University Press, 1995).

This new sensibility inevitably coloured the Christian understanding of human destiny. How did Christ himself experience death? How should I interpret my death, if it means my soul leaving my body but also my leaving behind other persons whom I love? Where will my soul be and what will its experience be like? The new personalism affected Christian thinking about the afterlife, the resurrection of the body, divine judgement, a post-mortem purification, and an eternal reward or punishment. At times personalist attitudes towards the afterlife lapsed into regrettable individualism. In Western Catholicism, official teaching during the Middle Ages and at the time of the Reformation reflected and reinforced a dominant interest in the eternal fate of individual Christians, which led to the attempt to secure salvation for oneself and one's immediate family.

The new religious climate partly shifted the Christian focus from the 'Eschatos', or the Lord coming at the end in person, to the 'eschata', or last things. Often listed as four (death, judgement, heaven, and hell) the 'last things' include six items, or seven if we distinguish death and particular judgement: (1) death and particular judgement, (2) purgatory, (3) heaven, (4) hell, (5) bodily resurrection of all at the end of time, and (6) general judgement. In the twentieth century, the Second Vatican Council redressed the balance by presenting (7) the Church as the pilgrim community awaiting Christ's final coming and avoiding any unilateral focus simply on the moment of death. Christian hope, nourished by the life of grace, is not to be reduced to the mere expectation of things to come beyond death; such hope inspires and assists Christians in their progressive growth to a final encounter with God. Let us take up in turn these themes.

1. The conviction that 'life is changed not taken away' has always characterized the Christian attitude towards death (see the preface used during many centuries at Masses for the Dead). A specifically Christian understanding of death can be gleaned primarily from the rites for the dying, prayers written for Masses on behalf of the dead, burial rites, and inscriptions on tombs.

The scriptures had seen death both as natural (e.g. Ps. 49: 11–12; Isa. 40: 6–7) and as the consequence of sin (e.g. Gen. 3: 19; Rom. 5: 12). Paul called death 'the last enemy to be overcome' by the risen Christ (1 Cor. 15: 26). From the earliest times, post-NT writers expressed their hope of sharing in Christ's victory and being delivered from death through the resurrection. Tertullian (d. *c.*225) opened his *On the Resurrection of the Flesh* with the

FIG. 9. A funeral Mass being celebrated in Mali, West Africa. Priest and people face each other as they celebrate Jesus as Lord of life and death. (© Abbas/Magnum Photos.)

memorable statement: 'The resurrection from the dead constitutes the confidence of Christians. By believing it we are what we claim to be.' Early Christians committed their deceased to 'cemeteries' (or sleeping places), where the dead 'waited' for the Lord's coming and their resurrection. The inscriptions and art from the catacombs, underground burial places found in Rome and around the Mediterranean world, witness to the tranquil hope with which Christians faced their own death or experienced that of their dear ones. They were not devoured by death, but rested 'in peace'—a very common inscription carved on Christian sarcophagi and tombstones. Pagan sarcophagi often carried sculpted lions and other voracious creatures to underline death's destructive nature; Christian sarcophagi and tombs sometimes carried scenes of Jesus raising to life Jairus' daughter, the son of the widow of Nain, or Lazarus—episodes that expressed and encouraged the Christ-centred hope with which Christians faced death.

From the outset, Christians accepted the once-and-for-all character of life and death. With death the story of each person assumes its complete, irreversible character, and is 'judged' by God in what came to be called 'the particular judgement'. 'Particular' judgement was understood to be passed when the individual soul separated in death from the body. The parable of the Rich Man and Lazarus (Luke 16: 19–31) and the words of the dying Jesus to the 'good thief' (Luke 23: 40–3) encouraged the idea of a particular judgement in which the soul at death knows at once its state in relationship to God. In the late Middle Ages, Christian asceticism came to include a hardy tradition that presented life as a persistent 'preparation for death'. *The Imitation of Christ* by Thomas à Kempis (*c.*1380–1471) warned: 'You ought so to order yourself in all your thoughts and actions, as if today you were to die' (1. 23). After the catastrophe of the Black Death in the mid-fourteenth century, books on 'the art of dying' enjoyed great popularity[23] and reinforced the portrayals of death in art. European cemeteries often featured the 'dance of death'; in these compositions, death, normally represented as a skeleton, led men and women, depicted in various conditions and states of life, in a dance towards the grave. Visitors to the Church of Santa Maria Novella in Florence will not easily forget the words at the foot of Masaccio's masterly portrayal of the crucifixion. A skeleton tells the viewer: 'What you are I once was. What I am you one day will be.' The warning coincides with the advice from *The Imitation of Christ*: 'If at

---

[23] See J. Wicks, 'Applied Theology at the Deathbed. Luther and the Late-Medieval Tradition of the *Ars moriendi*', *Gregorianum*, 79 (1998), 345–68.

any time you have seen another man die, realize that you must also pass the same way' (ibid.).

Down the centuries, *The Imitation of Christ* has fed the spiritual lives of innumerable Catholics and other Christians. It offers much more advice than the warning to 'remember death' and not forget one's mortality. But it does unmask the temptation to ignore or even deny death. At the same time, as the Second Vatican Council urged, a realistic recognition of death and the provisional nature of earthly life should not lead to a passive, world-denying disengagement. True hope should inspire Catholics to make human life even now 'more human' (*Gaudium et Spes*, 38), 'to build a better world based on truth and justice' (ibid. 55), and to promote 'the unity of the one human family' (ibid. 56).

Earlier church councils did not have much to teach about death. The Second Council of Orange appealed to Romans 5 in presenting death as the 'punishment' for Adam's sin (DH 372; ND 505). The Council of Trent mentioned the 'power of death' as a direct consequence of sin incurred by Adam but immediately defined that same 'power of death' as the 'power of the devil' (DH 1511–12, 1521; ND 508–9, 1925; see Ch. 5). The Second Vatican Council dedicated an entire section to the 'mystery of death'. It opens by reflecting on the dread and self-questioning that the fear of death arouses, and moves to the answer that faith in Christ provides (*Gaudium et Spes*, 18). Far from being merely the consequence of sin, and little more than an 'enigma', death allows us to be conformed to Christ's own dying *and rising* (ibid. 22). Hence the Catholic Church prefers, where possible, burial to cremation; the former can express more clearly that death is not the end of human existence. This 'Easter' sense of death enjoyed its liturgical counterpart when the Second Vatican Council's Constitution on Sacred Liturgy decided that 'the rite for the burial of the dead should show more clearly the Easter character of Christian death' (*Sacrosanctum Concilium*, 81). In other words, a shared hope that we enter through death into Christ's risen life should characterize funeral rites.

Nowadays the presence of the Easter Candle at the casket illustrates this hope. Christ, who has been the dead person's light and life since baptism, will continue to be that light now that the deceased is born into never-ending life. This helps to retrieve the style of burial services in early Christianity, when the day of one's death was referred to as *dies natalis* (day of birth). Those attending such services in the fourth century symbolized their faith and their joy by wearing white. From the eighth century liturgical services turned to 'black', underscored feelings of loss, and stressed deliverance from hell and the speedy purification of sins.

With their death, individuals appear before God and face the irreversible truth of their lives. They die, one may always hope, enjoying full union with God. But are they ready for the face-to-face vision of God which will bring them eternal happiness?

2. From the second century Christians prayed to God for those who had died. On the basis of some scriptural texts, which, apart from 2 Maccabees 12: 40–5, had little direct relevance, they took for granted the efficacy of prayers for the dead. They acknowledged that many of their dear ones who had died were not yet fully prepared to enjoy at once the vision of God but needed first to pass through some post-mortem process. Eastern Christians considered this process to be a final purification, maturation, and spiritual growth. Western Christians understood it to be a process not only of purification but also of satisfying or expiating for sins—an interpretation eventually summarized by the Council of Florence in 1439:

If they [the deceased] are truly penitent and die in God's love before having *satisfied* by worthy fruits of penance for their sins of commission and omission, their souls are *cleansed* after death by *purgatorial penalties*. In order that they may be *relieved from such penalties*, the acts of intercession of the living faithful benefit them, namely the sacrifices of the Mass, prayers, alms and other works of piety which the faithful are wont to do for the other faithful according to the church's practice.   (DH 1304; ND 2308; italics ours)

The Council of Florence repeated here, more or less verbatim, the teaching of the Second Council of Lyons, held in 1274. This earlier Council spoke, slightly more fully, of 'purgatorial and purifying penalties', but kept its distance from grotesque images of purgatory, legends about apparitions of souls suffering in purgatory, and the imaginary journeys there which many medieval preachers graphically described.

These two councils officially clarified and endorsed what Christians had implied for a thousand years when praying for their dead—a classic example of 'the law of praying being the law of believing' (*lex orandi lex credendi*). Neither council used the noun 'purgatory', let alone called purgatory a place, as Dante did when vividly describing what the travellers, Virgil and Dante himself, saw on their journey in the *Divine Comedy* (completed in 1320).

The First Council of Lyons, which met in 1245, had, however, spoken of 'purgatory' and 'a place of purgation' (DH 838) but refrained from indicating the 'whereabouts' of purgatory. Jacques Le Goff has argued that, since the *noun* 'purgatory' appeared in the twelfth century and was then accepted by the First Council of Lyons, the doctrine of purgatory itself was 'invented' in the Middle Ages by the official Church—in connection with various political and social structures and to meet new religious expectations. Nevertheless, the adjective 'purgatorial' had already been used for centuries, and Le Goff himself gathers evidence that shows how the idea emerged from prior practices and convictions: intercessory prayer for the dead, the sense that purification after death completes the process of salvation, and envisaging such a purification as distinct in time and place from heaven and hell.[24] Thus the official doctrine of purgatory, far from being a teaching imposed 'from above', simply articulated the implications of what rank-and-file Christians had been practising for centuries and what Dante vividly articulated by the case of Nella Donati's prayers and tears reducing the purgatorial sufferings of her husband Forese (*Purgatorio*, 23. 85–8).

In the sixteenth century Luther objected to the doctrine of purgatory by at first denying its scriptural foundations, raising doubts about the state of souls in purgatory, and querying the possibility of their making expiation for their sins (DH 1487–90). He went on to deny the very existence of purgatory, since such expiation of sins after death would be incompatible with salvation coming simply through the gift of God's justifying grace. Calvin denounced the notion of purgatory as a 'deadly fiction of Satan' and a 'dreadful blasphemy' against Christ.[25] The Catholic Church reacted to Luther's challenge, most notably at the Council of Trent. When explaining the nature of justification, the Council rejected the notion that after the grace of justification has been received, 'no debt of temporal punishment remains to be paid, either in this world or in the other, in purgatory, before access can be opened to the kingdom of heaven' (DH 1580; ND 1980). At its twenty-second session in 1562, when explaining the sacrifice of the Mass, the Council maintained that the Mass can be 'rightly offered' not only for the living 'but also for those who have died in Christ but are not yet wholly purified' (DH 1743; ND 1548; see DH 1753; ND 1557). The Council of Trent discussed purgatory more fully at its twenty-fifth or last session in 1563. The Council reaffirmed the existence of

---

[24] *The Birth of Purgatory* (Chicago: University of Chicago Press, 1984).
[25] *Institutes of the Christian Religion*, 3. 5. 6.

purgatory and the usefulness of prayers for the dead, but did not say anything about what suffering in purgatory is like or precisely how those 'in' purgatory are helped by prayers on their behalf.

When explaining the union of the pilgrim Church on earth with those who have died and gone to God, the Second Vatican Council spoke not only of those already in the glory of heaven but also of those 'still being purified' after death (*Lumen Gentium*, 49 and 51). Some years later, on 4 August 1999, Pope John Paul II drew together the teaching on purgatory when he stated: 'The term [purgatory] does not indicate a place, but a condition of existence. Those who, after death, exist in a state of purification, are already in the love of Christ who removes from them the remnants of imperfection.'[26] One might describe those passing through purgatory as being purified by the fire of divine love. But how should one describe the condition of existence for those whose purification has been completed and who, as Dante put it, are 'pure and ready to mount to the stars' (*Purgatorio*, 33. 145)?

3. In the Middle Ages, church teachers and theologians commonly held that the blessed, on entering the heavenly state (either immediately after death or, if that is needed, after some post-mortem purification), enjoyed *at once* an immediate and eternal vision of God. The Second Council of Lyons taught this in 1274:

> As for the souls of those who, after receiving holy baptism, have incurred no stain of sin whatever, and those souls who, after having contracted the stain of sin, have been cleansed, either while remaining still in their bodies or having been divested of them . . . they are received immediately into heaven.   (DH 857; ND 26)

A vigorous controversy over the immediacy of the vision broke out, with some Catholic theologians holding that after death the blessed enjoy only the vision of Christ's glorified humanity; the vision of the tripersonal God will begin for them after the general resurrection of the dead and on the day of the general judgement.

In 1336 Pope Benedict XII put an end to this controversy by solemnly defining, in the Constitution *Benedictus Deus*, that the souls of the blessed see God face to face immediately after death and prior to the general resurrection. In passing, we should note that the Constitution presupposes,

---

[26] *L'Osservatore Romano* (English edn., 11/18 August 1999), 7. On the way the doctrine of purgatory retains its relevance and has shaped Western views of time, see R. K. Fenn, *The Persistence of Purgatory* (Cambridge: Cambridge University Press, 1995).

but does not teach, an intermediate state of bodiless souls—that is to say, a state between death and resurrection. On the earthly time-scale there is an interval between death and resurrection. Does that entail a 'period' of bodiless existence in heaven, an intermediate state for souls in purgatory, heaven, or hell that 'lasts' until the general resurrection? The vision of God enjoyed by the blessed was described by Pope Benedict as follows:

These souls have seen and see *the divine essence* with an intuitive vision and even face to face ... *The divine essence* manifests itself immediately to them, plainly, clearly and openly, and in their vision they delight in *the divine essence*. Moreover by this vision and delight the souls of those who have already died are truly blessed and have eternal life and rest. (DH 1000; ND 2305; italics ours)

Later Catholic teaching preferred not to describe the beatific vision as seeing the 'divine essence', but as personally seeing face to face and relating immediately to the Father, Son, and Holy Spirit. In other words, the divinization that is the life of grace leads to a glorious communion with the persons of the Trinity. Thus the Council of Florence in 1439 spoke of seeing God who is 'one *and three*', as well as stating that the merits of the deceased would determine the degrees of intensity of their vision of the tripersonal God (DH 1305; ND 2309; italics ours). This Council did not repeat Benedict XII's language about seeing 'the divine essence', but agreed with him and differed from Eastern Christians in affirming that the vision of God enjoyed by the blessed would not be delayed until the general resurrection at the end of history.

What will heaven be like? What can we say if we follow Dante's final canto of the *Paradiso* in an attempt to evoke even a little of the nature of heaven? What will be the fundamental quality of heavenly life? We could 'define' the core of eternal happiness as the blessed dwelling forever with God and enjoying the immediate and fulfilling vision of the infinitely good and beautiful God. Such seeing 'face to face' rests on NT witness (1 Cor. 13: 12; 1 John 3: 2). But we need to add three comments.

First, in some way the redemption and glorification of the created world will attain their completion (Rom. 8: 18–25) and form 'the new heavens and a new earth' (2 Pet. 3: 13; Rev. 21: 1–22: 5). A transformed existence of embodied human beings will call for a transformed material environment. Not only humanity but also the whole cosmos will be transfigured through and with the glory of Christ. Second, just as the life of grace means being adopted in *Christ* as God's sons and daughters, so heavenly life perfectly incorporates the blessed into Christ and allows them to share in his final glorification. This is the ultimate 'being with him' which the NT promises (e.g. John 14: 3; 1 Thess. 4: 17). Heaven, according to the 1992 *Catechism of the Catholic Church*, 'is the blessed community of all who are perfectly incorporated into Christ' (no. 1026). Third, the change from the earthly life of grace to the heavenly life of glory brings the goal of a lifelong process of 'divinization' (see the first part of this chapter). The blessed will share in the ecstatic communion of mutual love that is the eternal life of the three divine persons. The indwelling of the Holy Spirit or life of grace will move to its heavenly climax, an intense participation in the life of the Father, Son, and Holy Spirit. 'Resting' fully in God we, who have been created as God's image, can at long last contemplate our divine model: 'Beloved, we are God's children now; it does not yet appear what we shall be, but we know that when he appears we shall be like him, for we shall see him as he is' (1 John 3: 2).

If such glory awaits the blessed in heaven, what has Catholic teaching to say about those who definitively close themselves to God's saving love?

4. The NT warns that the great judgement at the end of time will bring a separation between the 'good fish' and the 'bad fish' (Matt 13: 47–52), or between the 'sheep' who have cared for neighbours in distress and the 'goats' who have failed in that duty (Matt. 25: 31–46). The 'bad fish' and the 'goats' will be banished to 'eternal fire', 'eternal punishment', or 'into the outer darkness' where they 'will weep and grind their teeth' (Matt. 25: 30). On the basis of these and further biblical texts, Christians came to develop the doctrine of hell, a place or state where the devils and unrepentant sinners will suffer forever (DH 1002; ND 2307). This eternal punishment which was said to vary according to the gravity of the sins committed (DH 1306; ND 2309) was understood to consist in exclusion from God's presence (this is the pain of loss or damnation proper) and in suffering from an inextinguishable but unspecified 'fire' (see DH 443, 780; ND 1409).

Such an important creed as the Nicene-Constantinopolitan Creed of 381 did not include anything about the possibility or actuality of eternal damnation, but confined itself to professing faith in the final judgement of 'the living and the dead' and in 'the life of the world to come'. In the following century, the Pseudo-Athanasian Symbol, *Quicumque*, confessed that after the general resurrection and judgement 'those who have done evil will go to eternal fire' (DH 76; ND 17). In 1274 the Second Council of Lyons, in an appendix to a profession of faith, taught that even before the general resurrection of the dead, the souls of those who die in mortal sin will pass immediately after death to eternal punishment in hell (DH 858; ND 26). This movement from sober silence about hell professed by the Nicene-Constantinopolitan Creed to the details offered by the Second Council of Lyons mirrored how Christian teachers and believers had become more 'knowing' about the fate of those who seemed to die without repenting of their serious sins.

Christian literature, art, and preaching vividly filled in the official teaching. Stone carvings elaborated the parable of the wise and foolish bridesmaids (Matt. 25: 1–13), which ended with the latter group coming late and being excluded from the wedding banquet. These carvings represented the foolish bridesmaids being chained and led away by demons into hell. Painters ran riot in representing the fearful punishments meted out to the damned by the Devil and his cohorts. The journey through hell by Dante and his travelling companion, Virgil, depicted with painful brilliance the variety of sufferings that corresponded to the gravity of the sins that the damned had committed.

Nowadays, Catholic teaching speaks of hell in terms not of a punishment imposed externally by God but of a free and ultimate rejection of God. Out of respect for the freedom with which they are endowed, God never forces any person against his or her will to respond positively to the good. Given human freedom, hell remains a possibility for those who through deliberate malice refuse to love God and their neighbours. Thus, as Pope John Paul II stated, damnation or 'definitive separation from God' follows, when it is 'freely chosen by the human person and confirmed with death that seals his or her choice for ever. God's judgement ratifies this state.'[27]

But, unlike the many canonized and beatified men and women who are officially declared to be 'in heaven', the Catholic Church has never officially declared anyone to have been damned to hell. It makes no claims about the number, if any, of the damned. As John Paul II observed, we do not know 'whether or which human beings' are found in hell.[28] We may pray that the terrible possibility will never be realized for anyone. Unques-

---

[27] *L'Osservatore Romano* (English edn., 4 August 1999), 7.   [28] Ibid.

tionably Jesus left terrifying warnings about the possible outcome for serious sin. Yet we may hope that God's saving purpose for everyone (1 Tim. 2: 3–6) will be effective and that, finally, God will be 'all in all' (1 Cor. 15: 28)—that is to say, will achieve the divine purpose of saving the whole of creation which we know to suffer and need reconciliation.

Over the centuries some Christian writers have expressed this hope. Thus Isaac of Nineveh, who was also called Isaac the Syrian and who died *c*.700, stressed the infinite goodness and love of God when he wrote:

I am of the opinion that he is going to manifest some wonderful outcome, a matter of immense and ineffable compassion . . . It is not [the way of] the compassionate Maker to create rational beings in order to deliver them over mercilessly to unending affliction . . . God is not one who requites evil, but he sets aright evil. (*Homily* 39, 6, 15)

5. The general resurrection, called the 'resurrection of the flesh' by many early creeds or the 'resurrection of the dead' by the Nicene-Constantinopolitan Creed of 381, was always intimately linked in the Christian faith with Christ's own resurrection from the dead. It implies the ultimate consummation of God's plan for the whole of creation and the final completion of Christ's saving work. As the ancient hymn in the Letter to the Colossians indicates, at the general resurrection the two birthrights of Christ will finally coincide: the Firstborn over all creation becomes the Firstborn from the dead, who have all been brought to everlasting life (Col. 1: 15, 18).

6. The general resurrection was also persistently connected with Christ's future coming 'to judge the living and the dead'—the ultimate act of history and hence God's final word on the whole universe. God's mysterious plan will then be complete (see Eph. 1: 3–14). The creeds did nothing else than repeat Jesus' announcement that he would come in glory at the end to judge all people—the final judgement on both mankind as a whole and each individual. What we said above about the particular judgement applies even more to the final judgement. Rather than God the judge passing sentence on each and every individual at the general judgement, the whole of humanity and all creation will definitively experience the truth about themselves in the presence of God.

7. In the late twentieth century the Second Vatican Council, by presenting freshly the general resurrection and Christ's final coming in judgement and glory, helped many believers to recover the central vision

of early Christians: the Last One or Christ as the *Eschatos*, for whom we wait together, has priority over the last things or the *eschata*. The Council understood the Church to be the pilgrim people of God moving towards its final destiny and waiting for the risen Saviour to be definitively and powerfully manifested at the end (*Lumen Gentium*, 51).

The Council set the final future of the Church within the ultimate destiny of all humanity. The whole of humanity is moving towards its final goal, Christ's heavenly kingdom in which all people are to be united as one 'family beloved of God and of Christ their Brother' (*Gaudium et Spes*, 32). With Christ as the focal point, humanity as a whole and the created cosmos will be transformed and fulfilled (ibid. 39, 45). Such was the Council's renewed vision of all human beings and the entire creation finding in Christ their glorious destiny, the ultimate culmination of God's gracious self-communication.[29]

---

[29] J. Ratzinger, *Eschatology: Death and Eternal Life* (Washington, DC: Catholic University of America Press, 1988), which purports to be a comprehensive Catholic treatise, regrettably does not contain even one reference to the rich eschatological doctrine of Vatican II.

7

The Sacraments

We were buried with him by baptism into death, so that, just as
Christ was raised from the dead through the glory of the Father, we
too might walk in newness of life.   (St Paul, Rom. 6: 4)

The sacrament is one thing, the power of the sacrament another.

(St Augustine, *In Evangelium Johannis*, 26. 11)

On his way to martyrdom in Rome at the start of the second century AD,
Ignatius, bishop of Antioch, wrote to 'the Church which is in Smyrna of
Asia' to thank them for the welcome they had given him. Ignatius sent
abundant greetings 'in the blameless Spirit and in the Word of God' to
that community, which he called 'the Church of God the Father, and of
the beloved Jesus Christ, which has obtained mercy in every gift,
which . . . has been rendered most worthy of God and bearer of holiness
(*hagiophoros*)'. Just as his other name, 'Theo-phoros', made Ignatius a
'God-bearer', so the Church which had hosted him was a 'bearer of
holiness' (introd.).

What were the gifts that, through the Spirit and the Word of God,
made the Church a 'bearer of holiness'? In that same *Epistle to the
Smyrnaeans* Ignatius mentioned baptism and the Eucharist, which were
later to be called 'sacraments' and which continue to be celebrated by the
overwhelming majority of Christians. Like the Orthodox and unlike
many Protestants, the Catholic Church recognizes seven sacraments:
baptism, confirmation, Eucharist, penance, anointing of the sick, orders,
and matrimony. Unquestionably the divine gifts celebrated by Ignatius
and such NT writers as St Paul are not limited to the seven sacraments. But
they are seven privileged means that have been entrusted to his Church by

Christ and make his saving work (Ch. 4) personally present for men and women until the end of time. These sacraments are both perceptible signs (which can be seen, heard, tasted, touched, and smelled), central means for the common worship of God, and special vehicles of grace (Ch. 6) provided by the glorified Christ. They confer and strengthen the life of grace in the particular form that each sacrament symbolizes. How the Catholic sacramental system came to be and what the seven sacraments mean provide the themes for this chapter.[1]

We begin with the rites of Christian initiation: baptism, confirmation, and Eucharist. The intrinsic connection between these three sacraments causes them together to constitute full initiation into Christian life— something firmly expressed by the Second Vatican Council (*Ad Gentes*, 14). Like rites of passage in various human communities, these ecclesial initiation rites mark a movement from one kind of identity and status to another. The initiated 'die' to a former way of life and are 'resurrected' or 'reborn' to another. Right from NT times Christian initiation rites, or at least baptism, have been interpreted as rites of death, burial, and resurrection (Rom. 6: 1–14) and 'rebirth' (John 3: 5; Titus 3: 5). In a way that has resembled (without being identical with) other rites of passage, the stages of Christian initiation have included one of *separation* (entrance to the catechumenate), of *preparation* or transition when catechumens are instructed in Christian teaching and life (and learn to pray with the community), and of *celebration* (baptism, confirmation, and First Communion) by which the catechumens 'put on' Christ (Gal. 3: 26–7) and are incorporated into the 'one body' of the community (1 Cor. 12: 13). The process of Christian initiation has been followed by a period of 'mystagogy' or explanation of the mysteries, when the bishop or some other pastor spells out the fuller significance of the mysteries received at initiation and of the 'mystery' celebrated in every liturgy or public act of common worship. We look first at the history of Christian initiation,[2] and at its recent restoration for Catholics mandated by the Second Vatican Council (*Sacrosanctum Concilium*, 64).

---

[1] See L.-M. Chauvet, *The Sacraments* (Collegeville, Minn.: Liturgical Press, 2001).

[2] See M. E. Johnson, *The Rites of Christian Initiation: Their Evolution and Interpretation* (Collegeville, Minn.: Liturgical Press, 1999). P. Cramer, *Baptism and Change in the early Middle Ages c.200–c.1150* (Cambridge: Cambridge University Press, 1993).

THE SACRAMENTS OF INITIATION

From the start of Christianity the rite of baptismal purification and initiation was understood to be one process of justification and sanctification, in which the tripersonal God gave new life, and in which human beings were converted and entered into the Body of Christ: 'You were washed, you were sanctified, you were justified in the name of the Lord Jesus Christ and in the Spirit of our God' (1 Cor. 6: 11). We begin with baptism.

Baptism

We take up the celebration and understanding of Christian baptism in three stages: in the NT and beyond; the contribution of St Augustine; and the 1977 Rite for Christian Initiation of Adults.

The New Testament and Beyond

The baptized knew themselves to be assumed once and for all into the dying and rising of Christ, who had himself referred to his coming death as a 'baptism' (Mark 10: 38; Luke 12: 50). Having become God's adopted sons and daughters, they were initiated into the Church, 'a people claimed by God' (1 Pet. 2: 9–10). Their 'old self was crucified with him [Christ], so that the sinful self might be destroyed' and they 'might no longer be enslaved to sin' (Rom. 6: 6). Baptism, therefore, called on them to 'make no provision for the flesh' nor 'gratify its desires' (Rom. 13: 14). There was no room for half measures. Their rebirth through water and the Holy Spirit meant believing tenaciously in the 'good news', by which they were to be saved, provided they held fast to it (1 Cor. 15: 1–2). They were to live to the full the gift of baptism, and refrain from all behaviour that failed to witness to their new life.

Like birth itself and the coming resurrection from the dead, the rebirth and new life of baptism can be granted only once. From the outset, Christians acknowledged the once-and-for-all nature of baptism. Just as there is only 'one Lord', 'one Spirit', 'one God and Father of all', one Church, and 'one faith', so there is only 'one baptism' (Eph. 4: 4–6), which may never be repeated. Only once can we become adopted sons and daughters of God. In later times the Council of Trent was to insist that, after baptism is 'truly and rightly conferred', it cannot be repeated, even in the case of those who have denied their faith and then repented (DH 1624;

ND 1430). More than a century earlier the Council of Florence had explained why baptism, like confirmation and orders (and unlike the Eucharist, reconciliation, anointing of the sick, and matrimony) can never be conferred a second time. Baptism, along with confirmation and orders, imprints an 'indelible character' on the soul of the recipient (DH 1313, 1609; ND 1308, 1319). This way of expressing the once-and-for-all nature of baptism differed from the NT, but the point was the same. In any case those who spoke of an indelible character imprinted on the soul aligned themselves with the NT language of the 'seal of the Spirit' received at baptism. St Augustine, recalling the image of Jesus as the Good Shepherd, wrote of 'the Lord's brand-mark' on his sheep, an enduring sign by which the baptized are to be 'recognized, not disallowed' (*De Baptismo contra Donatistas*, 6. 1).

The last NT text to be recalled here, one that provided the threefold structure for the post-NT creeds with their 'articles' dedicated to the Father, the Son, and the Holy Spirit, is the mandate from the risen Christ at the end of Matthew's Gospel: 'Make disciples of all nations, baptizing them in the name of the Father and of the Son and of the Holy Spirit' (Matt. 28: 19). This baptismal formula in the name of the Trinity, rather than coming from the risen Jesus himself, reflects the practice of Matthew's community in the 70s who experienced the risen Lord present in their midst. At first Christians seem to have baptized converts in the name of Jesus Christ (e.g. Acts 2: 38). Even so, naming Christ inevitably brought in God (the Father) and the Holy Spirit, as 1 Corinthians 6: 11 illustrates. 'Washing in the name of the Lord Jesus Christ' led Paul to add at once: 'in the Spirit of our God [the Father]'. Baptismal initiation was always a radically new orientation 'in Christ', 'through the Spirit', and 'to the Father'.

When they wrote about Christian initiation, the second- and third-century Fathers highlighted two major consequences of baptism: the remission of sins and the new life in Christ through the Spirit. Thus Clement of Alexandria (d. *c*.215) understood baptism to be a 'washing' by which 'we are cleansed from our sins', 'adoption' as God's sons and daughters, 'enlightenment', and being 'made perfect' (*Paedagogus*, 1. 6). In Eastern Christianity 'enlightenment' or 'illumination' was to become a dominant motif for baptism.

Tertullian (d. *c*.225) was the first to write a treatise on baptism. He distinguished between (*a*) the 'simplicity of the divine works which are seen in the act' of baptism celebrated 'without pomp' (i.e. without the complexity and trappings of pagan rituals), and (*b*) 'the grandeur which is promised in the effect' (*De Baptismo*, 2). Through the primeval hovering of the Spirit over the waters (Gen. 1: 2), 'the nature of water' received 'the power of sanctifying'. Hence any 'waters' used in baptism, 'after the invocation of God, attain the sacramental power of sanctification' (ibid. 4).[3] Quoting the Lord's mandate, 'Go . . . teach the nations, baptizing them in the name of the Father, and of the Son, and of the Holy Spirit,' Tertullian concluded: 'The law of baptizing has been imposed, and the formula prescribed' (ibid. 13). In the same section of *De Baptismo* Tertullian not only used the adjective 'sacramental' but also the noun 'sacrament'—in the sense of a ritual action through which a salvific deed (Christ's 'birth, passion, and resurrection') becomes present, so that those performing the rite share in the deed's saving power. Here the Latin 'sacramentum', which originally referred to oath-taking, consecration, or ritual obligation, acquired the meaning of some ritual action that let human beings participate in the saving grace provided by God through Christ's death and resurrection. In a wider sense the Latin term became a rough equivalent of the NT Greek word *mysterion*, the whole divine plan realized in Christ for reconciling all people and all things to God (e.g. Rom. 11: 25; Eph. 1: 9; 3: 2, 4, 9).

Tertullian clarified at least three points: the sacramental act or sign (in particular, baptism with water), the effect of that sign through the power of the Spirit (sanctification), and the official regulation (within and for the community's worship) of those signs (here the law of baptism and its formula).[4] He also bequeathed to Western Christianity the noun 'sacrament' and the adjective 'sacramental', proving himself once again the creator of what was to become official terminology (see Ch. 1).[5]

Soon after the death of Tertullian, and unlike him, St Cyprian of Carthage (d. 258) strongly defended the practice of infant baptism and

---

[3] Where Tertullian attributed 'sacramental power' to the baptismal waters 'after the invocation of God', St Ambrose of Milan (339–97) was to contrast the cleansing effect of the waters with that of the Spirit: 'The water is that in which the flesh is dipped, so that all carnal sin may be washed away'; yet 'it is not through the waters but through grace that a person is cleansed' (*De Mysteriis*, 3. 11. 17).

[4] Many centuries later the Council of Trent sustained Tertullian's sense of the need to follow 'prescribed formulas', by insisting that 'accepted and approved rites' be used in the administration of all the sacraments (DH 1613; ND 1323).

[5] Tertullian called both baptism and the Eucharist 'sacraments' (*Adversus Marcionem*, 4. 34).

offered some theological justification for it (*Epistola* 64). Cyprian also witnessed to the custom of baptized infants receiving the Eucharist at the conclusion of the baptismal rite (and so making what would later be called their 'First Communion'), a practice that continues today in the churches of the Christian East.[6]

But apropos of baptism administered by those outside the unity of the church (i.e. heretics or schismatics), Cyprian followed Tertullian (De Baptismo, 15) and denied the validity of such a rite. It was in that context that Cyprian delivered his dictum, 'no salvation outside the Church' (*Epistola* 73. 2), and emphasized the ecclesial setting of baptism: 'he can no longer have God for his father who does not have the Church for his mother' (*De Catholicae Ecclesiae Unitate*, 6). Other third-century Christians, such as St Hippolytus in the *Apostolic Tradition*, argued that, since the Holy Spirit is not be found 'outside the Church', heretics cannot have valid sacraments.

Cyprian drew practical conclusions from his view that valid baptism did not exist 'outside the Church': that is to say, among schismatics and heretics. If and when they sought reconciliation, they were not 'rebaptized' but simply baptized—validly and for the first time (*Epistola* 71. 1). Over this issue Cyprian profoundly disagreed with Pope Stephen I, who held that baptism administered in the name of the Trinity and with the intention of incorporating someone into the Church was always valid, even when the baptizers were separated by heresy or schism. Hence penitent heretics were not to be baptized but simply reconciled through 'an imposition of hands by way of penance' (DH 110; ND 1401). The teaching of Stephen, who suffered martyrdom in the same persecution as Cyprian, was to prevail. But the issue between Stephen and Cyprian returned with a vengeance in the Donatist controversy that confronted Augustine, and prompted him into clarifying what constitutes the valid administration of the sacraments, especially baptism, and their proper minister (see Ch. 1).

St Augustine

The Donatists accused the Catholic Church in North Africa and elsewhere of being 'traitors' or real schismatics. Hence, so they argued, its ministers, like Judas Iscariot himself, were incapable of administering

---

[6] See D. Holeton, *Infant Communion. Then and Now* (Bramcote, Nottingham: Grove Books, 1981).

valid baptism or other sacraments. Augustine had a triple response to make. First, any baptism that uses the proper element of water and the proper words (the trinitarian formula) is 'valid' (*Contra Litteras Petiliani*, I. 6. 6). Second, he distinguished between the formal (the words) and the material (the water) dimensions that together make up the sacramental sign of baptism: 'Take away the word, and the water is neither more nor less than water. The word is added to the element, and there results the sacrament, as if itself also a kind of visible word' (*In Evangelium Johannis*, 80. 3). Eventually this distinction led to the medieval terminology of the 'matter' and the 'form' of the sacraments, a terminology approved by the Council of Florence (DH 1307; ND 1312). In the case of baptism, for instance, the 'matter' is the action of pouring the water or immersing someone in the water, whereas the trinitarian formula ('I baptize you . . .') provides the 'form'. Third, Christ himself is the real minister of baptism (*In Evangelium Johannis*, 6. 7). Hence even Judas Iscariot could administer a 'valid' sacrament, provided he used the required elements and words. Since the invisible Christ, not the visible minister, is the 'origin, root and head' of the baptized, even sacraments administered in schism (e.g. by the Donatists) should be recognized as valid (*Contra Litteras Petiliani*, I. 5. 6). Elsewhere Augustine put this point more forcefully: 'The baptism which is consecrated by the words of Christ is holy, even when conferred by the polluted, and on the polluted, however shameless and unclean they may be.' It is 'the power of God' that 'supports his sacrament, whether for the salvation of those who use it aright, or the doom of those who employ it wrongly' (*De Baptismo*, 3. 15).

Augustine bequeathed here two major themes to sacramental teaching in the West. First, the sheer performance of the act (*ex opere operato*, or the prayer of faith of the community that has received the Spirit) rather than the personal holiness of the visible performer (*ex opere operantis*) guarantees the efficacy of the sacrament, especially baptism. This is because it is primarily the invisible Christ (made visible in his Body which is the Church) who performs the baptizing, the ordaining, and what would later be called the dispensing of all sacramental graces. The medieval theologians who spoke of the *opus operatum* were in fact referring to the *opus Christi* or Christ himself working in the sacraments, as Thomas Aquinas put it (*ST* III q. 65 a. 1). The Council of Trent was to use the language of *ex opere operato* (DH 1608; ND 1318). In his 1947 encyclical on 'Christian Worship (*Mediator Dei*)' Pope Pius XII repeated (*a*) the

Tridentine language of *ex opere operato* and *ex opere operantis* (no. 29), but also (*b*) wrote of Christ's active 'presence' in the sacraments (no. 19). The Second Vatican Council left the (*a*) terminology behind and spoke of the powerful, personal 'presence' of Christ in the administration of all the sacraments (*Sacrosanctum Concilium*, 7), and indeed in the whole pastoral ministry of bishops and priests (*Lumen Gentium*, 21). But the point is the same: sacraments are primarily things God does for us through Christ, not vice versa.

Second, Augustine's stress on the priority of the divine initiative means that the validity of the sacraments does not depend on the worthiness of the human minister. God gives the grace, whether or not the particular minister is worthy. This issue was to flare up again in the twelfth century with the Waldensians (see Ch. 2) and even more in the fourteenth and fifteenth centuries, when John Wyclif and John Huss argued that sacraments administered by a sinful priest or bishop are not effective. In 1415 the Council of Constance and three years later Pope Martin V insisted that even 'a bad priest', provided he (*a*) 'uses the correct matter and form' and (*b*) 'has the intention of doing what the Church does', truly and validly administers the sacraments (DH 1262; ND 1304; see DH 1154; ND 1303). In the sixteenth century the Council of Trent reiterated this teaching but expressed (*a*) in a slightly less technical way—as the minister observing 'all the essentials that belong to the performing and conferring of the sacrament' (DH 1611–12; ND 1321–2). (Nowadays one should mention the prayer of the liturgical assembly among 'the essentials that belong to the performing and conferring of the sacrament'.)

In his controversies with the Donatists, Augustine never held, however, that merely 'valid' sacraments are necessarily 'fruitful'. He drew a distinction between the sacrament or sign itself, *sacramentum*, and its fruitfulness, or *res sacramenti*. Those outside the unity of the Church, such as the Donatists, were validly baptized but did not enjoy the fruit of baptismal regeneration, which is charity or love (*De Baptismo*, 1. 3) and the presence of the Holy Spirit (ibid. 1. 12). Unless they returned to visible unity with the one Church, they would not experience the proper effect of baptism; they were truly baptized but to their 'doom' (ibid. 3. 15).[7] What was enduringly important in Augustine's position against the Donatists was his conscious departure from the views of his North African predecessors,

---

[7] See J. L. Maier, *Le dossier du donatisme*, 2 vols. (Berlin: Akademie, 1987–9).

Tertullian and Cyprian: sacraments—in particular, baptism—exist 'outside' the Catholic Church. They may fail, as in the case of the schismatic Donatists, to enjoy their full and fruitful effect. But Augustine's insight in the long run opened the way for the Catholic Church (and other Christian communities) to acknowledge one, true baptism for the forgiveness of sins beyond their boundaries.

Back in Chs. 1, 5, and 6 we saw how Augustine also entered into a major controversy with the Pelagians. Against this group he appealed to the practice of baptism for infants; the newly born inherit original sin and need to be baptized, so as to be freed from it through the Holy Spirit and reborn to the new life of grace. It was partly through Augustine's influence that infant baptism, administered as soon as possible after birth, came to be seen as the norm. In any case a high infant mortality rate encouraged the practice. This also meant that baptism during the Easter season or at one of the feast-days—for instance, at the Epiphany—gradually disappeared.

But Augustine witnessed to one, integrated sequence of Christian initiation: baptism at the end of the catechumenate, followed at once by an anointing, the laying on of hands, and reception of the Eucharist. It was only in Rome that, before the reception of the Eucharist, the newly baptized received a *second* postbaptismal anointing *from the bishop*. The reservation of this anointing to the bishop spread and helped to trigger the emergence of confirmation as a separate sacrament. We return to this development below. As regards the season for Christian initiation, evidence from the fourth and fifth centuries shows how Christian communities preferred to celebrate the rites of Christian initiation at the Easter Vigil and after a forty-day preparation during Lent.

The Rite for Christian Initiation of Adults

Since the Rite for Christian Initiation of Adults (RCIA) was introduced in 1972, Catholics have been blessed by a retrieval of the ancient process for a conscious, grace-filled entry into the life of the Church. Formally elected and welcomed by the local community on the First Sunday of Lent, the catechumens, who have already been formed by the assembly in the ways of worship, justice, and personal prayer, begin their final period of preparation to receive the three sacraments of Christian initiation. The gospels of the Samaritan woman in search of water (John 4: 5–42), the man born blind (John 9: 1–41), and the raising of Lazarus (John 11: 1–45) are proclaimed at Mass on the Third, Fourth, and Fifth Sundays of Lent, respectively. These gospels incorporate three important themes of Christian initiation: cleansing through water and yearning for eternal life; faith understood as sight and vision; and death to one's 'old' self so as to rise again with Christ. After the homily on those Sundays the candidates, now called the 'elect' or the chosen, kneel before the presiding priest. After the assembly has risen to intercede for them, the president in a prayer of exorcism asks that God will deliver them from the power and wounds of sin. The ancient customs of *traditio* (handing over) and *redditio* (handing back) also enjoy their place in the Lenten preparation. The community of believers 'hands over' to the catechumens the Creed or symbol (summary) of the Church's faith, the 'Our Father' which is the model of all Christian prayer, and sometimes other special signs of Christian life, such as the Bible, which records and symbolizes the history of salvation into which the baptized enter, and copies of the Beatitudes and of the Ten Commandments, the guidelines for Christian living. After instruction on these items and a short period of living them out, the candidates are invited to 'hand back' what they have received by giving witness or by praying.

The rites of the Easter Vigil conclude the catechumenate. The lighting of the Easter Candle from a fire, the singing of the Easter Proclamation (*Exultet*) which announces Christ's victory over sin and death, and the extended readings from scripture that recount the divine work of creation and redemption lead up to the baptismal liturgy. Accompanied by their godparents, adult believers who offer the support of their own life of faith, the catechumens choose the name of a Christian saint to indicate the new life that will follow their baptism. They publicly renounce sin, 'the glamour of evil', and the power of Satan, profess their faith in a threefold interrogation that follows the wording of the Apostles' Creed, and are then baptized. They are clothed in a white garment to show the new, purified life they have received with and through Christ. Lighting a small candle from the great Easter Candle, the tall symbol of the risen Christ's presence in the believing community, the godparents hand it to the neophytes or newly baptized as a sign that they have shared with them their faith. The neophytes take the small candle and make it their own; Christ has called them to ensure that the light of faith, hope, and love shines before the world (Matt. 5: 14–16). The neophytes are then confirmed by a laying on of hands and an anointing, so that the gift of the Holy Spirit will strengthen their new life in Christ. The whole process of Christian

FIG. 10(a). A Catholic wedding in Kampala, Uganda in February 2002. (Carlos Reyes-Manzo/ Andes Press Agency.) (b). A christening in Brixton, London. The water of baptism brings new life, and the Easter candle symbolizes the light of Jesus who will guide the newly baptized. (Carlos Reyes-Manzo/Andes Press Agency.)

initiation reaches its conclusion when the newly baptized share in the Eucharist and make their First Communion.

The Churches of Eastern Christianity continue to celebrate the three sacraments of initiation together, even in the case of infants. In the Catholic Church of the West, as well as with many other Western Christians, parents are expected to bring their children to be baptized in early infancy. The parents and godparents profess their own faith in the name of the children, and promise to educate them in the Catholic faith and help them to live a life that befits the baptized. But First Communion and confirmation are delayed. The 1983 Code of Canon Law requires that, before receiving their First Communion, children should be carefully prepared and, 'according to their capacity', able to 'understand what the mystery of Christ means' (913. 1). It prescribes that candidates for confirmation be 'suitably instructed, properly disposed, and able to renew their baptismal promises' (889. 2). The Code prefers confirmation 'about the age of discretion' (canon 891), which would be around the time for First Communion. Hence confirmation could be celebrated during the same liturgy as First Communion—which would better express the unity between the three sacraments of initiation. We turn now to the development of confirmation in Western Christianity and Catholicism.

Confirmation

In describing the baptismal washing, which involved several ordained ministers, the early third-century *Apostolic Tradition* distinguished a first anointing administered by a priest from a second one administered by the bishop (nos. 21–2). Writing around the same time, Tertullian observed that this second, postbaptismal anointing was associated with a laying on of hands and an invocation of the Holy Spirit (*De Baptismo*, 7–8). The neophyte was thus 'confirmed' in the Spirit, something that the Western Church was to establish as a separate and subsequent rite. In early Christianity, however, there was only one unified ceremony of initiation presided over by the bishop, who reserved to himself the second anointing. He thus *confirmed* all that had just been done, and it was this that led to the name for a separate sacrament.

Some ancient witnesses report that the bishop anointed the baptized with holy chrism; others, such as Tertullian, mention the laying on of hands and invocation of the Spirit. While Eastern bishops reserved to themselves the blessing of the chrism but allowed priests to do the anointing in their stead, Western bishops insisted that the anointing with holy chrism was their exclusive right (DH 215; ND 1406). In both cases (the right to bless the chrism and the right to anoint with it) implied that only the bishop, as head of the local Church, can incorporate someone fully into it. Until the eighth century, bishops continued to anoint infants at their baptism. As Christianity moved into rural areas, it became increasingly difficult for bishops to attend all the baptisms. Easter Week, the week 'in albis' when adult neophytes dressed in white, offered the chance of approaching the bishop and receiving the second anointing. But with many people being baptized by pastors out in the countryside, such 'confirming' could be delayed until the bishop's next visitation. People baptized as infants might not have their baptism 'confirmed' until they were 6, 8, or 10 years old. Only after that did they receive Holy Communion.

During the first millennium, with some exceptions, the traditional order for the sacraments of initiation remained the same everywhere: baptism, confirmation, and Eucharist. But in Western Christianity, however, the delay between baptism and confirmation eventually led to the situation: baptism was conferred in early infancy;[8] First Communion came at the age of reason; and confirmation, delayed until adolescence or early adulthood, became the sacrament of mature faith commitment. Any sense of the unified process of Christian initiation was widely lost.

When examining what 'perseverance in Christ' means, Augustine explained it as 'the gift of God' to cope with 'the peril of falling' that characterized our entire life (*De Dono Perseverantiae*, 1). Some theologians of the Middle Ages used Augustine's concept of perseverance to express the meaning of confirmation. Aquinas himself stated that 'in the sacrament of confirmation we receive the fullness of the Holy Spirit in order to be strengthened . . . against the infirmity of the soul' (*ST* III q. 65 a. 1). 'Confirmation is to baptism as growth is to birth,' he added (*ST* III q. 72 a. 6).

Moving beyond notions of perseverance, strength, and growth, Vatican II retrieved from ancient Christianity the ecclesial dimension of confirmation: through this sacrament the faithful 'are more perfectly bound to the Church' and 'are, as true witnesses of Christ, more strictly obliged to spread the faith by word and deed' (*Lumen Gentium*, 11). This sacrament

---

[8] Martin Luther, who was born on 10 November 1483, was baptized the very next day, the Feast of St Martin of Tours—a typical Western example of baptism (but not confirmation and First Communion) following very quickly after birth.

constitutes in the Western Church a rite of passage for young adults who were baptized when they were babies. Confirmation comes at a time when they are expected to show themselves more mature and courageous witnesses. Hence many emphasize that confirmed Christians become 'soldiers of Christ' and enjoy maturity through 'the seven gifts of the Spirit': wisdom, understanding, counsel, fortitude, knowledge, piety, and the fear of the Lord. It might be better to highlight the communication of the divine Gift, the Holy Spirit in person. Already given in baptism, the Spirit now descends more fully upon those being confirmed. At the celebration of confirmation, the bishop or priest who presides over the liturgical ceremony accompanies the anointing with the words, 'Be sealed with the Gift of the Holy Spirit.' Through this transforming gift, or what John Paul II called this 'Person-gift' (*Dominum et Vivificantem*, 23–3), the faithful enjoy the indwelling of the Spirit, bring Christ to the world, and await the day when they will attain the full inheritance: God's own glory (Eph. 1: 13–14). Even now confirmation draws believers into the witness that the Spirit gives to the Father. As Paul writes to the Romans: 'the Spirit bears witness with our spirit that we are children of God, and if children, then heirs—heirs of God and fellow heirs of Christ' (8: 16–17).

Eucharist

In a single, interconnected process of Christian initiation, baptism and confirmation reach their goal in the Eucharist (Greek for 'thanksgiving'), the greatest of the sacraments and the central act of worship in the life of the Church.

The NT Origins

Unlike the other sacraments that Christ indirectly instituted, this sacrament comes directly from something that Jesus said and did during his earthly life: the institution of the Eucharist at the Last Supper. Convergent NT traditions about the Last Supper support this conclusion, while differing slightly over details. For instance, on the one hand, Paul (1 Cor. 11: 23–6) and Luke (22: 14–20) report the instruction to 'do this as a memorial of me', and, on the other hand Mark (14: 22–5) and Matthew (26: 26–9) report 'this is my body' (without the 'for you' found in the tradition from Paul and Luke) and 'my blood of the covenant' (without qualifying it as the 'new' covenant as do Paul and Luke). But these and further differences are secondary. The convergence of NT witness supports the constant Christian tradition and the teaching of the Council of Trent (DH 1640; ND 1517): Christ himself directly instituted the Eucharist before he died. At that sacrificial meal, he invited his disciples to share, by eating and drinking, in his covenant offering to the Father.

In this sacrifice of praise, thanksgiving, and expiation for sins, Christ functioned as both priest and victim. His priestly words and gestures (the 'breaking' of the bread/body, reported by Paul and all three evangelists, and the 'pouring out of my blood', reported by the three evangelists) were clearly to be understood sacrificially. These words and actions symbolized and enacted the new covenant effected by Jesus' life, death, resurrection, and sending of the Spirit, a covenant of reconciliation that bound human beings in a new relationship with God and with one another. Sealing the covenant with blood unmistakably recalled the Jewish sacrificial background: in particular, the ceremony at Mount Sinai when Moses in his role as mediator dramatized the union between God (represented by the altar) and the twelve tribes of Israel[9] by flinging some blood from the sacrifices over the altar and over the people and said: 'This is the blood of the covenant which the Lord has made with you' (Exod. 24: 1–8).

The Letter to the Hebrews developed at length the themes of the unique priesthood and unique sacrifice of Christ. This sacrifice, offered once and for all, redeemed all and mediated the new covenant (Heb. 4: 14–10: 39). Hebrews, while treating Christ's death and glorious exaltation, did not appeal to what immediately preceded the crucifixion and resurrection: the sacrificial meal on the night before he died.[10] The imagery of Hebrews drew from the levitical priesthood, the tent shrine of Exodus, and the ceremony of the Day of Expiation (Heb. 9: 7), as well as from the ratification of the covenant at Mount Sinai. In radically reinterpreting priesthood, sacrifice, and covenant, Hebrews filled out what Jesus said and did at the Last Supper. While the Last Supper was a sacrifice, even more obviously it was a meal involving the consecrated bread and wine: 'take and eat' and 'drink all of you' (Matt. 26: 26–7). This meal formed the

---

[9] For the evangelists, early Christians, and presumably for Jesus himself, the presence of 'the twelve' (Mark 14: 12, 17, 20; Matt. 26: 17, 20) or 'the (twelve) apostles' (Luke 22: 14) at the Last Supper recalled the covenant scene of the twelve tribes at Sinai. That, however, is not to say that only the Twelve and no one from the wider group of the disciples attended the Last Supper (see Matt. 26: 26).

[10] Some scholars, however, find in Heb. 9: 12, 14; 10: 19 a reference to communion in Christ's blood and to the eucharistic cup.

FIG. 11. Caravaggio (d. 1610) catching the dramatic moment at Emmaus when the two disciples recognize the risen Jesus as he blesses and 'breaks bread'. (© The National Gallery, London.)

highpoint of the previous meals of Jesus with sinners. During his ministry he ate with sinful men and women; that table fellowship was a major means for initiating people into a new, close relationship with God. What Jesus had repeatedly done during his lifetime he did at the end. All four Gospels make a point of stressing the moral weakness of those with whom he shared the Last Supper: Judas was about to betray him, Peter was about to deny him, and the other male disciples (at least according to Matthew, Mark, and Luke) were all to abandon him at his arrest. They needed to be initiated into a fresh relationship with God.

In its 1963 constitution on the liturgy (*Sacrosanctum Concilium*) the Second Vatican Council entitled ch. 2 'The Most Holy Mystery of the Eucharist'. By 'mystery' the Council pointed to a reality that, although revealed to us, can never be pinned down or defined by human reason, but which constantly discloses to us different aspects of its inexhaustible truth. By adding 'most holy' the Council indicated that the reality of the Eucharist, even more than the other sacraments, brings an encounter with the awesome and fascinating reality of God. Thus the title for that chapter should alert readers to the fact that any reflection on the Eucharist must reckon with its boundlessly rich significance in truth and grace. Historically this richness has also been reflected in the variety of its other names, such as the Breaking of Bread, the Lord's Supper, the Divine Liturgy, the Mass, the Christian Passover, and Holy Communion.

Over two millennia of Catholic and Christian life, however, six themes have recurringly emerged from prayerful consideration of the Eucharist: (1) the trinitarian aspect; (2) the unifying meal; (3) the sacramental sacrifice; (4) the special presence of the crucified and risen Christ; (5) the past, actual, and future dimensions; (6) the call to fraternal and social commitment in and through the Church. This is not to deny that other themes have turned up in official teaching and eucharistic theology. But our list of themes can help to organize much of what Catholics (and many other Christians) have believed and taught about the Eucharist. We begin with the NT writers.

Even before his Gospel ends, Luke begins to touch on theme 2 with his references to the Eucharist as 'the breaking of bread' (Luke 24: 35; Acts 2: 42, 46). At the start of a meal Jewish fathers broke the (flat) bread and shared it with those present while saying a prayer or singing a hymn of thanksgiving—a ceremony that Jesus himself followed when instituting the Eucharist.[11] Matthew, Mark, Luke, and Paul all recall that Jesus 'broke bread' at the Last Supper. When the risen Lord 'was at table' with the two disciples at Emmaus, they recognized him when he 'took bread, said the blessing, broke the bread, and offered it to them' (Luke 24: 30–1). But, not surprisingly, we glean more about the Eucharist from Paul and John, rather than from Luke. Paul wrote of taking part in the 'Lord's Supper' (1 Cor. 11: 20), and John of eating 'the bread of heaven' (John 6: 51). Only towards the end of the first century was the name 'Eucharist' to appear (*Didache*, 9. 1, 5).[12]

When correcting the Christians of Corinth, who were divided about such issues as meat that came from pagan sacrifices and divisions among themselves (which also involved tensions between rich and poor Christians), Paul invoked the Lord's Supper and interpreted it. The apostle condemned taking part in pagan sacrifices as simply incompatible with sharing in the sacrifice of the body and blood of Christ (1 Cor. 10: 14–22).[13] Here Paul contrasted Christ's sacrifice with those of pagans in Corinth and, in passing and with no vehemence, with the Jewish sacrifices that still continued at that time (the middle 50s) in the Jerusalem Temple. As well as touching in this context the theme of sacrifice (theme 3), Paul appealed also to what the Eucharist means as a sacred meal (theme 2). He may have had that in mind when he recalled the 'spiritual' food and drink provided by the manna and the water from the rock in the desert (1 Cor. 10: 3–4), a hint of what the Spirit of God provided during the Exodus and would bring to completion in the bread and wine consecrated and consumed at the Eucharist.[14] In any case

[11] The action and prayer of the bread blessing were completed when those at table ate the bread and with it the blessings given by God through the meal.

[12] Paul, nevertheless, applied the verb *eucharistein* to Jesus' actions at the Last Supper (1 Cor. 11: 24) as did the Gospel accounts (Matt. 26: 27; Mark 14: 23; Luke 22: 19). Those who date the *Didache* a little later find the first use of 'Eucharist' for the sacrament in St Ignatius of Antioch (*Epistle to the Philadelphians*, 4).

[13] Back in 1 Cor. 5: 7 Paul reminded his readers that 'Christ our paschal lamb has been sacrificed'. In the chapter under examination, as well as referring to Jews 'eating the sacrifices' and so 'sharing the altar' (1 Cor. 10: 18), he writes of 'food sacrificed to idols' (1 Cor. 10: 19), twice of pagans 'sacrificing' (1 Cor. 10: 20), and once of 'the table of demons' (1 Cor. 10: 21). On a 'table' in the temples of various divinities, pagans shared in the altar by eating cult meals with food offered to idols. In comparing the Lord's Supper to Jewish sacrifices and sharply contrasting it with pagan sacrifices, Paul indicates that he thinks of the Lord's Supper as a sacrifice and probably also of 'the Lord's table' (1 Cor. 10: 21) as an altar.

[14] Later the *Didache* was to refer to the eucharistic elements as 'spiritual food and drink' (10. 3); that connection may have already been intended by Paul. See A. C. Thiselton, *The First Epistle to the Corinthians* (Carlisle: Paternoster Press, 2000), 726.

Paul repeatedly referred to the 'eating' and 'drinking' that the eucharistic celebration entailed (1 Cor. 11: 17–34). Apparently only the baptized share in this meal—a requirement clarified later (in the *Didache* and by St Justin[15]). Paul vividly expressed the presence (theme 4) of the crucified and risen Christ by questioning his readers: 'The cup of blessing which we bless, is it not a sharing in the blood of Christ? The bread which we break, is it not a sharing in the body of Christ?' (1 Cor. 10: 16). The apostle also repeated the words with which Christ had identified himself with the elements: 'This (bread) is my body; this cup is the new covenant in my blood' (1 Cor. 11: 24–5). Paul's sense of the special presence of Christ in the Eucharist came through the warning that 'whoever eats the bread or drinks the cup of the Lord unworthily will profane the body and blood of the Lord' (1 Cor. 11: 27).[16]

Further, in a lapidary fashion Paul incorporated theme 5: 'As often as you eat this bread and drink this cup, you proclaim [in the present] the Lord's death [in the past] until he comes [in the future]' (1 Cor. 11: 26). The re-presentation here and now (in the shared eating, drinking, and 'pro-claiming' of the paschal mystery), the memorial of the past foundational event of salvation (the 'doing in remembrance' of Jesus handed over, symbolically in the Cenacle and physically on Calvary), and the anticipa-tion of his coming (which makes the sacrament a foretaste and advance presentation of the final kingdom and the future 'marriage supper of the Lamb' (Rev. 19: 9)) are woven wonderfully together in the liturgy of the community. More than a thousand years later, the Pauline theme of eucharistic experience, memory, and hope was classically expressed in a text for the Feast of Corpus Christi (instituted in 1264): 'O sacred banquet in which Christ is received: his suffering is remembered [past], (our) mind is filled with grace [present], and we receive a pledge of the glory that is to be ours [future].'[17]

---

[15] The *Didache* forbade communion being given to the unbaptized: 'Let no one eat or drink of your Eucharist except those who have been baptized into the name of the Lord' (9. 5; see Justin, *First Apology,* 66. 1).

[16] Paul's sense of Christ's presence in the Eucharist cannot be separated from his sense of Christ's presence in the assembly, a presence that those who eat and drink without thinking of the others in the assembly do not recognize (theme 6).

[17] 'O sacrum convivium, in quo Christus sumitur; recolitur memoria passionis eius; mens impletur gratia; et futurae gloriae nobis pignus datur.' In 1963 the Second Vatican Council quoted this antiphon, but omitted some words dear to Lutherans and other Protestants: 'his suffering is remembered (recolitur memoria passionis)' (*Sacrosanctum concilium,* 47).

Finally, Paul underlined vigorously how unity among Christians was both expressed and built up by the eucharistic sharing (theme 6): the 'divisions' and 'factions' (1 Cor. 11: 18–19) at Corinth were simply incompatible with the unity in Christ that partaking in the Eucharist expressed for the Church, his social body—a theme that the Apostle went on at once to develop (1 Cor. 12: 4–31).[18]

Although the Fourth Gospel, unlike those according to Matthew, Mark, and Luke, provides no narrative of the institution of the Eucharist, it contains a rich eucharistic theology, to be found in two sections: the presentation of Jesus as the bread of life (John 6: 22–71) which comes after the miraculous feeding of the five thousand (John 6: 1–15); and the story of the final meal with his disciples (John 13: 1–38), with the farewell discourse and prayer that follow (John 14: 1–17: 26).

When telling the story of Jesus feeding the five thousand, Mark (whose words were adopted by Matthew and Luke) and/or the tradition from which he drew used language coloured by the eucharistic liturgy: '*Taking* the five *loaves* and the two fish and looking up to heaven, he *blessed* (*eulogesen*) and *broke* the loaves, and *gave* them to his disciples... And all *ate* and were filled' (Mark 6: 41–2). The terminology foreshadowed what would be said about the institution of the Eucharist (Mark 14: 22–4). The 'gathering' of the 'broken pieces' (Mark 6: 43) would find parallels in what was apparently a eucharistic prayer at the end of the first century (*Didache*, 9). John, who also includes the story of the feeding of the five thousand, introduces even more eucharistic overtones. Unlike the other Gospels (where Matt. 14: 19 and Luke 9: 16 follow Mark 6: 41 in using *eulogein*), John describes Jesus as 'giving thanks' (*eucharistesas*) and later likewise summarizes the actions of Jesus in the feeding as 'giving thanks' (John 6: 11, 23). What is even more important, John takes up the miracle to develop the theme of Jesus being himself 'the bread of life'.[19]

Many commentators on John 6 remark that 'my flesh for the life of the world' (John 6: 51) corresponded approximately to Paul's 'this is my body

---

[18] On Paul's theology of the Lord's Supper see J. D. G. Dunn, *The Theology of Paul the Apostle* (Grand Rapids, Mich.: Eerdmans, 1998), 599–623; on 1 Cor. 11: 17–34 see A. C. Thiselton, *The First Epistle to the Corinthians*, 848–99.

[19] In a scene with eucharistic colouring at the end of John's Gospel, the risen Jesus will feed seven of his disciples with bread *and fish* (John 21: 9–13)—an echo of the miraculous feeding with five loaves and two fish.

for you' (1 Cor. 11: 24). What they do not always add is that John not only used 'flesh' in place of 'body' but also four times replaced 'eat', as in 'eat Jesus' flesh' (John 6: 52–3) by the graphic verb *trogein* (munch or chew) (John 6: 54–8). Evidently John wanted to counteract tendencies to spiritualize eucharistic teaching about feeding on Jesus' flesh and drinking his blood. No NT writer approaches the vivid realism with which John stressed the presence of Christ in the Eucharist (theme 4). In centuries to come, the character of this presence was to be explored and controverted.

In ch. 6, John has anticipated the institution of the Eucharist at the Last Supper; in this chapter John provides his direct, major teaching on the Eucharist. Nevertheless, in the story of what Jesus said and did on the night before he died, John includes a certain eucharistic colouring. What is blatantly obvious is the humble hospitality that Jesus expresses by the footwashing. This episode, repeated in Western Catholicism at Mass on Holy Thursday, embodies the loving service the Eucharist calls for (theme 6). What might be missed is the way in which John accentuates by what follows the trinitarian content of the sacrament (theme 1). His attention to Jesus' high-priestly prayer to the Father and the promise of the Paraclete foreshadow the trinitarian shape that would clearly emerge in the eucharistic prayers of Eastern Catholicism and less so in the Roman Canon of Western Catholicism.

In that eucharistic worship an *anamnesis* and an *epiclesis* have their inseparable but distinct places in leading up to the *doxology*. Let us explain these terms. The *anamnesis* as 'remembering' involves bringing to mind the saving actions of God in history, especially in the passion, death, resurrection, and glorification of Christ. As 'anticipation' *anamnesis* means looking forward to the time of final fulfilment and doing so with an expectation that already receives and perceives something of that ultimate future. In the eucharistic prayers the *epiclesis* or 'invocation' normally asks that the Holy Spirit descend upon the gifts to change them into the body and blood of Christ for the transformation of those who receive them. In the new eucharistic prayers introduced by the Catholic Church after Vatican II, the *epiclesis* before the institution narrative prays that the Spirit may descend on the gifts of bread and wine to change them, while the *epiclesis* after the institution narrative prays that the communicants be changed. In *epiclesis* the Spirit is invoked, and in *anamnesis* Christ is remembered and anticipated; through the presence of the Spirit, the eucharistic presence of Christ is actualized. Then the *doxology* (or 'giving glory to God') completes the eucharistic prayer, by directing 'all glory and honour' to God the Father 'through, with, and in' Christ 'in the unity' effected by the Holy Spirit. Although John 13–17 does not deploy any such clear eucharistic structure of *anamnesis*, *epiclesis*, and *doxology*, nevertheless, its trinitarian language and convivial setting are not alien to the emergence of that threefold structure. One might mount a similar argument for what comes after Paul's eucharistic teaching in 1 Corinthians 11. What is said about the Spirit, the Lord Jesus, and God the Father in the very next chapter (e.g. in 1 Cor. 12: 4–11) gives the Eucharist some kind of trinitarian setting, which will flourish in coming eucharistic prayers. They have always been prayers addressed to the Father, in the indissoluble union between Son and Spirit.

Let us note a further and final point where John and Paul also coincide in foreshadowing the development of the Liturgy of the Word and the Liturgy of the Eucharist. The former constitutes the first part of the Mass, with opening prayers of praise and repentance, readings from the Bible, followed ideally by a homily, intercessions for the Church and the world, and (on some days) the Creed or confession of faith. Then follows the Liturgy of the Eucharist, with the preparation of the gifts, the thanksgiving to the Father for the marvels of creation and redemption, the consecration and *anamnesis*, the *epiclesis*, the Lord's Prayer, some sign of reconciliation and peace, sharing in communion, and a final blessing. Unquestionably, we have nothing like this formalized sequence in John and Paul. Nevertheless, the eucharistic discourse in John 6 begins with the theme of eating and drinking the revealed teaching offered by the Word of God, and then turns to the life-giving bread who has come down from heaven (John 6: 25–59). This entire section in John 6 yields thus a certain analogy to the Liturgy of the Word and the Liturgy of the Eucharist. Similarly Paul seems to have in mind two different (but not opposed) gatherings: one for the 'word' and worship in 1 Corinthians 12–14, and one for the eucharistic meal in 1 Corinthians 11: 17–34. The former was a 'coming together' (1 Cor. 14: 23, 26) which, seemingly, interested outsiders could attend (1 Cor. 14: 24); the latter was a 'coming together' (1 Cor. 11: 17, 18, 20, 33–4) as a eucharistic assembly which was apparently restricted to the baptized. The two assemblies were to become united in one rite which moves from word and worship to the eucharistic meal.

Early Christianity

We listed above six themes that have characterized Catholic (and other Christian) reflection on the Eucharist. The development of the sacramental rite, official teaching, and popular devotion conspired to carry forward the understanding and interpretation of the Eucharist.[20] Let us first see what believers wrote of the Eucharist in the first two hundred years of Christianity, looking at the *Didache*, and the writings of Justin, Ignatius of Antioch, Irenaeus, and Tertullian. (We recommend for study the eucharistic prayer from the third-century *Apostolic Tradition*; in an adapted form it came into use as the Second Eucharistic Prayer in 1969, and in that way is readily available.)

The notion of the Eucharist as sacrifice was quickly supported by an appeal to the prophet Malachi: 'From the rising of the sun to its setting my name is great among the nations, and in every place incense is offered to my name, and a pure offering' (Mal. 1: 11). Apropos of the Sunday celebration of the Eucharist, the anonymous author of the *Didache*, when instructing some early community, connected the purity of the sacrifice (theme 3) with the unity of the community (theme 6).

On the Lord's own day gather together, break bread and give thanks, having first confessed your sins so that your sacrifice may be pure. Let no one who has a quarrel with a companion join you until they have been reconciled, so that your sacrifice may not be defiled. For this is the sacrifice concerning which the Lord said: 'In every place and time offer me a pure sacrifice, for . . . my name is marvellous among the nations.' (no. 14)

About a century later Irenaeus called on the same passage from Malachi to vindicate his faith in the Eucharist as the 'pure sacrifice' for all nations (*Adversus Haereses*, 4. 17. 4). Many centuries later the Council of Trent would appeal to the same, now classical, passage when expounding the sacrificial character of the sacrament (DH 1742; ND 1547). In the late twentieth century the post-Vatican II Third Eucharistic Prayer includes a clear echo of the same verse in its opening paragraph.

St Clement of Rome, who wrote around the time the *Didache* was composed, endorsed a sacrificial reading of the Eucharist. He did so by

---

[20] See J. Jungmann, *The Mass of the Roman Rite: Its Origins and Development* (2 vols.; Westminster, Md.: Christian Classics, 1981); E. Mazza, *The Celebration of the Eucharist: The Origin of the Rite and the Development of its Interpretation* (Collegeville, Minn.: Pueblo, 1999); N. Tanner, 'The Eucharist in the Ecumenical Councils', *Gregorianum*, 82 (2001), 37–49.

applying the regulations of the Book of Leviticus to Christian worship, and used (for the first time in Christian history) the term 'layperson' to distinguish priests from people (*Epistle to the Corinthians*, 40). Later Christians were to take Clement's appeal to the OT orders in the Jerusalem Temple further, and equated the high priest with the bishop, priests with the presbyters, and levites with the deacons.

The second-century philosopher Justin was the first post-NT writer to attest clearly the consecratory character of the eucharistic prayer (theme 4), which means that the 'eucharistic gifts' are not 'ordinary food or ordinary drink'. Just as Jesus Christ 'took flesh for our salvation', so 'the food over which thanksgiving has been offered' (what Justin calls 'the eucharisted bread'), from which 'our blood and flesh are nourished by transformation', is 'the flesh and blood of Jesus who was made flesh' (*First Apology*, 66. 2). Thus Justin connected the transformation of the bread and wine over which thanksgiving has been offered with the transformation of the communicants.

The spiritual nourishment effected by the Word of God who truly assumed the human condition and became present among us (theme 4) had already been emphasized by Ignatius of Antioch. He wrote of his desire for 'the bread of God, which is the flesh of Jesus Christ', and 'for drink I desire his blood, which is incorruptible love' (*Epistle to the Romans*, 7. 3). This bishop, martyred as was the philosopher Justin, linked the reality of the incarnation with that of the eucharistic presence and with Christ taking flesh in those who offer, eat, and drink. He denounced the Docetists, who denied a true incarnation (see Ch. 4), for staying away from the sacrament, 'because they do not admit that the Eucharist is the flesh of our Saviour Jesus Christ', who suffered 'for our sins' and was 'raised up by the goodness of the Father' (*Epistle to the Smyrnaeans*, 6). In a passage to become famous, Ignatius took further the link between the Eucharist and the resurrection, when he wrote of 'breaking one bread, which is the medicine of immortality, the antidote against death which gives eternal life in Jesus Christ' (*Epistle to the Ephesians*, 20. 2). Thus Ignatius linked, albeit briefly, the reality of the incarnation and the eucharistic presence with the reality of the resurrection, both that already achieved by Christ and that hoped for by believers. Even more, the unity of the worshipping community (theme 2) ran through the letters of Ignatius. There was only 'one Eucharist', 'one flesh of our Lord Jesus Christ, and one cup for union with his blood, one altar', and 'one bishop' or his delegate to preside at the ritual itself and the one 'agape (love-feast)', the common meal of Christians in which the Lord's Supper was initially embedded (*Epistle to the Philadelphians*, 4; *Epistle to the Smyrnaeans*, 8).

Where Justin had touched on the trinitarian aspect of the eucharistic assembly (theme 1) which 'blessed the Maker of all things through his Son Jesus Christ and through the Holy Spirit' (*First Apology*, 67), Irenaeus took this theme further. Opposing the Gnostics who denigrated the material world (see Ch. 1), Irenaeus understood the institution by Jesus of the Eucharist to entail 'offering to God [the Father]', with 'firm hope and fervent love', 'the first fruits of his own created things', bread and wine. When 'the bread, which comes from the earth, receives the invocation of God [the *epiclesis*]', it 'is no longer common bread but Eucharist', and believers are 'nourished by the body and blood of the Lord' (*Adversus Haereses*, 4. 18. 4, 5). At the Eucharist Western Catholicism echoes the language of Irenaeus (and of the Jewish tradition) when, during the preparation of the gifts, the priest blesses the 'God of all creation' for 'the bread which earth has given' (which will 'become the bread of life') and for the wine, 'the fruit of the vine' (which will become 'our spiritual drink'; see 1 Cor. 10: 3–4). As Irenaeus observed, the Eucharist invariably involves gratitude both for the gifts of divine creation and for those of redemption. The Gnostics could not logically accept the Eucharist if they refused to accept Christ as being also the Son of the Creator and the Word through whom (with the Spirit) all things were created:

How will they [the Gnostics] allow that the bread over which thanksgiving has been said is the body of the Lord and that the chalice is the chalice of his blood, if they deny that he is the Son of the Creator of the world, that is to say, his Word through whom the tree bears fruit and the fountains flow and the earth yields first the blade, then the ear, then the full corn in the ear? (ibid. 4. 18. 4)

The trinitarian aspect of the Eucharist belongs inseparably with faith in the tripersonal God of creation. Any denial of this was dismissed by Irenaeus as heresy masquerading as orthodoxy.

Irenaeus also took further a theme already initiated by Ignatius, the impact of the Eucharist on our coming resurrection (part of theme 5): 'our bodies, after partaking of the Eucharist, are no longer corruptible, having the hope of eternal resurrection' (ibid. 4. 18. 5). Against the Gnostics who denied 'the salvation of the flesh' and alleged 'the flesh incapable of immortality', Irenaeus maintained that our 'flesh' can enjoy 'eternal life', since it is 'fed on the flesh and blood of the Lord' (ibid. 5. 2. 2–3). It was left to Tertullian to express this hope for 'the resurrection of the flesh' in the larger context of Christian initiation and life. Through the indissoluble link between bodily baptism, confirmation, and reception of the Eucharist and the cleansing, consecrating, fortifying, illuminating, and nourishing of their soul, human beings are enabled to live a life of faith and service that prepares their entire existence for the glorious reward of bodily resurrection. Tertullian wrote:

No soul whatever is able to obtain salvation unless it has believed while it was in the flesh. Indeed, the flesh is the very condition on which salvation hinges . . . The flesh is washed [baptism], so that the soul may be cleansed. The flesh is anointed, so that the soul may be consecrated. The flesh is signed [with the cross], so that the soul too may be fortified. The flesh is overshadowed by the imposition of hands [confirmation], so that the soul may be illuminated by the Spirit. The flesh feeds on the body and blood of Christ [the Eucharist], so that the soul likewise may feed on its God. They [the body and soul] cannot then be separated in their reward, when they are united in their service.   (*De Resurrectione Carnis*, 8. 2).

Down to the Present: Presence, Sacrifice, and Participation

After centuries of peaceful endorsement, eventually two eucharistic themes were to become controversial: first, the presence of Christ in or under the elements (theme 4), and later, the Eucharist as sacrifice (theme 3). In the twentieth century the participation of the entire liturgical assembly in eucharistic celebration drew more attention and encouragement. Let us take up these three points.

1. *Eucharistic Presence.* Despite the lack of serious controversy for many centuries, Church writers attended to the change that occurs in the elements used to celebrate the Eucharist in the liturgical assembly. How should one express that change when the elements obviously continue to look like bread and wine? What new presence of the crucified and risen Jesus takes place through the *epiclesis* and the words of institution from the Last Supper?

The third-century writer Origen seemed to encourage in certain texts a 'purely' spiritual understanding of the eucharistic presence, based on the first part of John 6 (vv. 25–51*b*). Thus he indicated in one homily: 'That bread which God the Word proclaims as his body is the word which nourishes our souls' (*In Matthaeum*, 85). Yet Origen could also remind his readers in another homily: 'you know how carefully and reverently you guard the body of the Lord, when you receive it, lest the least crumb of it should fall to the ground, lest anything should be lost of the hallowed gift' (*In Exodum*, 13. 3). Such reverence for the consecrated elements expressed a realistic sense of the presence involved.

In the fourth century Athanasius of Alexandria, relying on St Paul (1 Cor. 10: 3–4), wrote of the Eucharist as 'heavenly food' and 'spiritual nourishment' (*Epistola ad Serapionem*, 4. 19). Yet eventually it became a commonplace to appeal to the miracle at Cana and to affirm more clearly a change in the reality of the eucharistic elements. Thus Cyril of Jerusalem reminded his hearers: 'In Cana of Galilee he [Christ] changed water into wine (and wine is akin to blood). Is it incredible that he should change wine into blood? . . . Therefore with complete assurance let us partake of those elements as being the body and blood of Christ' (*Mystagogic Catecheses*, 4, 2. 3). With reference to the *epiclesis*, Cyril commented on the words that at the time followed the Preface and Sanctus in the eucharistic rite: 'We call upon the compassionate God to send out his Holy Spirit on the gifts that are set out, that he may make the bread the body of Christ and the wine the blood of Christ. For whatever the Holy Spirit has touched is assuredly sanctified and changed' (ibid. 5. 7).

Where Cyril spoke of a 'change', Gregory of Nyssa wrote of the bread and wine being 'transformed' into the Lord's body and blood. Hence 'we are right in believing' that 'the bread which is consecrated by the Word of God is transformed into the body of God the Word' (*Oratio Catechetica*, 37). Where Gregory used 'transformation' to express the change in the eucharistic elements, Ambrose of Milan wrote of the bread and wine being 'transfigured' into Christ's flesh and blood (*De Fide*, 4. 125). In support of the changed 'character' of the elements, Ambrose appealed to an OT story about Elijah (1 Kgs. 18: 38): 'if the words of Elijah had the power to call down fire from heaven, will not the words of Christ have power enough to change the character (*species*) of the elements?' (*De Mysteriis*, 52). Around the same time John Chrysostom inculcated in his homilies a strongly realistic faith in the eucharistic presence. He appealed, for instance, to Matthew's story of the Magi, who 'worshipped this body even when it lay in a manger', and added: 'you behold him not in a manger, but on an altar; not with a woman holding him, but with a priest standing before him'. Chrysostom taught that Jesus is no longer wrapped in swaddling clothes but is entirely enfolded in the Holy Spirit. Thus this presence is to be attributed to 'the Spirit descending with great bounty upon the oblations'

(*In Epistulam Primam ad Corinthios*, 24). With graphic and almost excessive realism Chrysostom declared: 'Not only ought we to see the Lord; we ought to take him into our hands, eat him, put our teeth into his flesh, and unite ourselves with him in the closest union' (*In Johannem*, 46).

By the end of the fourth century Christians were using such terms as 'changed', 'transformed', and 'transfigured' to describe what happens to the elements in the Eucharist. In all this reflection the NT accounts of the institution of the sacrament played a decisive role, along with the discourse on the bread of life in John 6. That chapter's appeal to the eating of the manna in the desert prompted Augustine to remark about Moses and others who 'pleased God': 'they understood the visible food in a spiritual sense; they were spiritually hungry, they tasted spiritually, so that they were spiritually satisfied'. This enabled Augustine to distinguish between the visible sacrament or sign of bread and wine and its invisible power: 'the sacrament is one thing, the virtue of the sacrament is another'. Communicants were to eat 'inwardly' and not merely 'outwardly', consume 'the sacrament' in their 'heart' and not merely 'crush' it with their 'teeth' (*In Evangelium Johannis*, 26. 11, 12). Augustine spelt out in a more sophisticated and unambiguous way what Chrysostom intended by the Eucharist 'uniting' us with Christ 'in the closest union'.

It was only in the ninth and even more in the eleventh century that controversy about the nature of the change in the eucharistic elements and of the presence of Christ's body and blood triggered more precise reflection and teaching. (Since sacramental communion had already gone into a decline, the transformation of the elements could be considered without a strong link to the transformation of the communicants.[21]) Berengar (1005–88), head of the school of St Martin at Tours, attempted to correct the ultrarealism of Paschasius Radbertus (*c*.790–*c*.860) by explaining the eucharistic presence as 'spiritual' in that it entailed no physical but a metaphysical change in the bread and wine. Berengar was forced to admit that Christ becomes present by a change of 'substance' (or essential reality) in the elements (DH 700; ND 1501). By the late eleventh century some theologians began to use the noun 'transubstantiation' to avoid the other extreme of ultrasymbolism. A few years later, in 1215, the Fourth Lateran Council employed the verb 'transubstantiated' to describe the

---

[21] By that time the Western Church was well on the way to a Mass at which only the presider communicated, and in which the sacramental action was considered to be the recital of Jesus' words from the institution narrative.

metaphysical mutation in the eucharistic elements: the bread and wine are 'transubstantiated' into the body and blood of Christ (DH 890; ND 28). Later in the same century Thomas Aquinas was to elaborate this teaching by adopting terms from Aristotelian philosophy: the words of consecration bring a change in the 'substance' of the bread and wine, while the 'accidents' (the secondary characteristics that do not belong essentially to the substance) remain. Developments in eucharistic theology went hand in hand with a widely renewed devotion to the Eucharist (which sadly did not always involve its reception) and with the establishment in 1264 of the Feast of Corpus Christi, a feast that involved public processions of 'the Blessed Sacrament' or consecrated host and that for many centuries remained very popular in Europe and beyond.

With the movements initiated by John Wyclif (d. 1384), by John Huss (d. 1415), and, even more, by the sixteenth-century Reformers, controversy over the eucharistic presence broke out again. Martin Luther (1483–1546) proposed a doctrine of 'consubstantiation', according to which after the consecration both the bread and wine and the body and blood of Christ co-exist on the altar. The Swiss reformer, Ulrich Zwingli (1484–1531) maintained that the elements underwent no change whatsoever; he affirmed that the Lord's Supper is a mere memorial whose meaning in simply symbolic. John Calvin (1509–64) and his followers attributed the entire efficacy of the sacrament to the Holy Spirit, and thus held a mediating position: while denying any change in the elements, they acknowledged the 'virtue' of Christ's body and blood in the soul of believers by the power of the Spirit—a view which became known as 'virtualism' and was accepted by some of the leading Anglican Reformers. Faced with the challenges from Zwinglians and Calvinists (and with less of a quarrel with Luther, who allowed for Christ's real presence), the Council of Trent affirmed the doctrine of 'transubstantiation' more vigorously than Lateran IV, distinguished between the 'substance' and the 'outward appearances (*species*)' of bread and wine, but refrained from employing the pair of terms, 'substance' and 'accidents', which after Aquinas had become the normal usage in eucharistic theology. After acknowledging that 'we can hardly find words to express' Christ's eucharistic presence, the Council taught: 'by the consecration of the bread and wine there takes place a change of the whole substance of bread into the substance of the body of Christ our Lord and of the whole substance of wine into the substance of his blood. This change the holy Catholic Church has fittingly and properly named transubstantiation' (DH 1636, 1642; ND 1513, 1519; see DH 1652; ND 1527). This was the careful attempt of Trent to find a middle ground between a purely symbolic and a crudely realistic view of the presence of Christ's body and blood in the Eucharist. 'Transubstantiation' became 'the preferred terminology and touchstone of orthodoxy'.[22]

In the twentieth century some Catholic theologians groped for other ways of expressing the change in the eucharistic elements, so that it might be more intelligible, once problems arising from contemporary ways of understanding 'substance' had been avoided. Hence Karl Rahner (1904–84) reintroduced the Augustinian concept of 'real symbol', and Edward Schillebeeckx (b. 1914) and others suggested 'transignification' and 'transfinalization' based on modern approaches to metaphysics. In his 1965 encyclical *Mysterium Fidei*, Pope Paul VI expressed his fear that such emphases on the change of significance or of purpose did not *by themselves* safeguard sufficiently the real and wonderful presence of Christ in the Eucharist. He reiterated the doctrine of transubstantiation, but added that 'as a result of transubstantiation, the species of bread and wine undoubtedly take on a new meaning and a new finality' (ND 1577, 1580).

Beyond question the most eloquent passage on the eucharistic presence of Christ and his presence in all liturgical celebrations came from Vatican II (*Sacrosanctum Concilium*, 7):

Christ is always present in his Church, especially in her liturgical celebrations. He is present in the sacrifice of the Mass not only in the person of his minister... *but especially in the eucharistic species.* By his power he is present in the sacraments, so that when anyone baptizes it is really Christ himself who baptizes. He is present in his word, since it is he himself who speaks when the holy scriptures are read in the church. Lastly, he is present when the church prays and sings. (italics ours)

This striking list of the liturgical celebrations (the assemblies of the baptized), rites (the Mass and other sacraments), persons (the ministers and all those who take a specialized role in the liturgical celebrations), modes (reading of scriptures, as well as the singing and praying of the Church) that mediate the presence of Christ reaches its high point with the consecrated bread and wine on the altar. There his real and fullest encounter with Christians combines with his other liturgical presences (including his living and revelatory voice when sermons proclaim the

---

[22] Tanner, 'The Eucharist in the Ecumenical Councils', 42.

good news (ibid. 33)) and reaches its high point in the sacramental communion of the liturgical assembly.

In this Constitution on the Sacred Liturgy the Council made an inclusive, rather than an exclusive, statement. It recalled the range of the liturgical presences of Christ without denying that he is also present both non-liturgically and beyond the visible community of Catholics and other Christians: for example, in all those who suffer and need our practical love (Matt. 25: 31–46). We return to this point below.

2. *Eucharistic Sacrifice*. In the history of Christianity, the Eucharist as sacrifice (theme 3) became controversial much later than the real presence of Christ (theme 4). Hence we deal now with theme 3, only after tracking the development of Catholic teaching on the real presence. We noted above how OT texts like Malachi 1: 11 quickly encouraged post-NT writers to recognize the sacrificial character of the Eucharist. In any case the words employed by Christ when instituting the Eucharist had rich sacrificial associations: 'covenant', 'memorial', and 'poured out'. After some time talk of sacrifice, without losing its connection with the sacrificial offering and living of the Christian assembly, inevitably involved talking of the priests (or bishops) who presided at the rite. Thus Cyprian of Carthage wrote:

If Christ Jesus...is himself *the high priest* of God the Father and first *offered* himself as a sacrifice to the Father, and commanded this to be done in remembrance of himself, then assuredly *the priest acts truly in Christ's stead*, when he reproduces what Christ did, and he then *offers a true and complete sacrifice* to God the Father, if he begins *to offer as he sees Christ himself has offered*.

(*Epistola* 63, 14; italics ours)

The authority of the Epistle to the Hebrews supported calling Christ 'the high priest' and speaking of his self-offering in sacrifice. The question then emerged: is the Christian leader of the liturgical assembly who celebrates the Eucharist in 'memory' of Christ truly a priest 'acting in Christ's stead' and offering 'a true and complete sacrifice to God'? If we join Cyprian in answering yes, further questions arise: what is the connection between the Church's celebration of the Eucharist and the historic sacrifice of Calvary (Ch. 4) and between the priest (and the Church) and Christ himself?

John Chrysostom, as emphatically as anyone, insisted that there is only one sacrifice. He spoke of the daily Eucharist in a homily: 'We offer every day, making a memorial of his [Christ's] death. This is one sacrifice, not many. And why? Because it was offered once ... We always offer the same person ... the same oblation: therefore it is one sacrifice.' Just as there are not 'many Christs' but only one in every place, so there is only 'one sacrifice'. Chrysostom added: 'We offer now, what was offered then, an inexhaustible offering ... We offer the same sacrifice; or rather we make a memorial of that sacrifice' (*In Hebreos*, 3, 17). What is more, the human ministers ('we who offer') of this memorial sacrifice are just that, (secondary) ministers of the invisible Christ: 'He who did this at the supper is the same who now performs the act. We rank as ministers; it is he who consecrates and transmutes [the elements]' (*In Matthaeum*, 82). In controversy with the Donatists, Augustine—as we mentioned earlier in this chapter—stressed that Christ is the primary minister of baptism and hence also of the Eucharist.

Augustine further argued that sacraments enjoy 'a kind of likeness to those things of which they are sacraments'; it is from this likeness that they can 'receive the names of the things themselves'. Moreover, 'we speak of some sacred event which we celebrate as happening' now, when 'in fact it happened long ago'. Thus 'Christ was once sacrificed in his own person; and yet he is sacramentally (*in sacramento*) sacrificed for the peoples not only throughout the Easter festival [with its special, calendar connection with the sacrifice of Christ], but every day' (*Epistola* 98. 9). There are uncountable eucharistic sacrifices (lower case) but only one historic Sacrifice (upper case) of Christ, just are there many priests offering the Eucharist but only one primary high priest who always 'performs' the eucharistic act.

It was only many centuries after Cyprian, Chrysostom, Augustine, and other ancient writers commented on the sacrificial (and priestly) dimension of the Eucharist that we find full-scale attempts to define the nature of this self-giving. A vast literature built up from the fourteenth century and increased when many theologians of the Reformation either denied the sacrificial nature of the Eucharist or 'explained' it in an unconvincing way. A widespread tendency was to speak of the Eucharist as being a memorial meal, which recalled the loving self-offering of Christ, but not as being a redemptive sacrifice. Many Reformers feared that to admit the saving value of the Eucharist would be to take away from the unique sacrifice of Christ. The Council of Trent dedicated its twenty-second session (1562) to the sacrifice of the Mass. It restated traditional Catholic teaching: the bloody sacrifice Christ offered once and for all 'on the altar of the cross' is 'offered' 'in an unbloody manner', but not repeated, 'under visible signs' to celebrate 'the memory' of Christ's 'passage from this world' and to apply 'the salutary power' of his sacrifice 'for the forgiveness of sins' and 'other necessities' of the faithful, both living and dead (DH 1740–3; ND 1546–8).

In the twentieth century and, especially from the 1920s, Catholics realized more and more that it was a false choice to speak of the eucharistic liturgy as either a sacrifice or as a memorial meal. It is the sacrificial meal of the new covenant. 'This is my body given up for you' includes and does not exclude 'take and eat', just as 'the cup of my blood poured out for you' includes 'take and drink'. The properly enacted sacramental sacrifice calls for this eating and drinking. Second, while proposing different theories about the precise nature of sacrifice, many have recognized the term's rich range of meanings in the scriptures: one should value sacrifices not only for expiating sins and imploring the divine mercy but also for praising and thanking God, as well as for sealing and renewing covenantal relationships with God and with his people.[23] Some have argued for the primary 'direction' of sacrifice as coming not from human beings to God, but vice versa, inasmuch as 'sacri-fice' primarily means the 'holy-making' achieved by the divine initiative alone. Thus those who believe in Christ and share in his sacrifice are likewise 'consecrated' and sanctified by Christ and the Holy Spirit (Heb. 10: 14–18). Third, modern Catholic teaching has generally not been content to limit the event of the sacrifice of Christ to his crucifixion. One must take into account what came before (in the sacrificial nature of Christ's life of faith identified as sacrifice by his words and gestures at the Last Supper), and what came after (in his resurrection, exaltation, and sending of the Spirit). A fourth insight has been rediscovered, refined since the 1920s, and encouraged through dialogues with other Christians: a renewed sense of the import of the liturgical word *anamnesis* (remembrance). The Eucharist as *anamnesis* makes effective in the present the past event of Christ's sacrifice; it 're-presents' the whole event of his dying and rising, or makes the past effectively present now.

3. *Eucharistic Participation.* Finally, before leaving the Eucharist, we should add something on the participation by the entire assembly of the faithful in the liturgical re-presentation of Christ's living, dying, and rising. Ignatius of Antioch and other early witnesses let us picture the

---

[23] Along with the common elements between the OT and the NT, Christ's non-cultic sacrifice differs from the previous cultic sacrifices. They are ended, but for Christians the self-offering of Christ continues in the Church's self-offering or spiritual sacrifice.

bishop leading the eucharistic celebrations, with his priests and deacons standing around him on one side of the altar, a central sign of Christ's presence. The faithful, gathered on the other side of the altar, completed the sense of being grouped around Christ in the one community of God and with the bishop speaking in the name of the whole assembly. Apparently the bishop or his delegate initially improvised the prayers, drawing on extant Jewish blessings and the words of Christ at the Last Supper. The first clear example of a eucharistic prayer comes from the early third-century *Apostolic Tradition*. The fourth and fifth centuries witnessed the composition of the wonderful eucharistic prayers or 'anaphoras' attributed to Basil of Caesarea, John Chrysostom, and others. Eastern Catholicism has continued to enjoy a variety of anaphoras composed in Greek, Syriac, and other languages. In Western Catholicism, the Roman Canon or First Eucharistic Prayer was virtually the only one in use from the sixth century onwards.

By that time, after the freedom that came with Constantine (see Ch. 1), the places for Christian worship were no longer private houses but public churches, sometimes built into or on top of old pagan temples. The altar was usually moved against the Eastern wall; the celebrant at the Eucharist turned around, so that all the people of God could face in one direction, eastwards. The long defunct liturgy in the temple at Jerusalem served, in part, as a model for medieval Christians. Just as the high priest had approached the altar on behalf of God's people and offered sacrifices in their name, so too did the NT priests with the Christian offering of the Eucharist. Basil of Caesarea had recommended 'daily communion and participation in the holy body and blood of Christ' as a 'good and helpful practice' (*Epistola* 93). But in the Europe of the Middle Ages a profound sense of unworthiness caused the number of communicants to decrease. Western and Eastern Christians lost sight of St Paul's clear conviction: the worthy sacramental communion of the assembly is not optional (see above). Although many adored the consecrated species, most believers communicated rarely, some only once in a lifetime.

Believers came to 'hear' Mass and 'gaze on' the host, with such 'ocular' communion or adoring of the elevated host replacing sacramental communion. Early in the thirteenth century priests began to raise the consecrated bread after the words of institution; later an 'elevation' of the chalice was introduced. Some people wanted to be present at as many consecrations as possible, so that they could pray even more for the living and the dead. A bell called their attention to the fact that a consecration and elevation were approaching. The need for more masses became so great that some medieval cathedrals, such as St Alban's to the north of London, constructed several altars around the columns of the nave, so as to permit people to attend more consecrations.

The Council of Trent, knowing that the Eucharist was the bread of Christian life and nourishment for the life journey of the believer, encouraged frequent communion (DH 1649; ND 1524). At the same time, the Council set aside as inappropriate the Reformers' demands that the Mass be celebrated in the vernacular (or spoken language of different areas) and that the laity receive communion also from the chalice (communion under two kinds), without rejecting either change in principle. To promote stability and uniformity in the Western Church, the bishops at Trent asked for a reform of the liturgical texts. The Tridentine Missal was introduced in 1570 and replaced various missals that had appeared since the tenth century.

Building on the directives of St Pius X (pope 1903–14) and Pius XII (pope 1939–58) and inspired by leaders of the liturgical movement (see Ch. 8), Vatican II aimed to promote a more active and joyful participation in the celebration of the Eucharist (and of the other sacraments). Mass was translated into the vernacular languages, the altar turned to face the people, sacramental communion encouraged as 'the most perfect form of participation in the Mass' (*Sacrosanctum Concilium*, 55), and communion under both kinds made available to the laity under a wide variety of circumstances. Eventually the new Roman Missal was promulgated by Paul VI in April 1969. It contains four eucharistic anaphoras: Prayer I is a slightly revised version of the old Roman Canon, Prayer II an adaptation of the prayer in the third-century *Apostolic Tradition*, Prayer III a modern composition, and Prayer IV an adaptation of the Anaphora of St Basil. The aim of the Council and that of the Pope were identical: all the faithful should take part in the Eucharist, 'conscious of what they are doing, with devotion, and full collaboration'. Being 'instructed by God's word [the Liturgy of the Word]' and 'nourished at the table of the Lord's Body [the Liturgy of the Eucharist]', and 'offering the immaculate victim not only through the hands of the priest but also together with him, they should learn to offer themselves' (ibid. 48).

This continual self-offering implies that Christians should view the Eucharist not only as presupposing the existence of the Church, but also as contributing to its constant vitality. Thus, partaking in this sacrament in a conscious and active manner entails becoming ever more united with Christ the Head and all the other members of the Mystical Body. This modern theme retrieves the primarily ecclesial understanding of the Eucharist advocated by St Augustine. Attempting to clarify the unifying effect of the sacrament, he claimed that the *totus Christus* or 'whole Christ' (the glorifed Lord and the faithful) is present in the species on the altar, since the earthly Jesus identified himself with bread in the Cenacle and since all Christians 'become bread' at their baptism. In receiving communion, therefore, the faithful are 'to be' what they see, and 'to receive' what they are, the Body of Christ (*Sermo* 272). In fact, Augustine held that Christ and the Church are symbolized and conjoined in the eucharistic elements. St Thomas Aquinas, constrained by the medieval controversies to take a more christocentric and metaphysical view, found it necessary to modify the mystagogical insight of Augustine, without losing sight of the chief consequence of the Eucharist: the unity of the Church. He thus made the distinction, which has dominated ever since in the West, that 'Christ is signified and contained in the Eucharist, while the Church is only signified' (*ST* III q. 80 a. 4). Many Catholic theologians, writing in the post-Vatican II period, strive to show that the christological dimension of the Mass is not lessened by accentuating the ecclesial aspect of the eucharistic sacrifice, of the reception of Holy Communion, and of the life of grace which flows from them.

Thus self-offering, or sacrifice in union with Christ, should promote a eucharistic style of life, which manifests itself not only in charity towards members of the Church but also in generous service of the needy in society, with whom Jesus identifies himself in a special way (Matt. 25: 31–46). During a visit to Columbia for the 1968 International Eucharistic Congress, Pope Paul VI spoke of a real presence of Christ in the poor workers (ND 1587a). John Paul II was to take further the social implications of the Eucharist as empowering work for development and peace in the service of the coming kingdom of God (*Sollicitudo Rei Socialis*, 48; ND 1592).

SACRAMENTS OF THE SICK

After presenting the three sacraments that together constitute Christian initiation, we move now to two sacraments available for sinful and sick Catholics (penance and the anointing of the sick) and then two sacraments in the service of communion by creating and sanctifying the ordained ministry and married life (orders and matrimony).

Penance

The forgiveness of sins belonged essentially to the earthly Jesus' ministry for the kingdom of God. He imparted the divine pardon not only through his words (e.g. Luke 7: 47–50) but also through his action of establishing table fellowship with sinners and reconciling them with God. Jesus responded to those who criticized his ministry of reconciliation by declaring: 'Those who are well have no need of a physician, but those who are sick. I have not come to call the righteous but sinners to repentance' (Mark 2: 17). This notable saying summed up a major purpose of the mission of Jesus ('I have come') in terms that supported a post-NT title for him ('doctor'), which remained popular down to the time of St Augustine of Hippo, who preached Christ as the 'humble doctor' (*humilis medicus*). In what came to be known as the 'Our Father' or 'Lord's Prayer', Jesus asked his followers to keep praying for the forgiveness of their sins (Matt. 6: 12 = Luke 11: 4)—which presupposed that they would continue sinning even after an initial conversion and decision for him and his message. Their receiving forgiveness was conditional on their forgiving others, and so carrying out a mission of reconciliation received from Jesus.

The Gospel of John portrays the risen Jesus communicating the Holy Spirit to his disciples. This gift, which will be passed on to those who, as a result of the disciples' mission, come to believe and join the community, includes essentially the forgiveness of sins (John 20: 22–3). For John, the Holy Spirit, forgiveness, and membership in the new community are inseparable. Here John converges with what the Acts of the Apostles reports. Peter and the other apostolic leaders preach Jesus crucified and risen; those who 'repent of their sins', accept the good news, and are baptized will receive the gift of the Holy Spirit and forgiveness of their sins (e.g. Acts 2: 37–9).

But what of Christians who commit sins and even revert to a sinful lifestyle they have renounced at their baptism? Here and there the NT alerts us to the fact that some Christians lapse back into sin after entering the community. The Gospels indicate that there are procedures to be followed for the 'brother who does wrong' (Matt. 18: 15–18). Paul too shows his anxious concern over sins committed by Christians in Corinth and prescribes remedies. For instance, a man who is living in concubinage with his stepmother should be expelled from the community, 'so that his spirit may be saved on the day of the Lord' (1 Cor. 5: 5). The apostle also writes of someone who has suffered for some wrongdoing, but now should be forgiven and reconciled with the community (2 Cor. 2: 5–8).

Sinners in the Early Centuries

Towards the end of the first century Clement of Rome was shocked at divisions and 'sedition against the presbyters' among the Christians of Corinth. He begged them: 'Let us then quickly put an end to this [state of affairs]; and let us fall down before the Master and beseech him with tears that he may have mercy on us, be reconciled to us, and restore us to our seemly and holy practice of brotherly love' (*Epistle to the Corinthians*, 47–8). Around the same time another Christian writer exhorted the faithful to repent of and confess their sins before celebrating the Eucharist: 'On the Lord's own day [Sunday] gather together, break bread, and give thanks, having first confessed your sins so that your sacrifice may be pure' (*Didache*, 14. 1). A few decades later Hermas, in his third vision, pictures the Church as a tower. Some building stones have been rejected and thrown away, but they can still be incorporated into the structure. These stones symbolize sinful Christians who can still repent and rejoin the Church: 'Those then who are to repent—if they do repent—will be strong in faith, if they now repent while the tower is being built' (*Shepherd*, 3. 5. 5).

Early Christians distinguished between lesser, daily sins and death-dealing sins. Daily sins could be forgiven through prayer (in particular, through the Lord's Prayer), fasting, works of mercy, and the eucharistic celebration. Such death-dealing or serious sins as apostasy from the Christian faith called for a process of reconciliation. In the third century the sacrament of penance as reconciliation with and through the liturgical assembly emerged for the first time in a recognizable form. Christians publicly acknowledged their sins (confession) and were temporarily excommunicated or kept apart from community worship for a period of penance (involving plain food and squalid clothing), contrite prayer, and almsgiving—a process called 'satisfaction' by the Carthaginian Tertullian (*De Poenitentia*, 9). The penitents confessed God's mercy and asked prayers from other members of the community, and particularly from the widows and presbyters who were considered to be people especially dedicated to God. Reconciliation essentially involved the whole community praying for the penitents' conversion and renewed life.

When the bishop judged the repentance adequate, he summoned the sinners and restored them to full communion through the imposition of his hands (absolution). Recalling the original forgiveness of sins in baptism, Tertullian named postbaptismal forgiveness 'the second penitence'. But it could be received 'only once'; there could not be a second 'second time' (ibid. 7). After having initially accepted that all sins could be forgiven, Tertullian became fiercely rigorous, turned to Montanism (see Ch. 1), and towards the end of his life argued that some sins are 'too serious and ruinous to receive pardon': 'murder, idolatry, fraud, denial [of Christ], blasphemy. . . adultery, and fornication' (*De Pudicitia*, 19). With reference to 'the power of binding and loosing' given by Jesus to Peter, Tertullian denied that such power referred to the seven 'capital sins' he had listed; such 'sins against God are not to be remitted' (ibid. 21). He ridiculed a contemporary 'Supreme Pontiff' or bishop of Rome for presuming to absolve the sins of adultery and fornication. Such mockery on the part of Tertullian provided, however, a vivid picture of what might happen during the period of 'satisfaction', when penitents prostrated themselves and asked for the prayers of widows and presbyters:

You bring the penitent adulterer into the church to beg for readmission into the brotherhood . . . He is in a hair shirt, covered in ashes, in a condition of shame and trembling: you make him prostrate himself in public before the widows, before the presbyters, seizing the hem of their garments, licking their footprints, catching hold of them by their knees; and for this man you use all your aids to compassion, and you preach like the 'good shepherd' and 'blessed Papa' that you are.   (ibid. 13)

Tertullian's younger contemporary, Origen of Alexandria, showed a similarly rigorous attitude in distinguishing between sins for which presbyters 'should offer sacrifice' and sins that 'admitted of no sacrifice'. He dismissed as not being 'fully versed in priestly knowledge' those presbyters or bishops who prayed for grave sinners and forgave the deadly sins of idolatry, adultery, and fornication. Origen justified his rigorism with an appeal to the teaching about 'deadly' sins in 1 John 5: 11 (see above).

The anonymous author of an early third-century work on Church order from Northern Syria, the *Didascalia Apostolorum*, was, however, more compassionate about receiving sinners back into eucharistic fellowship. The writer, who was probably a physician converted to Christianity from

Judaism, encouraged bishops to remember their duty to 'give absolution to the penitent', even in cases of idolatry. With the power of the Holy Spirit, the bishops were to say: 'The Lord also has forgiven your sin; be of good cheer; you shall not die' (2. 18; see 2. 23).

We saw earlier in this chapter how the persecution of Christians by Decius (emperor 249–51) and others led to important clarifications about baptism, in particular baptism administered 'outside the Church'. Decius decreed that every household must have a notarized certificate attesting to the father's offering sacrifice to the gods of Rome. During this persecution in the mid-third century some Christians denied their faith by publicly worshipping the old Roman gods, others by producing false certification that they had done so, and others again by surrendering to government agents their sacred books. In the Church of Carthage the last two groups were readmitted to communion, after repentance and suitable satisfaction, but the public apostates were obliged to undergo lifelong penance and could be readmitted to fellowship only on their deathbed.

Fourth-century Christianity began with the Council of Nicaea (325) insisting on the authority of the Church to reconcile great sinners, even those who had lapsed under the Great Persecution which had broken out in AD 303 (DH 127; ND 1601). From an expanding Christian Church, which now enjoyed the freedom granted by the Emperor Constantine, we have abundant information about the administration of penance for the baptized who fell into serious sin. Previously 'confessors' or those who had suffered for having confessed their faith but without being killed, as living martyrs and representatives of Christ's forgiving love, had reconciled sinners on their own authority. The end of the persecutions and the death of the last confessors brought the forgiveness of grave sins more fully under the bishops' control.

Sinners acknowledged their guilt before an assembly of Christians presided over by the bishop and were enrolled in the order of penitents. Canon 11 of Nicaea prescribed that those who had denied the faith should spend three years among the 'hearers' or those who listened to the readings at the liturgy. Through the Word and prayers for them, the penitents were gradually reconverted. Next they had to face six years as 'prostrators' or those who heard the readings and homily, prostrated themselves in front of the celebrant, and were then dismissed with a blessing. The time and forms of penitential practices, now commonly called 'satisfaction', varied according to the gravity of the sins committed; bishops could lessen the severity of the penance. In any case the whole period of conversion was regarded as an opportunity to grow in renewed faith rather than as a punishment. The process ended with the bishop reconciling the sinners on Holy Thursday and readmitting them to the eucharistic table. This act of reconciliation was available only once in a lifetime—an ancient principle endorsed by Hermas, as we saw above. On account of this once-only reconciliation, sinners under the age of 35 were normally not admitted into the order of penitents; they could too easily go through the whole process of reconciliation but relapse later into serious sin. To sum up the picture from the fourth-century administration of penance: it was a public, communal action of reconciliation that led to a lasting change of heart, involved the whole community, and was presided over by the bishop.[24]

Preaching around AD 408, Augustine put the public reception of penance into a fuller context by distinguishing three kinds of reconciliation with God through the Church: the remission of all previous sins through baptism; the daily remission through prayer and fasting of 'light and small' sins; the formal remission of 'serious and deadly' sins granted through public penance but only once in a lifetime (*Sermo* 278). But before Augustine died in 430, changes were already coming in the administration of penance. No longer was such administration totally public and necessarily limited to bishops alone. At some point in the fifth century or perhaps earlier, in central Italy presbyters were delegated to be ministers of the sacrament, which now required a certain secrecy. Leo the Great objected to a 'public confession of sins in kind and number being read' from a written list: 'it is enough that the guilt of conscience be revealed to priests alone in secret confession' (DH 323; ND 1606).

---

[24] Written later in the fourth century, the three 'Canonical Letters' from Basil of Caesarea to Amphilochius, bishop of Iconium, give detailed regulations for penitential discipline. Someone who has committed murder and repented was to be excommunicated for twenty years: 'For four years he must weep, standing outside the door of the house of prayer, beseeching the faithful as they enter to pray for him, and confessing his sin. After four years he will be admitted among the "hearers" and for four years he will leave [the assembly] with them. For seven years he will leave with the "kneelers" (i.e. the prostrators). For four years he will merely stand with the faithful, not partaking of the offering. On the completion he will be admitted to partake of the sacrament.' Adulterers received fifteen years, to be divided as above into two, five, four, and two years; fornicators were let off with seven years, to be divided into two, two, two, and one years. Those who had denied Christ and repented had to spend the rest of their life in penitence, and could receive the Eucharist only at the time of death (*Epistola* 217, canons 56, 58, 73).

Two factors within the Church contributed to the breakdown of the administration of penance that had flourished after Nicaea I: the vastly increased numbers of Christians and the development of restrictions in the post-reconciliation life of penitents. They could not hold office in the community, they had to live with their spouse as brother and sister, and so forth. Add too the disruption caused by the barbarian invasions. As we saw in Ch. 1, between 410 and 455 invading forces had put Rome itself under siege eight times, occupied the city six times, and sacked it twice (in 410 and 455).

Penance from the Sixth Century

The sacrament of penance underwent a dramatic change from the end of the sixth century; Irish and Anglo-Saxon monk-missionaries, who had not known the older system of public penance, began fanning out across Europe, founding or refounding Christian communities, and introducing the 'monastic' practice of penance. This involved private confession to a spiritual father (or mother), reception of an appropriate penance (which was aimed more at restoring the balance of the moral universe than at reconciliation with the community), and private prayer of pardon or blessing after the penance was completed. The monk-missionaries brought with them 'penitentials' or handbooks for hearing confession on a one-to-one basis. Originally developed in sixth-century Ireland by such figures as St Finnian (d. 549) and St Columbanus (d. 615), the penitentials were composed over a period of three centuries in Latin and Old Irish, and varied in length and sophistication. The earlier models provided little more than lists of sins and the penance or 'tariff' appropriate to right the balance for each sin. The tariff was adjusted according to the rank of the sinner, the rank of the person offended against, and the objective seriousness of the sin; later penitentials drew on the Bible and early Christian writers. Besides making penance a private and non-liturgical matter, the monk-missionaries put an end to the practice of once-in-a-lifetime reconciliation for grave sins and to any necessary connection of penance with Lent and Easter. Satisfaction for the sins committed loomed large and became more punitive and less therapeutic or medicinal. Severe and sometimes long-lasting penances were imposed in the spirit of the punishment fitting the crime.[25]

[25] On the penitentials see H. Connolly, *The Irish Penitentials: Their Significance for the Sacrament of Penance Today* (Dublin: Four Courts Press, 1995).

The Third Council of Toledo tried to maintain the old system of reconciliation only once in a lifetime, which entailed groups of penitents completing a period of 'satisfaction' before being readmitted to communion. It rejected the Celtic practice as an abominable presumption (ND 1607). Around 650, however, we find the new penitential practice approved by another regional council, the Council of Chalons-sur-Saône, which also tried to establish some episcopal control over the monastic practice of penance. The severity of the penances imposed meant, however, that fewer Christians practised sacramental penance. Some penitent sinners found other persons to take on the penance and prayers for them. 'Chantries' or foundations to support a priest or a group of priests were endowed to celebrate Mass for the soul of the founder or foundress. The reception of the sacraments of reconciliation and of the Eucharist fell into decline.

In an attempt to correct this situation, the Fourth Lateran Council prescribed that the faithful who had 'reached the age of discretion should at least once a year faithfully confess all their sins in secret to their own priest' and receive communion (DH 812; ND 1608). Strict sanctions were imposed for any breach of the secrecy or 'seal' of confession: any priest who revealed a sin 'manifested to him in the tribunal of confession' was not only to be deposed from his priestly office but also 'consigned to a closed monastery for perpetual penance' (DH 814; ND 1609). This conciliar decree shows that repeated absolution for sins committed by the baptized was officially accepted and deemed necessary for their proper Christian life. The spread of the Dominican, Franciscan, and other orders in the thirteenth century made the practice of confession more frequent in some Christian circles.[26] But despite the desire of Lateran IV to increase sacramental practice, many limited themselves to confession and communion once a year.

In 1439 the Council of Florence spelled out more fully what the sacrament of 'penance' involved: (1) 'contrition of the heart, which requires that one be sorry for the sin committed with the resolve not to sin in the future'; (2) 'oral confession which requires that sinners confess to their priests in their integrity all the sins they remember'; (3) 'the words of absolution spoken by the priest who has authority to absolve';

---

[26] See P. Biller and A. J. Minnis, *Handling Sin: Confession in the Middle Ages* (Woodbridge: Boydell & Brewer, 1998).

(4) 'satisfaction for the sin according to the judgement of the priest, which is mainly achieved by prayer, fasting, and almsgiving' (DH 1323; ND 1612).

In 1551, in response to the claim of some of the Reformers that sinners could and should renew their baptismal justification by means of interior conversion, the Council of Trent pushed to an extreme the non-communal, individualistic approach to the sacramental rite of penance as effecting the sinner's 'reconciliation with God' (DH 1674; ND 1621).[27] The Council distinguished two kinds of contrition: 'perfect' or 'sorrow of the soul and detestation of the sin committed together with the resolve to sin no more' motivated by love of God; and 'imperfect' which 'commonly arises either from the consideration of the heinousness of sin or from the fear of hell and of punishment'. Such imperfect contrition or attrition 'disposes one to obtain the grace of God in the sacrament of penance' (DH 1676–8; ND 1622–4). More was said about the confession of sins than was the case with Lateran IV and the Council of Florence: the former had enjoined 'faithfully confessing all one's sins'; the latter had referred to Christians naming 'in their integrity all the sins they remember'. Trent also distinguished between what the sacrament required of the faithful and what it did not: 'all mortal sins of which penitents after a diligent self-examination are conscious' had to be confessed 'specifically and in particular'. As regards 'venial sins', the Council stated that it is 'right and profitable' to confess them, but there is no strict need to do so: they may be omitted and 'can be expiated by many other remedies' (DH 1679–80; ND 1625–6). Whereas the Council of Florence had attributed to the priest both a 'judgement' in deciding on some 'satisfaction' to be performed and an 'authority to absolve', Trent, wanting to show the insufficiency of the evangelical language of Martin Luther, specified that absolution does not merely consist in 'proclaiming the Gospel [of divine mercy] or of declaring that the sins have been forgiven'; absolution 'has the pattern of a judicial act in which the priest pronounces sentence as a judge' (DH 1685; DH 1628). The Council thus encouraged many subsequent generations of Catholics to speak of 'the tribunal of penance'. Finally, whereas the Council of Florence, as we also saw above, recognized the judgement of the priest in imposing satisfaction, which 'is mainly achieved by prayer, fasting, and almsgiving', Trent insisted on 'the duty' of priests 'to impose salutary

---

[27] See K. J. Lualdi and A. T. Thayer (eds.), *Penitence in the Age of Reformation* (Aldershot: Ashgate, 2000).

and proportionate satisfactions . . . in accordance with the nature of the crime and the ability of the penitents'. They should not 'connive at' the sins of others and 'deal too leniently with them by imposing only some sort of light penance for very grave faults'. The Council added that satisfaction imposed 'is meant not merely as a safeguard for the new life and as a remedy to weakness, but also as a vindicatory punishment for former sins' (DH 1692; ND 1633).

The institutes of priests that came into existence in the sixteenth century, as well as such later groups as the Passionists and the Redemptorists, propagated this teaching on penance. The elaborate confessionals in baroque and then neo-gothic churches across Europe and other parts of the world bear witness to the diffusion in Western Catholicism of the practice of sacramental penance along the lines prescribed by the Council of Trent. The new institutes for religious women which sprang up in the nineteenth century played a major role in spreading the Tridentine discipline when they prepared small children for their first confession and communion (see Ch. 2). In the twentieth century, through the parish schools they staffed, religious women also did much to promote more frequent communion, which brought with it more regular reception of the sacrament of penance or 'confession' as it had come to be called.

What many centuries of Catholics largely ignored was its relevance to the community. They considered 'confession' a private event and means of personal grace. They did not appreciate that, unlike sins committed before baptism and entrance into the Christian community, the sins of the baptized affect the Church and, in smaller or greater ways, rupture the communion of the people of God. The once-in-a-lifetime penitential discipline of early Christianity was obviously severe, in that it excluded sinners from participating in the Eucharist and readmitted them only when they had completed a notable period of satisfying for their sins. But that old discipline clearly appreciated both the harm baptized Christians did to the whole body of Christ by their sins and the fact that repentance entails the desire to be reconciled and share again fully in the life of the community. In a brief but important paragraph, the Second Vatican Council signalled a recovery of a communal perspective of sin, repentance, and reconciliation: 'Those who approach the sacrament of penance receive pardon from the mercy of God for the offences committed against him, and at the same time are reconciled with the Church which they have wounded by their sins and which by charity, example, and prayer works for their conversion' (*Lumen Gentium*, 11).

The enduring fruit of this renewed sense that sacramental penance reconciles sinners with God *and with the Church* came in December 1973 with the *Ordo Paenitentiae* (Order of Penance) of Pope Paul VI. This document introduced a new name, 'the sacrament of reconciliation'; treated the sacrament from an ecclesial perspective; and provided a formula of absolution that corresponds to that reality:

God, the Father of mercies, through the death and resurrection of his Son has reconciled the world to himself and sent the Holy Spirit among us for the forgiveness of sins. Through the ministry of the church may God give you pardon and peace, and I absolve you from your sins in the name of the Father, and of the Son, and of the Holy Spirit.

The 1973 *Ordo* offers three rites for celebrating the sacrament: reconciliation of individual penitents, reconciliation of many penitents who are absolved individually, and reconciliation of many penitents who make a public confession of sins and together receive a general absolution.

The first rite incorporates the personal caring for sinners, introduced by the monk-missionaries from the sixth century and officially endorsed by Lateran IV, the Council of Florence, and the Council of Trent. While allowing for something traditionally dear to Eastern Christians, spiritual direction, nevertheless, the first rite does not clearly exhibit its communal dimension. The second rite brings penitents together for a service of prayer, hymns, readings from the Bible, and a homily before they are absolved individually by one or other of a group of priests who attend the service. This rite combines a personal ministry (the monastic tradition) with the social and ecclesial dimension retrieved in modern times from the public penance of early Christianity. The third rite patently maintains the communal character of reconciliation, has proved popular in parishes across the world, but does not include the personal attention to penitents of the first and second rite. Moreover, the obligation of confessing grave sins individually, affirmed by the Council of Trent (see above), is not replaced by general confession and absolution. When such grave sins are absolved in such a communal rite, they are afterwards to be explicitly confessed to a priest.

Finally, just as baptism entails a salvific encounter with Christ, so too does the sacrament of reconciliation. He brings about the forgiveness of all sins, those committed before and after baptism (see 1 John 2: 2). In special, albeit different, ways both baptism and the sacrament of reconciliation actualize the ministry of Christ to sinners which he initiated in his earthly lifetime and will continue to the end of time. He never ceases to be the 'humble doctor', so cherished by Augustine.[28] The reformed rite of penance, with its Liturgy of the Word and its prayers of thanksgiving and praise, makes clear that the sacrament involves an encounter with Christ who is present in the assembly (of at least two persons), in the proclamation of the word, in the sacramental sign of the imposition of hands, and in the person of the minister, who is to embody Christ's forgiving love.

The Anointing of the Sick

The anointing of the sick is a sacrament closely associated with that of reconciliation, and follows the example of Christ who showed his love for the sick and sinful by healing them and forgiving their sins (e.g. Mark 2: 1–12). Both then in his earthly ministry and now through that of the Church, the remission of sins and the care for the sick announce that the kingdom of God is already powerfully working to bring the whole human family to its final fulfilment. When Mark recalls how Jesus sent the Twelve on a trial mission for the kingdom, we see the same care for the sick and sinful: 'they proclaimed the need for repentance, drove out many demons, anointed many sick people with oil, and cured them' (Mark 6: 7–13).

After the resurrection of Jesus from the dead and the coming of the Holy Spirit, the Acts of the Apostles reports many healing miracles worked through the mediation of Peter, Paul, and others. When Paul, for instance, spent three months on Malta as a prisoner en route to Rome, he visited the sick father of Publius, the island's chief official; Paul prayed, laid his hands on the sick man, who had been suffering from recurrent bouts of fever and dysentery, and cured him. This gesture recalled the tender care of Jesus in touching and curing the sick and suffering (e.g. Mark 1: 40–2; Luke 13: 11–13). After the healing of Publius' father, Paul also cured other sick people on the island (Acts 28: 7–9)—the last examples of a healing ministry,

---

[28] See R. Arbesmann, 'The Concept of "Christus Medicus" in St Augustine', *Traditio* 10 (1954), 1–28. For a summary account and basic bibliographies, see 'Penance', *Oxford Companion to Christian Thought*, 528–9; and 'Penance', *Oxford Dictionary of the Christian Church*, 1250–1. On the contemporary situation see D. M. Coffey, *The Sacrament of Reconciliation* (Collegeville, Minn.: Liturgical Press, 2001).

which come at the very end of Luke's two-volume work on Christian origins. The ministry to sick people carried on by Jesus and then by his followers belongs essentially to the proclamation of the kingdom of God, a theme that runs through the Gospel and serves to close the whole story Luke wants to tell (Acts 28: 31).

As a sacrament, the anointing of the sick took shape from the practice of Jesus and his first followers, and was inspired, in particular, by a passage from James:

Are any among you sick? Let them call for the elders of the church and have them pray over them, anointing them with oil in the name of the Lord. The prayer of faith will *save* the sick and the Lord will *raise* them up; and if they have committed sins, they will be *forgiven*. Therefore confess your sins to one another, and pray for one another, so that you may be *healed*. (Jas. 5: 14–16; italics ours)

James invited the entire community to acknowledge to one another their sinfulness and intercede for one another. The 'elders' had the specific role of 'praying over' the sick and anointing them with oil, understood to be endowed with special power from the Spirit. As the four italicized verbs indicate, believers should expect the power of the risen Lord to be at work to save, raise, forgive, and heal the sick and sinful.

From the early third century the *Apostolic Tradition* included a blessing for oil to be used for anointing the sick (5. 2). Innocent I, when writing in 416 to the bishop of Gubbio, quoted James 5: 14–15 and spoke of the ministry to the sick. The bishop was instructed to bless the oil to be used; yet the sick could be anointed not only by bishops and priests but also by any Christians (DH 216; ND 1603). The Pope, relying on the Letter of James, talked of 'the sick' as being candidates for this anointing. But neither James nor Innocent I excluded anointing those whose illness had brought them to death's door. During the first millennium the sacrament became associated with the end of life and hence called 'extreme unction'. Penance before readmission to the Eucharist, as we saw from the letters of Basil, could last fifteen or twenty years, and, as in the case of apostates who repented, even a whole lifetime. Some sinners preferred to delay their request for the sacraments until they were dying; they feared lapsing back into sin after receiving a 'once-in-a-lifetime' absolution. Thus absolution, anointing with oil, and Eucharist were administered to those on their deathbed or 'in extremis'.

In 1439 the Council of Florence reflected the shift from the anointing of the sick to 'extreme unction': 'this sacrament may not be given except to a sick person whose life is feared for'. The minister for the sacrament is a priest, and 'its effect is the healing of the mind and, as far as it is good for the soul, of the body as well' (DH 1324–5; ND 1613). It was customary in the fifteenth century for a priest to be accompanied by a procession of believers when he visited the dying. After the whole group arrived, the dying received absolution, the Eucharist as *viaticum* or food for the journey into the next life, and extreme unction, in that order. When the sick came near death, some or all of the penitential psalms were read, as was one of the Gospel accounts of Our Lord's passion and death. A commendation for a dying person and prayers for the dead developed, along with prayers for the bereaved after a person died. This tradition of prayers with and for the dying remains in the current rituals of the Church.

In the sixteenth century the Council of Trent followed the teaching of Florence when insisting on the sacramental status of 'extreme unction' against Luther, Calvin, and other Protestant Reformers, who appealed to the permanent efficacy of baptism throughout Christian life. Trent stated that the sacrament is 'to be administered to the sick, especially to those who are so seriously ill that they seem near to death; hence it is also called the sacrament of the dying'. Thus it 'protects the end of life' with 'a very strong safeguard'. Trent summed up the effects of this sacrament: 'it confers grace, remits sin, and comforts the sick'. Without condemning him by name, the Council maintained against Calvin that 'the elders' of James 5: 14 are 'priests ordained by a bishop' and not simply 'senior members of a community' (DH 1694, 1698, 1717, 1719; ND 1635, 1638, 1657, 1659).

When restoring the original name of the sacrament, 'the anointing of the sick', the Second Vatican Council emphasized that 'it is not a sacrament only for those who are the point of death'. It can and should be received by those suffering from serious illness and the onset of old age (*Sacrosanctum Concilium*, 73). Through the 1972 renewal of the rite for the anointing of the sick, this sacrament has come to be celebrated much more frequently, and with a number of people often receiving it together in church. When the sacrament of anointing is celebrated at home or in a hospital room, its ecclesial dimension is brought out by the presence of the family and other caregivers. They take their proper place in the liturgy, with readings, songs, and prayers. If the sick person receives communion, the rest of the assembly should do so as well. This renewal of the sacrament has also encouraged suffering Christians to find, through faith in the crucified and risen Christ, a spiritual value in their pain that can contribute to the good of the Church and the whole world. While maintaining the promise of saving and healing expressed by the Letter of James, the new rite invites the sick and the old to let their suffering become part of the passion and redeeming mission of Jesus.

SACRAMENTS IN THE SERVICE OF COMMUNION

Holy Orders

To introduce holy orders, we refer readers back to the opening pages of Ch. 1, which traced the emergence of institutional leadership in the NT Church and immediately thereafter. The first Christians, while enjoying the basic equality of all the baptized and so sharing the same 'holy' or 'royal priesthood' (1 Pet. 2: 5, 9), were, nevertheless, led and served by some who had performed specific ministries for them. We read that some received such ministries through the imposition of hands (e.g. Acts 6: 6; 1 Tim. 4: 14; 2 Tim. 1: 6), and we know the names for some office holders: *episcopoi* (overseers), *presbyteroi* (elders), and *diaconoi* (deacons). The development varied from place to place. The precise roles of these settled pastoral leaders are not made fully clear by the NT. Who, for instance, were responsible initially for baptizing converts and for presiding at the celebration of the Eucharist?

As we saw earlier in this chapter when dealing with the Eucharist, Clement of Rome appealed to the OT distinction between the high priest, priests, levites, and laypersons. Others followed up this reference: Tertullian, for example, was the first Christian writer clearly to apply the title of 'high priest' (*summus sacerdos*) to a bishop (*De Baptismo*, 17. 1).[29] When intervening with Corinthian Christians around AD 96, after several *episcopoi* had been deposed from office, Clement seemed to have equated them with the *presbyteroi* (*Epistle to the Corinthians*, 42, 44).

A decade or so later, however, the letters of St Ignatius of Antioch distinguish the one *episcopos* or 'bishop' from the many *presbyteroi, diaconoi*, and laypeople. The gathering of the whole worshipping community

[29] Many centuries later Vatican II in 1964 referred to 'Christ, the Supreme High Priest' being present and active through the bishops, 'his high priests' (*Lumen Gentium*, 21).

around the bishop resembles the unity of God the Father with the Son. The *Epistle to the Magnesians* by Ignatius could not have been more vigorously explicit on one bishop leading one community and 'presiding in the place of God [the Father]', who is the invisible 'Bishop of all':

As then the Lord was united to the Father and did nothing without him, neither by himself nor through the apostles, so do you do nothing without the bishop and the presbyters. Do not make anything appear right for you by yourselves, but let there be in common *one* prayer, *one* supplication, *one* mind, *one* hope, in love, and in the joy which is without fault, that is Jesus Christ, than whom there is nothing better. Hasten all to come together as to *one* temple of God, as to *one* altar, to *one* Jesus Christ, who came forth from the *one* Father, and is with *one*, and departed to *one*. (nos. 3, 6–7; italics ours)

Ignatius did not specify how the bishop entered into his ministry, still less what form any 'ordination' ceremony took. But he clarified the monarchical model of the Christian communities in Asia Minor: a united community gathered around one bishop, who was assisted by presbyters and deacons.

From the early third century the *Apostolic Tradition* of Hippolytus provides prayers for the ordination of bishops, presbyters, and deacons. The first prayer calls the bishop 'high priest', invokes on him the power of the Holy Spirit, understands him to have the authority 'to forgive sins' and to unite the cultic ministry of offering the Eucharist (interpreted in the light of the OT sacrifices) with the 'feeding' of the 'holy flock' of God (a ministry interpreted in the light of Jesus' own pastoral ministry) (no. 3). The formula for the ordination of a presbyter prescribes that the bishop should lay hands on his head, invoke the Holy Spirit, and, recalling the elders chosen by Moses, pray that he assist with 'a pure heart' in governing the people of God (ibid. 8). Deacons are likewise ordained by the bishop, who lays hands on them and invokes the Holy Spirit for their ministry of 'service' and collaboration with him (ibid. 9). The *Apostolic Tradition* also provides details about the ways in which the presbyters and deacons assist the bishop in baptizing, distributing communion, in serving at community meals, and in leading daily meetings for prayer and instruction (ibid. 23–4, 33). This third-century document describes the ordination and ministry of bishops, presbyters, and deacons; its guidelines for these holy orders remain thoroughly recognizable today in the Catholic Church, among the Orthodox, and beyond.

For many centuries after the apostolic era, the ordination and ministry of those in holy orders remained uncontested. The changes and crises we recalled in Ch. 1 and the first part of Ch. 2 concerned varying ways in which such orders were exercised as societies and cultures developed and collapsed. When, for instance, the Roman Empire was reorganized into fifteen 'dioceses' or administrative divisions, this provided Western Christianity with a standard term for the territory governed by a bishop (or archbishop). From the third century bishops adopted the seat or 'cathedra' of Roman magistrates to symbolize their episcopal authority in teaching, preaching, and presiding in their 'cathedral', the chief church in a diocese. The vestments or special clothes worn by bishops, priests, and deacons for liturgical functions came from Graeco-Roman customs. For example, the alb or long white tunic was modelled on an everyday garment that reached to the ankles. The stole, or long, narrow strip of cloth worn over the left shoulder by a deacon and over both shoulders by bishops and priests, derived from scarves worn by Roman officials to show their rank. The chasuble (Latin *casula* or 'little house'), worn as the outer liturgical vestment for the celebration of the Eucharist, was originally a cone-shaped, outer garment with a hole for the head. After the barbarian invasions, this garment went out of style, but continued to be the special dress for priests and bishops when celebrating Mass.

When Christianity spread through the Mediterranean world and beyond (see Ch. 1), the cathedral liturgy still brought together the bishop, the presbyters, and the deacons. But in rural parishes, often several days' journey from a city large enough to have a bishop, presbyters presided alone at the Eucharist. The vision of one sacrament, perceptibly shared by members of these three orders, disappeared from view. After being originally applied only to the bishop, the title of 'priest' was extended to the 'presbyters' and one spoke of their being 'ordained' by bishops to the priesthood, which essentially meant the power to celebrate the Eucharist. Thus the Fourth Lateran Council stated in 1215: 'No one can perform this sacrament, except the priest duly ordained according the [power of the] keys of the church, which Jesus Christ himself conceded to the apostles and their successors [the bishops]' (DH 802; ND 21). Seven years earlier in a letter to the bishop of Tarragona (near Barcelona), Pope Innocent III had stated: 'No Christians, however honest, religious, holy, and prudent they may be, either can or should consecrate the Eucharist and perform the sacrifice of the altar, if they are not priests regularly ordained by a bishop' (DH 794; ND 1703).

Difficulties already caused by the Waldensians and much more by other 'wounds of the Church', not least by the Great Schism when for thirty-nine years (1378–1417) Western Christianity was divided between eight popes and antipopes, raised serious questions about the sacramental power of bishops and priests, the differences in intrinsic and canonical status between clergy and laypeople, and the prevalent one-sided stress on the ministerial priesthood. Things came to a head when sixteenth-century Protestant Reformers, in the name of retrieving the common priesthood of all the baptized, denied that a sacrament of holy orders derived from Christ and the NT Church. Proper ministry, many of them argued, was a function delegated by Christian communities to some of their members, so as to assure primarily that the Word of God be preached well. To preside over the worship of Christian assemblies, ministers do not require a special sacramental power instituted by Christ but a charism of the Spirit to serve the common good with responsibility. Furthermore, by denying the sacrificial value of the Lord's Supper, the Reformers regarded ordin-ation to the priesthood as superfluous. No sacrifice, and so no priests. Yet the emphasis placed by the Reformers on the need to render the Lord's Supper fully effective through solid preaching beforehand and by pastoral care afterwards reflected major NT dimensions of ecclesial service.

In its twenty-third session (1563) the Council of Trent, having upheld the sacrificial character of the Eucharist in its previous session (1562), insisted on the essential connection between 'sacrifice and priesthood' and drew the conclusion: since 'the Catholic Church has received from the institution of Christ the holy, visible sacrifice of the Eucharist, it must also be acknowledged that there exists in the Church a new, visible, and external priesthood', which has 'the power of consecrating, offering, and administering his body and blood', as well as that of 'remitting sins' (DH 1764; ND 1707). The Council also maintained that bishops are 'superior' to priests, inasmuch as they 'govern the Church', 'ordain ministers', and 'confer the sacrament of confirmation' (DH 1768; ND 1711). Besides reiterating in a crisis situation traditional Catholic teaching on holy orders, Trent recommended such practical reforms as requiring that bishops and parish priests manifest a new commitment to the pastoral care of people, which included a renewed concern for preaching and teaching and a proper training for the priesthood. The Council's 1563 decree on the responsibility of bishops for such training encouraged the formation of seminaries across the Catholic world: from such sixteenth-century foundations as the Venerable English College (which replaced the medieval English Hospice in Rome), eighteenth-century foundations (e.g. St Mary's College, Baltimore, and St Patrick's College, Maynooth), down to huge twentieth-century seminaries in such countries as India, Korea, and Nigeria. The Second Vatican Council was to issue a decree on the training of priests (*Optatam Totius* of October 1965), which directed the bishops of each country to devise their programmes for the educational, pastoral, and spiritual preparation of candidates for the priesthood.

The 1947 encyclical letter *Mediator Dei* of Pope Pius XII signalled developments in teaching about holy orders which prepared the way for Vatican II. All priesthood is founded in the one and unique priesthood of Jesus Christ, but the ministerial priesthood (conferred by the sacrament of holy orders) is to be distinguished from the common priesthood of all the faithful (conferred by baptism) and is exercised differently in the eucharistic sacrifice, where priests 'represent the person of our Lord Jesus Christ' and 'act in the person of Christ' (DH 3850, 3852; ND 1734, 1736). Here the Pope took up an expression officially used for the first time in 1439 when the Council of Florence said of the celebration of the Eucharist: 'The priest effects the sacrament by speaking *in the person of Christ*' (DH 1321; ND 1510). At the same time, as Pius XII stressed, all share in the one offering of Christ, with the people offering the sacrifice 'through' and 'with' the priests (DH 3851–2; ND 1735–6). In *Sacramentum Ordinis* (the Sacrament of Order) also issued in 1947, the Pope authoritatively restated the ancient usage that we cited above from the third-century *Apostolic Tradition*: this sacrament is conferred by the imposition of hands and the invocation of the Holy Spirit. Significantly Pius XII wrote in the singular of the one sacrament of 'the holy orders of diaconate, presbyterate, and episcopate' (DH 3858–9; ND 1737).

Vatican II maintains some of the expressions of Pius XII: for instance, that 'the ministerial priest', by 'acting in the person of Christ, makes the eucharistic sacrifice present and offers it to God in the name of all the people' (*Lumen Gentium*, 10). But a number of emphases are significantly different. First, Vatican II accents even more the 'holy' or 'royal priesthood' of those who have been baptized (ibid.). Second, episcopal ordination confers on a bishop the fullness of holy orders (ibid. 21), with priests and deacons sharing in the one sacrament, albeit in different degrees (ibid.

28–9).[30] Third, the purpose of ministerial priesthood entails not only consecration to God but also a mission to the Church and the world, which aims 'to eliminate division of every shape or form, so that the whole human race may be led into the unity of the family of God' (ibid. 28). Fourth, a new attention to the redeeming role of Christ as prophet/herald, priest, and king/shepherd repeatedly illuminates Vatican II's teaching on the common priesthood of the faithful (ibid. 9–12, 34–6), the ministry of bishops (ibid. 25–7), and that of ordained priests. The scheme of Christ as the 'Teacher, Priest, and King' provides the major structure for the 1965 Decree on the Ministry and Life of Priests, *Presbyterorum Ordinis* (1, 4–6, 13) of the same Council. The prophetic, sanctifying, and pastoral role of presbyters means that priesthood may not be reduced to fulfilling the cultic function that is exercised supremely in offering the sacrifice of the Eucharist.

In 1972, during the aftermath of the Second Vatican Council, Paul VI instituted certain lay ministries in the Western Church. Catholics in many countries have experienced how well lectors (who proclaim the scriptures at the liturgical assemblies), acolytes (who assist priests and deacons at the altar), catechists, eucharistic ministers, and other such ministers can function. Vatican II also mandated the restoration of the permanent diaconate, one that is not simply a stepping-stone to priestly ordination (*Lumen Gentium*, 29). Many parishes profit greatly from the ministry of such permanent deacons who are often married. But what does or should the future hold for married deacons, as well as for catechists, especially since the latter have contributed immensely in Africa and elsewhere to the spread and good state of Catholic Christianity? Clearly the theme of holy orders brings up these and some further challenging questions: for instance, about the non-admission of women to the ordained ministry. Our concluding chapter will return to these issues. Even before then, the next chapter on 'The Catholic Church and Its Mission' will enlarge and shade our account of holy orders.

---

[30] At ordination ceremonies not only the prayers that accompany the imposition of hands during ordination but also the 'explicatory rites' show the difference between episcopate, presbyterate, and diaconate. For example, to signify their participation in Christ's high-priestly mission, bishops and priests are anointed with chrism; deacons are not anointed but are presented with the Gospel Book.

Matrimony

When treating 'the sexual order', Ch. 9 will contribute to our picture of marriage. But what of the sacrament of matrimony? How did Christian marriage come to find its place among the seven sacraments? To acknowledge it as a visible sign instituted by Christ and conferring grace takes us beyond arguing for an equal dignity for the wife and the lifelong nature of the marriage bond.

In the OT, wives became more or less the property of their husbands, who could divorce them for 'something offensive' (Deut. 24: 1). In earlier times polygamy was practised; later Judaism became more aware that monogamy represented the ideal. Jesus himself drew images from weddings for some of his parables (e.g. Matt. 21: 1–14; 25: 1–13). John's Gospel reports how Jesus attended a wedding during his public ministry (John 2: 1–11); the other Gospels show how Jesus strove to safeguard the institution of marriage. He wanted to restore the original plan of God for a married partnership as expressed in the story of creation (Gen. 2: 18, 24); hence Jesus excluded divorce and remarriage as contrary to the divine will: 'what God has joined together let no one put asunder' (Mark 10: 9).

New Testament Christians recognized the crucified and risen Jesus to be their divine Spouse; collectively they were united to him like a wife to a perfectly loving husband (e.g. Rev. 21: 9). The Letter to the Ephesians appeals to this 'great mystery' of the union of all the baptized with Christ to encourage a startlingly elevated view of the loving relationship between Christian husbands and wives (Eph. 5: 25–33). This powerful comparison implies the sacramental status of Christian marriage. Yet it took centuries for this implication to be fully elaborated.

As we saw in Ch. 1, Ignatius of Antioch held that it was up to the local bishop to approve marriages between Christians (*Epistle to Polycarp*, 5. 2). But he mentioned nothing about a sacramental celebration of the marriage contract. The early third-century *Apostolic Tradition* prescribed no particular ceremony for a married couple seeking entry into the church: the husband 'should be taught to be content with his wife' and vice versa. A bachelor who asked for baptism should be taught to avoid fornication and, if and when he decided to marry, to do so 'according to the [civil] law'. A man living with a concubine should either stop doing so or marry her legally (16. 6–7, 24). But from the third century, Christians, while following the forms of marriage current in civil society, practised some service of blessing, and replaced the sacrificial rites of solemn Roman weddings with a celebration of the Eucharist. Moral teaching from the NT guided, of course, the way in which they lived out their married and family life.

During the first Christian millennium and later, Manichaeans, Montanists, and other groups denigrated marriage, and even attributed it to the forces of evil. Early regional councils such as the First Council of Toledo in 400 (DH 206) and the Council of Braga in 561 (DH 461–2; ND 402/11, 12) rejected such errors, and upheld the essential goodness of marriage and the procreation of children. Some like Tertullian, at least at the time when he wrote *Ad Uxorem* (of which more in Ch. 9), did not condemn marriage but only second marriages: widows and widowers should not remarry. Centuries later in 1208 Pope Innocent III was to defend the right of widows and widowers to remarry (DH 794; ND 1802). The shorter life expectancy during the Roman Empire and the Middle Ages made this provision particularly relevant.

As we shall see in Ch. 9, Tertullian wrote for his wife a beautiful account of how shared Christian faith should bless the life of a married couple—a vision of marital union that understood it to be much more than the means for avoiding sexual sin. St Augustine of Hippo seems to have been the first (in 401) to list the purpose and shape of matrimony; he wrote not only of 'offspring' (*proles*) but also of 'fidelity' (*fides*) and 'mutual consent' (*sacramentum*) (*De Bono Coniugali*, 3). He played here on the fact that the Latin word *sacramentum* not only denoted the act of legal consent but also corresponded to the meaning of 'mystery' in Ephesians 5: 32, in which the 'mystery' of the love of Christ the divine Spouse for his bride the Church is related to Christian marriage. There was more to Augustine's view of marriage than simply the procreation and education of children.

By the beginning of the second millennium, European rulers had turned over to bishops and their assistants the celebration of marriage and the administration of matrimonial matters. The liturgy for Christian marriage adopted many of the symbols used in civil ceremonies: for instance, the veil worn by the bride, her ring, and her joining hands with the bridegroom. But there were also changes: instead of the bride's father, the priest led her to the bridegroom. Church control over marriage was reflected in the seventh canon from the Second Lateran Council of 1139, which denied the validity of marriages 'contracted against ecclesiastical law'. The work of Thomas Aquinas and other leading medieval theologians clarified finally the sacramental status of Christian marriage;

hence in 1274 the Second Council of Lyons put marriage down on its list of seven sacraments (DH 860; ND 28). In 1439 the Council of Florence appealed to the Letter to the Ephesians when affirming the sacramental status of Christian marriage, 'the sign of the union of Christ and the church'; it followed Augustine and other Fathers of the Church in recognizing in matrimony a 'triple good':

The first is the begetting of children and their education to the worship of God. The second is the faithfulness which each spouse owes to the other. Third is the indissolubility of marriage, inasmuch as it represents the indissoluble union of Christ and the church. But, although it is permitted to separate on account of adultery, nevertheless it is not permitted to contract another marriage, since the bond of a marriage legitimately contracted is perpetual.   (DH 1327; ND 1803)

Within a century this teaching came under fire from those motivated by a growing sense of personal and Christian freedom and, in particular, by a sense that life in the Spirit requires no law.

Many of the Protestant Reformers, while maintaining the holiness and goodness of marriage in the order of creation, (1) denied its sacramental status and canonical restrictions in the order of grace. Hence (2) they rejected the juridical function of the Church in matrimonial matters. (3) Adultery and sometimes other causes could justify divorce. (4) Because it seemed to contradict the order of created nature, many Reformers disparaged a celibate priesthood and the vow of chastity observed by religious men and women. The Council of Trent in 1563 took its stand on all four issues. (*a*) It upheld marriage as a sacrament instituted by Christ, whose 'grace perfects the natural love' of a married couple, 'confirms' their 'indissoluble union, and sanctifies' them (DH 1799; ND 1806); (*b*) it insisted on the competence of the official Church in matrimonial matters, which included the right to determine the necessary conditions for contracting a valid marriage (DH 1803–4, 1812; ND 1810–11, 1819). To put an end to injustices arising especially from secret marriages, the Council laid down legal procedures to be followed: the banns or public notification of an impending marriage (which in any case had been compulsory since Lateran IV in 1215 (DH 817)); the spouses to be questioned before two or three witnesses about their free decision to marry; their consent to be blessed by the parish priest or his delegate (DH 1813–16).[31] The priest who

---

[31] On this decree of Trent see 'Tametsi', *Oxford Dictionary of the Christian Church*, 1576, and 'Ne Temere', ibid. 1139.

blessed the marriage was viewed as acting as an official witness and not as the minister of the sacrament. Here matrimony stands apart from the other six sacraments, inasmuch as those who 'minister' the sacrament to each other are the bride and bridegroom.

On the question of (c) adultery as grounds for divorce, the Council wanted to avoid offending Orthodox Christians who allow remarriage in such cases. In a carefully worded canon it reiterated the Western teaching and tradition that, during the lifetime of the two spouses, 'the marriage bond cannot be dissolved because of adultery' (DH 1807; ND 1814). The Gospel of Matthew stood behind this difference between East and West. Unlike Luke 16: 18 and Mark 19: 9, Matthew 5: 31–2 and 19: 9, respectively, presumed that, in the case of 'unchastity', Jesus intended an exception to his unconditional prohibition of divorce. The Orthodox understood the Matthean clause, 'except for reason of unchastity', to allow divorce and remarriage in the case of adultery. Catholics regarded this clause as justifying separation but not remarriage. More recently some Catholic and other scholars have interpreted the Matthean clause as prohibiting marriage within the forbidden degrees of kinship (see Lev. 18: 6–18).[32] Such an incestuous union would in fact not be a genuine and valid marriage, and in Church law would require not a divorce but a decree declaring it to be null and void.

Against (d) the Reformers who belittled a celibate way of life, the Council of Trent took a strong line, 'anathematizing' those who asserted that 'the married state surpasses that of virginity or celibacy' and who denied that 'it is better and happier to remain in virginity or celibacy than to be united in matrimony' (DH 1810; ND 1817). The teaching of Christ remained the point of reference. But what had he taught? He introduced something new in the history of the Jewish religion by recognizing the value celibacy could have for the kingdom of God (Matt. 19: 10–12). Jesus invited his hearers to be ready to leave everyone and everything for the sake of the kingdom he proclaimed, mentioning in particular 'brothers, sisters, mother, father, children, and land' (Mark 10: 29). Luke 18: 29 added 'wife' to the list of those whom an individual might have to leave for the sake of Christ and the kingdom. In view of the coming end of all things, St Paul agreed with Luke and recommended celibacy, recognizing

---

[32] See J. A. Fitzmyer, *To Advance the Gospel: New Testament Studies* (New York: Continuum, 1981), 79–III.

at the same time that it is a gift granted only to some. The Apostle held that marriage is good but in the final age of the world celibacy could be better (1 Cor. 7: 1–40). But he never claimed that, in general and apart from the particular calling of individuals, celibacy is essentially 'better or happier' than matrimony.

The Second Vatican Council was to locate the question of married and celibate ways of life within an overarching context by following the NT teaching that *all* the baptized are called to holiness (*Lumen Gentium*, 39–42)—married people no less than celibate priests and consecrated religious men and women.[33] Married life, the 'primary form of interpersonal communion' (*Gaudium et Spes*, 12), embodies the 'unity and fruitful love which exists between Christ and his church', is a path to holiness, and makes the family into 'the domestic church' (*Lumen Gentium*, 11). To be sure, the Council of Trent acknowledged, as we saw above, how the 'grace of Christ perfects the natural love' of married couples, 'confirms their indissoluble union and sanctifies' them. But the language of Vatican II is more effective and personal in calling marriage an 'intimate partnership of life and love'[34] that involves 'total fidelity' and 'unbreakable unity', and in highlighting the importance of sexual love for the total married relationship (*Gaudium et Spes*, 48–9).

In presenting the sacrament of marriage, we have obviously followed once again the route of history. One can understand the seven sacraments of the Catholic Church by being informed about where they came from and how they developed. That is not to disparage other ways of presenting these sacraments: for instance, by showing how they are celebrated today in Church life, both among Eastern and Western Catholics. The post-Vatican II reformed rite of Christian marriage sets out beautifully the Catholic view of this sacrament. But we decided on a historical exposition. After completing it, we want to stand back and summarize what the sacraments mean.

'THE SACRAMENTS OF FAITH'

In its first document the Second Vatican Council described the sacraments as follows:

[33] Religious life entails a special and more radical, but not *exclusive*, call to holiness; all the faithful receive the same call to perfection (*Lumen Gentium*, 32).
[34] In his 1930 encyclical *Casti Connubii* Pope Pius XI had already called marriage 'a complete and intimate life-partnership' (DH 3707; ND 1829).

The purpose of the sacraments is to sanctify human beings, to build up the Body of Christ, and, finally, to offer worship to God. Since they are signs they also instruct. They not only presuppose faith, but by words and ritual elements they also nourish, strengthen, and express faith. Hence they are called 'sacraments of faith'. They do indeed impart grace but, in addition, the very act of celebrating them most effectively disposes the faithful to receive this grace fruitfully, to worship God in a manner that is due, and to practise charity. (*Sacrosanctum Concilium*, 59)

This dense summary calls for some detailed comments.

1. It begins with the threefold purpose of the sacraments: sanctifying, building, and worshipping. The celebration of sacraments lets men and women share more and more in the holiness of the Spirit—a theme that we drew from Ignatius of Antioch at the very beginning of this chapter and to which we shall return below under (4). Second, every sacrament also enables Christ to construct and foster the community of his disciples. Baptism and confirmation initiate new members into his Church, where all receive together his eucharistic Body. Reconciliation and the anointing of the sick communicate his forgiveness and healing to the benefit of everyone. Married love increases his community with the offspring of parents who believe in him. The ministry of those who have received holy orders nourishes the life and growth of the Church by prolonging his words, gestures, and love for all. Third, the sacraments constitute structured ways of worshipping God the Father, which anticipate the praise and glory that will be given, no longer through sacramental signs but face to face, to the divine Creator in the heavenly kingdom to come.

2. As 'signs' which 'instruct', sacraments do their work most effectively when the ministers and people join together in carefully preparing the ceremonies. The revised rituals for the sacraments offer a rich variety of choices in prayers, readings, and blessings, as well as providing for appropriate music, hymns, and actions to accompany the service. A little preparation goes a long way in allowing the sacraments to communicate the salvific intentions and to reactualize the gestures of Jesus Christ, the invisible minister of all the sacraments. In this way the liturgy of the sacraments becomes, for each local community, an attractive and instructive icon of the manner in which he stood on the banks of the Jordan, identified himself with those willing to be baptized with the justice of God, sat at table with religious and social outcasts, and made his own their yearning for the reconciling love of God. In effect, each sacrament

re-enacts the 'change of position' that Jesus created by sharing in our sinful world and offering us his prophetic gestures of salvation: we sinners are to become the justice and love of God in the world. Thus each of the sacramental celebrations restates in a particular way the marvellous interchange that St Paul boldly claimed: 'For our sake, God made him [Jesus] to be sin who knew no sin, so that in him we [sinners] might become the righteousness of God' (2 Cor. 5: 21).

3. The description provided by Vatican II highlights the manner in which sacraments both 'presuppose faith' and also 'nourish, strengthen, and express faith'. The reforms mandated by the Council included the reading and explanation of passages from the scriptures—a service of the word to introduce the celebration of every sacrament. The inspired word of God repeatedly proves 'inspiring' by effectively calling forth and energizing the faith of those about to receive the sacraments. The fact that the reading of the scriptures and a homily form a normal part of sacramental celebration means that the 'words' spoken in administrating a sacrament include, but go beyond, the formulas used, such as 'I baptize you in the name of the Father, and of the Son, and of the Holy Spirit.'

This 'going beyond' the formulas of the liturgy also means that our faith is to be strengthened not only as orthodoxy (i.e. as proper assent to the salvific force of the rite being celebrated) but also as orthopraxy (i.e. as a privileged responsibility with the tripersonal God of salvation for the material and spiritual well-being of those in our social ambience and, indeed, of all people. Sacraments prompt and empower us to put our faith into practice, to act more responsibly among our relatives, friends, associates at work, and fellow citizens. The third eucharistic prayer implies this moral mandate when it directs the attention of the members of the assembly beyond themselves: 'Lord, may this sacrifice which has made our peace with you advance the peace and salvation of all the world.' What we ask the Lord to grant is what we should also strive to promote: the redemptive joy of universal reconciliation with God on the planet.

4. The Council's description also highlights receiving 'grace', which—as we have seen in Ch. 6—can be best expressed as a personal sharing in the divine life of the Trinity. Whatever the grace of a specific sacrament, the Holy Spirit or Sanctifier is always the gift in person, the One who nourishes and consolidates our common life in Christ to the glory of God the Father. This can be seen best through the two great sacraments, baptism and the Eucharist.

Paraphrasing the words of St Paul, 'we who are many are one loaf, one body' (1 Cor. 10: 17), St Augustine reminded the newly baptized, in a good example of the 'mystagogy' that followed Christian initiation, how bread is made: many separate grains of wheat are crushed, moistened with water, and baked with fire to make a single loaf. So at baptism the neophytes were 'ground' by the rite of exorcism, 'moistened with water' at the font, and fired by the anointing of the Holy Spirit (*Sermo* 272). Augustine wanted to show how, above all through the Eucharist, the Spirit continues what was done at baptism, by converting multiplicity into the harmonious unity of the Church which is the Body of Christ. The same Spirit, who is invoked in the first eucharistic *epiclesis* to effect the consecration of the bread and wine into the Body and Blood of the Son, is called on in the second *epiclesis* to transfigure believers and let them share together in the life of the all-holy Father. Because of the constant, dynamic presence of the Holy Spirit, the Church of Jesus Christ is the 'bearer of holiness' for the world and for the greater glory of the Creator Father.

8

The Catholic Church and its Mission

The bishops [are] those to whom the apostles entrusted the churches
... The message of the Church is true and solid; with her there is
only one and the same way of salvation which appears in the whole
world. To her is entrusted the light of God ... The Church preaches
the truth everywhere, and she is the seven-branched candlestick
which bears the light of Christ.

(St Irenaeus, *Adversus Haereses*, 5. 20. 1)

Where the Church is, there is also the Spirit of God; and where the
Spirit of God is, there is the Church and every grace.

(St Irenaeus, *Adversus Haereses*, 3. 24).

Our earlier chapters have reported and explained many aspects of the
Church's origins and life. Chapter 1, for instance, set out the way in which
leadership roles emerged and shaped the government of Christian communities in the first and second centuries: St Paul, later books of the NT,
St Ignatius of Antioch, and St Irenaeus were cited as witnesses for the case
we developed. In his controversies with the Donatists St Augustine supported what had already emerged from Paul's First Letter to the Corinthians and other NT works: right from the outset the Church has been a
community that embraces saints and sinners.

Subsequent chapters added much to our account of the Church: for
instance, in dealing with our common call to final glory, Ch. 6 attended to
the image of the whole Church as the eschatological people of God, a
people on pilgrimage towards God's fulfilment for us in the glorious life of
heaven. Throughout Ch. 7 we were describing the life of the Church: from
the sacraments that initiate men and women into that life, the roles for the
community of those who are then married and/or ordained, and the

sacraments that the ministers of the Church administer to those who are sick and sinful (penance and the anointing of the sick).

Why then do we not address the Church and its mission until Ch. 8? It is because systematic theological reflection and major official teaching on the Church began quite late in the story of Catholicism. St Thomas Aquinas, for example, dealt more or less only in passing with the Church, the mystical Body of Christ that forms with him one 'mystical person' (III q. 19 a. 4; q. 49 a 1).[1] The first treatises on the Church came well over a century later: from two other Dominicans, Ivan Stojkovic of Dubrovnik (d. 1443) and the Spaniard Juan de Torquemada (d. 1468), who is not to be confused with his notorious nephew, Tomás de Torquemada.[2] In 1417 the young Juan de Torquemada attended the Council of Constance and from 1432 to 1437 the Council of Basle; we will say more below of these two councils. In his *Summa de Ecclesia* (published posthumously in 1489), he defined the Church as the 'totality of the faithful, good or bad, who retain the right faith and together participate in the celebration of the sacraments'. He defended the infallibility of papal teaching and, while defending the fullness of the Pope's spiritual power received directly from Christ, took a moderate view of his temporal power. The first attempt from a general council or a pope to present some major teaching on the nature and mission of the Church occurred only with the First Vatican Council. Hence, in line with our policy to treat matters chronologically as far as possible, we come only now to a chapter on the Church. We begin with Jesus and some early developments in the life of the Church down to the middle of the third century. We will then move beyond the founding period to various themes that fill out our picture, before we reach the full flowering of teaching on the Church in the nineteenth and twentieth centuries.

THE CHURCH'S ONE FOUNDATION

By calling the Church 'the seven-branched candlestick which bears the light of Christ' (see the opening of this chapter), Irenaeus expressed two

---

[1] Aquinas reflects on the Church, particularly but not exclusively, when he deals with the grace of Christ as the head of the Church (*ST* III q. 8 a. 1–6) or with the sacraments (*ST* III. qq. 60–90). The Blackfriars translation of the *Summa Theologiae* gathers together in a general index his scattered references to the Church (London: Eyre & Spottiswoode, 1981), lxi. 82–4.

[2] Head of the Spanish Inquisition from 1483 until 1498, the year of his death, Tomás de Torquemada was confessor to the sovereigns, Ferdinand V and Isabella, and apparently influential in their decision to expel Jews from Spain in 1492.

things: the origin of the Church in the Jewish people and the role of Jesus in founding this new assembly of God's people. The OT spoke of the people at Mount Sinai when they received the Ten Commandments and entered a solemn covenant with God as 'the gathering' or 'assembly' (e.g. Deut. 5: 22; the *synagoge* in the LXX or Greek version) or as their *ecclesia* ('that which has been called out' in the Greek of Deut. 9: 10; 18: 16). The NT applies *synagoge* ('synagogue' in English) to Jewish schools or places of worship. Jesus visited synagogues (e.g. Mark 1: 39; Luke 4: 16–30, 31–8, 44); later St Paul and other early Christians used synagogues for dialogue and debate with non-Christian Jews (eg. Acts 13: 14–23; 17: 1–2, 10–12).

For Christian assemblies or congregations the NT uses *ecclesia*,[3] and does so in various ways. There are 'house' churches or believers meeting in particular homes (e.g. Rom. 16: 5); the 'local' churches or congregations of Christians living and meeting in particular regions or towns such as Jerusalem (e.g. Acts 8: 1; 11: 22); and the 'universal' Church or entire body of believers throughout the world (e.g. Matt. 16: 18; Acts 9: 31; Eph. 1: 22). This term occurs frequently in the Book of Acts, in the letters of Paul, and in the Book of Revelation, and only nine times elsewhere in the NT, including three occurrences in Matthew's Gospel but with no examples in the other three Gospels. The most famous of these three instances comes undoubtedly in Jesus' words to Peter: 'On this rock I will build my Church' (Matt. 16: 18).

Jesus the Founder

Even if Jesus did not speak of building 'my church' in response to Peter's confession at Caesarea Philippi[4] and even if he did talk of 'the church' twice in the context of discipline among his followers (Matt. 18: 17), one thing is quite clear: the present and future Kingdom of God constituted the heart of his proclamation. Over and over again Jesus announced by his

---

[3] The English term 'church' comes from the Greek *kyriakon doma* ('the Lord's house').

[4] Mark's Gospel, one of the two major sources apparently used by Matthew, does not include 'building of the church' in its shorter version of Peter's confession and Jesus' response (Mark 8: 27–30). At least part of the longer and more familiar version of the episode at Caesarea Philippi (Matt. 16: 13–20) may not have been simply fashioned by Matthew himself but have come from a source or sources he received. Nowadays more scholars, and not necessarily Catholic ones, argue that some or much of the interchange between Jesus and Peter is authentic—that is to say, derives from a historical event involving both of them; see C. S. Keener, *A Commentary on the Gospel of Matthew* (Grand Rapids, Mich.: Eerdmans, 1999), 423–30. On the wider question of Peter in the early Church, see the interdenominational study by R. E. Brown *et al.*, *Peter in the New Testament* (New York: Paulist Press, 1973).

words and deeds that through his presence (e.g. Luke 11: 20) the powerful rule of God had already come and would reach its consummation at the end of all human history. We must do justice to Jesus' message, and acknowledge that from the beginning the Church exists for the Kingdom. This is not to separate, let along oppose Church and Kingdom, but to insist on fidelity to Jesus' preaching: the universal Kingdom of God is the more encompassing reality. The Our Father does not mention the Church as such but prays 'Thy Kingdom come' and not 'Thy Church come'. When Christ appears in his glory at the end of all history, he will hand over the whole Kingdom, and not simply the Church, to God the Father (1 Cor. 15: 23–4). The famous last lines of Augustine's *City of God* describe the ultimate communion with God in terms of the Kingdom: 'We shall rest and we shall see; we shall see and we shall love; we shall love and we shall praise. Look what will be, in the end, without end. For what is our end but to reach that Kingdom which has no end?' The priority of the Kingdom leaves us with the question: did Jesus intend to found the Church?

One cannot reasonably argue that Jesus clearly and explicitly aimed at founding the Church with all the structural components with which we are familiar: for instance, the government of dioceses (or in the East eparchies) by bishops, the seven sacraments, and the erection of cathedrals and other church buildings. There is no hard evidence for claiming that during his ministry Jesus entertained, let alone proposed, such a blueprint which foresaw and planned in detail the various future developments of the Church. But, as Raymond Brown, Anthony Harvey, Ben Meyer, Tom Wright, and other biblical scholars have rightly concluded: Jesus intended to reform and restore the Jewish nation at its religious and political centre. His dramatic entry into Jerusalem, cleansing of the Temple (Mark 11: 1–11, 15–19), and statement about the rebuilding of the Temple (e.g. Mark 14: 58; 15: 29) indicated that intention. So too did his call and sending of twelve disciples. The choice of the Twelve, for which we summarized the evidence at the beginning of Ch. 1, expressed the desire to gather again the twelve tribes of Israel (Matt. 19: 28; Luke 22: 30). Nevertheless, while Jesus preached principally to his own people and saw them as the primary beneficiaries of God's final revelation and salvation, his vision was universal.

Jesus demanded a realistic love towards other human beings in need, a love ready to cross racial boundaries (Luke 10: 25–37). He called for a new brotherhood and sisterhood that denied any sacrosanct value to family or tribal bonds within Israel: 'Whoever does the will of God is my brother, and sister, and mother' (Mark 3: 35). There was the same kind of universal ring to the parable of the tax-collector and the Pharisee (Luke 18: 9–14). There Jesus asserted that the extent of God's generosity had been hitherto ignored: the divine pardon was offered to all. Hence Jesus' vision of Israel's future entailed 'many coming from the East and the West to sit at table with Abraham, Isaac, and Jacob in the Kingdom of heaven' (Matt. 8: 11). The restoration of Israel to be effected through Jesus' ministry would gather and bring salvation to the nations. The reformation of the twelve tribes would benefit the human race.

Thus evidence from the public life of Jesus supports two conclusions that involve some measure of continuity between his personal mission for the Kingdom of God and the subsequent rise of the Christian Church. The gathering of disciples, from whom twelve were called for some leadership role(s), represents at least a minimal organization. Second, in various ways Jesus showed that he was aware of the universal import of his mission. Hence not only in the historical sequence of events but also in his conscious intentions, some line led from Jesus' proclamation of the divine rule to the establishment of Christianity as a new religious movement.

This second conclusion can be confirmed by what we can glean about Jesus' intentions when faced with death. Material from the Gospels of Matthew, Mark, and Luke back the view that Jesus anticipated his coming death and accepted it as an obedient service that would atone for the sins of others and in some way bring a new relationship between God and the human family. Jesus' death was not unrelated to his proclamation of the divine rule. The message of the Kingdom led more or less straight to the mystery of the passion. That message included and culminated in the suffering ordeal to come: a time of crisis and distress that was to move towards the final judgement, the restoration of Israel, the salvation of the nations. Thus his arrest, condemnation, crucifixion, and resurrection dramatized the very project that totally engaged Jesus: the final rule of God which, through a time of ordeal, was to come for all humankind.[5]

Hence we can follow the NT in its language about Jesus as the cornerstone or foundation-stone of the new Christian community (e.g. 1 Cor. 3: 11; Eph. 2: 20). The image of Jesus as the rejected stone that became the cornerstone or even 'the Living Stone' may well go back to his preaching (Mark 12: 10–11). In any case a number of NT books use that picture (e.g. Acts 4: 11; 1 Pet. 2: 4–8).

---

[5] On this see G. O'Collins, *Christology* (Oxford: Oxford University Press, 1995), 67–81.

The imagery links Christ as *the* (primary) Foundation-stone (in upper case) with the apostles as secondary foundation-stones (lower case) of Christianity (Rev. 21: 14; see Eph. 2: 19–22). Undoubtedly, events that went beyond the life, death, and resurrection of Jesus, above all the outpouring of the Holy Spirit, collaborated in the founding of the Church. Nevertheless, what Jesus preached, did, and endured should encourage Catholics to endorse the conviction expressed in the hymn by S. J. Stone (1830–1900): 'The Church's one foundation is Jesus Christ, her Lord.'

In equivalent terms we may speak of Jesus as the Founder (upper case) of the Church and others as the founders (lower case). In the narrower sense the Twelve, Paul, and other apostles were the founders of the Church.[6] In a wider sense all Christians of the first century can be considered to have been in a variety of ways the founding fathers and mothers of the Church. Let us summarize now something of their Church-founding work, and what ensued, through to the third century.

The Church after Pentecost

The first Christians thought of the Church as inseparable from the risen Christ and from the Holy Spirit. He was the heavenly Spouse of the Church (e.g. Eph. 5: 25–7) or 'the head of the body' which is the Church (e.g. Eph. 5: 23). Baptism in the name of Jesus (e.g. Acts 2: 38) or, with what became the normative formula, 'in the name of the Father, and of the Son, and of the Holy Spirit' (Matt. 28: 19) brought consecration by the Holy Spirit. The baptized knew themselves to be the living temples of the Spirit (1 Cor. 3: 16–17; 6: 19)—language that eventually led to calling the Spirit 'the soul of the Church'.

Baptism initiated believers into the Church, in which the Eucharist nourished their ongoing life. As we showed in Ch. 7, the trinitarian nature of baptism was eventually unfolded in the eucharistic *anamnesis*, *epiclesis*, and *doxology*, with their particular reference to the Son, the Spirit, and the Father, respectively. In the twentieth century Henri de Lubac (1896–1991) coined the axiom that the Church makes the Eucharist, and the Eucharist makes the Church.[7] What we drew in the last chapter from Paul, the

---

[6] For the language that has been traditionally used of the apostles as founders, see M. L. Held and F. Klostermann, 'Apostle', *New Catholic Encyclopedia*, i. 679–82.

[7] *Splendour of the Church* (London: Sheed & Ward, 1956), 106; the same principle is found in de Lubac's earlier and more academic work, *Corpus Mysticum* (Paris: Aubier, 2nd edn. 1949), 104. In *Dominicae Cenae* ('Of the Lord's Supper'), a letter to the bishops of the Church, John Paul II adopted this principle; *Acta Apostolicae Sedis*, 72 (1980), 119.

Gospels, and some post-NT writers illustrates strikingly the truth of that axiom. The Eucharist effects and nourishes the communion of believers among themselves and in the life of the Trinity.

Chapter 1 described the development from the functioning of charismatic endowments and institutional structures in early Christian communities, which we glean from Paul's letters, through to the emergence of leadership roles and authoritative offices. Ignatius of Antioch offers the first classic witness to the life of the Church organized around the local bishop, with his priests and deacons. Chapter 1 also told of Irenaeus' later role in defending the role of monarchical, or single presiding, bishops, who drew their authority from the apostles and succeeded one another in proclaiming one, orthodox faith.

The two passages from Irenaeus that head this chapter illustrate his consciousness of the trinitarian life of the Church, entrusted with 'the light of God' or 'the light of Christ' and blessed with 'every grace' by the Holy Spirit. The Church is *one* by enjoying 'one and the same way of salvation'; *holy* through 'the Spirit of God'; *catholic* in preaching 'the truth everywhere' and encompassing 'the whole world'; and *apostolic* in enjoying the 'true and solid' tradition coming through the bishops from the apostles. In his struggle against the Gnostics, Irenaeus insisted perhaps most of all on apostolicity: the faith and practice both of the community he led and of those with which he was in communion were essentially in continuity with the faith and practice of the earliest Christians led by the apostles and their first successors. The fourth-century Nicene-Constantinopolitan Creed (see Ch. 1) would enshrine unity, holiness, catholicity, and apostolicity as the four marks or essential characteristics of the Church. But we find them already endorsed two hundred years earlier by Irenaeus.

In the late second century Irenaeus fought for the unity of the Church and so too did Cyprian of Carthage half a century later (see Chs. 1 and 7). Sadly Cyprian overemphasized the setting of baptism in the Catholic Church. Hence he argued that valid baptism did not exist 'outside the Church': that is to say, baptism administered by those Christians who were separated by heresy or schism was simply null and void. Fortunately, as we saw in the last chapter, the position of Augustine prevailed in the worldwide Church. Heretics and schismatics can truly and validly administer the sacrament of baptism. But Cyprian's dictum 'outside the Church no salvation', as extended beyond Christian heretics and schismatics, was applied to all those who never request baptism (or who, very frequently, never have a genuine chance of being baptized), and has haunted Christian history down to the third millennium. Would that some early Christian writer had coined and spread the phrase 'outside Christ no salvation'! Such an axiom maintains that the crucified and risen Jesus, together with his Holy Spirit, brings about the eternal salvation of all human beings. *That* this is so is mainstream Christian faith. *How* it happens can be and is often a matter of debate. But such a Christ-centred axiom could well have inhibited some excessively Church-centred approaches to the issue of the salvation of those who are never baptized, an issue to which we return below.

THE CHURCH THROUGH MANY CENTURIES

We have looked at some major points in the Church-founding period of the NT and the first three centuries of Christianity. Although it is true that official teaching and vigorous theological reflection on the nature and mission of the Church emerged only from the nineteenth century, some earlier developments set the stage for what happened in modern times and should be recalled.

To the Protestant Reformation

Various lights and shadows characterize any stocktaking we care to make about the theory and practice of the Church's life from the third to the sixteenth century. The seven general councils, from Nicaea I in 325 to Nicaea II in 787, proved lastingly fruitful in laying down the main lines for Christian faith in Christ and the tripersonal God. The Creed that came from Constantinople I in 381 spread in the East and West, and became commonly professed at the Eucharist, as well as being used by Eastern Christians at baptism. But after the time of the Patriarch Photius in the ninth century, the unilateral addition in the West of the *Filioque* ('from the Son)' became a running sore in relations between Catholics and Orthodox (see Chs. 1 and 4). For some centuries the sacraments of initiation were administered together. But then, in Western Christianity, baptism, First Communion, and confirmation could be separated by years; any lively sense of a single rite of passage through which new members of the Church were justified and sanctified disappeared. The spread of 'auricular' ('in the ear') confession or penance from the end of the sixth century undoubtedly meant some gain, inasmuch, for example, as the earlier system of communal reconciliation through the bishop could be excessively rigorous. But it also meant loss, since penance became an affair between God and a sinful individual and no longer a sacrament of reconciliation with the Church as well as with God. The vivid consciousness of the Church as a people on pilgrimage to the final Kingdom (see the end of Ch. 6) waned. And so too did the awareness that all the baptized make up the Church and share in a common priesthood (see 1 Pet. 2: 5, 9). More and more the Church seemed divided into a lay majority and a clerical minority, and even limited to the clerical minority—an unfortunate misunderstanding still expressed in some ways of speaking. To say that 'so and so went into the Church' does not mean that the person in question accepted Christian baptism but rather that he or she was ordained and entered the clerical profession. When people ask, 'What does the Church think?', sadly one has to recognize that they want to know the views either of the local bishop, or of the all bishops of a country, or of the pope himself. Many Catholics and others still use the 'Church' in a way that refers only to the official leaders and teachers.

Our first two chapters drew attention to fresh initiatives, which appeared in the early centuries and continue to enrich today the Catholic Church and much of Christianity: the rise of monasticism; ongoing missionary activity that spread faith in Jesus Christ; the practice of pilgrimages; the growth of Christian art, architecture, and music; and the founding of religious orders that knew no national frontiers and strengthened the growth of higher learning. Many things happened in and to the Church, and at least in some cases the lasting fruits show the presence and power of the Holy Spirit. Yet for many centuries official teachers and learned theologians (down to the time of Anselm of Canterbury very often the same persons) hardly offered any explicit reflections on the nature and mission of the Church.

This absence of ecclesiology or study of the Church was no 'bad thing' in the sense that down to the Second Council of Nicaea in the eighth century much energy was spent in elucidating and defending basic Christian faith in Jesus Christ and the Trinity revealed through his life, death, and resurrection. In an image used by some early writers, Jesus is the sun and the Church is the moon. Clarifying Christology or doctrine about Jesus Christ obviously takes precedence over any development of ecclesiology.

In any case, from the early fifth century barbarian invasions from the North ravaged Europe and parts of North Africa, and checked doctrinal developments that might otherwise have taken place. From the early seventh century Muslim forces began to take over much of the Middle East; by the early eighth century Islam had taken possession of North Africa and Spain. This pressure from the South also played its part in limiting theological reflection. Christian leaders were forced to make the survival of Church life their major priority.

In those turbulent times the spiritual and, to some extent, political authority of the bishop of Rome emerged. As we noted in Ch. 1, in the early second century Ignatius of Antioch greeted the Church of Rome as 'worthy of honour' and 'presiding in love', recalled Peter and Paul who had been martyred there, but mentioned no bishop of the city (*Epistle to the Romans*, opening greeting, and 4. 3). More than a century later Cyprian, as the same chapter observed, in the first version of his work on the unity of the Catholic Church, put the rhetorical question: 'if someone deserts the Chair of Peter upon which the Church was built, has he still confidence that he is in the Church?' Although all seven of the first general councils of the Church took place in the East (in what is modern Turkey), the primacy in authority of the bishop of Rome featured. At the Council of Ephesus in 431, the Legate of the Pope made a declaration that would be cited at Vatican I in 1870 to support St Peter's primacy continuing in his successors (DH 3056; ND 822). Like Cyprian, this declaration and subsequent ones quoted or at least echoed the language of Matthew 16: 18–19 about the founding of the Church on the rock of Peter and his being given the keys of the Kingdom. Twenty years after the Council of Ephesus, when the bishops at the Council of Chalcedon had listened to the *Tomus* or Letter to Flavian written by Pope Leo I, they exclaimed: 'Peter has spoken through the mouth of Leo.'[8]

From the sixth century the title of 'Patriarch' was given to the bishops of Rome, Constantinople, Alexandria, Antioch, and Jerusalem. The patriarchs

---

[8] On biblical and theological issues about the papal ministry see B. Byrne, 'Peter as Resurrection Witness in the Lucan Narrative', in D. Kendall and S. T. Davis, *The Convergence of Theology* (Mahwah, NJ: Paulist Press, 2001), 19–33; J. M. Miller, *The Shepherd and the Rock: Origins, Development and Mission of the Papacy* (Huntington, Ind.: Our Sunday Visitor, 1995); G. O'Collins and D. Kendall, 'The Petrine Ministry as Easter Witness', *The Bible for Theology* (Mahwah, NJ: Paulist Press, 1997), 117–30; P. Perkins, *Peter: Apostle for the Whole Church* (Minneapolis: Fortress Press, 2000); B. Steimer and M. G. Parker, *Dictionary of the Popes and the Papacy* (New York: Crossroad, 2001); J. M. R. Tillard, *The Bishop of Rome* (London: SPCK, 1983); and many articles in P. Levillain (ed.), *The Papacy: An Encyclopedia* (3 vols.; London: Routledge, 2002).

exercised wide authority in such ways as appointing bishops to major dioceses and judging appeals to their jurisdiction. With a proper sensitivity to East–West tensions, a few months after his election Pope Gregory the Great, as we noted in Ch. 1, sent a circular letter in AD 591 to the Eastern patriarchs to assure them of his fidelity to the four Gospels and to the first four general councils of the Church (from Nicaea I in 325 down to Chalcedon in 451). But, as we also saw, various forces conspired to bring a tragic break, traditionally dated to the mutual excommunications of July 1054, between the patriarch of Constantinople or Ecumenical Patriarch and the bishop of Rome or Patriarch of the West. That formalized the still unhealed break between the Orthodox (Greek for 'right belief') and the Catholic Churches. The Orthodox acknowledge as normative guides to faith only the first seven general councils (up to Nicaea II in 787). The particular Orthodox churches are autonomous or 'autocephalous' (Greek for 'having its own head'), being governed by their own synods, led by patriarchs or metropolitan archbishops, enjoying communion with one another, and normally attributing the primacy of honour to the patriarch of Constantinople, but not in communion with nor acknowledging the universal primacy of the pope or Patriarch of the West.[9]

A new development followed soon after the official break between Constantinople and Rome: the development of Western canon law by Gratian, a twelfth-century monk from Bologna who put together in an organized way legal rulings from councils, popes, and the Church Fathers in his *Concordance of Discordant Canons* (usually known as the *Decree of Gratian* of 1141), a treatise which took for granted a sharp distinction between clergy and laity, or between what he called 'two classes of Christians' (2. 12. 1).[10] The stage was set for the growth of a canonical or juridical view of the Church, which further alienated the Orthodox, who

[9] For a brief, further account of such terms as 'Autocephalous', 'Orthodoxy', 'Patriarch', and 'Primacy', see G. O'Collins and E. G. Farrugia, *A Concise Dictionary of Theology* (Mahwah, NJ: Paulist Press, rev. edn. 2000). For a longer account see R. Roberson, *Eastern Christian Churches* (Rome: Pontifical Oriental Institute, 6th edn. 1999). For the role of patriarchs, see Y. Congar, 'Le Pape comme patriarche d'Occident: approche d'une réalité trop négligée', *Istina*, 28 (1983), 374–90; W. de Vries, 'The Origin of Eastern Patriarchates and their Relationship to the Power of the Pope', *One in Christ*, 2 (1966), 50–69, 130–42.

[10] Gratian's distinction (or should one say separation?) between clergy and laity prevailed for many centuries. Thus in his 1906 encyclical *Vehementer Nos* ('Our being extremely [concerned]'), Pope Pius X wrote: 'The Church is essentially an unequal society, that is, a society comprising two categories of persons, the pastors and the flock, those who occupy a rank in the different degrees of the hierarchy and the multitude of the faithful' (no. 8).

see the Church as the way to attain holiness and union with God through the process of divinization (see Ch. 6). Rivalry in the West between secular and ecclesiastical powers set the nature of Church authority high on the agenda. The centralizing policies of Gregory VII (pope 1073–85) and, even more of Innocent III (pope 1198–1216)—the first pope to use regularly a title dating from the eighth century, that of 'Vicar of Christ' (which completely superseded the older title of 'Vicar of Peter')—involved papal claims to exercise jurisdiction over the whole Church and even to dictate to temporal sovereigns in such major secular affairs as the election of the Holy Roman Emperor. This development, which reached its height in the theory and practice of Innocent III, took the power of the papacy well beyond the role envisaged by Cyprian, Leo the Great, and Gregory the Great. For them the bishop of Rome was the centre of unity in the true faith, and the final court of appeal in matters involving the authentic tradition that comes to us from the apostles.

Various spiritual movements, e.g. the Albigensians (see Ch. 2), which—along with false views about redemption—emphasized personal holiness and the fraternal communion of the faithful, protested against a vision of the Church dominated by clerical power. When condemning such movements in 1215, the Fourth Lateran Council applied the language of Cyprian to the current situation: 'there is one universal Church of the faithful outside which no one at all is saved' (DH 802; ND 21).

From the end of the thirteenth century and through much of the fourteenth, the relationship between the spiritual power of popes and the temporal power of princes dominated thinking about the Church. Medieval thinking associated the two powers with the 'two swords' produced by the disciples shortly before Jesus was arrested (Luke 22: 38). Boniface VIII (pope 1294–1303) reached for that image when he recognized the two 'swords' or powers, but went on to claim that his spiritual power should control any temporal power. He sought to exercise papal authority over the princes of his day, and claimed jurisdiction over every human being (DH 870–5; ND 804). He died a month after being briefly imprisoned by mercenaries sent by the French king. Six years later, the French Clement V (pope 1305–14) initiated the 'Babylonian Captivity' or seventy-year exile of the popes by fixing his residence at Avignon in 1309. Even after the papacy returned to Rome, 'the Great Schism' for thirty-nine years divided Christendom between various popes and antipopes, a situation that ended only when the Council of Constance elected Martin V (pope 1417–31).

In its famous decree *Haec Sancta* ('this Holy [Synod]') of 1415, one which some scholars hold to be intended only as a practical measure to deal with the crisis of the Great Schism, the Council maintained that it received its authority immediately from Christ and was vested with superiority over any pope. The same decree expressed the intention of 'uniting and reforming the Church in its head and members' (ND 806). When opening the First Council of Lyons in 1245, Innocent IV, as we saw, spoke of various 'wounds' of the Church. This language of 'head and members' and of 'wounds' implied a sense of the Church as the one, united, visible Body of Christ—a belief that would be severely questioned in the sixteenth century.

Just before the Protestant Reformation began, the arrival of the Europeans in the Americas challenged the universality of Christ's redemption and its mediation through the Church. Since the early centuries most Christians seem vaguely to have imagined that all human beings had somehow heard the Gospel proclaimed; unbelievers were those who refused to accept Christ and enter the Church through baptism. As we saw in Ch. 2, the discoveries initiated by Columbus in 1492 revealed the existence of millions of human beings who for many centuries never had the slightest chance of believing in Christ and joining the Church. How could one sustain the axiom 'outside the Church no salvation' in the rigorous way understood, for instance, by Boniface VIII and by a 1442 decree from the Council of Florence (DH 1351; ND 810, 1005)? It took centuries before Vatican II recognized that, whereas all are 'called' to belong to the Church, millions of people will never in fact have the chance of accepting the call, remain mysteriously 'related' to the Church (*Lumen Gentium*, 13, 16), and can find salvation through the power of the Holy Spirit who joins them to the crucified and risen Christ (*Gaudium et Spes*, 22). But we are jumping ahead of ourselves and must go back to the sixteenth century.

The Reformation and Beyond

The Protestant Reformers, led by Martin Luther, rejected papal authority, did not (at least initially) envisage a divided Christendom, and wanted to eradicate evils and bring the Church into line with NT faith and the scriptures. Luther, in his *Large Catechism* of 1529, wrote of the Church on earth as 'a little holy group and congregation of pure saints, under one head, Christ, called together by the Holy Spirit in one faith, one mind, and understanding, with manifold gifts, yet agreeing in love, without sects or schisms'. Believers are 'incorporated' into the Church 'by the Holy Spirit' through 'hearing and continuing to hear the Word of God'. The Holy Spirit 'abides with the holy congregation', 'brings us to Christ', and 'promotes sanctification, causing this congregation to grow daily and become strong in the faith and its fruits which the Spirit produces' (10. 3).

John Calvin, in his *Institutes of Christian Religion*, distinguished between the invisible Church of 'the elect of God' who are 'united in Christ' and live together 'in the same Spirit of God' and the visible Church whose members obey 'authority' and 'act as one flock' (4. 1. 2–3, 7). The Westminster Confession of 1646, the classic profession of Presbyterian faith, embodied much teaching from Calvin and later Calvinists: for instance, by upholding the distinction between the visible and the invisible Church:

> The catholic or universal Church, which is invisible, consists of the whole number of the elect . . . gathered into one, under Christ the head; and is the spouse, the body, the fullness of Him who fills all in all. The visible Church, which is also catholic or universal under the gospel (not confined to one nation as before under the law), consists of all those throughout the world that profess the true religion, together with their children; and is the Kingdom of the Lord Jesus Christ; the house and family of God, through which men are ordinarily saved and union with which is essential to their best growth and service. To this catholic and visible Church, Christ has given the ministry, oracles, and ordinances of God, for the gathering and perfecting of the saints, in this life, to the end of the world [through Christ's own presence and that of the Spirit]. (25. 1–3)

As Luther did, Calvin and the Westminster Confession expressed a trinitarian understanding of the Church, something that was to mark the teaching of the Second Vatican Council (*Lumen Gentium*, 2–4; *Ad Gentes*, 2–4).

Some points made by the Reformers recall views held in earlier centuries: for instance, Luther's language about a 'little holy group and congregation of pure saints' brings to mind the Donatists in North Africa (Chs. 1 and 7 above) or the spiritual Church championed by John Wyclif and others. Calvin's 'invisible' gathering of 'the elect' more than hints at the teaching of John Huss about the Church being the 'aggregate of the predestined' (DH 1201; ND 808/1). Certain themes from the Reformers recur in the later centuries. Into the twentieth century some and even many Catholics wrongly identified the Church with the Kingdom, even if they did not endorse Presbyterian ideas of ecclesial government. But the Westminster Confession includes themes that were to flourish in the documents of Vatican II: for instance, the plurality of images for the Church (as spouse, body, house, and family); the origins of ministry in the will of Christ and not in the arrangements of his followers; and union with the Church that offers all the ordinary means for salvation.

Although it was called to clarify teaching and reform abuses, the Council of Trent (1545–63) did not deal with questions of the Church or the papacy, but took up other issues such as scripture, tradition, original sin, justification, and the sacraments (see Chs. 2, 6, and 7 above). After the Council ended, Pius V (pope 1566–72) issued the *Roman Catechism* (1566), the revised Breviary (1568), and the Missal (1570). The *Catechism* understands the Church to be an 'assembly', but insists that it is 'very unlike all other societies', since it has been called forth through 'the kindness and splendour of divine grace'. The Catechism brings up other biblical names for the Church: in particular, 'house', 'flock', and 'body'. It distinguishes between the 'Church triumphant', which already enjoys the glory of the risen Lord, and the 'Church militant', 'the society of all the faithful still dwelling on earth'. The latter is 'composed of two classes of persons, the good and the bad, both professing the same faith and partaking of the same sacraments, yet differing in their manner of life and morality'. The Catechism adds that there are 'three classes of persons excluded' from the one Church: (*a*) 'infidels' who never belonged to the Church, (*b*) 'heretics and schismatics' who have separated themselves, and (*c*) 'excommunicated persons' who 'have been cut off' by an official decision and do not belong 'until they repent'. Finally, the Catechism is the first official document to develop the four 'marks' or main characteristics of the Church: as one, holy, catholic, and apostolic (1. 9).

A few years later St Robert Bellarmine (1542–1621) articulated in his *Controversies* (1586–93) a vision of the Church that remained more or less standard among Catholics for well over two hundred years. His basic definition runs as follows: 'There is but one Church, not two, and this one and true Church is the assembly of those who are brought together by the profession of the one and same Christian faith and by participation in the same sacraments, under the authority of legitimate pastors and above all under that of the one Vicar of Christ on earth, the Roman Pontiff' (3. 2). Bellarmine begins with the visible 'assembly' (*coetus*) which has been 'brought together' by God's grace, and then adds the three elements that unite the assembly: the same faith, the same (seven) sacraments, and obedience to a legitimate authority that comes from Christ. 'One and the same' echoes through the definition like an antiphon: 'one Church', 'this one and true Church', 'one and the same Christian faith', 'the same sacraments', and 'the one Vicar of Christ'. This 'public' version of 'but one Church' rejected that of those Reformers who distinguished the visible and invisible Church and privileged the latter. Bellarmine represented the 'one and true Church' to be as visible as the Kingdom of France or the Republic of Venice. Public affiliation, rather than virtuous behaviour, made one a member of the 'assembly'. At least in this key definition, Bellarmine highlighted the human, structural, and public elements and had nothing to say about the role of the Holy Spirit in animating the life of the Church.

Subsequent Catholic theology maintained Bellarmine's model of the Church as a 'perfect society', a highly visible, hierarchical institution that could, at least partly, be compared with sovereign states. From the sixteenth to the nineteenth century various events (such as the French Revolution, its aftermath, and the European uprisings of 1848) and movements (such as Gallicanism) encouraged the centralizing of authority more and more in the Roman Pontiff. Spreading from France across Europe from the late seventeenth century, political and other leaders who shared Gallican ideas claimed considerable independence from the papacy, asserted the supreme authority of general councils, and promoted national churches at the expense of wider Christian unity. Popes, many bishops, and other Catholics resisted Gallican-inspired interference in the life of the Church in a way that recalled the investiture controversy of the Middle Ages (see Ch. 2 above).

What helped to change, at least in the long run, prevailing views of the Church was the publication in 1825 of *Unity in the Church* by Johann Adam Möhler (1796–1838), a young Catholic professor at the University of Tübingen. Rather than stressing the juridical, centralized institution, he highlighted the nature of the Church as a living organism, a communion animated and sanctified by the indwelling Holy Spirit. The Spirit is the life-giving principle, made visible in a particular way by the bishop for a diocese and the pope for the universal Church.

Thus far this chapter has traced various forces and ideas that, from NT times and through subsequent centuries, prepared the ground for the full flowering of Catholic teaching on the Church. That happened only from the second half of the nineteenth century. We turn now to the work of the First Vatican Council (1869–70).

VATICAN I AND VATICAN II

In the run up to Vatican I and its definition of papal authority, the work of the French writer Joseph de Maistre (1753–1821) was seminal. In a world shaken by the French Revolution and its aftermath, he presented the papacy as an absolute monarchy that sustained the well-being of the whole Church. The pope's authority is sovereign: his decisions are not open to appeal, and his doctrinal declarations are infallibly binding. De Maistre argued that only such an absolute papacy could check abuses from national states in the temporal sphere and save separated Christian brethren from lapsing into religious indifference. Gallicans and many who championed liberal ideas dismissed de Maistre and others, such as William George Ward (1812–82), as 'ultramontanes (beyond the mountains)', since they looked 'across the Alps' to Rome, maximalized papal authority, and expected from the pope answers to every important question. In a saying that was widely quoted, Ward declared: 'I should like a new Papal Bull every morning with my *Times* at breakfast.'[11]

Vatican I and the Church

The constitution on Catholic faith, *Dei Filius* ('Son of God'), the first document solemnly accepted by the bishops at the First Vatican Council, made a passing reference in its introduction to the Church as 'the mystical body of Christ': the renewal brought about by the Council of Trent meant 'an increased vigour in the whole mystical body of Christ'. But the same introduction also listed among the blessings that followed Trent 'a closer union of the members with the visible head' (i.e. the pope) and the growth throughout the whole world of 'the Kingdom of Christ', which was obviously identified with the Catholic Church.[12] But Vatican I's second constitution, *Pastor Aeternus* ('the Eternal Pastor'), did not develop ideas either about the Church as the body of Christ or about the relationship of Church to Kingdom. It solemnly pronounced on two questions: (*a*) the

---

[11] Quoted by his son, Wilfrid Ward, in *The Life of John Henry Cardinal Newman Based on his Private Journals and Correspondence* (London: Longman, Green & Co., 1912), ii. 213.

[12] N. Tanner (ed.), *Decrees of the Ecumenical Councils* (London: Sheed & Ward, 1990), i. 804.

primacy of jurisdiction of the Roman Pontiff and (*b*) his infallible teaching function.

As regards (*a*), Vatican I taught that the pope exercised 'primacy of jurisdiction over the whole Church' (and not merely primacy of honour) and that this primacy of jurisdiction was 'immediately and directly promised and conferred' upon Peter alone by 'Christ the Lord' (DH 3053; ND 819). This universal papal authority is 'ordinary' and 'immediate' (DH 3060; ND 826): 'ordinary', in the sense that it 'goes with the job' of being pope and is not delegated to him by some other authority (e.g. a general council); 'immediate', in the sense that he can intervene anywhere without depending on the permission of the local bishop. In proposing this teaching, the Council maintained that, far from introducing an innovation, it was only reiterating what could be found earlier and was defined by the fifteenth-century Council of Florence (DH 3059; ND 825).[13]

Some at the Council, nevertheless, objected that such doctrine about papal jurisdiction could be taken to imply that the world is one, huge diocese, with the pope as its bishop. That would reduce the bishops to being papal assistants, officials of a centralized authority who did not exercise their episcopal mission and function in their own right. To avoid this false impression, *Pastor Aeternus* added:

This power of the Supreme Pontiff is far from standing in the way of the power of ordinary and immediate episcopal jurisdiction by which bishops who, under appointment of the Holy Spirit [see Acts 20: 28], succeeded in the place of the apostles, feed and rule individually, as true shepherds, the particular flock assigned to them. Rather this latter power is asserted, confirmed, and vindicated by this same supreme and universal shepherd.   (DH 3061; ND 827)

This reasonably clear statement did not, however, stop Otto von Bismarck (1815–98), the 'Iron Chancellor' of Germany, from issuing in 1872 a circular in which he attacked Vatican I over the direct and universal jurisdiction of the Roman Pontiff. Such a doctrine, he claimed, reduced the bishops to being no more than executive organs of the pope. The German bishops reacted by accusing Bismarck of 'completely misunderstanding' the Vatican decree, which did not make the bishops simply 'tools of the Pope, his officials, without responsibility of their own'. The German

---

[13] On the whole history of papal primacy, and not just the teaching from the Council of Florence and Vatican I, see K. Schatz, *Papal Primacy from Its Origins to the Present* (Collegeville, Minn.: Liturgical Press, 1996).

bishops insisted: 'it is in virtue of the same divine institution upon which the papacy rests that the episcopate also exists. It, too, has its rights and duties, because of the ordinances of God himself, and the Pope has neither the right nor the power to change them.' This, the bishops stressed, had been 'the constant teaching of the Catholic Church' (DH 3115; ND 841). A few weeks later Pope Pius IX came out in emphatic support of the declaration made by the German bishops (DH 3117). The text of *Pastor Aeternus*, along with the declarations by the German bishops and then Pius IX, demonstrated that the conciliar document about the direct and universal jurisdiction of the pope never intended to belittle the God-given 'rights and duties' of bishops around the world.[14]

The other major item from Vatican I about the nature of the Church as an institution concerned the teaching office of the pope. In carefully qualified language the status of the most solemn teaching, which—to the disappointment of the W. G. Wards of this world—has been exercised very rarely, was expressed as follows:

It is a divinely revealed dogma that the Roman Pontiff, when he speaks *ex cathedra* ('from the chair' of authority), that is, when, acting in the office of shepherd and teacher of all Christians, he defines, by virtue of his supreme apostolic authority, a doctrine concerning faith and morals to be held by the universal Church, possesses, through the divine assistance promised to him in the person of Blessed Peter, the infallibility with which the divine Redeemer willed his Church to be endowed in defining the doctrine concerning faith and morals; and that such definitions of the Roman Pontiff are therefore irreformable of themselves, not because of the consent of the Church.   (DH 3074; ND 839)

Various conditions are enumerated. To 'speak *ex cathedra*' is to teach solemnly (i.e. with the fullness of papal authority as universal pastor and successor of St Peter) some revealed truth that all Christians should believe. Hence such papal infallibility is not involved when the pope is teaching on matters other than revealed faith and morals, as, for instance, when John Paul II presented his valuable teaching on the relationship of faith and reason in his 1998 encyclical *Fides et Ratio* ('Faith and Reason'). Nor can infallibility be involved when it is not manifestly clear that the pope is teaching *ex cathedra*. Thus the 1968 encyclical on married life and love, *Humanae Vitae* ('Of Human Life'), which rejected the use of

---

[14] See W. Henn, *The Honor of my Brothers: A Brief History of the Relations between the Pope and the Bishops* (New York: Crossroad, 2000).

artificial means of birth control, cannot be considered an exercise of that infallible magisterium defined at Vatican I. Pope Paul VI did not propose his teaching with the type of language which would warrant it being considered an *ex cathedra* teaching; in fact, the Vatican official presenting the encyclical said what amounted to the same thing, when he pointed out that the encyclical did not claim infallible status. In short, no papal teaching should be credited with such status, unless it fulfils all the conditions enumerated—in particular, that the language used by the pope clearly indicates that he intends to teach in the way that Vatican I described as *ex cathedra*. The 1983 *Code of Canon Law* for Western Catholics makes this point in summary fashion: 'No doctrine is understood to be infallibly defined unless this is manifestly so' (749. 3).

Infallibility entails that the teaching in question is free from the possibility of error and not that it is necessarily expressed in the best and most helpful manner possible. In fact, one must always distinguish the meaning of the definition from its formulation, which will always be conditioned by the historical circumstances of the time. As we recalled in the last chapter, the truth that is proposed (e.g. the presence of the risen Christ in the Eucharist) and that remains 'irreformable' is not simply identical with the terms in which it is formulated and which can be reformulated (e.g. 'transubstantiation'). This instance taken from the Council of Trent (DH 1642; ND 1519) also reminds us of something we have already seen exemplified in many chapters of this book, especially in Chs. 4–7: infallible definitions have normally come from general councils of the Church and not from popes. When offering examples of the exercise of papal infallibility, authors generally cite two definitions: that of the Immaculate Conception of the Blessed Virgin Mary in 1854 (by Pius IX) and that of her Assumption into eternal glory in 1950 (by Pius XII).[15]

The first defined dogma, which supports the celebration by Western Catholics of a feast that goes back at least to the seventh century, teaches that, by a unique privilege and in view of her Son's merits, Mary of Nazareth was free of all sin, even original sin, from her very conception (DH 2800–4; ND 709). Partly because of differences over original sin, the Orthodox do not honour the Mother of God as immaculately conceived but simply as 'immaculate' or 'all-holy'. The second dogma declares that at the end of her

---

[15] In *Creative Fidelity* (Dublin: Gill & Macmillan, 1996), F. A. Sullivan presents arguments for recognizing the exercise of infallible definitions by popes in some other cases.

earthly life Mary was taken up body and soul into heavenly glory (DH 3900–4; ND 713–15). Where Christ 'ascended' by his own power, Mary was 'assumed' by divine power. From the fifth century Eastern Christians celebrated the *koimesis* ('falling asleep') of Our Lady. 'Assumption' replaced 'dormition' or 'falling asleep' when Rome adopted the feast in the seventh century. Popular faith and practice among Catholics supported both papal definitions for the feasts which they celebrated on 8 December and 15 August, respectively. Before defining the Immaculate Conception, Pius IX consulted bishops around the world, even if he did not go on to proclaim the dogma on the formal basis of 'the consent of the Church'. In a similar way, it was only after he consulted Catholic bishops and received requests coming from thousands of laypeople that Pius XII defined the Assumption of the Blessed Virgin Mary. Once again, 'the formal consent of the Church' was not the essential condition for his doing so.

A key feature of the 1870 definition of papal infallibility appears in the words about the pope sharing in 'the infallibility with which the divine Redeemer willed his Church to be endowed'. This infallibility with which the whole Church is endowed guarantees that the tradition of faith that comes from the apostolic Church will be handed on with essential reliability from generation to generation. As we noted in Ch. 3 when expounding the nature of tradition, all members of the Church share, albeit in different ways, in the task of transmitting tradition. John Henry Newman in his 1859 work *On Consulting the Faithful in Matters of Doctrine*[16] had drawn attention to the loyal sensitivity in matters of faith exercised by the whole body of believers; the Holy Spirit guides their discernment and transmission of revelation (see John 16: 13; 1 John 2: 20, 27). Vatican II was to vindicate the championing by Newman and others of this 'sense of the faithful', even if it spoke rather of 'the sense of faith', which means that the whole People of God, when in agreement, cannot err in matters of belief (*Lumen Gentium*, 12). The Council was also to spell out, in terms of the common teaching of the bishops around the world, other implications involved in the Redeemer's gift of infallibility to his Church (ibid. 25).

The Path to Vatican II

Vatican I represented the first major attempt on the part of a general council or a pope to produce an official document on the nature of the

---

[16] Ed. J. Coulson (London: Collins, 1986).

Church. The teaching remained, however, incomplete. The outbreak of the Franco-Prussian War and the advance of the Piedmontese troops on Rome forced the Council to adjourn hastily after defining the papal primacy of jurisdiction and infallibility, but without discussing and voting on an additional, longer document, which had been prepared to give more complete teaching on the Church as a whole. Italian troops seized Rome on 20 September 1870, and a month later the Council was formally suspended and never reconvened.[17] This turn of events left much unfinished business, including reflection on the Church's mission to evangelize the world. Sixty-seven other missionary bishops joined Blessed Daniele Comboni (1831–81) in presenting for the Council's discussion a stirring petition on behalf of the Black Populations of Central Africa. As regards evangelization and other aspects of doctrine on the Church, Vatican I left behind a lopsided view that highlighted the central mission of the pope and had little to say directly about the mission of bishops, priests, deacons, religious, and laity.

Many lights and shadows characterized the run-up to Vatican II and its ample teaching on the Church. Both before and after that Council, for better or worse, the theory and practice of the Catholic Church remained inextricably bound together.

Shadows covered Catholic relationships with other Christian bodies. Before the nineteenth century ended, Leo XIII (pope 1878–1903) in 1896 declared Anglican orders invalid (DH 3316–19; ND 1722–8)—a step that profoundly disappointed Viscount Charles Halifax (1839–1934) and other devout Anglicans who had initiated conversations in Rome (1894–6) with a view to promoting reunion between the Church of England and the Holy See. What Halifax and his friends attempted belonged within a wider ecumenical movement or common search for unity on the part of many Christian communities. The 1910 Edinburgh Missionary Conference, which brought together 414 delegates from 122 denominations and

---

[17] R. Aubert, C. Butler, G. Martina, G. Thils, and other scholars have produced helpful studies on Vatican I. But the best work is K. Schatz, *Vaticanum I. 1869–1870* (3 vols.; Paderborn: Schöningh, 1992–4). For a summary account, see H. J. Pottmeyer, 'Vatican Council I', in R. P. Mc Brien (ed.), *The HarperCollins Encyclopedia of Catholicism* (San Francisco: HarperSan Francisco, 1995) , 1296–8. For various themes which follow below, see in this order these entries in the *Oxford Dictionary of the Christian Church*: 'Comboni, Bl [Antonio] Daniele', 'Anglican Ordinations', 'Ecumenical Movement', 'Faith and Order', 'World Council of Churches', 'Malines Conversations', 'Anglican-Roman Catholic International Commission (ARCIC)', 'Couturier, Paul Irénée', 'Fisher, Geoffrey Francis', and 'John XXIII'.

43 countries, signalled the wide commitment to this search for Christian dialogue and, eventually, union. No Catholic delegation attended this conference, nor did any take part in the first meeting of Faith and Order, an ecumenical body founded to study theological problems underlying divisions between Christians, which first met at Lausanne in 1927. Likewise, the Catholic Church was not officially represented at Amsterdam in 1948, when 147 Protestant, Anglican, and Orthodox churches formed the World Council of Churches. Eventually, thanks to Pope John XXIII and others (of whom more below), the Catholic Church officially joined the Faith and Order Commission in 1968, and, while not becoming a member, has since 1965 enjoyed regular contacts with the World Council of Churches through the Joint Working Group. But for many decades Catholic leaders responded to the ecumenical movement with caution and even suspicion. Pope Pius XI, in his 1928 encyclical *Mortalium Animos*, even if it was officially dedicated to 'fostering religious union', judged that Catholic participation in assemblies with other Christians could all too easily give the impression that one religion or church was as good as another. Along with very many Catholics, the Pope's model of reunion was the return of non-Catholics to the Catholic Church, which he took to be simply coextensive with the One Church founded by Christ.

Some ecumenical initiatives involved Catholics and prepared the ground for what would come with Pope John XXIII and Vatican II. Viscount Halifax, supported by Cardinal Désiré Joseph Mercier (archbishop of Malines), brought together some outstanding Anglican and Catholic theologians to discuss such central themes as the Eucharist and the mission of bishops and popes. The Malines Conversations (1921, 1923, and 1925), while producing no immediate fruit, helped to open the way for the Anglican-Roman Catholic International Commission (ARCIC), which, after a preparatory Malta Report (1968), began its work with a nine-day meeting at Windsor in 1970. Cardinal Mercier died in 1926, and Viscount Halifax in 1934. By the early 1930s another enduringly valuable innovation was in place.

The First Lambeth Conference of Anglican Bishops (1867), in the preamble to its resolutions, had emphasized prayer for Christian unity. Fr. Paul Wattson (1863–1940), when still a member of the Protestant Episcopal Church in the United States, started in 1908 the Church Unity Octave, eight days of prayer for the religious unity of all Christians. The following year, with other friars, sisters, and laymen of his community, he

FIG. 12(a). On 25 March 1966 Pope Paul VI gives his own episcopal ring to Dr Michael Ramsey, Archbishop of Canterbury. (Topham Picturepoint.) (b). Pope Paul VI and Athenagoras, the Ecumenical Patriarch of Constantinople and head of Orthodox Christians, embrace on the steps of St Peter's Basilica on 28 October 1967. (Topham Picturepoint.)

was received into the Catholic Church. In 1934 Paul Irénée Couturier (1881–1953), a French priest who met many Orthodox Christian refugees from the Russian Revolution of 1917 and was impressed by the ecumenical initiatives of Cardinal Mercier, helped to universalize an octave of prayer for Christian unity (18–25 January). Through his vast correspondence and tracts on more inclusive prayer for unity, Couturier enjoyed contacts with Christians around the world and encouraged innumerable people to pray for 'the unity Christ wills, by the means he wills'. His work lives on in the widely observed Week of Prayer for Christian Unity, and enjoyed a moving outcome on 18 January, early in the Holy Year of 2000. The (Anglican) archbishop of Canterbury, George Carey, together with Metropolitan Athanasios, a representative of the (Orthodox) Ecumenical Patriarch of Constantinople, joined Pope John Paul II in opening the holy door of St Paul's Basilica (outside the old walls of Rome) and in the service for Christian unity that followed. Forty years before, the then archbishop of Canterbury, Geoffrey Fisher (1887–1972), had visited Pope John XXIII in 1960, the first archbishop of Canterbury to visit a pope since 1397.

All kinds of relations with other Christians played an essential role in moving Catholicism towards the teaching on the Church elaborated by Vatican II. Beyond question, one must list high among these relations the common suffering endured in two horrendous world wars and the persecution that faithful Christians endured from totalitarian regimes, especially from Communism and Nazism. Concentration camps, prisoner-of-war camps, and gaols fostered an ecumenism under the cross.

But what happened within the Catholic Church to make possible the teaching of Vatican II? Pope Leo XIII cautiously opened one or two doors. His 1897 encyclical on the Holy Spirit, *Divinum Illud Munus* ('That Divine Gift'), called the Holy Spirit the 'soul' of the Church, which is the 'mystical Body of Christ' (DH 3328). At least four developments should be recalled.

First of all, the initiatives of lay Catholics began to break down the division encouraged by a Gratian-style separation of the Church into clergy and laity. By championing human rights, Leo XIII's 1891 encyclical *Rerum Novarum* ('Of New Things') encouraged lay Catholics to become activists in trade unions and political parties. Much earlier in the nineteenth century an Irish layman, Daniel O'Connell (1775–1847), led the successful struggle for the Roman Catholic Relief Act of 1829, which removed most of the civil disabilities under which Catholics in the British Isles had suffered. From the early decades of the twentieth century, various large lay movements sprang up in Europe and around the world. Thus the 'Jocists' ('*Jeunes Ouvriers Chrétiens*') or Young Christian Workers formed a Catholic Action movement which was established after the First World War in Belgium by Joseph (later Cardinal) Cardijn (1882–1967) and spread to the United States, Australia, and other countries. It encouraged laypersons to become shining examples of Catholic faith and to share Christian values in their workplace. The Jocists helped to prepare Vatican II's vision of the role of laypeople in the Church and the world. So too did the Legion of Mary, a lay Catholic association founded by Frank Duff (1889–1980) in 1921 that spread from Dublin to many parts of the world. The Legion combined a serious life of prayer with apostolic activities.

Leo XIII's 1893 encyclical on the Bible, *Providentissimus Deus* ('the Most Provident God'), should have meant a new spring in Catholic biblical studies. Just three years earlier a great Dominican scholar, Marie-Joseph Lagrange, had opened the first Catholic institute of higher biblical and archeological studies in modern times, the École Biblique in Jerusalem. In 1909 another such centre for advanced study of the scriptures, the Pontifical Biblical Institute, opened in Rome and has been staffed by Jesuits. Shadowed often by the suspicions of Church leaders, Lagrange and other professors in both institutes needed intellectual and spiritual courage to carry on their work. The tide turned in 1943 when Pius XII's encyclical *Divino Afflante Spiritu* ('With the Divine Spirit Inspiring') strongly promoted biblical studies among Catholic scholars. A solid input from scriptural scholars enriched such Vatican II documents as *Dei Verbum* (see Ch. 3) and *Lumen Gentium* (see below). For these and other documents, biblical scholarship provided a scriptural perspective on the Church, something that Vatican I lacked. The biblical movement was an essential second development in the making of Vatican II.

A third movement, led by Benedictines in Belgium, France, Germany, Italy, and the United States, aimed to renew the forms of the liturgy and encourage community participation in worship. Prosper Guéranger (1805–75) led the way when in 1833 he refounded the Abbey of Solesmes (France) and made it a centre for liturgical life and publications. Other abbeys followed and fostered the liturgical movement: in Germany, Beuron (1867) and Maria Laach (1892); and in Belgium, Maredsous (1872) and Mont-César (1899). Pius X encouraged Gregorian chant (1903), frequent Communion (1905), and earlier First Communion (1910), but, to some extent, with the political and social aim of restoring a Catholic state system. Virgil Michel (1888–1938), a monk of St John's Abbey, Collegeville (Minnesota), worked for liturgical reform, however, in order to encourage social justice in the United States, as well as the spiritual lives of Catholics. Lambert Beauduin (1873–1960), who founded Chevetogne, the Benedictine Monastery of the Holy Cross (and also made it an enduring centre for ecumenical dialogue) and other leaders in Belgium taught priests and laypeople to recover a commitment to the liturgy as the heart of the Church's life. In Germany Odo Casel (1886–1948), a monk of Maria Laach, and Romano Guardini (1885–1968), a diocesan priest-scholar, inspired many Catholics to recover a sense of their sharing actively in the life and worship of the Church. *Mediator Dei* ('The Mediator of God'), the 1947 encyclical by Pius XII on the liturgy, endorsed the work of these and other pioneers (including, since 1952, those at San Anselmo in Rome). He also moved for an early reform of the liturgy of Holy Week (1951 and 1955), and so facilitated the changes initiated by Vatican II's 1963 Constitution on the Sacred Liturgy, *Sacrosanctum Concilium* ('The Sacred Council') (see Ch. 7 above). The reforming teaching of Vatican II on the Church has affected bishops, priests, religious, laypeople—both within the life of the Catholic Church and in relationships to others. That teaching could hardly have occurred without the liturgical developments initiated by Guéranger and his successors. The liturgy is decisive for the healthy state of the Church and, one should add, for healthy and well-balanced teaching on the nature and mission of the Church. To quote Vatican II: 'The liturgy is the summit towards which the action of the Church is directed; it is also the source from which all her strength flows' (*Sacrosanctum Concilium*, 10).[18]

Along with lay movements and biblical and liturgical studies, a return to the Fathers, St Thomas Aquinas, and other historical sources also played its part in eventually revitalizing an understanding of the nature of the Church, which God endows with holiness but which is also subject to human failings. Yves Congar (1904–95), Henri de Lubac, and their colleagues retrieved much from the past to construct a fresh vision for the future. The Dominican centre of Le Saulchoir breathed new life into Catholic theology by examining Aquinas's contribution within its historical context and then using it to address the questions of the twentieth

---

[18] For further information see 'Constitution on the Sacred Liturgy' and 'Liturgical Movement' in *The HarperCollins Encyclopedia of Catholicism*; and 'Liturgical Movement', 'Solesmes', and 'Maria Laach' in *The Oxford Dictionary of the Christian Church*.

century. The young Congar, already in contact with Beauduin, Couturier, and various Russian Orthodox and Protestant theologians, gave himself to teaching and writing on the Catholic Church and its relations with other Christians. He founded the important series *Unam Sanctam* ('One Holy') by publishing in 1937 his own *Chrétiens désunis*,[19] a prophetic work that spelled out principles for Catholic ecumenism. As prisoner-of-war in Colditz Castle (1940–5), he endured years of suffering with other Christians—an experience that fed into his call to reform wisely and lovingly the structures of the Catholic Church by 'returning to the sources': *Vraie et fausse réforme dans l'Église*.[20] Interventions from the Vatican led first to this book being withdrawn from circulation and then in 1954 to Congar being silenced and exiled to Jerusalem and Cambridge (England). But his lecturing, preaching, and writing from the 1930s had already opened up for many new vistas on the Church's tradition, ministry, leadership, and ecumenical relations. With the election of Pope John XXIII, the situation of Congar changed dramatically. As a theological consultor on the preparatory commission for Vatican II and then an expert at the Council, he influenced several of its most significant documents, not least *Lumen Gentium*, the 1964 dogmatic constitution on the Church.[21]

Historical studies of the Fathers of the Church and medieval theologians nourished the lecturing and writing of the Jesuit theologian Henri de Lubac. In 1938 Congar encouraged him to publish *Catholicisme*,[22] which reflected on the spirit of individualism that threatened the life of the Catholic Church. De Lubac's understanding of the Church centred on the Eucharist (see above) and on humanity's innate desire for the vision of God. His works on grace (1946 and 1965) enabled many to recognize how every human being, without exception, is called by God to a supernatural and everlasting life of glory. Purely 'natural' human beings, with a purely natural destiny or a purely natural religion, do not exist. This truth proves decisive for thinking about the situation of those who are not baptized

---

[19] Trans. *Divided Christendom: A Catholic Study of the Problem of Reunion* (London: Geoffrey Bles, 1939).

[20] (Paris: Cerf, 1950).

[21] See T. I. MacDonald, *The Ecclesiology of Yves Congar: Foundational Themes* (New York: University Press of America, 1984); J. Famerée, *L'Ecclésiologie d'Yves Congar avant Vatican II* (Leuven: Leuven University Press, 1992); 'Congar, Georges-Yves', *Oxford Dictionary of the Christian Church*, 397–8.

[22] Trans. *Catholicism: A Study of the Corporate Destiny of Mankind* (London: Burns & Oates, 1950).

and, often, have not even heard of Jesus Christ and his message. By co-founding in 1942 *Sources Chrétiennes*, a collection of patristic and medieval texts that by the end of 2001 included 463 volumes, de Lubac helped revivify Catholic theology in general and appreciation of the Church in particular. His writings on atheism, Buddhism, the thought of Pierre Teilhard de Chardin (1881–1955), and many other subjects facilitated the intellectual climate in which Vatican II prepared and promulgated its longest document, *Gaudium et Spes*, the pastoral constitution on the Church in the modern world. Like Congar, de Lubac served the bishops as an influential specialist at the Council.

Vatican II and the Church

Before the Council opened, Pope John XXIII in a 1961 encyclical recalled how Jesus had founded the Church 'to hold the world in an embrace of love, so that men and women, in every age, should find in her their own completeness in a higher order of being, and their ultimate salvation' (*Mater et Magistra*, 1). Through all four sessions of Vatican II the bishops and their advisers, together with other Christians who had been invited as observers, reflected on and prayed over the nature and mission of the Church, which, in one way or another, became the theme of all sixteen documents promulgated by the Council. At the end of Ch. 2 and in later chapters (e.g. Ch. 7), we have summarized some of the achievements of Vatican II; in Ch. 9 we will have much to say about *Gaudium et Spes*. But what was special or new about the teaching on the Church?

In particular, the dogmatic constitution of 1964 *Lumen Gentium* ('The Light of Nations'), to which ten other documents were attached either simultaneously or subsequently, expressed fresh teaching which filled out Vatican I's *Pastor Aeternus*. On the very day that the bishops and the Pope approved *Lumen Gentium*, 21 November 1964, they also approved a decree on Catholic Eastern Churches (*Ecclesiarum Orientalium*) and a decree on ecumenism (*Unitatis Redintegratio*). The former decree guaranteed the preservation of the spiritual heritage of Catholics who belong to Eastern Churches (e.g. their traditions for the Eucharist and the administration of the other sacraments and for government through patriarchs), and en-couraged relations with Eastern Christians not united with Rome.[23] The

---

[23] Chapter 4 above cited some later doctrinal results in the christological agreements with the Copts (1973) and with the Assyrian Church of the East (1994).

latter decree built on a key affirmation: the Church founded by Christ 'subsists in the Catholic Church, which is governed by the successor of Peter and by the bishops in communion with him'; yet 'many elements of sanctification and of truth are found outside its visible confines' (*Lumen Gentium*, 8). The document went on to list many ways in which the Catholic Church is 'joined' with other Christians (ibid. 15). In the aftermath of Vatican II, Catholics have also been 'joined' through dialogues and consultations with the vast majority of other Christians. By early 2002 twelve such official international dialogues or consultations were in progress with most Christian Churches, including the Orthodox Churches, the Ancient Oriental Churches, the Anglican Communion, the Lutheran World Federation, the World Methodist Council, the Disciples of Christ, the Pentecostals, the World Evangelical Fellowship, the World Alliance of Reformed Churches, the Mennonites, and the World Baptist Alliance.[24] In other ways the Catholic Church also has contacts with such groups as Old Catholics, Quakers, the Salvation Army, and Seventh-Day Adventists. Through the Pontifical Council for Promoting Christian Unity (Rome), similar offices at national and local levels, and all kinds of personal initiatives of individual Catholics, the ecumenical outreach of Vatican II's view of the Church has produced much fruit, even if organic Christian unity and the healing of the divisions triggered in the eleventh and sixteenth centuries still remains a matter for prayerful hope.

Lumen Gentium also went far beyond Vatican I's *Pastor Aeternus* by dedicating specific chapters to bishops, priests, and deacons (ch. 3), to the laity (ch. 4), and to religious (ch. 6).[25] These chapters, in their turn, were reinforced and applied in the fourth and final session of the Council by five decrees: on the Pastoral Office of Bishops in the Church (*Christus Dominus*), on the Ministry and Life of Priests (*Presbyterorum Ordinis*), on the Training of Priests (*Optatam Totius*), on the Up-to-Date Renewal of Religious Life (*Perfectae Caritatis*), and on the Apostolate of Lay People (*Apostolicam Actuositatem*). *Lumen Gentium*, along with *Apostolicam Actuositatem*, was also supplemented by a declaration on Christian Education (*Gravissimum Educationis*), which recognized that parents are

---

[24] The order follows the information provided by *8th Forum on Bilateral Dialogues*, Faith and Order Paper, 190 (Geneva: WCC Publications, 2002), 75–7.

[25] By including chapters on the laity (ch. 4), the universal call to holiness (ch. 5), religious life (ch. 6), and the Blessed Virgin Mary (ch. 8), Vatican II introduced remarkable innovations. Up to that time no council of the Church had ever dealt at such length with those themes.

'primarily and principally responsible' for the education of their children in faith and other matters (no. 3); apart from married Catholic priests who have children, the overwhelming majority of Catholic parents are laypersons. The three chapters of *Lumen Gentium* and the six subsequent documents present the Church as a richly varied community, brought into unity by the Father, Son, and Holy Spirit.

This sense of the origin of the Church in the tripersonal God's action to save all people emerges strongly from another decree that depends on *Lumen Gentium*, the Decree on the Church's Missionary Activity, *Ad Gentes* (7 December 1965). A paragraph of *Lumen Gentium* considered how those who have not yet received the Gospel are 'related to the People of God in various ways': from Jews and Moslems through to those who, without any personal fault, 'have not yet arrived at an explicit knowledge of God' (no. 16). In preaching to all the universal salvation brought about by Christ, the Church aims to 'heal, raise up, and perfect' everything good that God has already sown in 'the minds and hearts' of individuals and the 'rites and customs of peoples' (ibid. 17). *Ad Gentes* lends substance to those two paragraphs. It opens with a richly trinitarian picture of the divine plan to gather together the whole of humanity into the communion of eternal life (nos. 2–4). The message of Jesus Christ is to be preached everywhere, yet in ways that respect everything that is found to be good and true and that acknowledge how the Holy Spirit and the Word of God bless people before the missionaries of the Church arrive (nos. 4, 11).

The Declaration on the Relation of the Church to Non-Christian Religions, *Nostra Aetate* (28 October 1965), likewise recognizes both the activity of One who enlightens everyone and the Church's duty to proclaim Christ everywhere as the way, the truth, and the life (no. 2). This declaration unpacks *Lumen Gentium* (no. 16) by not only reflecting very positively on the faith of Jews and Moslems (nos. 3–4) but also by showing appreciation for the spiritual gifts of Hinduism, Buddhism, and 'other religions' (no. 2).

By illustrating the links between *Lumen Gentium* and ten other conciliar documents, we hope to have shown something of its wealth of teaching on the Church. But nothing substitutes for a careful, personal reading of its text. As a guide for such reading what further points do we underline as particularly valuable about its account of the Church? At least six themes deserve special mention.

First, *Lumen Gentium* remains faithful to the preaching of Jesus by insisting on the encompassing power and promise of the Kingdom of

God. The present and future reign of God is steadily growing to its final completion. The Church exists for this Kingdom and is to be understood in its light, and not vice versa.

Second, the biblical movement bore fruit in the variety of images for the Church listed and explored by *Lumen Gentium*: for instance, the Church as a flock or sheepfold; as a cultivated field or choice vineyard; as God's building, temple, or city; as Spouse of Christ; as Mother; and as the Body of Christ (nos. 6–8). The 1943 encyclical of Pope Pius XII, *Mystici Corporis*, displaced the long-standing model of the Church as a perfect society. Vatican II, while developing this theme, gave a certain preference to a model deeply rooted in the OT: the Church as the People of God (*Lumen Gentium*, 9–17). The generous variety of images and models witnessed to the spiritually rich reality of the Church which goes beyond any simple definition. Their exuberant multiplicity continues to pay tribute to the splendour of the Church, which shares something of the inexhaustible truth of Christ.[26]

In the last chapter we noted how baptism incorporates all believers into Christ, who is priest, prophet, and king. All the faithful share in these dimensions of Christ's redemptive work, even if the 'common priesthood' of the baptized is to be distinguished from that of the 'ministerial' or ordained priesthood (ibid. 10–13). This third theme of *Lumen Gentium* also provides the basic scheme for presenting the ministry of bishops: as 'heralds' or 'teachers', the supreme 'priests' of their dioceses, and 'shepherds' or 'pastors' (ibid. 25–7). A year later the Council used the same triple scheme in tracing the role of presbyters who take part in the function of Christ as 'Teacher, Priest, and King' (*Presbyterorum Ordinis*, 1, 4–6), and in describing laypersons as 'sharing in the priestly, prophetical, and kingly office of Christ' (*Apostolicam Actuositatem*, 2). Thoroughly biblical and traditional, this triple scheme of *Lumen Gentium* and of two decrees that depend on it shows the centrality of Christ, in whose life and work all members of the Church share.

Fourth, this teaching serves to follow through on the Christ-centred vision of the Church that *Lumen Gentium* developed from its first two words: it is Christ who is 'the Light of the nations'. The Constitution went on to sketch a comparison between the Incarnate Son of God, who unites in his person humanity and divinity, and the Church which is both a visible

---

[26] See A. Dulles, *Models of the Church* (Maryknoll, NY: Orbis, 2nd edn. 1992).

organization and the temple of the Holy Spirit. Nevertheless, there are limits to the comparison. Christ lived an utterly sinless life, whereas the Church is both 'holy and always in need of purification' (*Lumen Gentium*, 8). Through baptism the followers of Christ are 'truly sanctified' and 'made partakers of the divine nature'; they are all called to a life of holiness, i.e. to the 'fullness of Christian life and the perfection of love' (ibid. 40). Nevertheless, the holiness of the people of God on earth, while 'real', is always 'imperfect' (ibid. 48); the Church must constantly 'follow the path of penitence and renewal' (ibid. 8).[27] In a word, the Church is simultaneously holy *and* sinful—a description vividly and fully exemplified by what St Paul wrote in his First Letter to the Corinthians and by the confession of sins at the Eucharist celebrated in St Peter's Basilica on 12 March 2000. In a striking way that liturgy featured seven representatives of the Roman Curia asking pardon for sins of the present and past. The drawings created by Sandro Botticelli (1447–1513) to illustrate Dante's *Divine Comedy*, which were exhibited later that same year in Rome and early in 2001 at the Royal Academy of Arts (London), included the same vision of the Church. The illustration for Canto 32 of the *Purgatorio* juxtaposes (1) virtues who hold candlesticks, the four Gospel-writers, a healthy young tree, the beautiful Beatrice, and the chariot of the Church moving through history with (2) monstrous outgrowths and a prostitute being courted by a giant. By setting monstrosities alongside a group ascending into heaven, Botticelli powerfully conveyed a sense of the earthly Church as being both sinful and holy.

Fifth, we come to an issue not developed by Vatican I: the 'magisterial' or teaching role of bishops in and for the Church. We can summarize what *Lumen Gentium* says as follows (20–5). This magisterial role belongs to the whole 'college' of bishops (as successors to the college of apostolic witnesses) and to individual bishops united with the bishop of Rome. The bishops generally fulfil this magisterium on a day-to-day basis (various kinds of 'ordinary' magisterium). When assembled in an ecumenical council, they may teach some revealed truth to be held unconditionally

---

[27] The humble realism of Vatican II contrasts with Vatican I's robust but one-sided stress on the Church's holiness: 'To the Catholic Church alone belong all the manifold and wonderful endowments which by divine disposition are meant to set forth the credibility of the Christian faith. Nay more, the Church by herself, with her marvellous propagation, eminent holiness, and inexhaustible fruitfulness in everything that is good, with her Catholic unity and invincible stability, is a great and perpetual motive of credibility and an irrefutable testimony of her divine mission' (*Dei Filius*, DH 3013; ND 123).

and definitively (the 'extraordinary' magisterium). An exercise of the extraordinary magisterium obviously occurs only rarely, as, for instance, with the solemn teaching of the college of bishops at Vatican I or with the papal definitions about the Blessed Virgin Mary recalled above. It is the day-to-day teaching or ordinary magisterium that helps much more to enlighten and encourage the life of Catholics. They should listen respectfully to the teaching of bishops and popes, even when it is not a question of a papal *ex cathedra* teaching (see above) or a solemnly defined conciliar teaching being proposed about some matter of revelation. From *Lumen Gentium* we can glean three pertinent questions that should be posed. *Who* is teaching something (the pope, or the local bishop, or bishops gathered in a national conference, or an international synod)? *What* are they teaching about (matters which come directly from the divine self-revelation in Christ or other matters that, while often being extremely important, are not as such revealed truth)? *What* degree of authority is being claimed for the teaching? In the case of the Pope, for instance, the varying degrees of authority being claimed for non-infallible teaching are normally easy to identify: an encyclical letter addressed to all Catholics and sometimes to all men and women claims higher authority than what is said at papal audiences on Wednesdays.

Among other things, *Lumen Gentium* went here beyond earlier teaching in two significant ways: on the ordinary magisterium and collegiality. First, Vatican I in its first document, *Dei Filius*, had spoken very concisely of the 'ordinary and universal magisterium' of the Church being able to propose truths of faith which have been divinely revealed and are to be believed (DH 3011; ND 219). Vatican II spelled out the conditions for such infallible teaching coming from the ordinary magisterium: in communion among themselves and with the bishop of Rome, authentically teaching on matters of (revealed) faith and morals, and agreeing that some doctrine is to be held definitively, the bishops around the world pronounce infallibly on the doctrine of Christ (*Lumen Gentium*, 25). Such infallible truths from the ordinary magisterium, sometimes called non-defined dogmas, may sound remote and recondite. But they include all kinds of matters vital for the living of Catholic and Christian faith. No council or pope has ever, for example, solemnly and explicitly defined that Jesus is the Saviour of all men and women, from the beginning to the end of world history. This truth about human redemption is central to the life and mission of Catholics, but has never come up for formal definition.

The term 'collegiality' was new to Vatican II, even if its ultimate background is to be found in the college of apostles led by St Peter. Through their episcopal ordination and through being in communion with the head (the bishop of Rome) and the other bishops, new bishops become members of the worldwide college (ibid. 22). This doctrine of episcopal collegiality has been reflected in formal meetings: notably, episcopal conferences at the national level and, at the international level, episcopal synods which have met regularly in Rome since 1967. In both cases many bishops and other Catholics would like to see episcopal collegiality being more strongly encouraged and exercised. We return to this theme in our final chapter.

Sixth, *Lumen Gentium* also innovated by dedicating a chapter to the Mother of God in a way that rethinks her position within the history of human redemption and in reference to the Church founded by her Son (nos. 52–69). She was the first to benefit from his merits, as the dogma of the Immaculate Conception shows, and the first to share fully in his resurrection to glory, as the dogma of the Assumption shows (see above). She belongs within the Church as both Mother of the Church and the most eminent disciple of her Son—something expressed by the 'Lady Chapel' of many ancient and modern churches and by a scene cherished by Christian artists, the descent of the Holy Spirit on the disciples gathered in prayer around Mary (Acts 1: 14; 2: 1–4).[28] *Lumen Gentium* ended by praying that Mary would continue 'interceding with her Son in the fellowship of all the saints', until the whole human family 'may be happily gathered together in peace and harmony into the one People of God, for the glory of the Most Holy and Undivided Trinity' (no. 68). On the same day that Paul VI promulgated this constitution (21 November 1964), he proclaimed Mary 'the Mother of the Church'. In that way the Pope welcomed the Council's decision not to make extravagant claims about her but to recognize her significance when the Church was visibly constituted around her at Pentecost.

THE CHURCH AS COMMUNION AND MISSION

After presenting the teaching on the Church's nature and mission that Vatican I and II expounded, we want to conclude this chapter by drawing

---

[28] See also in Ch. 1 above how Jan van Eyck (and other artists) understood Mary, even at the Annunciation, to be the archetype of the whole Church.

on the Apostles' Creed and the Nicene-Constantinopolitan Creed. The former expresses belief in 'the communion of saints' and the latter calls the Church 'one, holy, catholic, and apostolic'—the four traditional marks of the Church of which the Apostles' Creed mentions only two (holy and catholic).

We noted in Ch. 6 what the communion of saints entails: a fellowship in Christian life with all the baptized, both still living and already dead, and with God. Such fellowship, created by union in the risen Christ and through the Holy Spirit with God the Father, extends to all the members of the Church, who by their baptism share in Christ's 'office' as priest, prophet, and king.

This communion makes the Church to be one, holy, catholic, and apostolic: one and holy in itself, catholic and apostolic in its missionary outreach. The basis of such unity is the Trinity, as the Letter to the Ephesians makes clear when it speaks of 'one body and one Spirit', 'one Lord [Jesus Christ], one faith, one baptism, [and] one God and Father of us all, who is above all and through all and in all' (4: 4–6). Two centuries later St Cyprian of Carthage eloquently witnessed to the oneness of the Church by using the images of rays from the sun, branches from a tree, streams from a fountain, and children born from a mother:

Separate a ray of the sun from the body of light, its unity does not allow a division of light; break a branch from a tree, and when broken, it will not be able to bud; cut off the stream from its fountain, and that which is cut off dries up. Thus also the Church, illuminated with the light of the Lord, sheds her rays over the whole world, yet it is one light which is diffused everywhere ... Her fruitful abundance spreads her branches over the whole world. She broadly expands her rivers, which flow liberally, yet her head is one, her source one. She is one Mother, plentiful in the results of fruitfulness: from her womb we are born, by her milk we are nourished, by her Spirit we are animated.   (*De Catholicae Ecclesiae Unitate*, 5)

The fruitful holiness cherished by Cyprian brings us to the second mark of the Church.

Through their baptism believers receive from Christ and the Holy Spirit a radical holiness (e.g. 1 Cor. 6: 11), which will be nourished, above all through the Eucharist. Hence St Paul addressed his communities, despite their blatant sins, as 'holy ones' or those 'called to be holy ones' (e.g. 1 Cor. 1: 2; 2 Cor. 1: 1). They are called to the fullness of life and true wholeness or the complete fulfilment of the purpose for their existence. The Spirit of God aims to make the entire Church community one holy temple of God, with its members sharing the divine life through grace and the sacraments (Chs. 6 and 7 above, respectively). Divinization means taking part in the holiness of God, the absolutely Holy One (Isa. 6: 3, 5). Bishop John Zizioulas (b. 1931) clarifies attractively that free collaboration in what the Holy Spirit does for our full sanctification:

In a christological perspective alone we can speak of the Church as *in-stituted* (by Christ), but in a pneumatological perspective we have to speak of it as *con-stituted* (by the Spirit). Christ *in-stitutes* and the Spirit *con-stitutes*... The 'in-stitution' is something presented to us as a fact, more or less a *fait accompli*. As such it is a provocation to our freedom. The 'con-stitution' is something that involves us in its very being, something we accept freely, because we take part in its emergence.[29]

The 'instituting' Christ and the 'constituting' Spirit have a universal mission; that moves us to the third mark of the Church.

The very first paragraph of this book quoted St Augustine's words about 'the unity of all peoples' in the worldwide Catholic Church. 'Catholicity' or 'universality' points to the all-embracing character of the Church which, through her missionary proclamation, has gathered into one People of God those of different races, languages, and cultures (*Lumen Gentium*, 13). At services held in great cathedrals we can sometimes see this all-embracing character of the Church right before our eyes. Catholics have come from different continents to share in the same Eucharist. On Easter Sunday in Rome television cameras let the same mark of the Church come through: when they move from one face to another in a vast crowd gathered in St Peter's Square, they show the worldwide nature of Catholicism.

Catholicity indicates the all-embracing character of the Church around the world, a characteristic in space to be matched in the passage of time by the fourth and final mark, apostolicity. This points to the essential identity between the faith and practice lived and proclaimed by the present Church and by the Church founded by Christ and his apostles. Apostolicity claims an unbroken continuity in life and mission between the Church today and that of the first century. The First Eucharistic Prayer or Roman Canon cites this mark when it speaks of 'the faith that comes to us from the apostles'. Often enough apostolicity is presented in terms of the continuity between the ministry of Catholic bishops today and that of

---

[29] *Being and Communion. Studies in Personhood and the Church* (New York: St Vladimir's Seminary Press, 1985), 140.

the apostolic leaders at the birth of Christianity. Certainly the college of bishops constitutes a visible sign of succession in apostolic faith and life. But the apostolicity of the Church should not be reduced to episcopal succession or the unbroken transmission through time of ordained ministers who visibly embody the Church's fidelity to its origins. All the baptized share in the role of maintaining apostolic succession or fundamental continuity in faith, practice, and mission with previous generations of Catholics and, especially, with the normative Church of the first century founded by Christ and his apostles.[30]

Such then is our concluding account of communion and mission in the one, holy, catholic, and apostolic Church. Once again let us add that many of the themes enunciated in this chapter, while distinctively Catholic, are not alleged to be uniquely so. We wished to make that point by citing John Zizioulas, a Greek Orthodox bishop. The following three chapters will fill out our vision of the life and characteristics of the Catholic Church.

---

[30] On the marks of the Church and related themes see W. Henn, *Church* (London: Continuum, forthcoming); P. C. Phan (ed.), *The Gift of the Church: A Textbook on Ecclesiology in Honor of Patrick Granfield, O.S.B.* (Collegeville, Minn.: Liturgical Press, 2000); F. A. Sullivan, *The Church We Believe In: One, Holy, Catholic and Apostolic* (New York: Paulist Press, 1988); id., *Magisterium: Teaching Authority in the Catholic Church* (New York: Paulist Press, 1983).

9

Catholic Moral Life and Teaching

Special attention needs to be given to the perfecting of moral theology. Its scientific exposition should be more thoroughly nourished by the teaching of Holy Scripture

(Vatican II, *Optatam Totius* (on priestly formation))

I have been an optimist all my life, trusting in reason, man's natural intelligence, and his conscience. (Julian Huxley, *Memories II*)

In Germany they came first for the Communists and I didn't speak up because I wasn't a Communist. Then they came for the Jews, and I didn't speak up because I wasn't a Jew. Then they came for the trade unionists and I didn't speak up because I wasn't a trade unionist. Then they came for the Catholics, and I didn't speak up because I was a Protestant. Then they came for me—and by that time no one was left to speak up.

(Martin Niemöller, John Bartlett, *Familiar Quotations*)

Previous chapters have highlighted the dignity of all human beings, created in the divine image and likeness (Ch. 5), enabled by Christ's grace and the power of the Spirit to share in the life of God, and called to eternal glory beyond death (Ch. 6). Catholics (and other Christians) are consecrated and nourished by the sacraments (Ch. 7) and by their communion in the Church's life and worship (Ch. 8). How then should Catholics (and other Christians) behave? What principles should guide their moral life and decision-making? How should the holiness with which they have been blessed express itself in their daily existence?

We wish to recall first the development of moral teaching in the Catholic Church, paying particular attention to three seismic shifts that have taken place in teaching and practice about usury, torture, and slavery. Against that background, we will dedicate the central part of the chapter to some distinctive Catholic moral convictions: about respect for life, the sexual order, truth, justice, care for the needy, human dignity, and human rights.

HISTORICAL DEVELOPMENTS

Jesus and the authors of the NT, as we saw briefly in Ch. 5, maintained much of the moral teaching that they had inherited from the OT. Jesus innovated by putting together in one love-command the hitherto distinct commandments to love God (Deut. 6: 5) and to love one's neighbour (Lev. 19: 18), by teaching a love for one's enemies (Matt. 5: 43–8), and by practising an equality that was shockingly new for the culture of his time (both Jewish and Graeco-Roman) in that women belonged to the travelling band of his disciples (Luke 8: 1–3). But, in general, both Jesus and the first Christians endorsed what Judaism had taught about right and wrong behaviour. Jesus and the early Christians, however, never endorsed armed violence, as did some texts of the Hebrew Bible, and drew rather on those passages that proclaimed peace.

The *Didache* shows that lengthy, pre-baptismal catechesis on moral matters, as well as on doctrines of Christian faith, emerged by the end of the first century. This concern with the conduct of believers had, of course, been preceded by the moral teaching provided by St Paul and other NT writers.[1] We will discuss below the *Didache* and the roughly contemporary *Epistle of Barnabas*. Here we simply want to recall that significant elements in teaching on the practice of virtue go back to the beginning of Christianity.

Subsequently such leading writers as Augustine of Hippo (d. 430) and Gregory the Great (d. 604) developed the centrality of love in their sermons and writings. Augustine addressed such particular moral issues as truth, lying, and human sexuality. Gregory spelled out the seven deadly sins or sins traditionally considered to be the root of all other sins: pride, avarice or covetousness, lust, envy, gluttony, anger, and sloth. At this period what we call 'moral theology' was not separated from 'spirituality';

---

[1] See F. J. Matera, *New Testament Ethics: The Legacies of Jesus and Paul* (Louisville, Ky.: Westminster/John Knox, 1996); R. Schnackenburg, *The Moral Teaching of the New Testament* (New York: Herder & Herder, 1965).

the list of the seven deadly sins, while specified by Gregory the Great, finds its origin in the spiritual instructions of the monk Evagrius Ponticus (d. 399). The penitentials, or handbooks for confessors promoted by the Irish and Anglo-Saxon monk-missionaries (see Ch. 7), flourished down to the eleventh century and helped to shape moral teaching and practice. In the thirteenth century Thomas Aquinas systematically reflected on many moral issues and, in particular, developed thinking about the 'natural law', the universally valid moral principles which are discoverable by human reason and should govern social institutions and personal morality. Rather than using the Ten Commandments as a framework, Aquinas elaborated his moral teaching in terms of the virtues. A little later Dante (d. 1321) brought together both doctrine and a detailed account of the moral life. His *Divine Comedy* remains a vivid handbook for the practical life of Christians. He constructed the long climb up the mountain of purgatory around seven terraces on which sinners were cleansed from the seven deadly sins, which began with the worst (pride) and ended with the least serious sin of lust. Thus Dante's order was: pride, envy, anger, sloth, avarice, gluttony, and lust. Then, on the popular level, such medieval 'morality plays' as *Everyman* typically contrasted virtues and vices and played a major role in inculcating good Christian behaviour.

But it was only at the end of the sixteenth century that 'moral theology', or that branch of theology which studies in a systematic way the ethical life and activity of Christians, began to emerge as a distinct branch of study. One unfortunate effect of this development was to separate moral theology from spirituality, and invest the former with a rather arid and legalistic character. What was true of academic theology applied also to the Church's official teachers. For well over a thousand years, councils, bishops, and popes, while producing some important pieces of official teaching in the area of morality, in general took for granted the Christian principles for human conduct. It was not until the nineteenth and twentieth centuries that they began to develop explicitly a body of moral teaching.

The notion of human rights, as we now understand them, had medieval roots, and early intimations of them can be found in the writings of the Dominican activist and theologian Bartolomé de las Casas (d. 1566). In modern Western philosophy John Locke (d. 1704) and other philosophers found a basis for human rights in a version of the natural law, Much later official church teaching took up the theme of such rights. Pope John XXIII in his 1963 encyclical *Pacem in Terris* grounded in the dignity of the human person created in the divine image an extensive treatment of such natural rights as the rights to life, to basic education, to religious freedom, and so forth. These rights, which 'the Creator of the world' has written into the natural order of things, imply a set of correlative duties (DH 3956–72, 3985; ND 2026–42, 2130, 2132–3), and apply also to the work of civil authorities and relations between sovereign states. Vatican II's 1965 Pastoral Constitution on the Church in the Modern World (*Gaudium et Spes*), which took further the theme of the dignity and value of the human person, became the first far-reaching and fairly complete official document on the moral life of Christians (and, for that matter, of all human beings). *Gaudium et Spes* also strongly endorsed Pope John's plea for the universal common good, which demands an end to war and peaceful methods for settling conflicts between nations.

Later in this chapter we will add considerably more on the official moral teaching of the Catholic Church. Here we want only to recall that, although there was an extensive body of instruction on Christian behaviour from the very beginning, doctrinal questions dominated the attention of church councils and papal teaching. The phenomenon of lengthy encyclicals and conciliar documents (in particular, *Gaudium et Spes*) on moral questions is new. This is our reason for coming to such teaching only in Ch. 9. Throughout this book we wanted to track matters more or less in chronological order, as we announced at the end of Ch. 2.

THREE SHIFTS

When we run back through time to examine the two thousand years of moral tradition in Catholic Christianity, we will find that, being a living tradition, it changed. There was a process of development in which, while the same basic values were preserved, certain theories emerged in particular historical circumstances that are seen as questionable. For example, in attempting to construct an ethical framework for war, which he believed to be a profoundly regrettable but inevitable element of sinful human reality, Augustine sketched reasons justifying war. Aquinas and subsequent authors such as Francisco de Vitoria (d. 1546) developed these reasons into full theories of a 'just war'.[2] Peace movements continue to keep alive

---

[2] For a summary and bibliography see 'War, Christian attitudes to', *Oxford Dictionary of the Christian Church*, 1719–20.

vigorous debate about the morality of any war. But we have other examples of moral teachings and practices from the story of Catholicism that have clearly moved from an earlier acceptance to a later rejection. Let us look at three examples: usury, torture, and slavery. After that we will come to some basic moral notions that have been positively and persistently developed.

Usury

Aristotle took the view that money is a 'barren' means of exchange and not capital that can produce wealth. Catholic teaching up to the Middle Ages and the Reformation followed suit and normally forbade any lending of money at interest. In 325 the First Council of Nicaea condemned the practice (canon 17), as did several later councils down to the Council of Vienne (1311/12). Bishops and theologians judged that charging interest on loans stemmed from greed and led to the poor being exploited. Money should be lent gratuitously. As late at 1745, Pope Benedict XIV in his encyclical *Vix Pervenit* endorsed this teaching, even though many Catholic teachers (and confessors of businessmen) had long recognized that money could be lent for productive purposes and at a just interest. Nineteenth-century official Catholic moral teaching came to accept such lending at reasonable rates of interest, while continuing to condemn usury or charging excessive interest for the use of money. One might cope with this shift by arguing that the nature of money itself had changed, that therefore just interest on loans became acceptable, and that usury or lending money at unfairly high interest rates has never ceased to be a sinful practice.[3]

Torture

Whatever our moral judgements about changes on the issue of loans, usury, and the function of money, no case can be made for a practice that Catholic teachers accepted for centuries and then firmly rejected in modern times: torture or the infliction of severe bodily (and/or psychological)

---

[3] For useful summaries and bibliographies see 'Usury', *Oxford Dictionary of the Christian Church*, 1672–3, and T. F. Divine, 'Usury', *New Catholic Encyclopedia*, xiv. 498–500. See also S. L. Buckley, *Teaching on Usury in Judaism, Christianity and Islam* (Lewiston, NY: Edwin Mellen Press, 2000). The question of lending money has acquired an international face, with many countries suffering a crippling burden from the interest charged on loans. The medieval concern about interest exploiting the poor has assumed a fresh meaning.

pain either to punish people or persuade them to say or do something. A letter sent to the ruler of Bulgaria in 866 by Nicholas I stands out as a refreshing exception. The Pope rejected using torture to extract confessions from those accused of crimes and any violent means for forcing people to accept the Christian faith which had just been officially accepted in Bulgaria (DH 647–8). Notoriously in 1252 Innocent IV authorized the use of torture to force suspected heretics to 'confess' and retract their errors and reveal the names of 'other heretics'; the Pope took for granted the use of torture on 'thieves and bandits'. In Ch. 2 (above) we recalled the way Catholic Christianity countenanced torture during the thirteenth-century anti-Albigensian crusade and later—in the cause of maintaining religious unity which underpinned social and political stability. Through the sixteenth century and beyond, faith commitments were woven into the fabric of life; rulers and their officials felt themselves answerable to God for supporting what they believed to be the true religion. Those who spread heresy brought eternal ruin on those who accepted their false views, and hence were deemed to be worse than thieves and murderers.[4]

A firm rejection of any 'physical and mental torture', as well as any 'undue psychological pressures', finally came in the Second Vatican Council's teaching on respect for the human person (*Gaudium et Spes*, 27). The Council insisted on the 'right to religious freedom', which 'means that all are to be immune from coercion' coming from 'any human power'; in 'religious matters no one is to be forced to act against their conscience nor prevented from acting according to their conscience' (*Dignitatis Humanae*, 2). Sadly such religious freedom is still not to be found in many countries around the world. Even worse many governments, as long as they can escape too much adverse criticism, still practise or allow torture to be practised by their police and military forces.

Slavery

Another seismic shift in Catholic moral teaching and practice concerns slavery, or the state of servitude in which human beings become (or remain) the property of others, available to be bought and sold, deprived of many basic human rights, and often treated with vicious cruelty by their

---

[4] For a cross-confessional study of (mainly) sixteenth-century Protestant, Anabaptist, and Catholic martyrs, see B. S. Gregory, *Salvation at Stake: Christian Martyrdom in Early Modern Europe* (Cambridge, Mass.: Harvard University Press, 1999).

owners.[5] The Mosaic Law, unfortunately, tolerated slavery, albeit in a mitigated form (Exod. 21: 1–11; Lev. 25: 44–55). In the ancient Mediterranean world slaves formed a large, integral, and seemingly necessary part of the social system. Aristotle had defended slavery as being for the good of both masters and slaves. But under the Roman Empire the latter had little legal protection. Juvenal (d. *c.*140) described a Roman matron who wanted a slave crucified and overrode her husband's objections with the notorious response: 'hoc volo, sic iubeo, sit pro ratione voluntas' (this is my will and my command. If you are looking for a reason, it is simply that I want it) (*Satires*, 6. 223). By the time of Juvenal the ease with which slaves could be crucified had long since encouraged the gallows humour of that subculture and their vulgar taunt of 'crux' (cross).

Their Jewish heritage, still less the Graeco-Roman society, did nothing to encourage the first Christians to challenge the institution of slavery, but they certainly moderated its worst features. St Paul, for instance, while never condemning the system of slavery as such, declared slaves to be equal to others in the Christian community (Gal. 3: 26–9), and encouraged a loving spirit between masters and slaves—something strikingly exemplified in his letter to Philemon. This letter was written to be delivered by Onesimus, a slave who had run away, made his way to Paul, and become a Christian, and was now returning to his master. Paul expected Onesimus to be received back by Philemon with forgiveness and to be accepted into the local church community as an equal member. Some NT letters contained household rules, including codes of conduct for slaves and masters. A Christian perspective and motivation meant that the former should serve obediently and cheerfully, and the latter should exercise their authority with understanding and loving-kindness: 'Masters, treat your slaves justly and fairly, for you know that you also have a Master in heaven' (Col. 4: 1; see Eph. 6: 5–9).[6]

Christian faith continued to modify dramatically the way slaves were treated. At least a few, such as St Felicity who died with St Perpetua in 203, suffered martyrdom together with their owners. Some male slaves became priests, bishops, or monks. In the fourth century the Emperor

---

[5] For summaries and preliminary bibliographies see 'Slavery', *Oxford Dictionary of the Christian Church*, 1508–9, and H. S. Pyper, 'Slavery', *Oxford Companion to Christian Thought*, 674–5.

[6] On household codes, see H. Moxnes (ed.), *Constructing Early Christian Families* (London/ New York: Routledge, 1997); C. Osiek and D. L. Balch, *Families in the New Testament World: Households and Household Churches* (Louisville, Ky.: Westminster/John Knox, 1997).

Constantine and in the sixth century Justinian I (see Ch. 1) greatly mitigated conditions imposed on slaves. Across Christian Europe slavery was gradually transformed into the much milder system of serfdom, which itself began to disappear from the fourteenth century. Sadly the discovery of America by Columbus in 1492 initiated a new outbreak of slave-traffic and slave-owning. Spaniards, Portuguese, British, and others made slaves of Indians and then brought thousands of slaves from Africa. The resistance of Dominicans such as Bartolomé de Las Casas and Jesuit missionaries in Bolivia, Paraguay, and elsewhere, along with condemnations of slavery by Paul III in 1537 (DH 1495) and successive popes, failed to persuade many Catholics into emancipating their slaves and renouncing the lucrative trade. Most regrettably St Augustine, a few other Fathers of the church, and St Thomas Aquinas had theological reasons for tolerating and justifying slavery as a state of life. Their authority made it easier for leading Catholic authors of the sixteenth and seventeenth centuries, e.g. Francisco de Vitoria (d. 1546) and Domingo de Soto (d. 1560), to consider slavery as not incompatible with the natural law and justifiable under certain circumstances.[7] Many Christians continued to argue that God had instituted servitude; the cursed children of Ham (traditionally identified as some North African people) were condemned to serve their brothers (Gen. 9: 25–6). The American Civil War (1861–5), which was fought over the issues of slavery and states' rights, brought the issue firmly to the notice of Pope Pius IX. Bishops in the northern states wanted slavery abolished, while some bishops in the southern states continued to support the institution. Pius IX wanted the American bishops to avoid all discussion of the issue; he himself opposed any immediate abolition of slavery and favoured a gradual evolution to emancipation.[8] In the USA a constitutional amendment of December 1865 prohibited slavery forever. But the following year in Rome the Holy Office published a statement claiming that slavery and slave-trading, under proper conditions, were not against 'the natural and divine law'.[9] As we saw in Ch. 2, the large Catholic country of Brazil maintained the institution of slavery until 1888.

---

[7] See S. F. Brett, *Slavery and the Catholic Tradition* (New York: Peter Lang, 1994).

[8] See G. Martina, *Pio IX (1851–1866)* (Rome: Gregorian University Press, 1986), 483–95.

[9] The date for the statement is 20 June 1866; see *Collectanea S.C. de Propaganda Fide*, i (Rome, 1907), n. 1239, 719; cited by J. F. Maxwell, *Slavery and the Catholic Church: The History of Catholic Teaching Concerning the Moral Legitimacy of the Institution of Slavery* (Chichester: Barry Rose, 1975), 78–9.

In the name of the essential equality of all human beings, the Second Vatican Council denounced 'any kind of slavery, whether social or political' (*Gaudium et Spes*, 29). In his 1993 encyclical *Veritatis Splendor* Pope John Paul II called slavery 'intrinsically evil' (no. 80).[10] When reflecting on the issue, one can only ask: why did it take Catholic teachers and writers so long to condemn slavery unequivocally? Why did we have to wait many centuries for the moral conscience of Catholics everywhere to reject slavery as an utterly repugnant system? When supporting torture, religious coercion, and slavery, many Catholics conformed to existing social patterns and drew their moral standards at least in part from civil society. In the case of lending money for a just interest, we see an opposite phenomenon: official Catholic teaching down to the nineteenth century stubbornly opposing what many morally sensitive persons had long accepted and continuing to reject as sinful usury any loans of money at interest. Here that official teaching diverged from what the majority of Catholics judged to be morally acceptable in the standards of society. Whatever else they do, these sobering examples from history illustrate the scrupulous care and openness to the Holy Spirit that should guide those trying to discern right from wrong, good from evil. The condemnation of slavery also illustrates what the Second Vatican Council observed about the way in which the Catholic Church has profited from secular developments and what it called 'the voices of our times' (*Gaudium et Spes*, 44). When they finally and firmly rejected slavery, Catholics and other Christians were influenced by Baron de Montesquieu (1689–1755), a French political philosopher, and some other Enlightenment thinkers who championed individual liberty and other inalienable human rights.

DISTINCTIVE MORAL CONVICTIONS

Before examining two central Catholic criteria for the moral life, it seems illuminating to track certain moral convictions deeply rooted in Catholic thinking and behaviour. We are not alleging that these convictions are unique, but only that they are distinctive and persistent.

---

[10] For accounts of this encyclical's important teaching on law, freedom, and intrinsically evil acts see J. A. DiNoia and R. Cessario (eds.), *'Veritatis Splendor' and the Renewal of Moral Theology* (Princeton, NJ: Scepter, 1999); R. Hütter and D. Dieter (eds.), *Ecumenical Ventures in Ethics: Protestants Engage Pope John Paul's Moral Encyclicals* (Grand Rapids, Mich.: Eerdmans, 1998); J. Wilkins (ed.), *Understanding 'Veritatis Splendor'* (London: SPCK, 1994).

Respect for Life

One of the earliest post-NT documents, written by an unknown author around AD 110 and attributed to St Barnabas, develops its moral teaching by contrasting 'the way of light' with 'the way of death'. It includes the following among the precepts for the way of light:

> *Love your neighbour more than your own life. Never do away with an unborn child, or destroy it after its birth.* Do not withhold your hand from your son or your daughter, but bring them up in the fear of God from their childhood. Do not cast covetous eyes on a neighbour's possessions. Do not be greedy for gain. Do not set your heart on being intimate with the great, but look for the company of people who are humble and virtuous. Whatever experience comes your way, accept it as a blessing, in the certainty that nothing can happen without God. Never equivocate either in thought or speech. A double tongue is a fatal snare.
>
> (*Epistle of Barnabas*, 19. 5–7; italics ours)

Much of this and further moral instruction on the two ways (ibid. 19–20) parallels what we read on 'the way of life' and 'the way of death' in a roughly contemporary document (*Didache*, 1–6). Like the *Didache*, the *Epistle* draws on a rich OT background: for instance, from Sirach and earlier books of wisdom. Some items directly echo the Ten Commandments (Exod. 20: 1–17): for example, 'do not cast covetous eyes on a neighbour's possessions' recalls the tenth commandment ('do not covet your neighbour's goods') and 'never equivocate in speech' recalls the eighth commandment ('do not bear false witness').

The opening precepts, however, take matters beyond OT morality. Loving 'your neighbour more than your own life' sets an even higher standard than 'you shall love your neighbour as yourself' (Lev. 19: 18). The *Epistle of Barnabas* brings to mind here St Paul's exalted guidelines for the practice of love (1 Cor. 12: 31–13: 13) and Jesus' words: 'No one has greater love than that he lay down his life for his friends' (John 15: 13). What interests us here, however, is the respect for life that is shown by the rejection of abortion and infanticide, and which draws particular conclusions from the general tenor of the fifth (also often listed as the sixth) commandment, 'You shall not kill.' The OT (and the NT) scriptures persistently express respect for innocent human beings and regard them at all stages as made in the image of God.[11] One text condemns violence that

---

[11] We prefer to express matters this way, rather than speak of 'the sacredness of human life', which is not a specifically biblical or Christian idea.

produces a miscarriage (Exod. 21: 22–5), but no biblical passage addresses itself explicitly to abortion, something practised along with infanticide in Roman society at the time of the birth of Christianity (see Ch. 1). The *Didache* (5. 2) joined the *Epistle of Barnabas* in condemning abortion, which we can describe as the intentional destruction of an unborn child either in its mother's womb or by removing it from its mother's womb.[12]

Later Christian authors such as Basil the Great (d. 379) treated abortion as murder. The Synod of Elvira (306) had excommunicated women obtaining abortions, allowing those who repented to receive communion only at the time of death (canon 63), whereas the Synod of Ancyra (314) readmitted them to communion after some years of penance (canon 21). The Quinisext Synod (691/2) called those who procured abortions 'murderers' (canon 91). Reference is sometimes made to an alleged late sixteenth-century change in the Catholic Church's position on abortion (1588–91). In fact there was no such change in the doctrine itself but only a change in the discipline regarding the imposition of a penalty for abortion. In the twentieth century, when it described infanticide and abortion as 'abominable crimes' (*Gaudium et Spes*, 51), Vatican II did so in a section devoted to promoting married love and respect for human life. Such concern for positive teaching, while often absent in what came from earlier Christian authors and synods, has also characterized the teaching of John Paul II. His authoritative 1995 rejection of 'direct abortion' as 'a grave moral disorder' and a decision 'against the weakest and most defenceless of human beings' is set in the context of a coherent ethic of concern for life (*Evangelium Vitae*, 28, 62, 70). That same encyclical also added these words for women who have undergone an abortion:

The Church is aware of the many factors which may have influenced your decision, and she does not doubt that in many cases it was a painful and even shattering decision. The wound in your heart may not yet have healed. Certainly what happened was and remains terribly wrong. But do not give in to discouragement and do not lose hope... You will come to understand that nothing is definitely lost and you will be able to ask forgiveness from your child, who is now living in the Lord.   (ibid. 99)

---

[12] An unborn child's unintended death during surgery to save its mother's life is 'indirect' abortion: the child's death is a tragic yet inevitable side-effect of surgery that is good in itself (e.g. the removal of a cancerous uterus). The child's death as such is not the means that produces the mother's restored health. Any such distinction between 'direct' or 'indirect' abortion was unknown in the Roman world, which, sadly, was familiar only with the first.

This encyclical repudiated the 'culture of death', which is also expressed both in the direct, 'gravely immoral' killing of the innocent and in euthanasia, 'a grave violation of the law of God' (ibid. 57, 64–6). The condemnation of the killing of the innocent was also directed against the practice of killing or deliberately shortening the life of handicapped infants, which is recommended by some modern authors and practised in some countries. Parents can be put under economic and other forms of pressure if they do not agree to the destruction of their genetically disabled children, particularly when they refused an abortion when abnormalities were detected before birth.

As regards euthanasia in the active or strict sense of the term, one must distinguish it from decisions to withhold futile or disproportionately burdensome means for prolonging life or to provide relief for gravely ill patients with the intention of reducing pain, even if the coincidental effect may also be to shorten life. Members of the medical profession cross, however, a major line into morally unacceptable killing when they claim the right, even in conjunction with patients and their relatives, to decide which lives are worth living, deliberately cause patients to die, or withhold treatment with the deliberate intention of bringing about death. The old and the incurably ill can feel that they are a burden on their families and that their earlier death would benefit others financially. Judged by productivity, they are an economic liability. It may take little to persuade them to accept a physician-assisted suicide. Stroke patients and the senile often have no choice in the matter; their death can result from others deciding to terminate their life directly.

Evangelium Vitae ('the Gospel of Life') also pleaded for life in two further ways. It called 'the use of human embryos or foetuses' for experiments 'a crime against their dignity as human beings who have a right to the same respect owed to a child once born' (ibid. 63).[13] It excluded the death penalty, 'except in the case of absolute necessity', or 'when it would

---

[13] Since *Evangelium Vitae* appeared in 1995, issues about stem-cell research and human cloning have continued to hit the headlines. In July 2001 the news broke that the Jones Institute for Reproductive Medicine in Norfolk, Virginia, was creating human embryos for the sole purpose of dismembering them for their stem-cells. Immediately after that news it was learned that a laboratory in Worcester, Massachusetts, was aiming to grow cloned human embryos to produce stem-cells. The same laboratory three years earlier had produced a hybrid human–cow embryo. The news inevitably brought to mind the criminal use of human beings as guinea pigs practised by twentieth-century totalitarian regimes. For some bibliography see T. A. Shannon, 'Human Embryonic Stem Cell Therapy', *Theological Studies*, 62 (2001), 811–24.

not be possible otherwise to defend society'. The Pope added: 'today, however, as a result of steady improvements in the organization of the penal system, such cases are very rare, if not practically non-existent' (ibid. 56).

The traditional teaching of the Catholic Church accepted the death penalty, provided that it was inflicted on those whose guilt for murder and other serious offences had been judicially established. Christians encouraged the Emperor Constantine to abolish crucifixion, a slow and atrocious form of execution, as a legal punishment. But for centuries most Catholics and other Christians accepted that a number of crimes could and should be punished by death. Gradually reflection on the fifth commandment ('You shall not kill') and other forces reduced in many countries capital offences to murder and treason or betrayal of one's country in time of war. Teachers of Catholic morality continued to accept that in these cases the death penalty was a justified punishment and the only possible way of effectively defending innocent lives against unjust aggressors. However, notorious miscarriages of justice that led to the execution of the innocent, the possibility of imprisonment bringing murderers to true repentance and conversion, the fact that secure gaols defend the public from dangerous criminals, and other considerations (e.g. that the threat of capital punishment is not an effective deterrent against murder) have convinced many Christians and others to support the abolition of the death penalty. In the Catholic Church John Paul II led the way with his almost unqualified opposition to capital punishment.

At the Second Vatican Council he had shared in the making of the Constitution on the Church in the Modern World, which devoted a whole chapter to the fostering of peace and establishing an effective community of nations (*Gaudium et Spes*, 77–90). The Council, in the face of modern weapons that 'can inflict immense and indiscriminate havoc', called for 'a completely fresh appraisal of war', and endorsed condemnations of 'total war' (which had already come from Pius XII, John XXIII, and Paul VI) and of 'the indiscriminate destruction of whole cities and vast areas'. The Council also condemned as 'frightful crimes' the 'extermination' of entire races, nations, or ethnic minorities (ibid. 79–80). In particular, it had in mind here the six million Jewish victims of the Nazi genocide, an unspeakable crime against God and humanity that John Paul II made a constant theme of speeches and sermons from the start of his pontificate.

The conciliar document, along with radical concern to 'curb the savagery of war', nevertheless, acknowledged that, 'as long as the danger of war persists and there is no international authority with the necessary competence and power, governments cannot be denied the right of lawful self-defence, *once all peace efforts have failed*' (ibid. 79; italics ours). This is tantamount to accepting the possibility of a just defence (to be distinguished from a holy war or a crusade), provided certain stringent conditions are met.[14] But in some tragic, recent examples we wonder whether war has been declared before 'all peace efforts' have been tried and failed. Vatican II's concern over the savagery of war sprang from its desire to prevent further slaughter of innocent civilians and to uphold in every way respect for human life. That respect characterizes the Catholic tradition, or at least the best features of the Catholic tradition, from the end of the first century and the teaching in support of life that came from the *Didache* and the *Epistle of Barnabas*. One can track a trajectory that supports naming respect for life a distinctive (but not unique) characteristic of Catholic morality. A right sexual ordering forms a second such characteristic.

The Sexual Order

Men and women were both created in the image and likeness of God and find through marriage their human and religious fulfilment (Chs. 5 and 7). From the start of Christianity respect for the personal and social values of human sexuality underpinned the teaching on sexual activity, a teaching that defended a middle ground between two extremes: the widespread licentiousness and shameful treatment of women in ancient times, on the one hand, and the repudiation of sexuality by such groups as the Marcionites, Montanists, Manicheans, and the Cathars, on the other (see Chs. 1 and 2, respectively).

In the immediate post-NT period we find the *Didache* and the *Epistle of Barnabas* warning against 'the way of darkness' by repudiating three kinds of sexual activity that the Catholic tradition would consistently repudiate, premarital sex, extramarital sex, and homosexual practices: 'You shall not commit fornication; you shall not commit adultery; you shall not engage in homosexual activity' (*Epistle of Barnabas*, 19. 4; *Didache*, 2. 2). In all three cases, down through the ages many people, including not a few Christians, have dissented from this teaching, but in doing so they have

---

[14] J. F. Langan summarizes these conditions: 'Just-war doctrine', in R. P. McBrien (ed.), *The HarperCollins Encyclopedia of Catholicism* (San Francisco: HarperSan Francisco, 1995), 728–9.

been overriding the clear judgement of the NT scriptures and the main-stream tradition. But what of sexuality and Christian married life?

St Paul's teaching on the equal status of men and women who had been baptized into Christ (Gal. 3: 28) seemed to make marriage a partnership of equals. However, subsequent domestic rules for Christian households followed patriarchal practice, by inculcating the subordination of wives to husbands. Yet these rules insisted on husbands showing loving respect: 'Husbands, love your wives and never treat them harshly' (Col. 3: 19). Nowadays, many societies take their distance from such first-century household codes of behaviour. But those codes insisted on something that was often missing in ancient and later cultures: Christian husbands were expected to cherish, protect, love their wives with a tenderness that took its standard from Christ himself (Eph. 5: 22–33; see 1 Pet. 3: 1–7). In Ch. 1 we saw how respect for wives and mothers made Christian faith attractive to many women in the Roman Empire.

In a treatise written around 200 (before he lapsed into the extreme views of Montanism) and addressed to his wife when both were in the prime of life, Tertullian left us a most moving appreciation of the beauty of Christian marriage:

How beautiful the marriage of two Christians, two who are one in hope, one in desire, one in the way of life they follow, one in the religion they practice. They are as brother and sister, both servants of the same Master. Nothing divides them, either in flesh or in spirit. They are, in very truth, two in one flesh [Gen. 2: 24]; and where there is but one flesh there is also but one spirit. They pray together, they worship together, they fast together, instructing one another, encouraging one another, strengthening one another. Side by side they visit God's church and partake of God's banquet; side by side they face difficulties and persecutions, share their consolations. They have no secrets from one another; they never shun each other's company; they never bring sorrow to each other's hearts. Unembarrassed they visit the sick and assist the needy. They give alms without anxiety; they attend the Sacrifice [the Eucharist] without difficulty; they perform their daily exercises of piety without hindrance. They need not be furtive about making the sign of the cross, nor timorous in greeting the brethren, nor silent in asking a blessing from God. Psalms and hymns they sing to one another, striving to see which one of them will chant more beautifully the praises of the Lord. Hearing and seeing this, Christ rejoices. To such as these he gives his peace. Where there are two together, there also he is present [Matt. 18: 20]; and where he is, there evil is not.   (*Ad Uxorem*, 2. 8)[15]

---

[15] Trans. W. P. Le Saint, *Tertullian: Treatises on Marriage and Remarriage*, Ancient Christian Writers, 13 (Westminster, Md.: Newman Press, 1951), 35–6.

Unsurpassed in its power to evoke the sanctity of marriage in early Christianity, this passage did not, however, anticipate the teaching of Vatican II on the beauty and wonder of married sexuality as a precious gift from God. In particular, the Constitution on the Church in the Modern World celebrated the tender, life-giving quality of dignified married love (*Gaudium et Spes*, 49, 51).

From the time of Pius XI's 1930 encyclical letter *Casti Connubii* ('Of Chaste Marriage') Catholic teaching has taken up the challenge of holding together the two obvious purposes of marital intercourse: the fostering of mutual love and the begetting of children. Clearly tensions can and do arise between these two purposes. Responsible parenthood must reckon with such factors as the lack of proper housing for a larger family, the precarious health of one or other of the spouses, economic difficulties, and some dramatic demographic challenges. Between 1960 and late 1999, the population of the world was to double: from three thousand million to six thousand million. Pius XI had recognized as legitimate choosing the safe or sterile period for intercourse (or natural family planning), but rejected contraception as morally wrong, 'an offence against the law of God and nature' (DH 3717; ND 2202). Vatican II couched its teaching in general terms, encouraging in spouses 'a sense of human and Christian responsibility'. With 'docile reverence towards God' and 'common counsel and effort', they should reach 'a right judgement' about having further children: 'taking into account their own good and that of the children already born or to be born, they will consider carefully the material and spiritual conditions of their times and of their own situation; and, finally, they will consult the interests of their own family, of the temporal society, and of the church herself'. The Council felt confident that 'there can be no real contradiction between the divine law of transmitting life and that of fostering genuine conjugal love' (*Gaudium et Spes*, 50–1).

At the request of Paul VI, the particular question of methods of birth control was left to a commission of experts appointed in 1965 by the Pope himself (see ibid. 51 n. 14). The majority on the commission came out in favour of a change in teaching. After prayerfully examining their report and consulting with others, Paul VI published in 1968 his encyclical *Humanae Vitae* ('Of Human Life'). While recognizing the importance of married love and endorsing responsible parenthood, the Pope rejected contraception. He appealed to the inseparable connection between the unitive and procreative meaning of sexual intercourse, and declared that 'each and every marriage act' must be open to the transmission of life (no. 11). Although an authoritative statement, the encyclical was not an infallible document. The bishops of many countries introduced mitigating nuances into its teaching: the French bishops, for instance, would not unconditionally exclude artificial means of birth control, which they considered 'a lesser evil', when periodical continence proves impossible or spouses are faced with a conflict of duties.

Whatever one discerns or decides, we must firmly distinguish between abortion and infanticide, on the one hand, and contraception, on the other. Catholic teaching, right from the first century, has rejected the former. As regards the latter, Vatican II should be heard: 'it is the spouses themselves who ultimately must make this judgement in the sight of God', doing so with their 'conscience dutifully conformed to the divine law' and 'submissive toward the church's teaching office, which authentically interprets that law in the light of the Gospel', and aware that the 'divine law reveals and protects the integral meaning of conjugal love, and impels it toward a truly human fulfilment' (*Gaudium et Spes*, 50). It is worth recalling here the relevant examination of conscience before approaching the sacrament of reconciliation proposed in 1977 by the patriarch of Venice, Cardinal Albino Luciani (to become Pope John Paul I the following year), and by the archbishops or bishops of fourteen neighbouring dioceses: 'In agreement with my spouse, have I given a clear and conscientious answer to the problem of birth control? Have I prevented a conception for egotistical motives? Have I brought a life into the world without a sense of responsibility?'[16] These questions test the loving and responsible decision of the two spouses; nothing is asked about the methods used to prevent what they together judge would be an 'irresponsible' pregnancy.

In his papal teaching John Paul II, while saying nothing about any means adopted, repeatedly condemned contraception as gravely wrong and 'a falsification of the inner truth of conjugal love' (*Familiaris Consortio*, 32). He also firmly distinguished contraception from abortion:

From the moral point of view contraception and abortion are *specifically different* evils: the former contradicts the full truth of the sexual act as the proper expression of conjugal love, while the latter destroys the life of a human being; the former is opposed to the virtue of chastity in marriage, the latter is opposed to the virtue of

---

[16] *Libro di preghiera per le diocesi della regione Triveneta* (Turin: Elle Di Ci, 2nd edn. 1977), 418; trans. ours.

justice and directly violates the divine commandment 'You shall not kill.' (*Evangelium Vitae*, 13; italics his)

Truth and Justice

A further moral commitment, once again a commitment of Catholic Christianity which is distinctive but not unique, concerns truth and justice. Two documents that open a window on the moral teaching of Christians around the end of the first century concur in advocating the telling of truth and the practice of justice. Those who follow 'the way of death' are 'haters of the truth, lovers of lies'; 'robbery' figures among the vices that 'destroy' their 'soul' (*Epistle of Barnabas*, 20. 1–2; see *Didache*, 5. 1–2).

1. Their convictions about Christ being the divine 'Truth' or the true 'Word of God' underwrote the emphasis many church writers put on speaking the truth and not lying (or making intentionally false statements). St Augustine, in particular, gave the highest importance to truth-telling and condemned lying as something that could not be changed from a bad to a good act by an added good intention. The unqualified obligation of confessors to maintain 'the seal' (see Ch. 7) and never reveal a sin confessed to them by penitents and the very serious obligation of 'professional secrecy', which concerns private and confidential matters communicated to doctors, lawyers, and others in the course of their professional work, have proved a testing-ground for grappling with the nature of truth-telling and lying. The seal of confession, the obligation to maintain professional secrecy, and other challenges have led many Catholic teachers to distinguish between real lying and false speaking. Lies or telling intentional falsehoods when others have a right to hear the truth, disrupt the ordinary trust necessary to maintain healthy human communication. But there can be occasions when other persons, whether they know it or not, do not have the right to hear the truth. Priests, doctors, lawyers, and others have a strict duty to keep secrets, and in the circumstances simply remaining silent or using merely equivocal language may not be enough to safeguard such secrets.

The modern world has often suffered from institutionalized sins against truth—in the systematic distortion or deprivation of information given to the public through press, radio, television, and textbooks produced for wide use in schools. George Orwell's prophetic 1949 novel, *Nineteen Eighty-Four*, indicts not only totalitarian states that have misrepresented reality through their 'ministries of truth' but also modern democracies, where the media controls and twists public opinion. After a tragedy, caused perhaps by a terrorist attack, interviews with survivors, eyewitnesses, and the relatives of victims perform a good service by personalizing the tragedy. But the impact becomes very slanted when the media has little or nothing to say about thousands of tragedies that happen outside the Western world. A very partial coverage of human life, suffering, and needs—not to mention the advantageous lies deliberately propagated by governments—sins against a general right to know what is happening. The media selectivity allows the public quickly to forget thousands, even millions, of refugees and other victims of conflicts, supposing that the public heard about such suffering in the first place. Regrettably many Catholics fail to share any sense of outrage against the structural perversion of truth. Courageous journalists have proved a refreshing exception; because of their tenacious pursuit of the truth, some have been eliminated by criminals and criminal politicians. Among the institutions that champion the truth, the Truth and Reconciliation Commission in South Africa deserves to be praised and imitated. Probably one cannot make a firm judgement on its long-term effects. Nevertheless, provided the perpetrators repent and the victims are ready to forgive, the Commission's core principle, that the discovery of truth will help to heal social wounds caused by years of ruthless trampling on human rights, seems to be better based morally and more effective politically than what has so often happened elsewhere. A general amnesty for past crimes stops the truth from ever being heard publicly and may well provide impunity for future horrors to happen. Augustine's passion for the truth has today a national and international importance that he never imagined.

2. One of Jesus' parables pictured an 'unjust' judge who initially was too lazy to hear the case of a widow whom an anonymous person has treated badly over some issue. She is not getting her rights and lacks the support of a husband and family, but her persistent appeals eventually win the day. Her case is heard and she is granted 'justice' or what is due to her. The Christian tradition came to call justice, along with prudence, temperance, and fortitude, one of the four *cardinal* ('hinge') virtues, because right human conduct pivots upon them. In the Middle Ages Thomas Aquinas described justice as 'the strong and firm will to give each his due' (*ST* II-II q. 58 a. 1). Citing Aristotle's *Nicomachean Ethics* (5. 1), Aquinas recognized general justice and and two kinds of particular justice, commutative and distributive (*ST* II-II q. 61 a. 1). In modern times Catholic

thought has elaborated what is 'due' on the basis of 'social' justice. Let us look in turn at commutative, distributive, and social justice.

Commutative justice calls for fairness in agreements and transactions between individual persons or groups. It requires, for instance, that employers pay employees a just wage and provide safe and decent working conditions. On their side, employees owe their employers serious and productive work. Commutative justice supports such recent practices as the adequate labelling of food; buyers have the right to know what they are purchasing and where the products come from.

Distributive justice, as this came to be understood in modern times, deals with the ways in which societies allocate their wealth, resources, and power. But how should equalities and differences determine the distribution of resources? Should allocation be structured merely according to what people contribute, or according to what they are deemed to merit, or according to some pattern of equality? From Pope Leo XIII's groundbreaking 1891 encyclical *Rerum Novarum* ('Of New Things'), Catholic teaching has emphasized the needs of people. As Leo XIII put it, 'justice demands that the interests of the poorer populations be carefully watched over by the administration' (no. 27).

A developing stress on need and a more egalitarian view of society led to the inclusion of 'social justice' as a key term in Catholic teaching from Pius XI's 1931 encyclical *Quadragesimo Anno* ('In the Fortieth Year': i.e. since *Rerum Novarum*). Such social justice obliges individuals to participate in and contribute to society, but at the same time society should facilitate such participation. Social justice aims to remove various ways in which individuals or groups are excluded from such participation or even condemned to live on the margins of society. Pope John Paul II emphasized the virtue of solidarity as complementary to justice: it is an awareness that can bring about community relationships in human society.[17]

In the aftermath of Vatican II various documents issued by Paul VI, John Paul II, national conferences of bishops, and some offices of the Roman Curia continued to develop the Catholic Church's social doctrine and, in particular, to champion the rights of those millions who are victims of injustice. A synod of bishops in Rome (1971) summed up the commitment to social justice in all its forms: 'Action on behalf of justice

[17] For a summary of and selection from documents on the Catholic Church's social doctrine from Leo XIII, see ch. 21 of ND, 899–972.

FIG. 13. Dorothy Day, peace campaigner and social activist, testifying in the USA before an official Catholic hearing on liberty and justice in preparation for the 1976 bicentennial celebration. (Catholic News Service.)

FIG. 14. On 3 February 1986 Pope John Paul II holds the hands of Mother Teresa of Calcutta after visiting one of her homes for the destitute and showing once again his deep regard for her holiness. (Popperfoto.)

and participation in the transformation of the world' are 'a constitutive dimension of the preaching of the Gospel, or, in other words, of the Church's mission for the redemption of the human race and its liberation from every oppressive situation' (*De Iustitia in Mundo*, 6; ND 2159). Gustavo Gutierrez (b. 1928), Jon Sobrino (b. 1938), and other leaders of Latin-American liberation theology endorsed this call for a worldwide justice that should deliver the great masses of poor people.

Care for the Needy

Love, even more than considerations of justice, has inspired Catholics and other Christians to care for the socially marginalized and any man or woman in need. Christianity inherited from the OT a healthy message of concern for widows, orphans, and strangers (e.g. Deut. 24: 17–21), along with prophetic opposition to those who used their wealth and power to oppress the economically and socially weak. The very early post-NT codes on which we have already drawn maintained the Jewish moral message by attributing to 'the way of death' the actions of those who 'attend not to the widow and orphan', 'turn away the needy', and 'oppress the afflicted' (*Epistle of Barnabas*, 20. 2; see *Didache*, 5. 2). The denunciation bears on sins of omission (failures to help widows and orphans) and those of commission (in positively turning away the needy and oppressing those who are already afflicted).

Those whom Jesus expected his followers to help included the hungry, the thirsty, strangers, the naked, the sick, and prisoners (Matt. 25: 31–46). The list of the suffering with whom he identified did not explicitly include widows and orphans, but the list was obviously open-ended. His parable of 'the Good Samaritan' powerfully illustrates what he wants from all: the willingness to reach across religious and cultural divides to help any human being in distress (Luke 10: 30–7). He left no room for a self-absorption that may not even notice the pain of others. Jesus' message fuelled the kind of commitment to the sick, the poor, and others in need symbolized by the figure of St Laurence (see Ch. 1). It fuelled also the powerful words St John Chrysostom addressed to rich Christians in Constantinople:

Consider that Christ is that tramp who comes in need of a night's lodging. You turn him away and then start laying rugs on the floor, draping the walls, hanging lamps on silver chains on the columns. Meanwhile the tramp is locked up in prison and you never give him a glance . . . Make your house beautiful by all means but also look after the poor, or rather look after the poor first . . . Adorn your house if you will, but do not forget your brother in distress. He is a temple of infinitely greater value.   (*Homily* 50. 4)

The words of Jesus from Matthew 25 and Luke 10, along with his parable of the rich man and the poor Lazarus (Luke 16: 19–31) have influenced and disturbed the moral conscience of Catholics and other Christians for two thousand years.

This moral message provided an important stimulus for the development of hospitals. St Basil of Caesarea (d. 379) founded what was perhaps the first Christian hospital. Innumerable doctors, nurses, and administrators have followed his lead, not least Catholic women who belonged to religious institutes founded specifically to care for the sick and the terminally ill.[18] They have 'come to the help' of the sick as enjoined by Jesus' message (Matt. 25: 36). Many others have realized that one should add to the list in Matthew's text those who are ignorant and in need of education. Part at least of the astonishing commitment by Catholics and other Christians to the work of educating children and older persons has been fired by the sense of Jesus saying to them: 'I was ignorant and you taught me.'

In an eloquent passage the Second Vatican Council recalled Christ's parable of the rich man who failed to care for the poor man, Lazarus, and spoke of the 'inescapable duty to make ourselves the neighbour' of all and 'to come to their aid in a positive way', whether the neighbour 'is an aged person abandoned by everyone, a foreign worker despised without reason, a refugee, an illegitimate child . . . or a starving human being' (*Gaudium et Spes*, 27). The ethical motivation in this section is clearly twofold: not only obedience to the message of Jesus, who practised and encouraged a 'fundamental option for the suffering', but also an unconditional respect for the human person, who has been created in the image and likeness of God.

Human Dignity and Human Rights

The dignity conferred on all human beings by their being created in the divine image provides the grounds for typically Catholic teaching on

[18] In 1288 Folco Portinari, whose beautiful daughter Beatrice captivated Dante forever, opened in Florence the still existing hospital Santa Maria Nuova, which brought together religious women serving the sick, the first such nursing staff on record.

universal human rights and their correlative duties (e.g. *Gaudium et Spes*, 26). Pope John Paul II developed this theme in a December 1978 message to the Secretary General of the United Nations Organization, from which he quoted a month later in his address in Puebla to the Third General Assembly of Latin American Bishops in denouncing

> the sometimes massive increase of human rights violations in many parts of the world... Who can deny that today individual persons and civil powers violate basic rights of the human person with impunity: rights such as the right to be born, the right to life, the right to responsible procreation, to work, to peace, to freedom and social justice, the right to participate in the decisions that affect people and nations? And what can be said when we face the various forms of collective violence like discrimination against individuals and groups, the use of physical and psychological torture perpetrated against prisoners and political dissenters? ... We cry once more: respect the human persons! They are the image of God! (ND 426)

Less than two months later the Pope's first encyclical *Redemptor Hominis* developed at length the unconditional dignity of human persons lovingly created by God and redeemed by Jesus Christ. He often had occasion to return to the themes of human dignity and basic rights, not least in his 1988 apostolic letter *Mulieris Dignitatem* ('The Dignity of Woman'), which expounded women's dignity and equality on the basis of women and men being created in the divine image and likeness.

In January 1979 John Paul II spoke to the Latin American bishops gathered in the Mexican city of Puebla. We have just quoted his words when writing this chapter shortly after the death of Digna Ochoa on 18 October 2001. One of Mexico's most prominent human rights lawyers, she often defended the defenceless, was repeatedly threatened for doing so, and was eventually shot dead in her law office in Mexico City. A devout Catholic, she put into practice her moral convictions about human rights and paid for that with her life. In Latin America and elsewhere champions of human rights have often suffered the same fate, not least the members of the Justice and Peace commissions that sprang up in many Catholic dioceses after the Second Vatican Council. Practical solidarity with those who are deprived and subjugated remains a dangerous commitment.

More than ever, as we move ahead in the third millennium, global economic development calls for human rights to be remembered and championed. The contemporary international financial system has spectacularly increased human wealth. But to what extent is that happening to the detriment of many human beings? We do not want to pretend that questions of the world economy are anything else than very complex. But we do strongly maintain that healthy ethical considerations must play a decisive part in policies involving such matters as the new biotechnology replacing conventional farming. Higher productivity by itself cannot be allowed to shape national and international decision-making. What health risks do genetically modified food crops pose to human beings? How will modern biotechnology affect the life, freedom, and basic rights of farming communities around the world?

Over fifty years ago Rachel Carson (1907–64) in her *Silent Spring* warned against the indiscriminate use of pesticides and weedkillers. Sadly governments and multinational corporations have continued to embrace new discoveries and adopt the related technologies, often with scarce attention paid to the ecological implications. Pollution and a reckless squandering of natural resources threaten everyone, perpetrators and victims alike. Our environment must be protected if it is to continue being a habitat for humanity.

At least as much in the field of bioethics, human values and well-based principles and standards about what contributes to the life and happiness of men and women must shape the new knowledge. Facile arguments about 'the need for research' or the 'proper progress of science' can notoriously cloak a hideous misuse of new medical knowledge and technology.[19] Once again we recognize how complicated bioethical and medical questions can prove. But we insist that human dignity, rights, and basic values must inform all bioethical and medical decisions. Let us raise three questions, which concern the end of life (question 1) and the beginning of life (questions 2 and 3).

1. Remarkable and often costly medical advances prolong life for a wealthy minority of the world's population, while millions continue to lack basic medical services and even safe drinking water. Is such a distri-

---

[19] In 1987 the Congregation for the Doctrine of the Faith commented wisely on the relationship between science and morality: 'It would on the one hand be illusory to claim that scientific research and its application are morally neutral; on the other hand one cannot derive criteria for guidance from mere technical efficiency, from research's possible usefulness to some at the expense of others, or, worse still, from prevailing ideologies. Thus science and technology require, for their own intrinsic meaning, an unconditional respect for the fundamental criteria of the moral law; that is to say, they must be at the service of human persons, of their inalienable rights, and their true and integral good according to the design and will of God' (*Donum Vitae*, intr. 2; ND 2072).

bution of medical resources just, or does it embody a complicity in evil that ignores the fact that human beings form one family under God?

2. New gene therapy, which aims to remedy genetic defects, can happily bring about the birth and growth of healthy children. But it may also be used to enhance particular traits such as height and so improve the athletic performance of children to be born. Thus wealthy parents may buy desirable characteristics through gene enhancement and so produce children with a biologically higher potential for 'success'—what one might call, more 'marketable' offspring. A new social class could emerge, comprised of those whose wealthy parents can afford to buy superior genetic endowments. Biotechnology firms are already busy creating and cultivating a market for their products and services, which promise to turn human reproduction into commercial breeding.

3. Alongside new genetic engineering, old eugenics has appeared in fresh forms but with the original project of altering the human race by breeding for inherited characteristics deemed to be desirable and eliminating those deemed to be unwanted. For the 'greater good of humanity' people who harbour 'dangerous' genes must be prevented from begetting children or the foetuses they produce must be aborted. Embryos are to be selected for implantation or destroyed because they display the 'right' or 'wrong' characteristics, respectively. By promoting on its own terms the 'needs' of society, the new eugenics makes the alleged 'greater good' of society dominate over the rights and dignity of individuals.

FORMING OUR CONSCIENCE

We have recalled some major distinctive (but, let us insist once again, not necessarily unique) moral convictions and concerns of Catholic Christianity: respect for all human life as sacred; a sexual responsibility located between selfish licentiousness and anti-body rigorism; a deep concern for truth and justice; care for all our neighbours in need; a defence of human dignity and rights. What is to be said when we move from moral principles to human decisions and actions? We conclude this chapter by proposing two fundamental principles for forming our conscience: the following of Christ and docility to the guidance of the Holy Spirit.

Notoriously the world has experienced and suffered from a 'morality' according to which we should create meaning and value for ourselves. In a spirit of unqualified self-determination and self-creation, some claim:

'The moral meaning of my acts is controlled by me and me alone.' In its own way such a moral stance recalls the Roman matron described by Juvenal: 'don't ask me for reasons; it is enough that I want something.' A self-directed self similarly allows the autonomous will by itself to justify deeds and their values; as John Paul II wrote, it 'grants to the individual conscience the prerogative of independently determining the criteria of good and evil and then acting accordingly' (*Veritatis Splendor*, 32).

But what of those noble 'liberal' thinkers, such as Sir Julian Huxley, who appeal to reason and conscience? In a book published two years before he died, this biologist and first director-general of UNESCO wrote: 'I have been an optimist all my life, trusting in reason, man's natural intelligence and his conscience.'[20] All power to Huxley and his appeal to the human conscience, which Vatican II invoked[21] and which John Paul II called 'the proximate norm of personal morality' (*Veritatis Splendor*, 60). Huxley's optimism was underpinned, however, by an unqualified confidence in the 'natural' goodness and perfectibility of human beings that the Enlightenment thinkers propounded (see the end of Ch. 2). The harm done by sin to human beings, not least the impact of sin on our intelligence,[22] and the help offered by the Holy Spirit to our ways of thinking, deciding, and acting simply did not enter Huxley's confident picture. Here St Paul proves much more realistic; he knew that our sinful minds need to be transformed and renewed before we can 'discern the will of God' and know 'what is good, acceptable, and perfect' (Rom. 12: 2). Before we discuss with the Huxleys of this world anything about conscience and moral decisions, we need to take them through the first eleven chapters of Romans and debate their picture of the human condition. They need to be ready to acknowledge not only our created condition but also that sinfulness which evoked the loving, redemptive activity of the tripersonal God.

At the same time, we should acknowledge how Huxley stood apart from those who facilely call on experience, science, and some supposed consensus in making up their moral minds. One must ask: whose experience counts? And then: what science counts? And how do we move beyond the

---

[20] *Memories II* (New York: Harper & Row, 1973), 258.

[21] 'In the depths of their conscience human beings detect a law which they do not make for themselves but which they must obey. Its voice always summons them to love and to do what is good and to shun what is evil' (*Gaudium et Spes*, 16).

[22] See the sombre words of Vatican II about those who 'take little care to seek what is true and good' and whose conscience 'through a habit of sin' gradually becomes 'almost blind' (*Gaudium et Spes*, 16).

facts, presented by science, to values, or beyond what is to what ought to be? Some cases we cited earlier in this chapter (that of slavery, torture, and capital punishment) should give us pause about appealing to a consensus, even supposing that it has genuinely been established to exist. History shows how for much too long Christians conformed to regrettable social standards and were slow in opposing the prevailing consensus.

If we drop any debate with the Huxleys and others, what do we intend to say about the eminently practical exercise of applying the moral law to our concrete circumstances and forming our moral consciences or allowing them to be formed (see John Paul II, *Veritatis Splendor*, 54–64)? When they weigh up what they should do or refrain from doing at home or in work situations, whether these are such public institutions as schools and hospitals or private business settings, what principles should ideally guide Catholics and other Christians in evaluating their moral obligations and choosing a course of action? Ultimately, for Christ's disciples such principles seem to come down to two: the expectant hearing of the divine intentions communicated through God's revealed word and through the testimony of conscience, and a sense of freedom as the gift of God's Spirit.

1. Catholic and, indeed, all Christian morality is a morality of discipleship, for those who want to follow Jesus faithfully and unconditionally. Jesus himself endorsed the Jewish faith in the Torah as a divine gift, in fact as the special sign of the fact that God had chosen and entered into a unique covenant relationship with Israel. More than being ten rules for decent behaviour or an excellent summary of a natural code of conduct with which all ethically serious persons should agree, the Decalogue offered a way of life with God. Beyond question, Jesus took matters further—not only by subsuming all law under love (Mark 12: 28–34) but also by being himself the Law in person. Nevertheless, he expected his followers to attend with utter seriousness to the claims of the divine law and let their lives be shaped accordingly. He wanted them not simply to join Psalm 118 in celebrating the Law as God's extraordinary gift to Israel, but also to interiorize it and let it shape their hearts and minds (e.g. Mark 7: 20–3).

The *Didache* bears striking witness to this first principle of the attentive hearing expected from disciples. Its moral instruction for Christians around the end of the first century fashions its teaching about 'the way of life' and 'the way of death' by blending Christ's teaching about the life of love with the Ten Commandments and related prescriptions from the OT

(*Didache*, 1–6). The *Didache* says here in a more homely fashion what Paul had already expressed in his masterpiece. Christ has brought the OT law to its peak and perfection (Rom. 10: 4), and his teaching on love is the 'fulfilment' of the law (Rom. 13: 8–10). One might sum up the moral instruction from the *Didache* and the apostle as hearing the Decalogue to the accompaniment of the Sermon on the Mount (Matt. 5–7).

Paul called this approach to moral living 'following' or 'imitating' Christ (1 Cor. 11: 1), an existence for which the primary aim is being like Christ or taking to heart his loving, generously self-forgetful style of life (2 Cor. 8: 9; Phil. 2: 1–12). The apostle pointed to Christ as the supreme moral exemplar, the paradigmatically good person, *the* teacher whose way of life we follow. St Irenaeus, among the most Pauline of the Church Fathers, expressed beautifully what such discipleship entails:

> There was no other way for us to learn than to see our Teacher and hear his voice with our own ears. It is by becoming imitators of his actions and doers of his words that we have communion with him. It is from him who has been perfect from before all creation that we, so lately made, receive fulfilment. (*Adversus Haereses*, 5. 1. 1)

Such an existence means being, or rather letting ourselves be, transformed into the likeness of the crucified and risen Christ through the power of the Holy Spirit (2 Cor. 3: 18). With this we move from the christological principle of moral existence to the pneumatological principle or 'life in the Spirit'. These two principles match Vatican II's conception of Christian life as involving the following of Christ (*Lumen Gentium*, 41) and the free acceptance of the call to holiness (ibid. 40).

2. Paul vividly describes the powerful, trinitarian transformation of human existence effected by the Holy Spirit. Through their adoption as God's sons and daughters, men and women are enabled through the Spirit to leave behind everything that is deadly, join the Son in praying to the Father, and live in expectation of a glorious, resurrected life to come (Rom. 8: 1–30). This moral transformation brought by the Spirit looks forward to the definitive liberation and glory to come. Christian pneumatological morality is nothing if not end-oriented, totally shaped by the new existence of the final, heavenly kingdom, which will bring a face-to-face sharing in the life of the tripersonal God. 'The end governs all,' as a classical maxim put it. It is such a hope which gives the courage to 'stand up' in the face of evil, a courage that Pastor Martin Niemöller found tragically lacking among too many Christians under the Nazi

regime.[23] The need to be totally oriented towards our final destiny probably prompts fewer questions than talk of 'liberation'.

John Paul II's 1993 encyclical *Veritatis Splendor* had as one of its major concerns the clarification of human freedom, and of the way it is limited inasmuch as it is 'called to accept the moral law given by God'. 'Human freedom', the Pope wrote, 'finds its authentic and complete fulfilment precisely in the acceptance of that law. God . . . knows perfectly what is good for the human being, and by virtue of his very love proposes this good in the commandments' (*Veritatis Splendor*, 35).[24] Vatican II had called the freedom with which we make 'this free choice of what is good' a 'freedom wounded by sin' and needing 'the help of God's grace' (*Gaudium et Spes*, 17). This teaching stands over against those false views of freedom that argue for an unqualified autonomy, as if less moral law would mean more freedom, and no law would bring perfect freedom. The OT story of the exodus, however, represents the God of the Sinai covenant and Decalogue to be precisely the faithful One who has delivered his people from bondage. God and God's law are liberating, not enslaving. The people of Israel were invited to accept their freedom as a gift that would bless their whole existence. Answerable to God for this gift, they pledged themselves in the covenant at Mount Sinai to avoid morally evil acts, which would destroy their freedom and make them slaves to sin.

At the time of the Babylonian Captivity prophets communicated the divine promise to give the people a 'new heart' created by God's 'spirit'. With this gift the people would be able to practice obedience to the Law and receive the divine blessings. In the words of the divine oracle, 'I will put my spirit within you, and make you follow my statutes and be careful to observe my ordinances' (Ezek. 36: 26–7). God promised to set his law 'within' his people and 'write it on their hearts' (Jer. 31: 33). Such language foreshadowed the NT gift of the Holy Spirit, who was be poured into human hearts (Rom. 5: 5) and dwell within the baptized as in a consecrated temple

---

[23] Niemöller, who was imprisoned in Sachsenhausen and Dachau concentration camps during the Second World War and later (1961–8) became president of the World Council of Churches, berated himself for not doing more in opposition to the Nazis, as we can see from the quotation with which this chapter opens. After the War, and especially in the United States, he often concluded his speeches with a version of those words. But there is no precise source. One must be content with J. Bartlett, *Familiar Quotations* (Boston: Little & Brown, 16th edn. 1992), 684.

[24] In his first encyclical John Paul II had written of our using the gift of freedom 'for everything that is our true good. Christ teaches us that the best use of freedom is charity, which takes concrete form in self-giving and in service' (*Redemptor Hominis*, 21).

(1 Cor. 3: 16–17; 6: 19). Guiding powerfully from within, the Spirit makes possible a life-giving obedience to the divine will (e.g. Rom. 8: 2, 4–6, 9, 14). Led by the Spirit, Christians can enjoy such fruits of the Spirit as joy, peace, gentleness, and self-control (Gal. 5: 22). Hence Paul can conclude that 'where the Spirit of the Lord is, there is freedom' (2 Cor. 3: 17).

The apostle presents here true freedom as participatory—that is to say, a freedom which comes through sharing in the new life given by the Spirit. Paul significantly speaks of the Spirit not only as 'the Spirit of God' (e.g. 1 Cor. 2: 11, 12, 14) but also as 'the Spirit of Christ' or 'the Spirit of God's Son' (e.g. Rom. 8: 9; Gal. 4: 6). The genitive is exquisitely rich with meaning. The Spirit originates and comes *from* God the Father or *from* the Son. But the genitive also suggests how the Spirit puts believers in a relationship *with* the Father and *with* the Son. Through the Spirit sent into their hearts, they can join the Son in praying 'Abba, Father' (Rom. 8: 15; Gal. 4: 6). The liberated and liberating life in the Spirit brings the faithful into a fellowship with the three divine persons.

Understood in this way, the gift of moral freedom comes from and leads to that communion in the divine life which we described above in Ch. 6. Here it is worth adding that the three persons of the Trinity set, so to speak, the standard for an authentically liberated life. Within the tripersonal God, utter self-giving and complete self-possession coincide. Within God unity (or communion) and distinction are in direct, not inverse, proportion: the unique unity and communion between the divine persons go hand in hand with the unique distinction. This truth of faith has enormous implications for human life with God. The closer one draws to the community of believers, to all suffering people, and in and through them to the tripersonal God, the more 'self-possessed' and 'distinct' one will become. Authentic self-possession grows in direct proportion to our self-giving union with the tripersonal God and all human beings.

In this way the following of Christ and the guidance of the Spirit make Catholic and all Christian morality utterly trinitarian. The christological and pneumatological principles we have proposed look here and hereafter to our deepest communion in love with the life of the tripersonal God (*Lumen Gentium*, 42).[25]

---

[25] For additional material see J. Mahoney, *The Making of Moral Theology: A Study of the Roman Catholic Tradition* (Oxford: Clarendon Press, 1989); W. J. Woods, *Walking with Faith: New Perspectives on the Sources and Shaping of Catholic Moral Life* (Collegeville, Minn.: Michael Glazier, 1998).

10

Basic Characteristics of Catholicism

After this I saw a great multitude which no one could number, of all nations and tribes and peoples and tongues.

(Revelation 7: 9).

When she had received the body of Christ, she beheld her soul . . . in the likeness of a tree fixing its roots in the wound in the side of Jesus Christ; she felt in some new and marvellous way that there was passing through this wound, as through a root, and penetrating into all her branches and fruit and leaves a wondrous sap which was the virtue of humanity and divinity of Jesus Christ.

(Gertrude the Great, *The Herald of Divine Love*, 3. 18)

After expounding the history of Catholic Christianity and its teaching, what should we say in drawing together and so summarizing the principal characteristics of the worldwide Catholic Church? Two thousand years of history and a current membership of a little over one billion people make this summary a daunting task. Before facing that task, let us repeat once again a point made in the Preface and subsequent chapters. The characteristics we present here will often hold true of other Christians and their communities. For that matter, some themes apply also to Judaism and to religions other than Christianity. But right to the end of this book we intend to write about Catholicism, without pausing to make elaborate comparisons and contrasts with other Christian churches and world religions. What is distinctive about the Catholic Church is not always and necessarily unique to Catholicism. Furthermore, we will continue to follow the advice from Aristotle that we invoked in the Preface: it is by examining the better or even the best features of something, rather than its defects, that we can more truly judge what we are looking at. We will not understand Buddhism, Hinduism, Islam, Judaism, or Catholicism by unilaterally attending to decadent and diseased expressions and adherents of these religions.

That said, any list of the key characteristics of Catholicism should include the following features: it is centred on Jesus, along with his mother Mary; it readily takes up material objects into its sacramental and devotional life; it practises the principle of 'both/and' (e.g. both grace and freedom; both faith and reason; both worldwide unity and new religious movements). The Catholic 'substance', to echo Paul Tillich's term, which we recalled in Ch. 2, will show forth at least those three characteristics.

CENTRED ON JESUS (AND MARY)

Any good anthology of spiritual writing witnesses to the way that Catholicism at its best and truest focuses its heart on Jesus, who came to live, die, and rise for our salvation.[1] In his *Epistle to the Romans*, written in the early second century when being brought in chains by soldiers to face death in Rome, St Ignatius of Antioch (d. *c*.107) showed his intense love for Christ. Being 'ground by the teeth of wild beasts' would make him 'God's wheat' and the 'pure bread of Christ' (4. 1). This martyr summed up his longing to die and be with Jesus: 'Let there come upon me fire and cross, and struggles with wild beasts: my being mauled and torn asunder, my bones racked, my limbs mangled, my whole body crushed, my being cruelly tortured by the devil, provided only that I may reach Jesus Christ' (ibid. 5. 3).

As we saw in Ch. 2, the medieval piety of St Francis of Assisi, St Clare, and so many other leading Catholic figures reflected a similar Jesus-centred life—something we find strikingly exemplified in the prayer by St Richard of Chichester (d. 1253): 'Thanks be to thee, my Lord Jesus Christ, for all the benefits which thou hast given me—for all the pains and insults thou hast borne for me. O most merciful Redeemer, Friend, and Brother, may I know thee more clearly, love thee more dearly, and follow thee more nearly.' A few years later St Gertrude the Great (d. *c*.1302) reported her own experiences in *The Herald of Divine Love*: 'Her most loving Jesus seemed to draw her toward himself by the breath of love of his

---

[1] See e.g. T. de Bertodano (ed.), *Treasury of the Catholic Church: Two Thousand Years of Spiritual Writing* (London: Darton, Longman & Todd, 1999); published in the USA as *The Book of Catholic Wisdom* (Chicago: Loyola Press, 2001).

pierced heart, and to wash her in the water flowing from it, and then to sprinkle her with the life-giving blood of his heart.' After echoing in this way the words of John 19: 34, she continued with the passage cited at the start of this chapter.[2] In his *Imitation of Christ* Thomas à Kempis (d. 1471) summarized what a Jesus-centred existence promised: 'Blessed are those who know how good it is to love Jesus . . . Love him and hold him for your friend; for when all others forsake you, he will not forsake you' (2. 7).

The Christ whom they knew and received in the Eucharist fostered the devotion of Ignatius of Antioch, Richard, Gertrude, Thomas à Kempis, and innumerable other Catholics. The initiative of Juliana of Liège, as we saw in Ch. 2, secured in 1264 the establishment of the Feast of Corpus Christi—for centuries celebrated with great devotion. St Francis de Sales (1567–1622) called the Eucharist 'the centre of Christian religion'.[3] In modern Ireland and around the world, many teachers used to quote the summary of Irish faith and practice offered by Augustine Birrell (1850–1933): 'It is the Mass that matters.' Beyond question, over the centuries eucharistic practice and piety have waxed and waned among Catholics, as we recalled in Ch. 7. But looking at the whole picture supports the conclusions: there is a special Catholic emphasis on attending the Sunday Eucharist,[4] and there is a particular Catholic intensity about receiving Christ in Holy Communion and praying before his presence in the Blessed Sacrament. One feels very close to the heart of Catholicism at a parish Mass on Sundays, especially in the moments after Holy Communion.

The Eucharist focuses a deep commitment to Christ, and so too does the widespread desire to have a crucifix and not simply a bare cross displayed in churches. Certainly an empty cross can emphatically recall Christ's rising into glory. He is no longer personally pinned to that terrifying instrument of suffering and death. All the same, Catholics want to see his body and its wounds. This instinct has also prompted them into erecting in different parts of the world wayside scenes of Calvary. At the foot of the cross Christ's Mother often keeps her lonely vigil.

---

[2] Trans. M. Winkworth, Classics of World Spirituality (Mahwah, NJ: Paulist Press, 1993), 176.

[3] See *Introduction to the Devout Life*, 2. 14. 1.

[4] This was vigorously recalled by John Paul II in his 1998 apostolic letter *Dies Domini* ('the Day of the Lord').

Catholics feel very comfortable with images of Mary standing by her dying Son or holding her new-born baby in her arms. To be sure, Christ does not appear in many wonderful paintings of the Annunciation left us by fifteenth-century Florentines and artists of other places and times. We see only Mary, the angel Gabriel, and sometimes one or two other figures. Christ's conception and birth are being announced; he is not yet visibly there. Nevertheless, he is not absent, as Andy Warhol (1928–87) brilliantly showed in his adaptation of an ancient masterpiece, a painting of the Annunciation by Leonardo da Vinci (1452–1519). Warhol has kept only the hands of Mary and the angel; between them he has highlighted a mountain, which one barely glimpsed in Leonardo's original painting. The change highlights effectively the coming down 'from above' of the divine Word in Christ's conception and birth. Even in the Annunciation and other compositions where Mary visibly stands or kneels alone, her Son is not missing. As we noted at the beginning of Ch. 2, a mosaic in St Mary Major's (Rome) shows her sitting on a throne beside her divine Son—in a work that commemorates the Council of Ephesus (AD 431) that upheld her already popular title of *Theotokos* (Mother of God). She conceived, gave birth to, and mothered Someone who was personally the Son of the God and the Saviour of the world.

Catholics, Orthodox, and some other Christians feel themselves understood and cherished by this woman and this mother.[5] A fourth-century papyrus gives us in a Greek version the first text of *Sub Tuum Presidium*, one of the oldest Christian prayers after those found in the Bible (e.g. the psalms in the OT and the Our Father in the NT). It begins: 'Beneath your protective shelter we flee, holy Mother of God.' This prayer, in an expanded form, continued to be used in the Middle Ages and beyond. Like the rosary with its joyful, sorrowful, and glorious mysteries—and, since 2002, mysteries of light—that commemorate the main stages in the story of Christ, the *Sub Tuum Presidium* moves from Mary to her Son: 'O glorious and blessed Virgin, our dear Lady, our mediator, our advocate, lead us to your Son, recommend us to your Son, present us to your Son.' An anonymous medieval poem, 'I sing of a maiden', in a courtly and charming manner honours Mary but does so precisely because of her Son. The opening verse says: 'I sing of a maiden that is makeless [matchless]:

---

[5] Nothing has expressed for us more forcefully a Catholic sense of Mary's loving concern than hearing the English soprano Lesley Garrett sing from Verdi's *The Force of Destiny* Leonora's plea to the Virgin to secure her pardon and protection.

King of all kinges to her Son she ches [choose].' The poem describes Christ being conceived as silently as the dew falling on the grass in April, and ends: 'Mother and maiden was never none but she: well may such a lady Goddes mother be.'

Millions of Catholics and other Christians have cherished Mary as the loving helper of the suffering and a compassionate advocate for sinful human beings. Statues of Mary with her Son, stained glass portrayals from medieval Europe, and Eastern icons from all centuries present Marian devotion at its best and truest, with Mary's beauty, nobility, and importance all derived through the Holy Spirit and from her Son. Hundreds of Marian legends emerged in the Middle Ages and were gathered in collections made in France, Germany, Italy, Spain, and elsewhere. Some of those legends, however, expressed and encouraged a flawed devotion to Mary, one that for selfish reasons neglected Christ. Erasmus of Rotterdam set out to correct this situation, by ridiculing and exaggerating in a 'colloquy' first printed in 1526 'the shameless entreaties' some people made to Mary. In an imaginary letter he quoted her as saying: 'they demanded everything from me alone, as if my Son were always a baby... Sometimes a merchant, off to Spain to make a fortune, commits to me the chastity of his mistress...A profane soldier, hired to butcher people, cries out to me: "Blessed Virgin, give me rich booty!" ' After listing these and other 'irreverent' prayers, Erasmus passed to what he called some 'absurd' ones: 'An unmarried girl cries: "Mary, give me a rich and handsome bridegroom!" A married one, "Give me fine children." A pregnant woman, "Give me an easy delivery." ... A doddering old man, "Let me grow young again." '[6]

Erasmus had been once (1512), or possibly twice (1514), to the shrine of Our Lady of Walsingham and was only too ready to embellish and embroider popular devotion to the Virgin Mary. But we can understand Reformers crying out against such a distortion of petitionary prayer and marginalizing of Christ as the Saviour of all sinners. But it is harder to feel much sympathy for the outbursts of iconoclasts, who turned many beautiful statues and pictures of Mary into their special target.

Martin Luther maintained some well-founded insights into the unique role and grandeur of Mary in the whole story of salvation. Musicians, even

---

[6] Erasmus, *Ten Colloquies*, trans. C. R. Thompson (Indianapolis: Bobbs Merrill, 1957), 60–1.

more than writers,[7] ensured much continuity with the happier aspects of medieval veneration of Jesus' Mother. Among the oldest Marian antiphons, the *Salve Regina* ('Hail, holy Queen, Mother of mercy') dates back at least to the end of the eleventh century. Its tenderly devotional language and its exquisite setting in Gregorian chant (or plainsong) have made it enduringly popular in the Catholic world and beyond. Three other ancient Marian antiphons are also much loved: *Alma Redemptoris Mater* ('Kind Mother of the Redeemer'), *Ave Regina Coelorum* ('Hail Queen of the Heavens'), and *Regina Coeli* ('Queen of Heaven'). The *Stabat Mater* ('The Mother was standing [at the cross]'), a dramatic medieval hymn describing the suffering of the Virgin Mary during her Son's passion and crucifixion, became widely used at Mass and for the Stations of the Cross (see Ch. 2). The fifteenth-century Litany of Loreto, the name coming from the Marian pilgrimage site in Italy, enumerates various titles and qualities of the Virgin Mary (e.g. 'Holy Mother of God', 'Seat of Wisdom', and 'Comforter of the Afflicted') and adds the invocation 'Pray for us.' Eventually it was set to music by Mozart. Along with the *Ave Maria* (inspired by Luke 1: 28, 42–3) and the *Magnificat* (Luke 1: 46–55), the *Stabat Mater*, and the four major Marian antiphons (see above) were set to music by Bach, Brahms, Dvořák, Gounod, Haydn, Palestrina, Schubert, Verdi, Vivaldi, and other famous composers. Not all of them composed settings for every one of these texts, but some of them composed many settings for one or other of the Marian antiphons and prayers: for instance, Palestrina left more than thirty settings for the *Magnificat*, and Vivaldi came up with four settings for the *Salve Regina*. The most celebrated setting of all is arguably Bach's composition for the *Magnificat*. Such music conveys perhaps best of all the enduring place of Mary in Catholic Christianity, just as the *Akathistos*, an ancient song of praise to the Mother of God, expresses the devotion to Mary among Eastern Christians, both Catholic and Orthodox.[8]

---

[7] Normally the three great figures in European literature are reckoned to be Dante (d. 1321), Shakespeare (d. 1616), and Johann Wolfgang Goethe (d. 1832). The Virgin Mary occupies a central place in Dante's *Divine Comedy*; she is very minor in the works of Shakespeare; in Goethe's masterpiece, *Faust*, she is tenderly invoked by the tragic figure of Gretchen.

[8] No book conveys better the place of Mary in the Catholic imagination than C. H. Ebertshäuser *et al.* (eds.), *Mary: Art, Culture, and Religion through the Ages* (New York: Crossroad, 1998). See also J. Pelikan, *Mary through the Centuries: Her Place in the History of Culture* (New Haven, Conn.: Yale University Press, 1999).

As our first characteristic of the Catholic Church, we have highlighted the way it is centred on Jesus Christ, along with his mother Mary. The fact that Catholicism has persistently taken up material objects into its sacramental and devotional life forms a second characteristic.

THE MATERIAL AND THE SPIRITUAL

In Ch. 1, we saw how Catholic Christianity, from the time of Ignatius of Antioch and Irenaeus of Lyons in the second century, fostered the sense that all human reality and, indeed, the whole material cosmos has been touched, blessed, and changed by the 'Word becoming flesh' (John 1: 14). The incarnation of the Son of God, understood together with the life, death, and resurrection, and sending of the Spirit that followed, transformed the physical, bodily reality of the created world. To be sure, the 'goodness' (Gen. 1: 1–25) and 'beauty' (Wis. 13: 1–9) of all that was made already showed forth the Author of all goodness and beauty. In a special way, being created in the divine image and likeness (Gen. 1: 26–7), all men and women have always symbolized God. Add too that in the life of God's chosen people certain persons (e.g. the OT kings, prophets, and priests) and places (e.g. the Temple in Jerusalem) manifested God and communicated the divine blessings. Nevertheless, the incarnation brought a quantum leap in the way in which such material realities as water, bread, wine, oil, and human bodies were lifted to a new level and spiritualized to become the channels of the tripersonal God's saving self-revelation or 'bearers' of the divine holiness (see the beginning of Ch. 7).

Through the seven sacraments of the Church, things that we see, hear, touch, taste, and smell bring us the divine truth and power. The water poured in baptism, bread and wine consecrated at the Eucharist, hands imposed in ordination, oil smeared on the foreheads and hands of the sick, bodies joined in matrimony, and the other perceptible signs that constitute the sacraments communicate various spiritual blessings and a share in the life of the tripersonal God. The Church's sacraments transfigure material things and actions of a world which is already 'charged with the grandeur of God' (Gerard Manley Hopkins, 'God's Grandeur').

The sacramentalizing of the material world finds its heart in the seven sacraments that initiate and nourish a share in the life of the all-holy God. But this spiritualizing of the world and human beings extends beyond the seven sacraments: in particular, to such sacramentals as the ashes Catholics receive on their foreheads on Ash Wednesday and the palms they carry home on Palm Sunday. In the proper sense, sacramentals are holy practices, prayers, and things officially approved and blessed in the Catholic Church. They include some of traditions that were fostered by Franciscans and Dominicans and have never lost their popularity: for instance, making the Stations of the Cross (especially during the weeks leading up to Good Friday), Christmas cribs, which recall Christ's birth among us, and the saying of the rosary. In Ch. 2 we noted how these and other practices aimed to sacramentalize or consecrate to God through Christ the whole of life. We also recalled in that chapter the much older practice of pilgrimages, which can bring a fresh start in life and inculcate a sense of human existence as one long spiritual journey. Along with pilgrimages and images, structures (catacombs and then churches) played their part in sacralizing life right from the early centuries of Christianity. Obviously buildings and images are central to the official worship of the Church. But even when the sacraments are not being administered, the churches, statues, mosaics, paintings, and stained glass windows are there to lift to God the minds and hearts of those who visit or simply pass by. For Eastern Christians, both Orthodox and Catholics, icons are endued with divine power and help the whole world to symbolize God. Almost as old as Christian art, 'holy water' or blessed water has been used for such religious purposes as spiritual cleansing and dedication from at least the fourth century.

Some of the sacramentals we have mentioned, such as the palms distributed on Palm Sunday, originate with the history of Jesus (Mark 11: 8). Others such as the usage of sweet-smelling incense, go back even further, in this case to rites followed in the Jerusalem Temple (Ps. 141: 2). The scented smoke of burning incense that rose to God meant 'squandering' something costly in a gift of unreserved love. Incense has maintained a central place in the worship of Orthodox Christians. Catholics use it frequently in processions and in the celebration of Mass.

Living for years in Italy, we have enjoyed the various eating customs associated with the religious feasts. During the Christmas season we eat *panettone*, a bread made with eggs, dried fruit, and butter. Easter brings the *colomba* or dove-shaped cake. In other countries hot cross buns or buns marked with a cross have been eaten on Good Friday. In Italy, Spain, and some Spanish-speaking countries, people eat sweets called 'the bones of the saints' when All Saints' and All Souls' Days come around on 1 and 2

November, respectively. Such customs link the secular (in this case, eating) with the sacred, and punctuate the year in a way that gently reinforces a feeling of moving through holy time to a final meeting with God.

Saints play their part in spiritualizing the year and the movement of human life. It can be a matter of the annual celebration of the feast-day of a saint who has a special connection with some nation, city, village, parish, shrine, or person. On 17 March Irish Catholics around the world continue to celebrate with gusto the feast of St Patrick; Scots and those of a Scottish origin do the same on 30 November, the feast of St Andrew, their patron saint. On 13 June Italians pack into Padua for the feast of St Antony (d. 1231), a Franciscan friar who spent the last period of his life in or near that city. Many Catholics, year by year, observe their 'name-day' or feast-day of the saint after whom they are called. Although the day of their birth may not coincide with the feast-day of their saint, it is the feast-day that often counts more for them and their families. Sometimes the 'special function' of a saint figures prominently on the feast-day. Thus St Antony (d. 356), an Egyptian Christian who organized the life of hermits in the desert, is celebrated in Italy and elsewhere as a friend and protector of animals—and, by extension, of goldfish, canaries, and other pets. On his feast-day, 17 January, the Mass ends with wine and special sweet bread distributed to the faithful as they leave the church, while an assortment of animals wait aside (and occasionally are brought inside) to be blessed. At St Eusebius' in Rome this event has become so popular that the cats, dogs, and horses, which used to be able to fit into the church, now have to wait for their blessing in the square outside with their owners.

Around the world Catholics use a wide variety of blessings for their homes, their workplaces, and for other material things that enter their lives and can be consecrated to become part of joining Christ in their pilgrimage home to God. Thus there are blessings for factories, farms, homes, hospitals, libraries, offices, shops, aircraft, motor cars, and ships (including fishing fleets). Blessings are available for engaged couples, families, nurses and doctors (with their patients), teachers (along with their students at the start of the academic year), travellers, and other categories of persons. The urbanizing of the world and the flight from the land may have meant, for a while, a decline in such practices. But now blessings seem to be booming again, and many families treasure, for example, the annual blessing of their homes around Easter time. Through such sacramentals, the powerful presence of Christ in every aspect of our bodily and human existence can become more perceptible. Some people fear that such practices bring a lapse into magical superstitions. But this will not happen so long as believers remember that blessings and other sacramentals aim at putting all times, places, and activities in relationship with Christ.[9]

The sanctification of *time* goes together with the sacramentalizing of material realities through sacraments and sacramentals. Such sanctification happens, of course, through the celebration of the seasons and feasts of the liturgical year. But time is also sanctified through the Liturgy of the Hours, when Catholics and other Christians gather at different times of day or night in cathedrals, parish churches, monasteries, and other places to hear passages of scripture (and other sacred writings) and to sing or recite together psalms and further prayers. Those who follow this daily programme of official worship give praise to God, share in Christ's priestly office, and intercede for the salvation of the whole world. Vatican II's first document, *Sacrosanctum Concilium*, sets out beautifully how the divine office or Liturgy of the Hours sanctifies the passage of time on a daily and annual basis.

BOTH/AND

The first two sections of this chapter on persistent characteristics of Catholicism have laid the ground for the third. It is typically Catholic to embrace 'both/and', and hold together things that some Christians may tend to oppose to each other. Hence Catholics, like Orthodox, do not accept an 'either/or' in the case of Jesus and his Mother. Many Protestant Reformers and their followers hold that honouring Mary (and, for that matter, other saints) somehow blurs the unique role of Christ as Saviour. But Catholics do not admit a choice here; they want Jesus *and* his Mother. It is likewise with the sacraments and that broad range of sacramental practices that we just summarized above. Sacramentals remain subordinate to baptism, the Eucharist, and the other five sacraments, but belong with them in consecrating to God through Christ our entire bodily and material existence.

Our opening two chapters provided numerous examples of the characteristically Catholic readiness to hold together, often in tension, things

[9] See M. Walsh, *Dictionary of Catholic Devotions* (San Francisco: HarperSan Francisco, 1993).

that others could separate or even oppose. Let us recall some examples of a Catholic 'both/and'.

1. Catholics unite in their confession of faith both divine grace and human freedom, rejecting, on the one hand, a Pelagian-style 'do it yourself' salvation, and, on the other hand, the kind of emphasis on divine predestination and sin's enduring harm to human freedom that would turn salvation into a puppet-show arranged by the omnipotent God. Debates flared up over works that St Augustine wrote late in his life and which pushed too far God's predestining will (Chs. 1 and 6), and over some Reformers' views on sin destroying human freedom (Ch. 2 above). Notoriously, no theological explanation is available for the mysterious interaction of God's sovereign grace with the human will, as we saw in Ch. 7 when recalling the sixteenth-century debates about grace and free will. The need to endorse both grace and freedom comes through the old advice: 'Pray as if everything depended on God, and work as if everything depended on yourself.' Dante knew that human salvation always comes through God's grace; yet he called free will 'the greatest gift God made to his creatures' (*Paradiso*, 5. 19–22).

2. A related Catholic 'both/and', one shared by other Christians, concerns the love of God and love of neighbour. Catholics want to give God time in prayer, either alone or with others, but they also want to care for all their neighbours in need (see Ch. 9). From the very beginning, a this-worldly and an other-worldly commitment have characterized Catholic Christianity. The ancient *Didache* enjoined not only the regular practice of daily prayer (8. 3) but also generous help to those in need (4. 5–8). Chapter 9 above quoted Tertullian's beautiful picture of how married life entailed both prayer and assisting the needy. Chapter 1 recalled the practical love towards the plague-stricken shown by second- and third-century Christians whose devotion to Christ could also bring them to martyrdom. Catholics, at their best, have always seen (*a*) satisfying the spirit's hunger for God through prayer and (*b*) feeding the hungry of this world as a 'both/and'. In modern times, an engagement with God in prayer and a practical love towards others have gone hand in hand for Catholic or Catholic-inspired groups that run soup kitchens, staff leprosaria, provide dying derelicts with care and digni-fied shelter, and give homes to the mentally handicapped.

Here a Catholic 'both/and' emerges strikingly through the sup-port gladly given to both contemplative and active religious institutes.

Rank-and-file Catholics happily accept a kind of 'division of labour': Benedictine, Camaldolese, Carmelite, Carthusian, Cistercian, and other monastic groups of men and women who lead a life of silence and prayer are understood to support spiritually the work of consecrated men and women who serve others through schools, colleges, hospitals, and other social 'ministries'. A vertical commitment to God unites with an horizontal commitment to human needs.

3. Mentioning schools and colleges already hints at a further Catholic 'both/and': both faith and reason. Catholicism never embraced the opposition between Athens (standing for reason) and Jerusalem (standing for faith) that we saw being vigorously supported by Tertullian. Through the Cappadocians (Ch. 1) and Thomas Aquinas (Ch. 2) and down to the 1998 encyclical of John Paul II, *Fides et Ratio*, Catholic Christianity has never accepted a separation between God's gift of faith and the cultivation of human reason. St Athanasius of Alexandria and nearly all the Fathers of the Church had received an excellent secular education in the classics of Greek and Latin literature. When barbarian invasions tore Europe apart, the Irish and other monasteries kept learning alive. Charlemagne (d. 814) gathered his court scholars, collected many valuable manuscripts in his library at Aachen, and promoted the professional study of Latin, a language that held together the Western world. With gratitude we recall the contribution of many scholarly religious, such as Rosvitha, a tenth-century canoness of an abbey in Saxony. She was not only very learned in the scriptures, the writings from the Fathers of the Church, and classical Latin literature, but also composed in Latin a number of poems and plays. A few hundred years later Carmelites, Dominicans, Franciscans, and members of other religious orders played a major role in developing European universities. By leading a renewal in theological learning and recovering the philosophy of Aristotle, Thomas Aquinas expressed for all times a harmony between faith and reason. Following his lead, Dante blended human learning and divine revelation in the *Comedy*. His two companions in that masterpiece were Virgil and Beatrice, the former symbolizing true humanism and the latter divine wisdom. From the sixteenth century Jesuits were 'the schoolmasters' of Europe, not to mention the role they played in education in the Americas, the Middle East, India, Japan, the Philippines, Australia, and other parts of the world.

Occasionally tensions grew between faith and reason or between the truths of revelation and worldly learning, above all after the rise of the natural sciences. Sometimes these tensions arose from rational, scientific, and materialist claims to enjoy total authority over the interpretation of reality. Sometimes Catholics, in particular Church officials, were to blame. After making the right decision to reform the calendar of Julius Caesar, Roman authorities proved disastrously intransigent in the case of Galileo Galilei (1564–1642), as we saw in Ch. 5. Since his observations that the earth moved around the sun seemed to challenge the Church's authority to interpret the scriptures, he was forced to deny those observations. His case came to symbolize for many people an antagonism between science and religion. But all truth is based in God, and there can never be final opposition between religious and scientific truths. Nowadays more and more people realize how advances in the life sciences and biotechnology need to be evaluated ethically and religiously; otherwise they can threaten the dignity, environment, and even survival of the human race (see Chs. 5 and 9). Full and genuine dialogue between faith and scientific reason is more urgent than ever. In the case of Galileo, ecclesiastical officials made a tragic mistake. Fairness, however, suggests retrieving other names from history: a Jesuit mathematician and astronomer, Christopher Clavius (*c.*1537–1612), led the team for Pope Gregory XIII that in 1582 reformed the calendar that Julius Caesar had devised and which had accumulated an error of ten days by the late sixteenth century. The new, 'Gregorian' calendar eventually became standard for the life of the world. Sadly Clavius, who confirmed in correspondence with other leading scientists the discoveries Galileo had made with his telescope, died before Galileo's problems began with some theologians of the Holy Office of the Inquisition. An Austrian abbot, Johann Gregor Mendel (1822–84), through his experiments with peas in the monastery garden, demonstrated the primary source of variability in plants and animals and became the father of genetics. In their different ways, Clavius and Mendel symbolize what Thomas Aquinas stood for: the basic harmony of all truth, whether known through divine revelation or human research.

4. We could pile up a long list of further 'both/ands' that typify Catholicism: for instance, both Eastern and Western ways of worship; both married and celibate priests (the first being typically the case in Eastern Catholicism and the second in Western Catholicism); both the (very many) lay members and the (comparatively few) ordained ministers; both saints and sinners belonging to the Catholic

Church;[10] both institutional structures and charismatic initiatives. The final 'both/and' provides the material for the closing section of this chapter.

From the time of Ignatius of Antioch, Cyprian of Carthage, and Augustine of Hippo (see Ch. 1), we find Catholic Christians shrinking from divisions and sharing a gut feeling that worldwide unity must be maintained. Inevitable and, one should add, healthy tensions have continued to arise between unity and diversity, and between the inherited institutions (essentially the pastoral government of bishops in communion with the bishop of Rome) and fresh movements inspired by the Holy Spirit. In a world that now includes around 20,000 separate Christian denominations, Catholics believe and hope that new movements, led by Spirit-filled and Spirit-guided men and women, should not lead to separation and any breaking of communion with others. Rather they should enrich the whole Church, whether these movements last for only a short time or for many centuries, as was the case with the religious families founded by Benedict, Scholastica, Dominic, Francis, Clare, and Ignatius.

Undoubtedly the institutional authority of bishops has at times been exercised foolishly and sinfully against men and women who emerged charismatically with fresh ideas and new commitments. But that authority has often worked to defend and promote people raised by the Holy Spirit to minister to others in times of crisis and challenge.

Our final 'both/and', both the institutional and the charismatic, leads naturally to the agenda for the closing chapter, dedicated to our vision of the major challenges facing the Catholic Church at start of the third millennium.

---

[10] We saw in Ch. 1 how strongly St Augustine upheld this 'both/and' against the Donatists.

II

Current Challenges

Babylon the great city will be violently thrown down, and will be found no more. (Revelation 18: 21)

One of the seven angels...showed me the holy city Jerusalem coming down out of heaven from God.

(Revelation 21: 9–10)

Our first ten chapters have been predominantly descriptive of the Catholic tradition. We set ourselves to summarize the history of the Catholic Church (Chs. 1 and 2), clarify its doctrines (from the nature of revelation in Ch. 3 to morality in Ch. 9), and spell out its basic characteristics (Ch. 10). Those chapters attended to the past and present state of Catholicism. Before ending this book, what dreams and concerns do we want to share about the future of the Catholic Church?

Professor Umberto Eco and Cardinal Carlo Maria Martini, when taking stock of Catholicism and, indeed, of the whole world, in a remarkable exchange of letters, began with the future of our race and planet. Should we fear the future or hope in the future? Eco had no difficulty in listing some ecological and other major threats:

the uncontrolled and uncontrollable proliferation of nuclear waste; acid rain; the disappearing Amazon; the hole in the ozone; the migrating disinherited masses knocking, often with violence, at the doors of prosperity; the hunger of entire continents; new, incurable pestilence; the selfish destruction of the soil; global warming; meltdown glaciers; the construction of our own clones through genetic engineering.

Eco even entertained the thought of humanity's 'necessary suicide': we must 'perish in order to rescue those species' that we have 'almost obliterated', and 'Mother Earth' herself, who is 'denatured and suffocating'. Without minimizing the terrifying portents listed by Eco, Martini insisted that no human or satanic power can destroy the hope of believers: the virtue of hope is, after all, a gift from God.[1]

But, if we look beyond the ecological, political, and social challenges that all human beings face, what particular issues confront the Catholic Church as it moves ahead in the third millennium? What are the challenges that arise from faith and invite discernment, action, and deeper commitment? At least four areas call for scrutiny: ongoing conversion to Jesus Christ; over-centralization; the ministry of laypeople and women; and dialogue and mission.

CONVERSION TO CHRIST

With a view to the Great Jubilee of the Year 2000 and the start of the third millennium, special assemblies of bishops from each of the five continents took place in Rome: the Assembly for Africa (1994), America (1997), Asia (1998), Oceania (1998), and Europe (1991 and 1999).[2] These assemblies, along with the 'apostolic exhortations' that Pope John Paul II published later on the basis of their work and recommendations, mirror the present state and future hopes of the Catholic Church around the world. The bishops, like committed Christians everywhere, wanted above all to promote among believers, and in particular among Catholics, a more vital encounter with the living Christ.

Ecclesia in America ('The Church in America') of 22 January 1999, the exhortation in which the Pope drew together the proceedings of the 1997 Assembly for America, highlighted the encounter with the living Jesus Christ as the path to a radical conversion for the Catholics of North, Central, and South America. Through the powerful presence of their risen Lord, Catholics will be enabled to maintain their Christian identity. Thus they will be guided through the Holy Spirit to renewed fellowship in the life of the Church, which will strengthen them to work in solidarity for the good of all human beings and to bring to the world the good news that is

---

[1] U. Eco and C. M. Martini, *Belief or Nonbelief?* (New York: Arcade Publishing, 2000), 21, 30.

[2] No document was issued after the 1991 Synod of Bishops for Europe; the apostolic exhortation *Ecclesia in Europa* ('The Church in Europe') to follow the 1999 assembly has not yet (in April 2002) been issued.

Jesus himself. What shows clearly through *Ecclesia in America* is that the road to evangelization and social action leads through a radical conversion to Jesus and a life nourished by ecclesial communion and, above all, by the celebration of the Eucharist. This apostolic exhortation proposes to Catholics a style of life totally centred on Jesus, experienced and known through a prayerful commitment to the scriptures and the Eucharist, 'the outstanding moment of encounter with the living Christ' (no. 35).

Much of the language of *Ecclesia in America* matches that of evangelical Christians, who have found in Jesus their 'personal Saviour' and whose deeply felt moment of conversion continues to support their adherence to one of the Protestant Churches. The language differs markedly from positive assessments of Christianity that one sometimes reads elsewhere. Take, for example, the following confession of faith, which Charles Davis composed in the 1970s:

I am a Christian because the Christian tradition, with its symbols, doctrines and values, with its communities and institutions, has in fact mediated for me an experience of transcendent reality and has opened for me a level of consciousness and way of living I recognize as valuable and liberating. I find much truth and value in it.[3]

Here Davis wrote of Christianity's 'symbols, doctrines and values', of an 'experience of transcendent reality' (lower case!), and of his own new 'level of consciousness' and liberating 'way of living'. It is not that all this was false, but recognizing 'much truth and value' simply did not reach the heart of the matter. A confession along the lines of *Ecclesia in America* would state: 'I am a Catholic because, through the scriptures, sacramental life, and fellowship of the Catholic Church, I have experienced deeply Jesus Christ, and through receiving his Holy Spirit have received the light and strength to share this good news and work in solidarity with a suffering world.' Davis's confession was incompletely personalist, in that it included 'I am', 'for me' (twice), 'I find', and a nod towards other believers, those 'communities' and 'institutions' which hand on 'the Christian tradition'. One missed a robustly personalist and communitarian faith, which would follow the apostolic exhortation in bringing repeatedly into the picture the living Jesus, his Holy Spirit, the Virgin Mary, and the wide range of human beings who make up the Catholic Church and the world in which Catholics live.

---

[3] C. Davis, *Temptations of Religion* (New York: Harper & Row, 1973), 23–4.

The conversion to Christ entails experiencing and believing in him as fully human *and* truly divine. Anything less, such as the deconstructed versions of Jesus offered by Richard Holloway and others,[4] cannot sustain a living faith, still less the kind of conversion *Ecclesia in America* and mainstream evangelical Christians want to encourage. To answer the utterly key question 'Who do you say that I am?' (Mark 8: 29) by presenting Jesus as an outstanding prophet who little by little was posthumously deified not only betrays the common creed that Christians recite every Sunday but also does not correspond to the data we summarized in Ch. 4. Jesus made some astonishing claims for his own personal authority and identity; a theological understanding about him as divine Lord and Son of God developed very early, even before Paul wrote his letters. Bishop Holloway calls on his readers to follow the way of Jesus. But following Jesus finds its power in our beliefs about him. Here the Bishop is simply out of touch with dedicated Anglicans, Catholics, and other Christians. Their faith in the crucified and risen Son of God supplies the strength to serve and, sometimes, to die for Jesus' brothers and sisters. Having visited South Africa and El Salvador, the Bishop should have known better. Who would risk death on the basis of his and others' deconstructed version of Christ and Christianity?

Belief and behaviour work vigorously together. Integrity in everyday life and faithful responsibility in human relationships draw their strength from faith in Christ and the God whom he revealed. The moral courage of Catholics and, indeed, of all Christians depends upon their belief in the tripersonal God revealed through Jesus' life and death and the coming of the Holy Spirit. Hence we share the dream of *Ecclesia in America*—that more and more Catholics and others will let themselves be drawn into a deep, life-transforming experience of Jesus. That kind of experience of him in prayer and community will give great vigour to their faith, which will then radically reshape their behaviour.

Here Catholics share common ground with many Methodists, Pentecostals, and other evangelical Christians. John Wesley (1703–91), the founder of Methodism, cherished his May 1738 conversion experience, when his 'heart was strangely warmed' and he began an intense missionary life thirsting for holiness and proclaiming the saving love of Jesus. In

---

[4] See R. Holloway, *Doubts and Loves: What Is Left of Christianity* (Edinburgh: Canongate, 2001); see the review by G. O'Collins, *The Tablet*, 27 October 2001, 1529–30.

spreading the good news to others and revitalizing the faith of their fellow believers, evangelical Christians of every kind emphasize personal conversion and a deep experience of Christ's presence and power. Pentecostal Christians, as the name indicates, highlight their experience of the Holy Spirit and the 'charisms' or gifts of the Spirit celebrated by St Paul (e.g. 1 Cor. 12: 1–11; 14: 1–40). The Charismatic Renewal, which Vatican II encouraged (*Lumen Gentium*, 12) and which from 1967 spread from Catholic groups on a number of university campuses in the United States, has shown deep affinity with Pentecostals, not least in the pursuit of personal holiness fostered by the Spirit.

Chapter 2 of this book recalled some of the medieval and later developments that invigorated a fresh attachment to Christ: the rosary; the Stations of the Cross; the *devotio moderna* ('modern devotion') of Thomas à Kempis; the spiritual teaching of Carmelites, Dominicans, Franciscans, Jesuits, and other male and female institutes of religious; devotion to the Sacred Heart of Jesus; the encouragement Pope Pius X gave to frequent Holy Communion; and the rest. Many of these aids to a Christ-centred life remain as strong as ever. But there are also such new developments as the Latin American 'base communities', local groups of Catholics (and other Christians) who worship and study the scriptures, seek a communal encounter with the risen Christ, and aim to revitalize the life of the Church and use their gifts in the service of others. The Second Vatican Council hoped, as we saw in Ch. 3, that a prayerful and constant contact with the scriptures would give new life and light to Catholics everywhere. Adopting the language of St Paul (Phil. 3: 8), the Council exhorted all the faithful to 'learn the surpassing knowledge of Jesus Christ by frequent reading of the divine scriptures' (*Dei Verbum*, 25).

What we read can feed a Christ-centred prayer. So too can what we see. And here we wish to express our hope that the Catholic faithful and, especially, Catholic families might once again put sacred images back on the walls of their homes. One can well understand what fuelled a certain dislike for such images: much popular religious art was sentimental kitsch. But many tasteful and moving crucifixes, statues, icons, and other religious pictures are now available around the world. Graceful images of Christ and his saints recall his presence and foster love for him. Western Catholics could well follow the example of Orthodox (and Eastern Catholics) who bring icons into their homes and thus create a 'beautiful corner' or 'holy place' in their lives.

DECENTRALIZATION

Many committed Catholics and not a few other Christians judge that the Catholic Church has become over-centralized, with too much power being exercised by those who run offices for the pope in the Roman Curia. The Second Vatican Council endorsed the principle of episcopal collegiality, or the role of bishops who together form a teaching, priestly, and pastoral college and who in communion with the bishop of Rome bear responsibility for the worldwide Church. Occasionally, when a general council of the Church takes place, the bishops meet to exercise this collegial role in a solemn fashion. But they exercise this role also, albeit in a more limited way, when they assemble in national conferences to plan policies and take decisions for the Catholic Church in their country.

The revolution in world communications and transport has made the Catholic Church also a kind of global village. Contacts with offices in the Roman Curia through letters, faxes, phone calls, and e-mails have been facilitated in unheard-of ways. From Rome it is possible to have instant access to and information from almost every Catholic diocese and even community. That new development in Catholicism has also its shadow side: central officials can be tempted to engage in micro-management of what belongs to particular communities. They can lack trust in the bishops and other leaders 'on the spot'. But this is to question Vatican II's understanding of the mission of the diocesan bishop: he has the primary responsibility for leading his people.

Early in the twentieth century many Catholics welcomed the new era encouraged by Pope Pius XI, when in so-called mission countries local priests, instead of foreign missionaries, became the bishops. 'Rome rule means home rule,' they announced proudly. Today the bishops around the world are generally natives of their own country. Yet home rule is at times spoiled by Rome rule. Instead of being the last court of appeal, some officials of the Roman Curia claim to be the 'judges' in the first instance. They seem to fear that the bishops and other leaders on the spot are almost sure to get things wrong when faced with major issues, and that they somehow lack guidance from the Holy Spirit to lead the local churches in the right direction. These officials want to maintain good order and Catholic unity (or is it sometimes a false uniformity?) by exercising centralized power over the particular churches.

Relationships between the centralized Roman Congregations (or papal ministries) and the national episcopal conferences do not always run smoothly. While local synods of bishops flourished in the first millennium of Christianity, since the sixteenth century Roman Congregations have been entrusted with the Pope's delegated authority. The whole Church would be blessed if the interaction were better co-ordinated between the curial officials in Rome, on the one hand, and the episcopal conferences and local bishops, on the other. Blessed John XXIII decided that the executive secretaries of the Roman Congregations should be bishops, so that they could deal as equals with diocesan bishops. Has this change continued to be fully helpful in the life of the worldwide Church?

In expounding the limits in the duty and rights of public authority to intervene in social and economic affairs, Pius XI introduced the principle of subsidiarity (*Quadragesimo Anno*, 79), a principle later approved and further applied by Pius XII and John XXIII (e.g. the latter's *Mater et Magistra*, 53, 80). In essence the principle teaches that decisions and activities which naturally belong to a lower level should not be taken to a higher level. This means, for instance, that central organs of a state should not intervene unnecessarily with local authorities. The Second Vatican Council appealed to the principle of subsidiarity in dealing with international co-operation in economic matters (*Gaudium et Spes*, 85–6) and when indicating the limits of the state's responsibility in education (*Gravissimum Educationis*, 3, 6). Although introduced into Catholic teaching on social and economic affairs, the principle has been extended to the life of the Church. On 2 February 1946 when addressing the cardinals in a consistory at which he created thirty-two new cardinals, Pius XII stated that subsidiarity could be applied to the internal life of the Church. He set the principle over against the centralization of totalitarian dictatorships that had crucified Europe in the first half of the twentieth century. Two international synods of bishops (1967 and 1969) voted in favour of applying the principle of subsidiarity to canon law and to the functioning of national conferences of bishops. Hence subsidiarity became one of the principles for the reform of the Code of Canon Law (promulgated in 1983).[5] Subsidiarity, or not taking to a higher level matters that can and should be dealt with at a lower, local level, clearly

---

[5] See J. A. Coriden *et al.* (eds.), *The Code of Canon Law: A Text and Commentary* (Mahwah, NJ: Paulist Press, 1985), 6, 21, 312.

constitutes a healthy principle for our lives together, both in human society at large and in the Catholic Church in particular. But some officials in the Roman Curia do not always honour the principle in practice and occasionally question it in theory.[6]

Some OT passages suggest an early implementation of the principle of subsidiarity when describing the co-ordination of Israelite life under the leadership of Moses. Prompted by his father-in-law, Moses reorganized the way disputes among the people were to be handled. Ordinary cases were to be heard by lay leaders and judges. Moses was to adjudicate only in those cases that lacked legal precedent and required a special divine oracle (Exod. 18: 13–27; see Deut. 1: 9–18). A similar practice of subsidiarity shows up when the Book of Deuteronomy legislates for ordinary cases to come before local, subordinate judges. Only difficult cases were to be taken to the priests or the presiding judge (Deut. 17: 8–13). The first books of the OT seem to support the value of the principle of subsidiarity for the people of God. Could we see Moses as an early role-model for the practice of healthy subsidiarity?

Our reflections on collegiality and subsidiarity go beyond administrative practicalities in a desire to promote the life of the Church as communion (see the last section of Ch. 8 above). The pope exercises a specific ministry of unity for and within the whole Church; he does so by fostering a global communion that reflects the exchange of love between the Father, the Son, and the Holy Spirit. Bishops, through the collegial mission that they have received by their episcopal ordination, will further solidarity among their own faithful more effectively when they can live out more fully the episcopal brotherhood to which they have been called.

MINISTRY OF LAY PERSONS AND WOMEN

In one of his most famous statements, St Paul pointed out how being baptized into Christ implies overcoming religious, social, and gender barriers: 'There is no longer Jew or Greek, there is no longer slave or free, there is no longer male and female; for all of you are one in Christ Jesus' (Gal. 3: 28). Paul himself struggled to break down the barriers between Jews and Gentiles. When the slave Onesimus ran away, Paul

---

[6] See J. Quinn, 'The Reform of the Roman Curia', in his *The Reform of the Papacy* (New York: Crossroad, 1999), 154–77.

pleaded with his owner (Philemon) to receive the slave back as a brother, and gently suggested that Philemon set him free. The final chapter of the Apostle's Letter to the Romans showed how much he valued the ministry of women such as Prisca (or Priscilla), who with her husband (Aquila) was a great support to Christian communities around the Mediterranean world. But there is obviously still much unfinished business in overcoming the barriers between Jews and Gentiles, in delivering from oppression those who suffer from different forms of slavery, and in establishing a true equality for women in the Church and society.

The First Letter of Peter acknowledged how the new life in Christ made all the baptized into a 'holy' or 'royal' priesthood (1 Pet. 2: 4, 9). Baptism confers on all who receive it 'a dignity which includes the imitation and following of Christ, communion with one another, and the missionary mandate' to bring 'their brothers and sisters to encounter the living Jesus Christ'. Any renewal in Catholic life is impossible without 'the active presence of the laity... they are largely responsible for the future of the church' (*Ecclesia in America*, 44). The apostolic exhortation named the two areas in which lay people, both men and women, live their vocation: (1) through their calling to embody the values of Christ's Gospel in secular society,[7] and (2) through the exercise of their charisms and ministries within the Church itself, provided that the common priesthood of all the faithful remains 'clearly distinguished' from that of the ordained priesthood (ibid.).

In the Western world and beyond, lay and religious women are prominent in ways for which it is hard to discover parallels from the long story of the Catholic Church. Women teach in theological colleges, university faculties, and seminaries. Some laywomen are chancellors of dioceses and judges in marriage tribunals; many administer parishes for which no ordained priests are available. A number of women are officials in the Roman Curia, while a woman (Professor Mary Ann Glendon) headed the Vatican delegation to the UN conference in Beijing in 1995. What of women and the ordained ministry within the Catholic Church? In his dialogue with Umberto Eco, Cardinal Martini had this to say: 'On the one

---

[7] Vatican II's Pastoral Constitution on the Church in the Modern World (*Gaudium et Spes*) remains the classic call to all Catholic (and indeed Christian) men and women to play their essential role in the whole human community: by promoting the well-being of families, an economic order at the service of all, justice in public life, peace between nations, cultural growth, and everything that contributes to the common good.

hand, the role and presence of women in all aspects of church life and society must be realized, far beyond the degree to which it has been previously. On the other hand, our understanding of the nature of the priesthood and ordained ministers must be more profound than ever before.' The Cardinal hoped and expected that the future would bring a fuller understanding of the 'mysteries' or sacraments that the Church 'lives and celebrates'. He ended by quoting the conviction St Thomas Aquinas took over from St Augustine: 'the liberation of the human being should show itself in both sexes (hominis liberatio in utroque sexu debuit appa-rere)' (*ST* III q. 31 a. 4).[8]

One recent international event, however, suggests that the talk of women's 'prominence' with which the last paragraph began may be somewhat premature. At the summit for world spiritual leaders held at Assisi on 24 January 2002, women were only 10 per cent of the two hundred delegates who came through wind and rain to gather with John Paul II under a huge tent. There was a striking imbalance, and not only on the Catholic side.

DIALOGUE AND MISSION

A fourth challenge that we wish to mention is that of continuing the move beyond the Western mould of Catholicism and, indeed, of much Christianity. The Catholic message about Jesus Christ and the way of living it in practice have, to some extent, already been indigenized in various cultures around the world. But more needs to be done, so as to adapt the language and life of Catholic faith to African, Chinese, Indian, and other cultural and religious forms.[9] Being Catholic means hearing *all* the voices, so as to respect and incorporate within a united tradition *all* the true, healthy, and life-giving elements from cultures and religions everywhere. Here the teaching and practice of Pope John Paul II were exemplary; right from the start of his pontificate he showed himself open to what he called 'the treasures of human wisdom and religion' (*Fides et Ratio*, 31) and to the 'spiritual riches' with which God has endowed the peoples of the world (*Redemptoris Missio*, 55).

---

[8] *Belief or Nonbelief*, 78, 79, trans. corrected.

[9] See what the post-synodal papal exhortations say on inculturation: from the 1995 *Ecclesia in Africa* (59–62, 78); from the 1999 *Ecclesia in Asia* (21–2); from the 2001 *Ecclesia in Oceania* (16–17).

The 'inculturation' of the Catholic proclamation of Jesus Christ is much more than a marketing device for adapting and selling the message. It comes right out of faith in Jesus himself. He is the Saviour who died for all (e.g. 2 Cor. 5: 14, 19) and who, in his risen glory, will be the final destiny of every man and woman of all times and places (Rev. 21: 22–22: 5). But right here and now he has already united everyone to himself, as Vatican II (*Gaudium et Spes*, 22) and John Paul II (*Redemptor Hominis*, 13) vigorously insisted. All human beings, both individually and collectively, are affected by the powerful presence of Christ but also, as the Pope repeatedly emphasized, of the Holy Spirit, whose activity affects not only individuals but also the world's 'cultures and religions' (see Ch. 4 above). The Pope's teaching here recalls for us what St Irenaeus wrote about the Son and the Spirit as the 'two hands of God' working inseparably together for the enlightenment and salvation of all.

Such a faith in the universal presence and activity of the Son of God and the Holy Spirit provides, from a Catholic and Christian perspective, the deepest motivation for the most respectful and prayerful dialogue not only with Jews but also with Buddhists, Hindus, Muslims, and the adherents of the other world religions. To be sure, admirable Catholics and other Christians have long ago initiated such a dialogue around the world. And they have frequently met remarkable partners in this dialogue. But the painful strife between Christians and members of other religions in the Balkans, Egypt, India, Indonesia, Nigeria, the Sudan, and elsewhere makes the call to patient and forgiving dialogue more urgent than ever. John Paul II's peace message for New Year's Day 2002 rightly emphasized the need for greater interreligious understanding and co-operation. Worn out with age, gunshot wounds, and sickness, he gave right to the end a shining example by trying to encourage greater respect and solidarity between all religions. It was precisely his faith in the powerful presence of the Son of God and the Holy Spirit in all cultures and religions that propelled him to such dialogue. The migrations of Muslim workers, the diaspora of Tibetan Buddhists, and further developments have brought peoples of different faiths into a new proximity with each other. But will they be true neighbours to each other? Catholics and Christians of every kind have an urgent obligation to bring about a true and gracious harmony. Their transparent faith in the ever-present Christ and Spirit should powerfully motivate every kind of harmonious dialogue.

Any interreligious dialogue and collaboration remain, however, hampered by the divisions between Christians. To the degree that Christians remain separated and at odds with each other, they are weakened in what they can do towards interreligious dialogue. Undoubtedly, the ecumenical movement has succeeded to some extent intellectually, as patient Catholic exchanges with Anglicans, Lutherans, Methodists, and other Christians have uncovered a remarkable amount of common ground. But institutionally the goal of Christian unity continues to be a matter of hope and of prayer. Nevertheless, some fruit of Christian ecumenism was strikingly symbolized on 18 January 2000, when the archbishop of Canterbury and a representative of the Orthodox patriarch of Constantinople joined the Pope in opening together the holy door of St Paul's Outside the Walls (Rome). The photograph of the three Christian leaders kneeling together in prayer at the open door of the basilica encouraged fresh hopes for a living and loving unity between all Christians.

Only courageous love can carry forward authentic mission and dialogue. Most people naturally think of love as following on knowledge; through seeing and knowing we come to love someone or something. But the experience of interpersonal relationships supports a view that goes back through St Augustine to St John's Gospel: we will know the truth, and especially the truth about persons, because we already love them. Love predisposes us to see. In Thomas Aquinas's lapidary phrase, 'ubi amor, ibi oculus' (where there is love, there is vision) (III *Super Libros Sententiarum*, 35. 1. 2). Only a deep love for Christ and all his brothers and sisters around the globe can enable Catholics to see the truth about all men and women and in all men and women.

Both within the Catholic Church and in all its contacts with those who do not or do not yet accept Catholic faith, it is love that will open up the future. Here we end with the greatest challenge to Catholicism and the greatest gift from God to human beings, the divine love that, as the final line of Dante's *Divine Comedy* attests, 'moves the sun and the other stars'. The Babylons of world history, built on human greed and ruthless power, will all fall sooner or later. But the heavenly Jerusalem, built on God's infinite love revealed at the coming of Christ and the Holy Spirit, will never fail.

We end by making our own the sentiments expressed by Clement of Alexandria (d. *c*.215): 'The eternal Jesus, the one high priest' cries,

'I summon the whole human race . . . Come unto me and gather together as one well-ordered unity under the one God, and under the one Logos of God' (*Protrepticus*, 12). Around the same time, Hippolytus of Rome expressed the same hope in his vision of Christ as 'the queen bee' who has come to gather around him the whole of humanity (*In Canticum*, 1. 16).

SELECT BIBLIOGRAPHY

ADAM, K., *The Spirit of Catholicism* (London: Sheed & Ward, 1929).

AQUINAS, ST THOMAS, *Summa Theologiae*, trans. T. Gilby *et al.* (60 vols.; London: Eyre & Spottiswoode, 1964–6).

AUGUSTINE OF HIPPO, ST, *Confessions*, trans. H. Chadwick (Oxford: Oxford University Press, 1991).

BAMAT, T., and WIEST J. P. (eds.), *Popular Catholicism in a World Church: Seven Case Studies in Inculturation* (Maryknoll, NY: Orbis, 1999).

BARRETT, D. B., *et al.* (eds.), *World Christian Encyclopedia* (2 vols.; Oxford: Oxford University Press, 2nd edn. 2001).

BEINERT, W., and SCHÜSSLER FIORENZA, F. (eds.), *Handbook of Catholic Theology* (New York: Crossroad, 1995).

BOKENKOTTER, T. S., *Concise History of the Catholic Church* (3 vols.; New York: Doubleday, 1977–90).

BOWKER, J. (ed.), *The Oxford Dictionary of World Religions* (Oxford: Oxford University Press, 1997).

Catechism of the Catholic Church (Vatican: Libreria Editrice Vaticana, 1992); various editions of the English translation.

CHADWICK, H., *The Early Church* (London: Pelican, 2nd edn. 1993).

—— *The Church in Ancient Society: From Galilee to Gregory the Great* (Oxford: Oxford University Press, 2001).

COLLINS, M., and PRICE, M. *The Story of Christianity* (New York: Dorling Kindersley, 1999).

CROSS, F. L., and LIVINGSTONE, E. A. (eds.), *The Oxford Dictionary of the Christian Church* (Oxford: Oxford University Press, 3rd edn. 1997).

DANTE ALIGHIERI, *The Divine Comedy*; we recommend the translation by D. L. Sayers (3 vols.; Harmondsworth: Penguin Books, 1950–62).

DONOVAN, D., *Distinctively Catholic: An Exploration of Catholic Identity* (Mahwah, NJ: Paulist Press, 1997).

DUFFY, E., *Saints and Sinners: A History of the Popes* (New Haven, Conn.: Yale University Press, 1997).

DULLES, AVERY, *The Catholicity of the Church* (Oxford: Oxford University Press, 1985).

EDWARDS, D. L., *What is Catholicism? An Anglican Responds to the Official Teaching of the Roman Catholic Church* (London: Mowbray, 1994).

—— *Christianity: the First Two Thousand Years* (London: Cassell, 1998).

FAHLBUSCH, E., *et al.* (eds.), *The Encyclopedia of Christianity* (Grand Rapids, Mich.: Eerdmans, 1999–).

FLANNERY, A. (ed.), *Vatican Council II: The Conciliar and Post Conciliar Documents* (Northport, NY: Costello, rev. edn. 1996).

HARRIES, R., and MAYR-HARTING, H. (eds.), *Christianity: Two Thousand Years Later* (Oxford: Oxford University Press, 2001).

HASTINGS, A. (ed.), *A World History of Christianity* (London: Cassell, 1999).

HELLWIG, M. K., *Understanding Catholicism* (New York: Paulist Press, 1981).

JEDIN, H., and DOLAN, J. (eds.), *History of the Church* (10 vols.; New York: Crossroad, 1981–2).

JODOCK, D. (ed.), *Catholicism Contending with Modernity* (Cambridge: Cambridge University Press, 2000).

KELLY, J. N. D., *The Oxford Dictionary of Popes* (Oxford: Oxford University Press, 1986).

KÜNG, H., *Christianity: Its Essence and History* (London: SCM Press, 1995).

LANGAN, T., *The Catholic Tradition* (Columbia, Mo.: University of Missouri Press, 1998).

LUBAC, H. DE, *Catholicism: Christ and the Common Destiny of Man* (San Francisco: Ignatius Press, 1988).

MCCLELLAND, V. A., and HODGETTS, M. (eds.), *From Without the Flaminian Gate: 150 Years of Roman Catholicism in England and Wales: 1850–2000* (London: Darton, Longman & Todd, 1999).

MCBRIEN, R. P., *Catholicism* (San Francisco: HarperSan Francisco, new edn. 1994).

MCGINN, B., *The Foundations of Mysticism* (New York: Crossroad, 1991).

—— *The Growth of Mysticism* (New York: Crossroad, 1994).

—— *The Flowering of Mysticism* (New York: Crossroad, 1998).

MCMANNERS, J. (ed.), *The Oxford Illustrated History of Christianity* (Oxford: Oxford University Press, 1990).

New Catholic Encyclopedia (19 vols.; New York: McGraw Hill/Catholic University of America, 1967–96).

NEWMAN, J. H., *Apologia pro Vita Sua* (London: Longman, Green & Co., 1873).

—— *Essay on the Development of Christian Doctrine* (London: Longman, Green & Co., 2nd edn. 1878).

NICHOLS, A., *Epiphany: A Theological Introduction to Catholicism* (Collegeville, Minn.: The Liturgical Press, 1996).

O'COLLINS, G., and FARRUGIA, E. G. *A Concise Dictionary of Theology* (Mahwah, NJ: Paulist Press, new edn. 2000).

O'COLLINS, G., and VENTURINI, M., *Believing: Understanding the Creed* (New York: Paulist Press, 1991).

PARRY, K., *et al.*, *The Blackwell Dictionary of Eastern Christianity* (Oxford: Blackwell, 1999).

RAHNER, K., *Foundations of Christian Faith* (New York: Crossroad, 1978).

RAHNER, K., *Theological Investigations* (23 vols.; London: Darton, Longman & Todd, 1961–92).

Select Bibliography

RATZINGER, J., *Introduction to Christianity* (New York: Herder & Herder, 1969).

REESE, T. J., *Inside the Vatican: The Politics and Organization of the Catholic Church* (Cambridge, Mass.: Harvard University Press, 1996).

STRANGE, R., *The Catholic Faith* (London: Darton, Longman & Todd, 2001).

—— *Living Catholicism* (London: Darton, Longman & Todd, 2001).

TANNER, N. P. (ed.), *Decrees of the Ecumenical Councils* (2 vols.; London: Sheed & Ward, 1990).

TIMMS, N., and WILSON, K. (eds.), *Governance and Authority in the Roman Catholic Church* (London: SPCK, 2000).

WEIGEL, G., *The Truth of Catholicism: Ten Controversies Explored* (New York: HarperCollins, 2001).

INDEX